Refugees from Nazi Germany
and the Liberal European States

Refugees from Nazi Germany and the Liberal European States

Edited by
Frank Caestecker and Bob Moore

SOMA[ ]CEGES

berghahn
NEW YORK · OXFORD
www.berghahnbooks.com

Published in 2010 by
Berghahn Books
www.berghahnbooks.com

©2010, 2014 Frank Caestecker and Bob Moore
First paperback edition published in 2014.

All rights reserved. Except for the quotation of short passages for the purposes of criticism and review, no part of this book may be reproduced in any form or by any means, electronic or mechanical, including photocopying, recording, or any information storage and retrieval system now known or to be invented, without written permission of the publisher.

Library of Congress Cataloging-in-Publication Data

Refugees from Nazi Germany and the liberal European states / edited by Frank Caestecker and Bob Moore. -- 1st ed.
   p. cm.
   Includes bibliographical references and index.
   ISBN 978-1-84545-587-3 (hardback) -- ISBN 978-1-84545-799-0 (institutional ebook) -- ISBN 978-1-78238-392-5 (paperback) -- ISBN 978-1-78238-393-2 (retail ebook)
   1. Jewish refugees--Government policy--Europe, Western--History--20th century. 2. Refugees--Government policy--Europe, Western--History--20th century. 3. Germany--Emigration and immigration--History--1933-1945. 4. Jewish refugees--Europe, Western--History--20th century. 5. Jewish refugees--Germany--History--20th century. 6. Refugees--Europe, Western--History--20th century. 7. Refugees--Germany--History--20th century. 8. Europe, Western--Emigration and immigration--History--20th century. I. Caestecker, Frank. II. Moore, Bob, 1954-
   HV640.5.J4R43 2010
   940.53'18142--dc22

2009047793

British Library Cataloguing in Publication Data
A catalogue record for this book is available from the British Library

Printed on acid-free paper

ISBN: 978-1-78238-392-5 paperback
ISBN: 978-1-78238-393-2 retail ebook

Contents

List of Tables	vii
List of Figures	viii
List of Abbreviations	ix
Acknowledgements	xi
Introduction *Frank Caestecker and Bob Moore*	1

Part I: National and International Analyses of Policies towards the Refugees from Nazi Germany

I.1.	International Refugee Policy and Jewish Immigration under the Shadow of National Socialism *Susanne Heim*	17
I.2.	The Danish Immigration Authorities and the Issue of Rassenschande *Lone Rünitz*	48
I.3.	Unwilling Refuge: France and the Dilemma of Illegal Immigration, 1933–1939 *Vicki Caron*	57
I.4.	Dwindling Options: Seeking Asylum in Switzerland 1933–1939 *Regula Ludi*	82
I.5.	The 1930s: The End of the Latin American Open-door Policy *Patrick von zur Mühlen*	103
I.6.	Shanghai: A Last Resort for Desperate Jews *Steve Hochstadt*	109
I.7.	Palestine as a Destination for Jewish Immigrants and Refugees from Nazi Germany *Aviva Halamish*	122
I.8.	American Refugee Policy in the 1930s *Bat-Ami Zucker*	151

I.9. Were Unaccompanied Child Refugees a Privileged 169
     Class of Refugees in the Liberal States of Europe?
     Claudia Curio

Part II: A Comparative Analysis of Immigration Policies of Liberal States in Western Europe and the Flight from Nazi Germany

II.1. The Legal Construction of Policy towards Aliens prior to 1933 193
     Frank Caestecker and Bob Moore

II.2 Refugees from Nazi Germany and the Development of 207
     Refugee Policies, 1933–1937
     Frank Caestecker and Bob Moore

II.3 The Deepening Crisis: March 1938–October 1938 244
     Frank Caestecker and Bob Moore

II.4 From *Kristallnacht* to War, November 1938–August 1939 276
     Frank Caestecker and Bob Moore

     Conclusion 313
     Frank Caestecker and Bob Moore

Appendix 325
Notes on Contributors 327
Select Bibliography 331
Index 337

List of Tables

I. 7.1	Palestine's Contribution to the Absorption of Jewish Immigrants (1932–1939)	144
I. 7.2	Jewish Immigration to Palestine, 1932–1938 (from selected countries)	144
I. 7.3	Percentage of Immigrants from Germany in Jewish Immigration to Palestine, 1932–1938	145
I. 7.4	Summary of Jewish Immigration into Palestine, 1932–1938 (from selected countries)	145
I. 7.5	Comparison of Immigration into Palestine from Germany and Poland, 1936	145
I. 7.6	Germany's Share in Labour Certificates, 1933–1937	146
II. 2.1	Country of Asylum of a Sample of 333 German Communists, 1933–1937	226
II. 2.2	The treatment of 6,280 Asylum Applications in France, 1936–1938	230
II. 3.1	'Jewish' Refugees' Official Destination when Applying for Passports in Vienna and Prague, 1938–1939	284
II. 3.2	Country of Asylum of a Sample of 333 German Communists, 1938–1939	288
II. 3.3	Number of Refugees Interned in Dutch Camps for Legally and Illegally Immigrated Refugees, 12.1938–8.1939	295

List of Figures

1. Refugees Newly Registered by Jewish Refugee Committees, 1933–1937 — 218

2. West European Countries from which HICEM Organized Emigration of Jewish Refugees from Nazi Germany, 1933–1935, 1939 — 325

3. Destination of the HICEM-organized Emigration of German-Jewish Refugees from West European Countries, 1933–1939 — 325

4. Newly Registered Refugees by Jewish Refugee Committees, 1938–1939 (by month) — 326

5. Official Registration of Refugees in Denmark and Luxembourg, 1938–1939 (by month) — 326

List of Abbreviations

AAD   Algemeen Rijksarchief Brussel, Belgian Ministry of Justice, Aliens' Department
AADi   Algemeen Rijksarchief Brussel, Belgian Ministry of Justice, Aliens' Department, individual files
AIU   Alliance Israélite Universelle
AMIA   Archive Belgian Ministry of Interior Affairs, Aliens' Department, individual files
AN   Archives Nationales, Paris
ABMFA   Archives of the Belgian Ministry of Foreign Affairs
BABL   Bundesarchiv Berlin-Lichterfelde
BCRC   British Committee for Refugees from Czechoslovakia
EJPD   Eidgenössische Justiz- und Polizeidepartment ([Swiss] Federal Police for Foreigners)
BBR   Bundesarchiv Berlin, R 58 (Reichssicherheitshauptamt)
CJA   Centrum Judaicum Archiv
CZA   Central Zionist Archives, Jerusalem
(UN)HCR   (United Nations) High Commissioner for Refugees
FRUS   Foreign Relations United States
HIAS   Hebrew Sheltering and Aid Society
HICEM   Hebrew Intergovernmental Committee for European Migration (an amalgam of several Jewish emigration and immigration organisations established in 1927)
HSTAD   Nordrhein-Westfälische Hauptstaatsarchiv Dusseldorf, RW 58 (Gestapo(leit)stelle Düsseldorf).
IfZ   Institut für Zeitgeschichte, Munich
IMG   Internationaler Militärgerichtshof (International Military Tribunal)
JCA   Jewish Colonization Association
JDC   American Jewish Joint Distribution Committee archives, if no mention of the collection it refers to collection 33/44.
IGC   Intergovernmental Committee for Refugees
JM   Justitsministeriet (Danish Ministry of Justice).
KPD   Kommunistische Partei Deutschlands (German Communist Party)

KPO	Kommunistische Partei Osterreich (Austrian Communist Party)
LBIYB	Leo Baeck Institute Year Book
LBI-NY	Leo Baeck Institute, New York
LPA	Labour Party Archive, Beit Berl, Israel
LSA	Luxemburg State Archives
NA	National Archives and Records Administration, Washington DC
PA AA	Politisches Archiv des Auswärtigen Amts
PRO	Public Record Office, London (now, The National Archives)
RCM	Refugee Children's Movement
RG 59	National Archives, Suitland Maryland US Department of State, Central Decimal Files, Record Group 59
SAP	Sozialistische Arbeiterpartei Deutschlands
SD	Sicherheitsdienst
SIG	Schweizer Israelitische Gemeindebund
SHEK	Swiss Agency for Refugee Children
TAJB	Tel Aviver Jahrbuch für deutsche Geschichte
UDL	Rigspolitiet, Tilsynet med Udlaendinge, UDL-sager (Danish State Police, Aliens Files).
UEK	Unabhängige Expertenkommission Schweiz-Zweiter Weltkrieg, *Die Schweiz und die Flüchtlinge zur Zeit des Nationalsozialismus*, Bern 1999.
UM	Udenrigsministeriet (Danish Foreign Office).
YIVO	Yiddisher Visns haftelekher Institut, New York
ZE	Zionist Executive

Acknowledgements

The idea for this book originated in two workshops organized by Frank Caestecker at the Studie en Documentatiecentrum Oorlog en Hedendaagse Maatschappij (SOMA-CEGES) in Brussels on 15–17 January 2004 and 20 January 2005. Both these events were made possible by generous financial contributions from the Goethe Institut, Brussels Capital Region, the Fonds voor Wetenschappelijk Onderzoek – Vlaanderen, the Fonds National de la Recherche Scientifique, the Programmatorische Federale Overheidsdienst (POD) Wetenschapsbeleid/Service Public Fédéral de Programmation Politique Scientifique and the Royal Flemish Academy of Belgium for Science and the Arts. The workshops benefited from the support and encouragement of José Gotovitch, the then director of SOMA, and its staff and scientific committee. In particular, we would like to thank Anne Bernard and Lut van Daele, two members of the administrative staff of SOMA who gave unstinting and invaluable help to the project. We are also delighted to acknowledge the help given by Professor Herman Balthazar (Universiteit Gent), Professor Els Witte (Vrije Universiteit Brussel) and Margareta Hauschild of the Goethe Institut, Brussels, as well as the hospitality afforded by Professor Pieter Lagrou (Université Libre de Bruxelles) and Dr Rudi van Doorslaer (SOMA-CEGES) which allowed us the time and space to edit the volume.

The final version of the book took shape when Frank Caestecker left SOMA-CEGES to take up an appointment in the Department of Modern and Contemporary History at the University of Ghent in 2005. The success of an edited volume depends heavily on the goodwill of its contributing authors and we were fortunate to gather together an excellent group of academic colleagues who responded to queries and questions promptly and with unerring good humour. The various contributions contained in this volume all have a specific function in providing insights into the field of refugee policy in a particular time and place. In this book refugee policy has been approached from different perspectives and from the different historical experiences of refugees, immigration officers, politicians, refugee advocates and public opinion. Although they did not contribute directly to this book, we are greatly indebted to a number of experts in this field who shared their insights with us, most notably Louise London, Stefan Mächler, Hans Uwe Petersen and Klaus Voigt.

Finally we would like to thank Dr Marion Berghahn of Berghahn Books for taking this project on board and seeing it through to completion, and to the publisher's anonymous readers for their invaluable suggestions.

Introduction

Frank Caestecker and Bob Moore

Europe in the twentieth century has been subject to a series of mass migrations; from the Jews fleeing tsarist persecution at its beginning, through the upheavals of two world wars to the more recent refugees from the conflicts in Africa and the Balkans and extensive attempted migration into and within the expanded borders of the European Union. All have had their commentators and analysts, but it is the refugees from Nazi Germany in the 1930s that have received by far the greatest attention from historians, social scientists and demographers. The reasons for this are not difficult to ascertain. The idea that large numbers of people could be displaced from a highly cultured and modernised state such as Germany flies in the face of contemporary ideas about civilisation and progress, but perhaps more importantly, the overwhelming attention given to the Holocaust within the historiography of Europe and the Second World War has created a situation in which the issues surrounding the movement of people from Nazi Germany prior to 1939 are seen as an essential pre-history; implicating the Western European democracies and the United States as bystanders in the impending tragedy.

The first publications on the refugees in the 1930s came at the end of that decade with the appearance of Sir John Hope Simpson's *The Refugee Problem* in 1939. Although undoubtedly prompted by the concerns surrounding the refugees from Nazi Germany, its scope included all the refugee movements of the post-First World War era, including the Armenians and White Russians who had been the first subjects of national concerns and of international action through the League of Nations. Simpson highlighted the ways in which the Nansen Office had been created to deal with the issue of de facto stateless people, and how this system had been rejected as a solution to the problem of refugees from Germany after 1933. His researchers often gave very detailed explanations of how state policies were applied in practice, but could give only limited insights into how such policies had been formulated. His was the only academic study to appear in the pre-1939 period, although other contemporary publications did add important information, most notably a special edition of the

Annals of the American Association for Political and Social Sciences in May 1939 that contained a series of article on aspects of the refugee problem. During the Second World War, there were attempts to analyse the problems of refugees, albeit without access to contemporary European sources.[1] After 1945, the tragedy of the Holocaust and the threat of a Third World War overshadowed any independent analysis of state refugee policies in the 1930s, and the main publications on the issue in the 1950s and 1960s came from those directly involved in private refugee relief work. Their analysis was often framed as explanations for what had, and what had not been done for the victims of Nazism before the outbreak of war. These few publications were rarely critical of the relief effort and most were concerned to reinforce the idea that the private and public sectors had done everything possible.[2]

The first general histories of the Holocaust focused on the tragic fate of the Jews during the German occupation and made few references to the pre-1940 period, and the same was true of the national studies that appeared. Academic interest was also limited, except in Switzerland where an edition of German documents published in 1953 highlighted that country's collusion in the introduction of the 'J'-stamp on German passports. This revelation caused a public outcry and led to an official report commissioned by the Swiss Parliament. The historian Carl Ludwig was granted full access to Swiss diplomatic archives and his research laid the foundations for a historical analysis of Swiss refugee policy of the 1930s.[3] Notwithstanding that the report clearly pointed out that Heinrich Rothmund, the Head of the Federal Police, had advocated the introduction of visas for Jewish Germans, but had considered the 'J'-stamp as contrary to Swiss interests, he was singled out as the scapegoat and had to resign. As a result, the Swiss political elite escaped any additional criticism and a further investigation of refugee policy had to wait another two decades.[4]

In the 1970s, the refugees became a focus of German historical research. Studies were commissioned by the German Democratic Republic on communist refugees who had later been active as founders of the East German state, and the appointment of a former political exile, Willy Brandt, as West German chancellor also helped to propel the wider study of refugees up the agenda of the influential Deutsche Forschungsgemeinschaft. A first major accomplishment was the *International Biographical Dictionary of Central European Emigrés 1933–1945*, a massive work of agglomerative scholarship on the political, cultural and scientific elite of the refugees. By the end of the 1970s, German refugee studies had lost much of its backing, but remained in the hands of a few committed historians, such as Patrick von zur Mühlen, Hans-Uwe Petersen, Ursula Langkau-Alex and Klaus Voigt, who continued the work of uncovering those who had continued to resist the Nazi regime in exile.[5] Latterly these so-called *'Exil-Studien'* have shifted into examinations of the cultural and literary legacies of the exiles and their impact on the postwar world.[6] The 1980s concentration on history from below can also be seen in the *Exil-Studien*. After the initial concentration on the flight of political activists, intellectuals and artists, there was a slow movement towards greater consideration of the masses. Ernst Loewy, Wolfgang Benz and Ernst Lorenz began studies of what they called the 'common people' among the refugees and through this new interest focused not only on the rank and file of the political exile organisations, but also on the Jewish refugees.[7] Nevertheless, their attention remained strongly German-centred and the countries of exile were only of secondary interest.[8]

Analysis of the flight of the émigrés and refugees from Nazi Germany, and the policies adopted towards them in their countries of refuge was almost exclusively in the hands of historians working on the national history of the countries of asylum. The first example of this came in the Netherlands, where the first volume of the official history of the Second World War was published in 1969.[9] Here the author, Louis de Jong, with unrivalled access to state and private documentation, placed the question of refugees into the wider context of Dutch–German relations, but followed this up with a detailed examination of the various Jewish and non-Jewish relief efforts. His purpose in so doing was clear and explicit – namely as an introduction to the issues and actors that framed the persecution of the Jews during the Nazi era. The book provided an excellent basis for future discussion. This came initially in the form of two doctoral theses: while Dan Michman reflected on the Dutch Jewish community and the Jewish refugee issue of the 1930s, Bob Moore combined this with an analysis of the factors that framed policies towards both Jewish and political refugees.[10] As an Anglo-Dutch historian he was fully aware of the British historiography on migration and applied these insights to the Dutch case.

Since the early 1970s, issues such as immigration and antisemitism had been widely discussed in British historical and social sciences and there was also an increasing interest in the experiences and social history of immigrants. In that decade the first publications on the longer-term trends of immigration to Britain and on the policies followed by successive British governments were published. Many of these focused on the non-white immigration after the Second World War, but were inevitably informed by development of immigration policies in the late nineteenth and earlier twentieth century that were primarily directed against an influx of Jews from Eastern Europe. This combination of anti-alien and antisemitic trends that helped to frame British immigration policies in the 1930s has been well documented, most notably by Colin Holmes, while the path-breaking work on antisemitism in the United Kingdom by Gisela Lebzelter has been complimented by other, more recent studies.[11] The first study specifically devoted to British refugee policy was Arieh Sherman, *Island Refuge*, which analysed the development of British policy towards refugees in the 1930s, although without the benefit of access to many government sources.[12] Austin Stevens, in *The Dispossessed*, concentrated more on the experiences of the refugees themselves who came to Britain in the 1930s, but he also drew conclusions about the nature of the British responses, as did later works by scholars such as Marion Berghahn and Gerhard Hirschfeld.[13] At the same time, the study of the refugees was being more closely associated with the wider analysis of Britain and the Holocaust, starting with *Britain and the Jews of Europe, 1933–1945* by Bernard Wasserstein.[14] One further notable addition to the canon came in 1994 with the publication of Tony Kushner's important work, *The Holocaust and the Liberal Imagination*. Although a broad ranging analysis of responses to the Holocaust, it also provided an analysis of British government responses to the plight of refugees in the 1930s.[15]

The shift in research interest towards the flight of Jews was evident in the publication of Frank Caestecker's book, *Unwanted Guests: Jewish Refugees and Migrants in the Thirties*.[16] Notwithstanding the subtitle, this book dealt with both Jewish *and* political refugees fleeing Nazi Germany, but the Jewish refugees took centre-stage. Moreover, by referring to the Jews as migrants, it also linked the study to the wider interest in migration as part of the historical experience of continental Europe epitomised by the work of Gérard Noiriel in France, but also of Jan Lucassen in the Netherlands, and Gérald and Silvia Arlettaz in Switzerland. These historians had analysed the history of migration in different West-European countries and also investigated the indigenous resistance to the increasingly multi-ethnic and multicultural societies as a result of colonial and economic migration.[17]

The 'asylum crisis' in the Western world during the 1990s also prompted investigations into the origins of national refugee and immigration policies.[18] This analysis had a strong focus on the Jewish refugees from Nazi Germany as they were seen as the refugees par excellence and thus the ideal example of how different interests, including the humanitarian concern for people in need of protection, shaped immigration and refugee policy. In Great Britain, Ariel Sherman's analysis of refugee policy was complemented by Louise London's, *Whitehall and the Jews*. London was able to make extensive use of the British government's by then declassified archival records to analyse policy development in depth. London's state-centred approach was complemented by Amy Gottlieb, who focused on Anglo-Jewry's efforts to bring relief to Jewish refugees.[19] Also Lone Rünitz in her analysis of the Danish policy towards Jewish refugees added immeasurably to the Danish historiography that, until then, had been exclusively concerned with political refugees.[20]

Until recently, French research on refugee policy remained scant, with only a few publications concentrated mainly on the refugees' political activities.[21] This changed with the publications on French government policy, popular opinion, and the native Jewish response by Vicki Caron.[22] Her research shows how popular attitudes fed policy and how policy fed attitudes, and she evokes not only the attitude of the French-Jewish community towards the refugees arriving from Nazi Germany and Eastern Europe, but that of all French society. Caron's historical research also seeks to explore the origins of Vichy antisemitism in the interwar period and she also points to tensions within the French Jewish community that would later influence Jewish responses to Vichy. Within migration studies, the strong tradition of French social history with its emphasis on the *longue durée* has tended to ignore political history. French historians of immigration in general, and Gérard Noiriel in particular, have focused their analysis of the political aspects of migration mainly on how administrative categories structured social reality in the long term. This has led to the neglect of a political history that analyses concrete political decisions and their administrative implementation.[23] In contrast, several Swiss studies have examined refugee policy in the 1930s in a very detailed manner. In the 1950s the investigation of Carl Ludwig on refugee and immigration policy had focused nearly exclusively on the federal level, but historians of the 1990s looked into the daily operation of alien policy. Not only the immigration policies of public actors, including cantonal and local authorities, but also of private actors, such as the refugee aid committees, in particular those imposed on Jewish refugees, were explored in depth.[24]

As a result of the recent growth of interest in the Holocaust, government agencies have played an increasingly important role in stimulating historical research on refugee policy in the 1930s. In the Netherlands, the Ministry of the Interior sponsored the publication *Joodse Vluchtelingen in Nederland, 1938–1940. Documenten betreffende toelating, uitleiding en kampopname*, a volume that made available previously classified documents of vital importance to the study of Dutch central government policy towards refugees in the two years before May 1940.[25] In Switzerland, the morality of the country's wartime history has been gradually eroded by the Swiss historical profession's attempts to provide a more objective analysis of the period. Scholars have demonstrated clearly that the Swiss could no longer regard themselves as heroic rescuers in the Holocaust tragedy nor even as innocent bystanders; a conclusion that has deeply troubled Swiss national identity. This was compounded in the mid 1990s by the scandal of the dormant accounts in Swiss banks that tarnished the country's international image and caused a major historical analysis of Swiss policy towards Nazi Germany and the persecution of Jews. In 1996 the Swiss Parliament voted for an historical investigation into the issue of dormant accounts and heirless assets. The use of new archival material that had not been accessible before and a comprehensive approach has thus deepened our knowledge of Swiss refugee and immigration policy.[26] In Denmark a similar, but less extensive research programme was initiated by the government. A newspaper article by Vilhjalmur Orn Vilhjalmsson that focused on the extradition of twenty-one stateless Jews by the Danish authorities during the occupation served to undermine the Danish self-image as rescuers of Jews. Likewise, Lone Rünitz's research added to the need for a reassessment of the Danes' long-held image of their past. This led to the Danish government commissioning a study on Danish refugee policy after 1933 and allowed Rünitz to analyse 8,000 police files on refugees who entered or tried to enter Denmark after 1933. On the basis of these individual case studies her latest book shows in a very detailed manner how the decisions of the legislative and executive agencies were implemented by local authorities on a daily basis at the border and in the country itself. These various historical commissions have added immeasurably to our knowledge of the actual policy towards political activists and Jews fleeing Nazi Germany.[27]

By the new millennium all over Europe, historical research on refugee policy had definitely shifted attention away from the political to the Jewish refugees. The recognition that the Holocaust was a crucial event in Europe's twentieth century has to be credited with this paradigm shift. Also a general shift in Holocaust historiography and a reassessment of its significance for Nazism can be seen as the driving force for this change, with most European societies being forced to consider their roles as bystanders in the persecution and rescue of Jews during the Nazi era.

The Need for an International and Transnational Perspective

Historiography on the refugees in the 1930s and on Western states' policy towards them remains largely based on a national perspective, with each country producing its own narratives and analyses. Such national studies are almost invariably preceded by a summary of the voluminous literature on Nazi Germany that explores in depth the nature and extent of persecution. Research on Nazi Germany has however paid little attention to how persecutees finally left the country. Moreover the influence of the emigration and expulsions policies pursued by the various agencies within Hitler's Germany on their flight has been given only scant attention.[28] Only recently has there been recognition that the failures of these emigration policies may hold a key to further the understanding of the twisted road to Auschwitz.[29]

A few publications have analysed the dispersal of the (Jewish) refugees using the watersheds of Nazi persecution as a means of periodization. The authors highlight national immigration policies as an important explanatory variable but do no more than juxtapose the national cases and do not embark on a comparative analysis of the similarities and differences between national policies.[30] Historiography on the policy towards refugees from Nazi Germany rarely provides an overview beyond the national case. The international dimension of refugee policy has also been neglected. Where the international refugee regime was discussed, it was merely to illustrate how national refugee policy was reflected in the attitudes of national representatives at international forums. The one exception to this is Claudia Skran, who approached the international refugee regime in the interwar period from a non-national angle but her very optimistic analysis concentrated primarily on the legal dimension of that regime. In her analysis, the international refugee regime of the interwar period was seen as the precursor of the 1951 Geneva Convention that introduced the idea of special treatment for refugees within a country's immigration policy. In examining the legal developments involved, Skran concentrates almost exclusively on the international scene and pays little attention to domestic determinants in the various countries of asylum. Thus she has nothing to say about how this international refugee regime affected the harsh reality of most refugees in the 1930s.[31] Until now there has been little or no investigation of how the international refugee regime affected national policies, or how individual states' policies were both dependent on those of their neighbours and subject to ongoing comparison throughout the period as all governments strove to make their policies equally, or ideally slightly less, welcoming than others. This comparison was inevitably complicated by the fact that there was no single policy in any country, but an agglomeration of measures related to citizenship, residence, entry and employment that, taken together, made up an immigration policy. Moreover, as will be shown in this analysis, no two countries entered the 1930s with policies based on the same set of principles, precepts or legislative history, let alone a common practice in the treatment of aliens.

The intention here is to undertake a comparative study of refugee policy in the 1930s among the liberal states of Europe; Belgium, Denmark, France, Luxemburg, the Netherlands, Switzerland and the United Kingdom. This concentration on the European liberal democracies has therefore deliberately excluded the reception of refugees from Nazi Germany in Fascist Italy, Spain and Portugal.[32] As a country of asylum until 1938 with a liberal regime, Czechoslovakia could have been included, but knowledge of its refugee policy is currently so limited that meaningful comparisons would have been impossible.[33] The focus on countries with a liberal regime is based on the contemporary social science theory that liberal norms affect alien policy, and that these norms are the key to understanding constraints on migration controls.[34] However, it is clear that these same contemporary norms and liberal values have had a much longer life span than social scientists might suggest. The liberalism of the nineteenth century caused a normative revolution which had a lasting impact on the ways in which the state functioned, not least on the whole question of immigration policies. The period in which these liberal values were under severe attack, the 1930s, is thus a good testing period for the lasting strength of these norms.

All the countries considered here, with the exception of the United Kingdom, had common land frontiers with Germany. The continental European countries faced common challenges to their immigration policies as their green borders were more difficult to control than the British sea borders. However, the United Kingdom was also included; because it was the most important European power at that time and because its decisions had far reaching influence: creating refugees through the Munich agreements and controlling access to the vast British overseas Empire and specifically to the Palestine Mandate. The United Kingdom also became an important country of asylum in the last years of peace, but was able to operate different and more selective immigration and refugee policies than its continental neighbours. The Scandinavian states of Norway, Finland and Sweden surrounded by the Atlantic Ocean and the Baltic Sea were not important countries of asylum in the 1930s and were thus not included in this comparative exercise, except insofar as their policies affected developments in Denmark, the only Scandinavian country that shared a common border with Germany.

The period covered by this study has been deliberately chosen to end at the outbreak of a general European war in September 1939. Inherent in this periodisation is a desire to rule out any teleological discussion of policy in 1930s in relation to the Nazis' later collective expulsion and extermination of the Jews. While there had been some discussion of the so-called Madagascar Plan in the 1930s, this had no basis in reality until the collapse of France in 1940, and the Lublin 'resettlement' scheme was only formulated after the success of the Polish campaign. The policy towards the victims of the prewar Nazi regime has to be analysed in its proper historical context. The policy makers in the 1930s could not yet know the horrors that would be visited on the Jews in Nazi-occupied Europe after 1940.[35]

The central focus of this book has been to provide a comparative survey of the main policy changes on refugees carried out by the liberal Western European states during the 1930s. In the first part of the book, 'National and International Analyses of Policies towards the Refugees from Nazi Germany', the main focus is on national case studies, all written by acknowledged experts in their respective fields. It begins with a chapter by Susanne Heim which gives an overview of the international refugee regime during the 1930s. She analyses the half-hearted efforts of the liberal democracies for a coordinated answer to the refugee crisis. Her article goes beyond the formal refugee regime, by outlining also what she calls an informal international refugee regime that influenced the Jewish exodus from Nazi Germany. Heim explains how the Jews in Germany interacted with a vast informal network of institutions wanting to accelerate, facilitate, slow down or stop their emigration.

The three following articles are national case studies, each with a different approach. Lone Rünitz focuses on individual cases of refugees applying for asylum in Denmark. These refugees had either fled Nazi Germany because of persecution due to the Nazi crime of *Rassenschande* or had counted on settling in Denmark as they had married Danish nationals (or intended to do so). On the basis of an analysis of individual cases, she concludes that these refugees were not considered deserving by the Danish authorities and shows how Copenhagen succeeded in denying most of them asylum. Rünitz also provides insights into administrative immigration practices. This daily policing of immigration is difficult to disentangle, because evolving administrative jurisprudence is mostly carried out by a few high ranking officers and seldom committed to paper. Thus the dividing line between migrants and refugees and between different groups of refugees is difficult to draw, both then and now, and there remain many grey areas which only painstakingly detailed research can disclose.

Vicki Caron gives a broad overview of the Jewish refugees' reception in France between January 1933 and September 1939. Using a broad range of sources including newspapers, state papers and the archives of Jewish aid organisations, she analyses French immigration policy and the extent to which those fleeing Nazi Germany were treated more generously than other immigrants. She points out the fluctuations in French refugee policy and focuses on how policy was implemented on the ground. She reviews numerous institutions involved in French refugee policy, be they part of the legislative, executive or judiciary and unearths a complex picture indicating how difficult it was for the French polity to develop a policy to address the pressure at its borders. Although at times French policy makers were fiercely determined to keep uninvited immigrants out, the authorities had to come to terms with the continuous infiltration of refugees and the liberal or merely pragmatic opposition to a wholly exclusionary policy.

The third national case study is the Swiss case. Regula Ludi provides a very broad picture of refugee policy, positioning it in a long-term analysis of the unease of the Swiss elite with a changing world. Their obsession with national identity that expressed itself in antisemitism and anti-Bolshevism forms the background for understanding the policy towards the refugees from Nazi Germany – a policy that evolved through the 1930s towards an ever-stricter regime and the eventual closure of the border to Jewish refugees in 1938.

In their different contexts, these four chapters demonstrate that the state-centred paradigm of migration control which forms the main focus of this volume has to be contextualized with reference to other actors; such as political parties, humanitarian organisations and civil society at large. This broader picture of the political system is essential for an understanding of developments in immigration and refugee policies. The refugees themselves have also to be considered as actors in this process, as they reacted both to Nazi persecution and to the measures taken to prevent them from entering countries of refuge by utilising whatever channels were available, both legal and illegal, to bypass control mechanisms.

The next four chapters provide insight into the refugee and immigration policies beyond Europe. Here the volume departs from its focus on liberal regimes in order to highlight the limited opportunities that refugees could find outside Europe. Patrik von zur Mühlen concisely outlines the manner in which refugees from Germany found homes in Latin America. Refugees were rarely offered asylum, but they were admitted as regular immigrants who had to be of benefit for the host country. However, by the end of the 1930s, refugees were being singled out by policy makers in Latin America as unwanted immigrants, for being Jews, for being politically unreliable, or for not having a desirable economic profile. The generally ineffective or corrupt nature of Latin American bureaucracy meant, however, that a large number of refugees could nonetheless still emigrate to these countries.

Aviva Halamish outlines British immigration policy for Palestine and the (limited) input of the Zionists in this policy. Although the Zionists favoured the 'repatriation' of all Jews to Palestine on ideological grounds, in practice they pursued a much more pragmatic policy taking into account economic and political constraints, while continuing to press for Palestine as the long term solution for the Jews of Central Europe. This ideologically based answer to the refugee crisis, although knowingly unrealistic, was intended as a lever for the cause of the Jewish state in Palestine. By September 1939, sixty thousand refugees from Greater Germany had found a safe haven in Palestine. This was a larger number than the British authorities had sanctioned, but was largely the result of Zionist-organised illegal immigration (sometimes in connivance with the Nazis). The readiness of German Jews to flee in makeshifts boats and enter Palestine illegally is proof of the refugees' desperation at the end of the 1930s. This is even more true of those leaving for Shanghai, an episode particularly revealing for the lack of (legal) alternatives for Jews wanting to leave Germany. Steve Hochstadt outlines the immigration policy in Shanghai and points out the reasons why this international settlement was, until the outbreak of the Second World War, the only place in the world where German Jews were still admitted without a visa.

Bat-Ami Zucker analyses the immigration and refugee policy of the United States. Here also, those fleeing Nazi Germany were not considered a privileged category in immigration policy. The very restrictive admission criteria meant that relatively few refugees were admitted. Only in 1938 did President Roosevelt take the initiative to use his administrative powers to open the door slightly more. This turned out to be a marginal concession to the pro-refugee lobby.

In the final chapter of this first section of the book Claudia Curio illustrates the desperation of the Jews most poignantly by examining the cases of the children who were sent abroad by their parents to be saved by strangers. She looks into the reception of the unaccompanied child refugees in four countries to provide comparative conclusions. Her study highlights the options open to policy makers and demonstrates the particularities of each individual country by highlighting the contrasts between them.

The second section of the book has been written by Frank Caestecker and Bob Moore, and attempts to provide a comparative approach to refugee policy in the 1930s as a whole. To do this effectively, the first chapter is devoted to a detailed pre-history of the policies towards aliens and refugees developed from the mid nineteenth century onwards. These formed the essential precedents and customs on which policies in 1933 were based. The following chapters are divided chronologically. Each chapter shows both the comparisons and contrasts in the responses of the various states to Nazi persecution policies and to the pressures on their borders from refugees. All European countries were exposed to similar challenges by Nazi Germany, but how these challenges were tackled often varied. Each of the national cases is illuminated and enriched by comparison. The analysis also shows the interplay between different national immigration policies, and between German emigration policy and the immigration policy of the countries of asylum.

Notes

1. A. Tartakower and K.R. Grossmann, *The Jewish Refugee*, New York 1944; M. Wischnitzer, 'Jewish Emigration from Germany 1933–38', *Jewish Social Studies* 2, 1940, pp.23–44.
2. M. Wischnitzer, *To Dwell in Safety*, Philadelphia 1948, p.199; N. Bentwich, *The Refugees from Germany April 1933 to December 1935*, London 1936; N. Bentwich, *They Found Refuge. An Account of British Jewry's Work for Victims of Nazi Oppression*, London 1956; N. Sutro, *Jugend auf der Flucht 1933–1948. Fünfzehn Jahre in Spiegel des Schweizer Hilfswerks für Emigrantenkinder*, Zurich 1952; B. Garfinkels, *Belgique, terre d'accueil. Problème du réfugié 1933/1940*, Bruxelles 1974; D. Cohen, *Zwervend en Dolend*, Haarlem 1955.
3. C. Ludwig, *Die Flüchtlingspolitik der Schweiz in den Jahre 1933 bis 1952* (Bericht des Bundesrates an die Bundesversammlung), Bern 1957. The Ludwig report was popularised in the late 1960s by A. Häsler, *The Lifeboat is Full: Switzerland and the Refugees, 1933–1945*, New York 1969.
4. R. Ludi, 'Waging War on Wartime Memory: Recent Swiss Debates on the Legacies of the Holocaust and the Nazi Era', *Jewish Social Studies* 10, no. 2, 2004, pp.116–52.
5. U. Langkau-Alex, 'Geschichte der Exilforschung', in *Handbuch der deutschsprachigen Emigration 1933–1945*, ed. C. Krohn, P. von zur Mühlen, G. Paul and L. Winckler, Darmstadt 1998, pp.1195–205. On exile politics, see among others W. Röder, *Die deutschen Exilgruppen in Großbritannien 1940–1945. Ein Beitrag zur Geschichte des Widerstandes gegen der Nationalsozialismus*, Hanover 1968; H. Maimann, *Politik im Wartesaal. Österreichische Exilpolitik in Großbritannien 1938–1945*, Vienna 1975; A. Glees, *Exil Politics during the Second World War: The German Social Democrats in Britain*, Oxford 1982; C. Brinson, *The Strange Case of Dora Fabian and Mathilde Wurm: A Study of German Political Exiles in London during the 1930s*, Bern 1996; U. Langkau-Alex, *Volksfront für Deutschland*, Frankfurt 1977; B. Herlemann, *Die Anleitung des Widerstands des KPD durch die Exilierte Parteiführung in Frankreich, die Niederlanden und Belgien*, Königstein im Taunus 1982; see also several articles in *Nederland en het Duitse Exil 1933–1940*, ed. K. Dittrich and H. Würzner, Amsterdam 1982 and in K. Bartosek, R. Gallissot and D. Peschanski (ed.), *De l'exil à la résistance: Réfugiés et immigrés d'europe centrale en France, 1933–1945*, Paris 1989. They also stimulated and assisted refugees to publish their memoirs see for example: B. Vormeier and H. Schramm, *Vivre à Gurs. Un Camp de Concentration français 1940–1941*, Paris 1977; R. Fabian and C. Coulmas. *Die deutsche Emigration in Frankreich nach 1933*. New York 1978; Y. Kapp and M. Mynatt, *British Policy and the Refugees 1933–1941*, London 1997; Ursula Langkau-Alex started in the 1970s with her research on the German Popular Front in exile and published a first volume in 1977: one had to wait to 2005 for two other volumes, in the mean time the first volume needed a re-edition (*Deutsche Volksfront 1932–1939. Zwischen Berlin, Paris, Prag und Moskau*). These three volumes give an important insight into the political activities of the political refugees in Western Europe.
6. E. Timms and R. Robertson, *Austrian Exodus: The Creative Achievements of Refugees from National Socialism*, Edinburgh 1995; J. Palmier, *Weimar en exil. Le destin de l'émigration intellectuele allemande antinazie en Europe et aux Etats-Unis*, Paris 1990; D. Vietor-Engländer, *The Legacy of Exile: Lives, Letters, Literature*, Oxford 1998.

7. W. Benz (ed.), *Das Exil der Kleinen Leute. Alltagserfahrung deutscher Juden in der Emigration*, Munich 1991; E. Lorenz, *Mehr als Willy Brandt : die Sozialistische Arbeiterpartei Deutschlands (SAP) im skandinavischen Exil*, Frankfurt 1997.
8. R. Thalmann, 'L'immigration allemande et l'opinion publique en France de 1936 à 1939', *Deutschland und Frankreich 1936–1939. Beihefte der Francia*, 10, 1981, pp.47–70; R. Thalmann, 'L'immigration allemande et l'opinion publique en France de 1933 à 1936' in *La France et l'Allemagne 1932–1936, actes du colloque franco-allemand tenu à Paris 10–12.3.1977*, Paris 1977, pp.149–72; B. Vormeier, 'La situation administrative des exilés allemands en France (1933–1945): 'Accueil-Répression-Internement-Déportation', in *Vivre à Gurs. Un Camp de Concentration français 1940–1941*, ed. B. Vormeier and H. Schramm, Paris 1977, pp.197–242. H. Walter, *Deutsche Exilliteratur 1933–1950* (4 volumes), Stuttgart 1978–2006, focused mainly on the literary exile, but Hans-Albert Walter drew at the same time a very broad picture of the exile experience, including refugee policies in the countries of exile.
9. L. de Jong, *Het Koninkrijk der Nederlanden in de Tweede Wereldoorlog Vol.1 Voorspel*, 's-Gravenhage 1967, see especially pp.446–505.
10. D. Michman, 'The Jewish Refugees from Germany in the Netherlands 1933–1940', PhD Thesis Hebrew University of Jerusalem, 1978 (in Hebrew); D. Michman, 'The Committee for Jewish Refugees in Holland (1933–1940), *Yad Vashem Studies*, 14, 1981, pp.205–32; B. Moore, 'Refugees from Nazi Germany in the Netherlands 1933–1940: The Political Problem and Government Response', PhD Thesis Manchester, 1983. A revised and updated version of the thesis was published as *Refugees from Nazi Germany in the Netherlands 1933–1940*, Dordrecht 1986.
11. C. Holmes, *John Bull's Island: Immigration and British Society, 1871–1971*, London 1988; C. Holmes, *Antisemitism and British Society 1867-1939*, London 1979; G. Lebzelter, *Political Antisemitism in England 1918–1939*, London 1978; G.C. Field, 'Antisemitism with the Boots Off: Recent Research on England', *Wiener Library Bulletin*, Special Issue (1983), pp.25–46; J. Steinert and I. Weber-Newth (eds), *European Immigrants in Britain, 1933–1950*, Munich 2003.
12. A. Sherman, *Island Refuge*, London 1973 see also, Arieh Sherman, 'The British Government, the Jewish Community and Refugee Agencies', *Journal of Holocaust Education* 4, no.1, 1995, pp.18–28.
13. A. Stevens, *The Dispossessed: German Refugees in Britain*, London 1975; G. Hirschfeld (ed.), *Exile in Great Britain. Refugees from Hitler's Germany*, Spa 1984; M. Berghahn, *Continental Britons: German-Jewish Refugees from Nazi Germany*, Oxford 1988 (revised edition 2007); M. Berghahn, *German-Jewish Refugees in England: The Ambiguities of Assimiliation*, New York 1984; Anthony Grenville (ed.), *Refugees from the Third Reich in Britain*, London 2003.
14. B. Wasserstein, *Britain and the Jews of Europe 1939–1945*, Oxford 1979.
15. T. Kushner, *The Holocaust and the Liberal Imagination*, Oxford 1994. Ignored here is William Rubinstein's flawed and sometime intemperate critique of American and British scholarship on the refugee issue. W. Rubinstein, *The Myth of Rescue*, London 1997.
16. F. Caestecker, *Ongewenste Gasten: Joodse Vluchtelingen en Migranten in de Dertiger Jaren in België*, Brussels 2001.
17. G. Noiriel, *Le Creuset Français. Histoire de l'immigration XIX–XXe siècles*, Paris 1988; G.and S. Arlettaz, *La Suisse et les étrangers. Immigration et formation nationale (1848–1933)*, Lausanne 2004; J. Lucassen and R. Pennix, *Nieuwkomers. Immigranten en hun nakomelingen in Nederland, 1550–1985*, Amsterdam 1985.

18. G. Noiriel, *La tyrannie du National. Le droit d'asile en Europe, 1793–1993*, Paris 1991 ; F. Caestecker, *Alien Policy in Belgium, 1840–1940 : The Creation of Guest Workers, Refugees and Illegal Aliens*, Oxford 2000; U. Gast, *Von der Kontrolle zur Abwehr. Die eidgenössische Fremdenpolizei im Spannungsfeld von Politik und Wirtschaft 1915–1933*, Zürich 1997; M. Leenders, *Ongenode gasten. Het vluchtelingenbeleid in Nederland, 1815–1938*, Utrecht 1993; C. Van Eijl, *Al te goed is buurmans gek. Het Nederlandse vreemdelingenbeleid 1840–1940*, Amsterdam 2005.
19. L. London, *Whitehall and the Jews, 1933–1948: British Immigration Policy, Jewish Refugees and the Holocaust*, Cambridge 2001; L. London, 'Whitehall and the Refugees: The 1930s and the 1990s', *Patterns of Prejudice* 34, no. 3, 2000, pp.17–26; A. Gottlieb, *Men of Vision: Anglo-Jewry's Aid to Victims of the Nazi Regime, 1933–1945*, London 1998.
20. R. Dinesen, B. Nielsen, H. Petersen, F. Schmoë, *Deutschsprachiges Exil in Dänemaken nach 1933. Zu Methoden und Einzelergebenissen*, Copenhagen 1986; L. Einhart, K. Misgeld, H. Müssener and H. Petersen, *'Ein sehr trübes Kapital'? Hitlerflüchtlinge im nordeuropäischen Exil 1933–1950*, Hamburg 1998; L. Rünitz, *Danmark og de jodiske flygtninge 1933–1940*, Copenhagen 2000.
21. A few essays addressed French refugee policy in the 1930s and in particular the role of the refugee committees in the reception of refugees in France: J. Omnès, 'L'accueil des émigrés politiques 1933–1938: L'exemple du Secours Rouge et la Ligue des Droits de l'Homme, et du Parti socialiste' and J. Joly, 'L'aide aux émigrés juifs: le Comité national de secours', in *Les Bannis de Hitler. Accueil et lutte des exilés allemands en France , 1933–1939*, ed. G. Badia et al., Paris 1984, resp. pp.65–104 and pp.37–64; C. Nicault, 'L'accueil des juifs d'Europe centrale par la communauté juive française (1933–1939)', in *De l'exil à la résistance: Réfugiés et immigrés d'Europe centrale en France, 1933–1945*, ed. K. Bartosek, R. Gallissot and D. Peschanski, Paris 1989, pp.53–59; A. Grynberg, 'L'accueil des réfugiés d'Europe Centrale en France (1933–1939)', in *Les Cahiers de la Shoah*, 1994, pp.131–48.
22. V. Caron, *Uneasy Asylum: France and the Jewish Refugee Crisis, 1933–1942*, Stanford 1999; V. Caron, 'Loyalties in Conflict: French Jewry and the Refugee Crisis, 1933–1935', *Leo Baeck Institute Yearbook* 36, 1991, pp.305–38; V. Caron, 'The Politics of Frustration. French Jewry and the Refugee Crisis in the 1930s', *Journal of Modern History* 65, no. 2, 1993, pp.311–56.
23. G. Noiriel, *La Tyrannie du national. Le droit d'asile en Europe 1793–1993*, Paris 1991; C. Zalc, 'Des réfugiés aux indésirables: les pouvoirs publics français face aux émigrés du IIIe Reich entre 1933 et 1939' in *Construction des nationalités et immigration dans la France contemporaine*, ed. E. Guichard and G. Noiriel, Paris 1997, pp. 259–74. New scholarship has started to tackle these issues. See for example P. Rygiel (ed.), *Le bon grain et l'ivraie: l'Etat-Nation et les populations immigrées fin XIXème siècle-début XXème siècle*, Lyon 2004.
24. Among others: F. Battel, *'Wo es hell ist, dort is die Schweiz' Flüchtlinge und Fluchthilfe an der Schaffhauser Grenze zur Zeit des Nationalsozialismus*, Zürich 2000; S. Keller, *Grüningers Fall. Geschichte von Flucht und Hilfe*, Zürich 1993; H. Wichers, *Im kampf gegen Hitler. Deutsche Sozialisten im Schweizer Exil 1933–1940*, Zürich 1994; J. Wacker, *Humaner als in Bern! Schweizer und Basler Asylpraxis gegenüber den jüdischen Flüchtlingen von 1933 bis 1943 im Vergleich*, Basel 1992; S. Machler, *Hilfe und Ohnmacht. Der Schweizerische Israelitische Gemeindebund und die nationalsozialistische Verfolgung, 1933–1945*, Zürich 2005.

25. C. Berghuis, *Joodse Vluchtelingen in Nederland, 1938–1949. Documenten betreffende toelating, uitleiding en kampopname*, Kampen 1990.
26. R. Ludi, 'Waging War on Wartime Memory: Recent Swiss Debates on the Legacies of the Holocaust and the Nazi Era', *Jewish Social Studies* 10, no. 2, 2004, pp.116–52. Unabhängige Expertenkommission Schweiz-Zweiter Weltkrieg, *Die Schweiz und die Flüchtlinge zur Zeit des Nationalsozialismus*, Bern 1999.
27. L. Rünitz, *Af hensyn til konsekvenserne, Danmark og flygtningespørgsmålet 1933–1939*, Odense 2005.
28. J. Toury, 'Ein Auftakt zur "Endlösung": Judenaustreibungen über nichtslawische Reichsgrenzen 1933–1939', in *Das Unrechts-Regime. Festschfit für Werner Jochmann zum 65. Geburtstag*, vol. 2, ed. U. Büttner, Hamburg 1986, pp.164–96; S. Heim, 'Vertreibung, Raub und Umverteilung. Die jüdischen Flüchtlinge aus Deutschland und die Vermehrung des "Volksvermögens"', in *Flüchtlingspolitik und Fluchthilfe* (Beiträge zur Nationalsozialistischen Gesundheids-und Sozialpolitik), Berlin 1999, pp.107–38; H. Berschel, *Bürokratie und Terror. Das Judenreferat der Gestapo Düsseldorf, 1935–1945*, Essen 2001.
29. K. Schleunes, *The Twisted Road to Auschwitz: Nazi Policy toward German Jews, 1933–1939*, Urbana 1970.
30. W. Rosenstock, 'Exodus 1933–1939: a Survey of Jewish Emigration form Germany', *Leo Baeck Institute Yearbook*, 1956, pp.337–90; H. Strauss, 'Jewish Emigration from Germany. Nazi Policies and Jewish Responses,' *Leo Baeck Institute Yearbook*, 1980–1981, 25–26, resp. pp.318–61 and pp.343–409.
31. C. Skran, *Refugees in Inter-War Europe: the Emergence of a Regime*, Oxford 1995; C. Skran, 'The Historical and Contemporary Context of International Responses of Asylum', *Journal of Policy History* 4, 1992, pp.8–35. Moreover the lack of attention to non-English sources inevitably limits the importance of her analysis.
32. K. Voigt, *Zuflucht auf Widerruf. Exil in Italien 1933–1945*, Stuttgart 1989; C. Villani, *Zwischen Rassengesetzen und Deportation. Juden in Südtirol, im Trentino und in der Provinz Belluno, 1933–1945*, Innsbrück 2003; P. von zur Mühlen, *Fluchtweg Spanien-Portugal, die Deutsche Emigration 1933–1945: Politische Aktivitäten und sociokulturelle Integration*, Bonn 1988.
33. Katerina Capkova and Michal Frankl of the Institute of Terezin Initiative at Prague are currently preparing a publication on Czechoslovakian refugee policy (1933–1938) which is due to be published by Paseka under the title *Nejisté útočiště: Československo a uprchlíci před nacismem, 1933–1938* (Uncertain Refuge: Czechoslovakia and the Refugees from Germany and Austria, 1933–1938).
34. J. Hollifield, *Immigrants, Markets and States: The Political Economy of Postwar Europe*, Cambridge 1992.
35. Some authors assume the genocidal intent of Hitler's regime and vest this knowledge into the minds of statesmen, governments and organisations in the 1930s. See, for example Jean-Pierre Deschodt and François Huguenin, *La république xénophobe, 1917–1939*, Paris 2001, p.108. The historian must avoid the distortion of hindsight.

Part I

National and International Analyses of Policies towards the Refugees from Nazi Germany

Chapter I.1

International Refugee Policy and Jewish Immigration under the Shadow of National Socialism*

Susanne Heim

Most of the about 500,000 Jews who lived in Germany when the Nazi takeover took place in 1933 did not initially consider emigration because they did not expect the regime to last. Within a few years however, this attitude changed. Although not particularly large in numerical terms compared to other refugee movements, the emigration from Nazi Germany caused major changes in the juridical systems and in the public policy of the main countries of refuge. This not only affected their migration management policies but also had an impact on their residents' access to the labour market as well as on welfare regulations.

By excluding the Jews from the *'Volksgemeinschaft'* and defining them as inferior and having fewer rights, the Hitler regime initiated a radical change in the international order and jeopardised the fragile equilibrium of the political system in interwar Europe. The Germans reclaimed the right not just to exclude 'foreigners' who wanted to enter the German territory, but went far beyond this to declare that sections of their 'own' national population was 'not of German blood' and thus not part of the ethnic community, which was considered as a prerequisite for full citizenship.[1] This policy set in motion a severe crisis by forcing other states to accept the consequences of this redefined German concept of citizenship and to cope with those who were forced out. Such action finally caused the breakdown of instruments of international conflict prevention like the system of minority protection and had the effect of spreading authoritarian methods into otherwise democratic countries.

As long as the countries neighbouring Germany accepted national interests and the definition of citizenship as the essence of the nation states' sovereignty and did not want to go into open confrontation with the Nazi state, they could only try to deal with the consequences of this German redefinition. Proceeding from a national understanding of citizenship and from the assumption that the refugee problem was a temporary one, they saw those refugees who had no nationality, i.e., the stateless people and the Jews who were forced to leave Germany, as the major problem, because these people could not be repatriated anywhere. Those countries most affected by the refugee influx reacted to the crisis by strengthening border controls, by inventing a variety of restrictions for refugees living in the country and finally by establishing camps for the detention of the 'unwanted' newcomers.

The main tendency in migration policy was – and is – the protection of national territory against unwanted immigration, no matter what this meant for the refugees or for the international climate. In cases of doubt, the national interest and a general attitude of accommodation and appeasement towards Germany (even before the Munich agreement of 1938) took precedence over humanitarian considerations and good relations with less powerful neighbours. This kind of national 'egoism' was also partly a reaction to the failure of international institutions to deal with the crisis. The old instruments of international migration management, which had been reasonably effective in dealing with earlier refugee movements, no longer worked. The reason for this was not merely the world economic crisis, which had changed the whole framework and made the transformation of refugees into manpower much more difficult. The system of minority protection was, at least half heartedly, respected only as long as it was enforced by the Great Powers on the new states emerging from the ruins of the great empires as a precondition for their independence. However, the Jews in Germany were not regarded as a national minority and the Great Powers did not even attempt to put the same pressure on Germany that they had imposed on the smaller central European states. This very fact would later encourage states like Poland and Romania to follow the German example and attempt to push their Jewish populations out and thus make the German refugee problem a European one. The other traditional instrument of international refugee policy, the Nansen Office, was never involved in helping the German refugees, for reasons that will become apparent.

Today, new forms of migration and border controls are initiated through the concerted actions of ministers of the interior (or secretaries of state) or international meetings of special police forces. In the 1930s, however, the establishment of migration control instruments was scarcely a coordinated decision-making process. Governments tended to develop (migration) policy independently from one another, and often at odds with one another. However, there were occasional adjustments of migration policy at a regional level and usually national interests were not defined in a way that was hostile to other states.

There were several attempts made to solve the refugee crisis through international agreements. The main steps towards an internationally coordinated answer to the refugee crisis focused on in this chapter were:

- The establishment of a High Commissioner of the League of Nations for Refugees (Jewish and others) coming from Germany in October 1933
- The Provisional Arrangement concerning the status of refugees coming from Germany signed in 1936
- A formal convention determining some basic rights of the refugees, approved two years later, in February 1938
- The Evian Conference in July 1938 as the last attempt to find an international solution of the refugee crisis before the outbreak of the war.

While some historians see these agreements as demonstrating a substantial progress towards an international consensus,[2] most authors have dismissed the League of Nations as a weak institution incapable of offering refugees any substantive protection.[3] Dealing exclusively with these attempts to find to a new consensus on migration rules would, however, limit the analysis to the classical repertoire of international politics such as international institutions, agreements and diplomatic efforts, in other words the formal refugee regime. The various indirect means used to limit and to control migration as well as the refugees themselves, their institutions and their reactions to migration restrictions would be ignored. Yet from the refugees' perspective, what shaped the international refugee regime was much more the conjunction of many formally unrelated actions to protect alleged national interests (German or others) than the actions of the international institutions.

Beside the formal structures, there existed what I would call an informal international refugee regulation. On various levels and in a variety of institutions – which ranged from the Jewish communities to the Gestapo – refugee policy was shaped by actors who were neither formally interrelated nor coordinated. Nevertheless their actions were often interdependent and served to influence what happened at an international level. To give only a few examples: the barriers set up in the countries of refuge to protect the national labour market or the interests of certain professional groups changed migration movements and often forced a refugee recently arrived in one country into further emigration; the British mandate authorities retaliated against Zionist efforts to bring Jews from Germany illegally to Palestine by establishing detention camps and by militarizing the control of shipping lanes; and, through the establishment of a special Central Currency Investigation Office (Devisenfahndungsamt) and other instruments, the Gestapo attempted to control the movements, contacts, and actions of the refugees, and forced Jews who wanted to leave the country and to get their assets out to evade the restrictive laws and provisions.

In this chapter, the refugee crisis of the 1930s will be analysed as a history of the development of national and cross-national instruments to control migration. This process has to be scrutinised from both formal or institutional and informal perspectives. Such a distinction between the two levels makes formerly invisible actors, such as the individual refugees and the relief organisations, recognisable as subjects of international politics; and it is based on a comprehensive understanding of migration politics going far beyond the direct means of migration control.

The High Commissioner – a New Institution on Fragile Foundations

When forced migration from Germany started in 1933, there was no international institution 'naturally' responsible for the refugees. The Leagues of Nations' 'traditional' refugee organisation, the Nansen Office, was not authorised to deal with any new group of refugees. The mission of the Nansen Office was limited to the Russian refugees (in the aftermath of the revolution, civil war, and later famine). An extension of its mandate to new groups of refugees would have required an amendment of the agreement establishing the office, as had been necessary for the Armenian refugees, among others, in the 1920s. Such an amendment would have been difficult to obtain, and would in any case have excluded the Soviet government who rejected the Nansen Office for its alleged anti-Soviet policy supporting the Russian refugees. The League, however, not only hoped to involve the Soviet Union in efforts to solve the new refugee crisis but also wanted her to join the League – which indeed happened in 1934. Strengthening the importance of the Nansen Office would have jeopardised such expectations. In any case the League of Nations was losing much of its authority in the early 1930s. At the same time, Europe was still struggling with the economic crisis and refugees were seen mainly as an unwanted burden instead of an asset to domestic labour markets.

Another international institution traditionally engaged in migration policy was the International Labour Office (ILO), which dealt with the refugees in one of its international conferences in the summer of 1933, but only insofar as they affected national labour markets. The head of the ILO, Albert Thomas, regarded the refugee problem in general as a question of settlement of 'excess population' and the control of migration as the basis of a 'rational population policy'.[4] The ILO commissioned a study on the problem. However, according to German sources, the Secretary General of the League of Nations did not even consider the ILO resolution concerning the refugees from Germany worth communicating to the member states of the League.[5]

Discussions about the necessity of establishing a new institution for the refugees from Germany began in the spring of 1933, but no country pushed for its creation because such a step might have offended the German government.[6] The Germans typically argued that the Jews leaving

Germany were not in fact stateless refugees (the usual clients of the Nansen Office) or not refugees at all,[7] as according the German Foreign Office they had left Germany in fear of losing their privileges.[8] Germany was still a member of the League of Nations and could have vetoed any League action on the refugees such as the establishment of a High Commissioner. In the autumn of 1933 Germany left the League, but any cancellation of membership was to become effective only after two years. Concerned about the decreasing authority of the League, the Secretary-General as well as many League members hoped that the Germans would revoke their decision if the intended reforms of the international body met their demands. Among the League's members, then, a consensus existed that an initiative to establish a new institution dealing with the refugees coming from Germany had no chance unless the German government agreed to it, at least tacitly. At length and reluctantly, the Dutch government finally took the initiative to suggest the foundation of a High Commissioner for the refugees from Germany, all the while stressing repeatedly in front of the Germans that this should not be seen as a criticism of Germany, but purely as a measure of self-defence.

The fact that no one wanted to confront the Germans led to a compromise that debilitated the High Commissioner's Office from the outset. During the preliminary discussions, the German representative at the League had made it clear that Germany would refrain from her right to veto only if the new refugee body was not an official institution of the League. In this way, the German anti-Jewish policy could not become a topic in the General Assembly of the League. This request had far-reaching consequences: The newly founded High Commission remained an institution not answerable to the League itself, and the Commissioner did not have the right to report on its activities before the General Assembly of the League. Thus the High Commission remained a somewhat marginalised institution in League circles. This 'distancing' even took on a concrete form with the proposal by the League's Secretary-General, Joseph Avenol, that the Commissioner reside at Lausanne, some distance from the headquarters of the League in Geneva. Due to the League's member states' unwillingness to finance the new institution, it was supported almost exclusively by private funds, mainly by Jewish organisations.[9] The 25,000 Swiss Francs the High Commissioner received from the League's Fund for organising purposes was merely a loan to be repaid within twelve months. By such restrictions Avenol hoped to appease the Germans who were about to leave the League.[10]

Eventually the first High Commissioner, James G. McDonald, a U.S. citizen, was appointed. He had been chosen largely because he was seen as a candidate the Germans could accept; he had strong contacts with Germany and had proved his goodwill to that country by defending it against claims of war atrocities during World War I. In fact, the U.S. Government had opposed the nomination of a U.S. citizen as High Commissioner, worrying that this could undermine U.S. immigration policy.[11] The promoters of the new institution within the League hoped that the choice would integrate the U.S. State Department into the efforts to solve the refugee problem even though the U.S. was not a member of the League. Supported by the American Foreign Policy Association, whose chairman he had been for many years, McDonald had been lobbying for the establishment of the High Commission for several months. However, most of the pressure for this had come from Jewish organisations and in a way, the creation of a separate institution devoted to refugee affairs was their accomplishment.

Whereas the High Commissioner was not accountable to the General Assembly of the League, it had to answer to the Governing Body. This consisted of representatives from twelve states: Belgium, Great Britain, Denmark, the USA, France, Italy, the Netherlands, Poland, Sweden, Switzerland, Czechoslovakia and Uruguay.[12] Most of the governments expected, at least tacitly, that their representatives would do their best to direct the refugees to other countries. 'Only countries that had received considerable numbers of refugees showed any interest in the High Commission's activities, but this was merely to exploit it as an instrument to get rid of "their" refugees'. France, for example, was convinced that the High Commissioner's only task should be colonisation: rapid evacuation of the refugees from the host countries.[13] The French delegate Henry Bérenger put it bluntly: 'La France c'est un passage, pas un garage.'[14]

In addition to the Governing Body, there was an Advisory Council to influence the High Commissioner's policy made up from representatives of the refugee relief organisations. Despite the competition between the various organisations, the Council played an important role in supporting the refugees in practical matters. Furthermore the most influential organisations in the Council, such as the American Jewish Joint Distribution Committee, the Jewish Agency for Palestine and the Jewish Colonization Association (ICA), were instrumental in financing the High Commissioner while the states represented in the Governing Body had declined to carry any financial burdens. One of the major problems McDonald was expected to solve was the transfer of Jewish property from Germany, thus enabling Jewish emigrants to start a new life abroad. The main obstacle hindering the High Commissioner's activities was the fact that he lacked backing from the member states of the League, and the Germans refused even to receive him. They claimed their anti-Jewish policy was an internal affair not only on principle but also because they were unwilling to make any compromise on the export of Jewish assets as, according to their antisemitic propaganda, Jews had achieved their wealth only by exploiting and cheating German non-Jews. As a result, McDonald could do little or nothing to expedite a solution to this particular problem and, as a result, devoted more of his attention to other aspects of the refugee issue.

In 1935, after two frustrating years in office, James McDonald resigned. He had not been able to negotiate with the German government and had not had much success in facilitating the settlement of refugees in foreign countries.[15] McDonald was not the only one to be disappointed about the results of his work. Some distinguished Jewish leaders expressed themselves dissatisfied with his 'lack of initiative and poor efforts' and commented that McDonald 'took credit for the actual relief work rendered by Jewish organisations'.[16] Long before his resignation, in September 1934, relief organisations in Britain and France considered discontinuing financing of the Commissioner's budget and wanted him to resign.[17] After his resignation McDonald was nonetheless still committed to the refugee work; he became a member of the President's Advisory Commission on Refugees in the United States and after the Second World War he served as U.S. ambassador in Israel.

Labour Restrictions and the Policy of Dispossession

During the first months of Hitler's chancellorship, neighbouring countries had received the refugees and tried to accommodate them, at least provisionally. As the Nazi government turned out to be more stable than initially expected and it became clear that the refugees would not return to Germany for quite a while, public attitude towards them in the receiving countries became more hostile. Due to the economic crisis and the high rates of unemployment, refugees were seen primarily as a threat to national labour markets. Consequently, among the first measures taken to limit the influx of refugees were restrictions on access to the labour market. In several countries employment of foreigners had to be approved by the state and this was not permitted if there were any native workers available for the job.[18] At the end of December 1934, a co-worker of the High Commissioner reported on the xenophobic atmosphere in the Netherlands, rooted in the 'general feeling ... that for several years the country has been overrun by foreigners who are competing unfairly in the labour market'.[19] While the Dutch Foreign Office expressed itself quite sympathetic to the situation of the refugees coming from Germany 'the economic and welfare departments are at present waging a sort of economic war on foreign labour, which is of course a very unfortunate break with the liberal traditions of the country'.[20] In Denmark the government uttered similar concerns about the competition that German refugees represented for the Danish unemployed.[21] In Austria, a High Commission staff member reported in early 1935 that 'only in very rare cases have permissions been given to employ refugees from Germany.'[22] According to the representative of the American Jewish Joint Distribution Committee (AJDC) in the autumn of 1934, hatred against foreigners and refugees was very strong in several European countries. Sometimes even parts of the Jewish communities in the countries of refuge took an anti-refugee attitude, fearing that their own social acceptance might be suffering from the growing antisemitism allegedly provoked by the huge number Jewish refugees from Germany.[23]

The increasingly restrictive policy in the countries of refuge was accompanied by an escalation of Nazi anti-Jewish policy designed to push even more Jews out of the Reich. After a chaotic series of atrocities during the first months of the regime, the Sicherheitsdienst (SD) and the Gestapo officials eager to find solutions to the so-called 'Jewish Question', and who gradually took over the initiative in guiding anti-Jewish policy in Nazi Germany, focused on forcing the emigration of young Jews. In 1934 the SD outlined its position in the following statement:

> For the Jews, living conditions have to be restricted – not only in the economic sense. Germany for them has to be a country without a future, where the remnants of the old generations can die, but the young can't live, so that the incentive for emigration remains vital.[24]

Such 'incentive' was, above all, the destruction of the material existence of German Jewry.

The Nazi policy of expelling the Jews was contradictory from its very beginning. Some of the bureaucratic measures and the harassment designed to chase the Jews out of Germany actually hindered their emigration. In particular, the policy of dispossessing Jews through taxes, fees, professional restrictions and prohibitions, as well as the restrictive rules concerning the transfer of assets to foreign countries, turned the emigrants into 'unwanted' individuals who, from the perspective of immigration authorities in the receiving countries were thus more likely to become a 'public burden'.

Like Jewish artists and journalists, who were not allowed to join the newly founded professional organisations which were open only to 'Aryans', Jewish workers were excluded from the Arbeitsfront, the official workers organisation. Yet only members of the Arbeitsfront could receive insurance and sickness benefits. As a consequence of this, and the exclusion of Jews from the civil service and many professions, the rates of unemployment and impoverishment in German Jewry increased considerably. As Herbert Strauss has noted, 'if small loans and other forms of social aid are included in the estimate of supported persons, as many as 33 per cent of the German-Jewish population may have received some form of social assistance in 1935 – about 52,000 Jews received assistance from the government welfare system.'[25] This was the case even years before the so-called 'De-Judaisation' of the German economy began in 1938.

While the German government deprived more and more Jews of any chance to earn their living it also prevented them from starting a new life abroad. In 1934, the amount of money emigrants could take abroad was reduced to RM 2,000 instead of RM 10,000.[26] One of the most important instruments for the dispossession of the refugees was the flight tax (*Reichsfluchtsteuer*). This tax had existed since 1931 and was designed to limit the emigration of wealthy people and protect the value of the German currency. It therefore also applied to those who left the country voluntarily. However, from 1933 on, this tax was primarily directed against Jewish emigrants, who were forced to leave a proportion of their assets in Germany when leaving the country. Initially only those earning more than RM 20,000 per annum or owning property worth more than RM 200,000 were obliged to pay the flight tax. 'In 1934, the tax base was changed to include those owning RM 50,000 at any time since 1931.'[27] During the following years the tax threshold was reduced step by step, thus expanding the number of those who were subject to the tax. Those unable to pay the tax were refused permission to leave the country. Emigrants had to deposit their money in a blocked account and only small amounts were released for their daily life. Thus even relatively wealthy people had to live at a very restricted level. In 1936, the establishment of the Devisenfahndungsamt considerably strengthened the control over the emigrants' financial affairs.

At the same time, the SD tried to influence Jewish life by hindering any so called assimilatory tendencies among Jewish leaders while encouraging the Zionists as they were seen as a driving force for emigration.[28] Jewish emigration to Palestine was thus supported by the Nazi authorities – at least as long as a Jewish state in Palestine seemed to be a rather unlikely prospect. However, after the Peel Commission had proposed the establishment of a Jewish state next to an Arab one in Palestine, this policy changed. In November 1937, officials in Department II 112, in charge of anti-Jewish policy of the SD, summarised that up to that date the 'main task' of the SD had been the repression of all 'assimilatory tendencies' in German Jewry. In future however, now that the German Foreign Office had taken position against a Jewish state, Zionists should no longer be supported by the SD. This change of policy was to be kept secret from the Jews. The crucial point was to make clear to the Jews living in Germany that emigration was the only way out.[29]

The Ha'avarah Agreement, which had been concluded in August 1933 between the German Minister of Economics and the Zionist representatives from Germany and Palestine, enabled Jewish emigrants to take at least some of their assets to Palestine and at the same time facilitated exports of German goods to that country.[30] For the German government, the expected benefit to its foreign trade was the main motive for signing the agreement. Among Jewish organisations there was a major controversy. On the one hand it was argued that the agreement indirectly supported the German economy and undermined the Jewish boycott of German goods, organised by a special committee residing in New York.[31] On the other hand, the Zionists argued that the German Jewish assets transferred to Palestine were desperately needed there for the building up of Jewish life.[32]

In the mid 1930s, similar plans for transferring Jewish money to countries other than Palestine were discussed by Jewish organisations in Germany and abroad. The British Zionist and department store owner, Simon Marks, had developed a scheme of action for the emigration of between 60,000 and 100,000 young German Jews. Their settlement in Palestine as well as other countries was to be financed by donations collected among Jews outside Germany. The Jewish banker Max Warburg, a member of the Reich Representation of German Jews (*Reichsvertretung der deutschen Juden*), who had comparatively good relations with the president of the Reichsbank Hjalmar Schacht, submitted another plan.[33] According to Warburg the assets and property of Jewish emigrants in Germany could be earmarked to serve as a security for credits given to the emigrants by a trust company to be set up in London. Warburg expected wealthy and influential Jewish personalities such as Anthony de Rothschild, Lord Bearsted and Simon Marks to found this company.[34] The 'Warburg Plan' to a certain extent met the same criticism as the Ha'avarah agreement, namely that it would assist the export of German goods.[35] A combined version of the Marks and the 'Warburg Plan' was discussed among representatives of the *Reichsvertretung* on the one hand and delegates of the *Reichsbank*, the Reich Ministry of the Economy,[36] and the Reich Interior Ministry on the other.[37] The German authorities expected to increase exports through such an agreement. Negotiations however reached a deadlock for various reasons.[38] As long as the emigrants' assets on the blocked accounts were reduced by the flight tax, there were only small sums available as security for loans abroad.[39] The limited results achieved by the Ha'avarah agreement did not justify the optimistic prospects of a transfer of large sums made in the 'Warburg Plan'.[40] Furthermore, once the emigrants had left the country their remaining property in Germany was considered to be worthless as a security for a loan in foreign exchange.[41] A special agreement did ease money transfer, but only on a very limited scale. By 1934, restrictions on transferring money abroad made it nearly impossible to send money from Germany to German citizens in other countries. This affected, among others, several thousand Jewish children, whose enrolment in schools outside of Germany could no longer be supported by their families.[42] Probably as a result of McDonald's negotiations with the German Reichsbank in late 1934,[43] the so-called 'education clearing' was set up, allowing Jews to transfer money to their children who attended schools or training centres abroad.[44]

The pace of 'Aryanisation' began to quicken as more and more Jews were effectively forced to sell their businesses and assets, almost always at prices far below their real market value. The increasing impoverishment of the Jews in Germany made any possible emigration more and more problematic. The financial restrictions imposed on German Jews and particularly potential emigrants, in conjunction with the restrictions on the labour market in the receiving countries, all conspired to complicate matters for would-be Jewish emigrants.

Restructuring the Jewish Community

While a considerable number of Jews were preparing to leave Germany in one way or another, the German Jewish organisations still hesitated about promoting emigration. The most influential of these was the Central Association of German Citizens of Mosaic Faith (*Centralverein deutscher Staatsbürger jüdischen Glaubens*, CV). The CV stressed the necessity to fight antisemitism in Germany and to stand firm against increasing discrimination. Like the Reich Association of Jewish War Veterans (*Reichsbund jüdischer Frontsoldaten*), the first reactions of the CV to the Nazi regime staggered between protest against antisemitic attacks, declarations of patriotic loyalty, and attempts to deal with the consequences of the anti-Jewish measures. Both organisations were opposed to Zionism and feared undermining Jewish positions in Germany by promoting emigration. As late as in spring 1935 the CV warned 'that nervousness should not be increased unnecessarily by rashly uttered slogans for emigration'.[45] The majority of the CV leaders, at least at the early stage of Nazi persecution, saw professional retraining as the right way to deal with the plight of the Jews. Through so-called restructuring (*Umschichtung*) they wanted to counterbalance the concentration of Jews in certain professions such as academic posts and trade and direct them into those professions and economic fields where they were still permitted to work.[46]

Gradually the focus of work of the Jewish community shifted towards new tasks. Training, restructuring, economic support and consultation about emigration became the main activities of both national and international Jewish organisations in Germany. Despite all the previous conflicts between Zionists and non-Zionists, both sides converged in the face of a growing common threat. On a practical level the CV, the Reichsbund and the Zionist Federation of Germany (*Zionistische Vereinigung für Deutschland*) cooperated in the various new institutions created to ease the crisis facing the Jewish community. Although many Jewish leaders did not regard emigration as a 'solution' for German Jewry in general, they tried to meet the needs of those who saw no future in Germany.

The new situation caused a far-reaching restructuring of German Jewish organisations. In April 1933 the Central Office for Jewish Economic Support (*Zentralstelle für jüdische Wirtschaftshilfe*) was founded, and only a few days later the Central Committee for Help and Reconstruction (*Zentralausschuß für Hilfe und Aufbau*) that united all Jewish institutions for welfare affairs, emigration and education matters. The aim of the *Zentralausschuß* was to open up new possibilities for Jews pushed out of their economic positions by facilitating a change of profession or preparing emigration. Although the focus was supposed to be the consolidation of Jewish life in Germany, this was not handled in a dogmatic manner.[47]

On 17 September 1933, the *Reichsvertretung der deutschen Juden* was established as an umbrella organisation in order to meet the need for a more powerful representation of Jewish interests to the Nazi authorities.[48] The Zionist movement, which had traditionally only attracted minority support from German Jewry, grew steadily after the Nazi assumption of power and played a decisive role in organising emigration, especially for Jewish youngsters. Within a short period, Zionists built up or expanded the infrastructure for organising and preparing emigration to Palestine: agricultural training centres for Jewish youngsters, Hebrew courses, classes on Jewish history and Palestinian geography, and discussion circles dealing with the political perspectives of Zionism.[49]

Self-help and Emigration

Notwithstanding their enormous efforts, the Jewish organisations were able to help only a limited number of emigrants. They tried to focus their work on those who had little chance of organising (and financing) emigration on their own. Many others who had financial means and relatives abroad to help them left on their own initiative.[50] Throughout the 1930s, organising one's emigration became a full-time job and this helps to explain why many Jews moved from small towns to the big cities; both to facilitate their emigration and to evade persecution by local Nazis. Would-be emigrants had to contact a huge number of agencies to obtain all the necessary documentation. Often an application was turned down because supporting documents had expired or because other documents were required before it could be processed.[51] In searching for a refuge, emigrants contacted far-away relatives even if they had never met them personally and asked them for financial guarantees, money or other kinds of support. Ultimately the Gestapo in Berlin restricted this desperate search for relatives abroad by prohibiting the Jews from writing letters to foreign citizens of the same family name simply because of the complaints from non-Jews who had received such letters.[52]

On a practical level the prohibitions on immigrants working in countries of refuge meant illicit work (and thus the risk of trouble with the authorities) or dependence on relief organisations. Consequently the immigrants developed a kind of black or informal economy in which women played an important role. They mended clothes for refugee men whose wives had remained in Germany, they produced toys, clothes or other things that could be sold without a shop, took in refugees as lodgers or did secretarial work for a rescue committee.[53] They gave courses in sewing, knitting, cooking or arts and crafts such as flower-arranging. Usually women were more disposed than men to accept a job that had nothing to do with their previous experience.

This informal economy was sometimes also supported by the Jewish immigrant or relief organisations in the receiving countries. They tried to convince the native population that refugees were not necessarily an economic burden and that immigrants could become at least partly independent from subsidies by selling goods and services among themselves.[54] In other cases, however, the Jewish communities in the receiving countries also regarded the immigrants from Germany as competition and wrote to the Hilfsverein in order to prevent further immigration to 'their' country.

Seen as a whole, there was a broad-based transfer of knowledge, money and practical support within Jewish families and at the community, and even the international, level that was vital for the emigration of many

Jews from Germany. This network had its parallel among the Jewish refugee organisations as well. Immediately after the Nazi takeover several international organisations had started to focus on aid for German Jews. Alongside the majority of the German Jewish leaders, these organisations shared the idea that *Umschichtung* was the right response to the plight of German Jews and that emigration was a possibility for young Jews but could not be considered as a general solution. Nevertheless the Joint financed a good deal of German Jewish emigration and together with HICEM, ICA and the Jewish Agency organised the transit to other countries and tried to provide opportunities for German Jews abroad. They cooperated closely with German Jewish organisations in order to arrange an 'orderly emigration' from Germany and to establish a system of selecting those Jews who were considered to be most in need for financial help as well as refuge.[55]

The Provisional Arrangement of 1936

In February 1936 the League of Nations appointed Sir Neill Malcolm, a retired British general, as High Commissioner for refugees from Germany. Malcolm was in an even weaker position and less dedicated to the task than his predecessor McDonald. Having been chair of the inter-allied military commission in Germany after the First World War, Malcolm had good contacts with the German aristocracy and high-ranking military men,[56] although he did not speak German. He was nevertheless completely inexperienced in refugee matters,[57] but this was not the only reason for the reservations harboured against him.[58] According to Myron Taylor, the U.S. representative at the Conference of Evian, Malcolm:

> does the work of the League Commission in time which he can spare from his duties as head of the North Borneo Company. ... Sir Neill's chief virtue is that he obeys the orders of the British Foreign Office and of the League Secretariat without question and does not even attempt to act independently.[59]

Immediately after his assumption of office as a High Commissioner in February 1936, Malcolm started to organise a conference, which finally took place in Geneva from 2–4 July 1936. At the end a 'Provisional Arrangement' was announced for the German refugees, which would guarantee them certain basic rights that had been given to the Russian refugees years before. In this Arrangement, which came into force on 4 August 1936,[60] the term 'refugee coming from Germany' was defined as 'any person who was settled in that country, who does not possess any nationality other than German nationality, and in respect of whom it is established that in law or in fact he or she does not enjoy the protection of the Government of the Reich'.[61] Thus Jews of Polish nationality who had been living in Germany for decades were excluded from protection. According to the Arrangement, refugees from Germany were to receive an identity certificate, valid usually for one year (and renewable for another six months), which would allow them to travel abroad and come back to the country where the ID card had been issued. This certificate, however, was granted only to persons 'lawfully residing' in the relevant country on the date when the Agreement became effective. As a transitional measure, the ID card could also be issued to refugees living illegally in the country if they reported themselves to the authorities within a certain time span 'to be determined by the Government concerned'.[62] In practice the interpretation of the Provisional Arrangement by national authorities only eased the situation of those who had managed to leave Germany comparatively early, but did not abolish the mechanism that continued to foster illegal immigration.[63] This met the requirements of most of the governments involved. They were prepared to deal with the refugees already in their respective countries, but did not want to give any guarantees concerning future arrivals as there was no finite limit to the potential European refugee problem.[64]

According to the agreement the expulsion of refugees was forbidden, 'unless such measures are dictated by reasons of national security or public order'.[65] In cases where a refugee protected by the international Agreement was told to leave the country, a 'suitable period' was to be granted to make necessary arrangements.[66] Under certain conditions refugees could even be sent back to Germany: for example where 'they had been warned and have refused to make the necessary arrangements to proceed to another country or to take advantage of the arrangements made for them with that object'.[67] The Arrangement contained no provisions concerning the issue of labour permits or welfare and relief. As these topics had been included in the convention of 1933 on the refugees from Russia, the fact that such fundamental issues were left out here reveals how limited the international consensus regarding the refugee problem was. The Czech government accordingly refused to sign the arrangement, claiming that the Czech practice of asylum was more favourable for the refugees.[68] The Provisional Arrangement was signed by eight states; Belgium, Denmark, France, Great Britain, Norway, the Netherlands, Spain and Switzerland.[69]

The Arrangement came nowhere near meeting the demands of the refugee relief organisations. A representative of the Joint criticised it as being too vague, 'unnecessarily precautious' and 'in need of clarification'. Terms like 'lawfully residing in their territory' or 'suitable period' were not defined precisely and thus could be interpreted to the detriment of the refugee. By emphasizing that the certificate should 'not contravene any law of regulation governing the supervision of foreigners', the impact of the arrangement was weakened and reading between the lines it was possible to see how its provisions might be circumvented.[70]

Refugee organisations such as the Central Association of German Emigration (*Zentralvereinigung der deutschen Emigration*), an umbrella organisation for German refugees regardless whether they left the country because of political or racial persecution, had requested amnesty for all those who had been expelled from a country of refuge and were now living there illegally.[71] The association suggested the establishment of an advisory commission in which the refugee organisations would be represented and which should ascertain if the person in question was to be regarded as a refugee.[72] Furthermore the refugees should be effectively protected against repatriation to Germany and have the right to appeal against their possible expulsion to another country. The international conference on the right of asylum, organised in Paris in June 1936, had even requested that the refugees should be free to choose the place they wanted to live and their way of earning a living.[73]

The German evaluation of the arrangement was unsurprisingly dismissive. The German Foreign office surmised that their representatives in Geneva had achieved a propaganda success without making any sacrifices, either in relation to the labour market or on financial or economic issues. The arrangement was not even as far reaching as the convention of 1933 on the refugees covered by the Nansen Office.[74]

The Convention of 1938

Less than two years later, at an international refugee conference that took place in Geneva from 7 to 10 February 1938, the definition of 'refugees coming from Germany' was expanded. The term now explicitly included stateless persons who had left Germany for the same reasons as the refugees of German nationality.[75] While the Provisional Arrangement of 1936 referred almost exclusively to refugees of German nationality, the convention approved in 1938 strengthened the rights of stateless people who had previously been in a much weaker position. According to an additional paragraph, 'persons who leave Germany for reasons of purely personal convenience' were excluded from protection. In fact this was meant to ensure that only a migrant forced out of the country by political, racial or religious persecution would be protected by the Arrangement while those who left Germany because they had got in trouble with criminal or fiscal law could still be excluded. The vague terms left a considerable space for interpretation and provoked a debate at the conference in February 1938 about who could be regarded as a 'voluntary emigrant'.[76] Gerhart Riegner, a co-worker of the World Jewish Congress in Geneva,[77] criticised the vague wording about the 'purely personal convenience', which, according to him, satisfied the wishes of the Belgian and the Swiss delegates and might cause some problems. The Swiss representative Heinrich Rothmund, head of the federal police, wanted even economic reasons to be interpreted as 'personal' ones; the French delegate however replied that Jews whose assets had been confiscated in Germany undoubtedly had to be regarded as refugees.[78] In order to prevent misinterpretation of the term 'purely personal convenience' the refugee organisations lobbied for the establishment of a control commission to prevent any misuse of the convention. This aspiration was indeed included in the final statement of the conference.[79]

According to the convention, refugees were not to be expelled back to Germany 'unless they [had] been warned and have refused, without just cause, to make the necessary arrangements to proceed to another territory or to take advantage of the arrangements made for them with that object'.[80] Compared to the Provisional Arrangement the words 'without just cause' were added to the text of the Convention. Perhaps Riegner was thinking of that addition when he considered this clause as a far-reaching restriction to the states' right to deport refugees to Germany. Only the Netherlands, he remarked, insisted on the right to send refugees back to Germany.[81] Also in contrast to the 1936 Arrangement, the Convention of 1938 included a chapter on labour conditions. Under certain circumstances, the restrictions for the protection of the labour market were to be waived for refugees who had been resident in the country for at least three years, who were married to a citizen of that country or had children possessing the nationality of the country of residence. This chapter, like most paragraphs of the convention, had been taken from its predecessor of 1933, the convention concerning the Nansen refugees. New, however, was article 15, providing professional training for the preparation of refugees for emigration to countries overseas. According to Riegner, the fact that these regulations had now also been adopted for refugees from Germany was one of the main achievements of the conference. Nevertheless he feared that the article on labour conditions that would benefit the majority of the refugees might reduce the chances of future refugees being accepted at all.[82]

The convention approved at this meeting was signed by only seven states: Belgium, the U.K., France, Denmark, Spain, Norway and the Netherlands – and each had reservations about individual articles.[83] Moreover, only the first two states mentioned actually ratified the convention before the outbreak of war in September 1939.[84] The Danish government did not ratify the convention before the end of the Second World War. As Hans Uwe Petersen assumes 'the reasons lie in the development of the refugee question in the following period on the one hand and the position of Norway and Sweden on the other hand'.[85] Denmark usually took the other Scandinavian countries as a point of reference and did not want to run any risks by making concessions towards the refugees if other governments were likely to take a more restrictive attitude.

The signatory states to the 1938 Convention made several reservations concerning the provisions related to labour and the equal treatment of refugees and foreigners, primarily because education and other rights were usually accorded to foreigners on the basis of reciprocity. In addition, the Netherlands refused to sign the paragraph restricting the expulsion of refugees to Germany. The United Kingdom stated that the definition of 'public order', which might be used as a reason for expelling a refugee, included 'matters related to crime and morals'.[86] The convention became effective on 27 October 1938.[87] By additional agreements the terms of both the Provisional Arrangements of 1936 and the Convention of 1938 were extended to the refugees from Austria and, on 17 January 1939, to the refugees from the areas ceded by Czechoslovakia to Germany (Sudetenland).[88] The various reservations as well as the imprecise wording of some paragraphs left many loopholes for national immigration authorities to circumvent the agreements. Their implementation in each country depended to a large extent on the public perception of immigration.

In a way, the Provisional Arrangement as well as the Convention of 1938 might be seen as an attempt by the governments concerned to cope with the ups and downs of public opinion about the refugees and to maintain sovereignty in the field of refugee policy. Both international agreements defined who were to be considered as 'refugees from Germany' as well as their rights. This included a limitation of to whom these rights should be conceded and a clear signal that these concessions would not be made to future refugees arriving from Germany or elsewhere.[89] Thus the governments involved hoped to discourage not only the refugees themselves, but also the German and other antisemitic governments who were looking to expel their Jewish minorities.[90] However the agreements failed to send a strong enough signal, as it was too obvious that the states involved were somewhat half-hearted. Consequently, the terms of the agreements had a much greater impact on the refugees than on the German authorities.

The main purpose of the agreements was to stabilise the actual refugee situation by deterring future refugees and by improving the chances of integration of those already in a country of refuge and by the strengthening of states' instruments to 'protect' themselves against alleged 'fake refugees'.[91] In some states this was to be achieved by integrating the voluntary organisations in the procedures used to distinguish between 'real' refugees worthy of asylum and those coming for 'purely personal reasons'. In assessing the 1938 convention, Tartakower and Grossmann wrote in 1944:

> In general, despite some inadequacies, this Convention was felt to be an important step towards legalization of the status of the refugees, and it was urged that it be extended to all emigrants and ratified by all democratic states. But apart from these legal achievements, not much was accomplished.[92]

More recently Claudena Skran passed a similar judgement.[93] In general, her view of refugee policy in the interwar period and the role of the League of Nations in this respect is, albeit carefully constructed, quite positive. She considers the League to be 'a forum for co-operation and a source of innovation',[94] not least because the international refugee regime, established in the 1930s 'led to the creation of the refugee as a special category of persons deserving preferential treatment.'[95]

As can be seen from the current discussion about international criminal law, changes in the international legal system usually start from noncommittal statements. The legal practices in such cases were, however, essentially determined by political circumstances and prevailing public opinion. The vague terminology could thus also be employed in a restrictive way against the best interests of the refugees. The Convention was a declaration of intent with no obligation. It could be used as a general guideline for dealing with the refugees, but left sufficient scope of interpretation or even evasion.

Even if the conventions are seen as progress at an international diplomatic level, they were in many respects insufficient to protect the refugees – especially after the events of 1938.[96] In July of that year, on the eve of the Evian conference, a newsletter circulated among refugee organisations analysing the results of the preceding conferences. According to this text, the conferences had been shaped by police spirit and rubber paragraphs. Even the Convention of 1938 gave them no opportunities to claim their rights. Most of the formal improvements, guaranteed on paper in the Convention, turned out to be illusionary in practice, when after the *Anschluss*, European countries closed their borders to the refugees from Austria and returned those arriving illegally back to the frontier.[97]

The End of 'Orderly Emigration'

The events of 1938 prompted a fundamental change at all levels of international refugee policy. The hesitant attempts to create common standards, which had been made by the agreements of 1936 and 1938, were swept away by a new wave of refugee movements after the *Anschluss* of Austria. The immediate reaction of nearly all potential countries of refuge was a hasty closing of borders and the invention of more rigid immigration controls. This is described in more detail elsewhere and therefore only some general trends are outlined here. The new restrictive rules in various countries were complemented by internal instructions to refuse visa applicants who were or at least seemed to be Jews, because they were suspected as wanting to stay permanently even when their visas expired.[98] Furthermore, the reaction towards illegal immigrants became much more rigorous. As a consequence, refugees and sometimes even those who supported them ran a higher risk of criminalisation and imprisonment.

There was a general dynamic to implement new restrictions as fast as possible and always with a view not to lag behind the policies of neighbouring countries. Nevertheless some attempts at a coordinated reaction towards the new refugee crisis were made. The most famous one is the Evian Conference, which took place in July 1938. Representatives of thirty-two states were invited by U.S. president Franklin Roosevelt in order to deal with the refugee disaster caused by the *Anschluss*. Most of the participants, however, declared from the very beginning that they were not willing to change their restrictive immigration laws. Diplomacy and the desire not to offend the Germans shaped the agenda of the conference as well as the final declaration in which there was no overt criticism of

German anti-Jewish policy. The results were even more disappointing as the conference not only failed to meet its original goal, but on the contrary initiated a chain reaction of further border closures.

In the history of international refugee policy, the conference nevertheless represents a landmark. It can be seen as an attempt to establish a new instrument of migration management – not guided by the League of Nations and its High Commissioner for Refugees but by the U.S. government.[99] The only concrete result of the conference was the establishment of the Intergovernmental Committee for Refugees (IGC) chaired by the American lawyer George Rublee, a friend of Roosevelt. His main task was to initiate negotiations with the German government aimed at making the transfer of Jewish assets possible in order to finance the settlement of German Jews abroad. Initially the Germans refused to even receive Rublee. After the November pogrom however, secret negotiations took place between Rublee and Schacht in London. The main reason why the Germans changed their mind was their foreign currency crisis that came to a head after the pogrom.[100] Throughout 1938 there had been several attempts to ease this problem – to the detriment of the Jews. Goering's Four Year Plan authority had initiated various steps to confiscate Jewish property, especially foreign currency accounts and obligations.[101]

In January 1939 Schacht was dismissed and replaced by Helmut Wohlthat, a foreign-exchange expert of the Four Year Plan and responsible for the confiscation of Jewish property in Europe.[102] After several months of negotiations, a plan was agreed for the emigration of Jews from Greater Germany whereby 150,000 of the approximately 600,000 'racial Jews' in Germany would emigrate within a three-year period and their relatives would follow them as soon as they had established themselves abroad. To fund this plan two organisations were to be established: the German government would create a trust fund from 25 per cent of the Jewish property in Germany to facilitate emigration; and a 'private international corporation for financing of refugee settlement [was to] be set up concurrently outside Germany'.[103] Following the model of the Ha'avarah Agreement, the money in the trust fund would be used to pay for additional German exports. The remaining Jewish assets would be retained in Germany and be used, among other things, to support the 200,000 German Jews who were supposed to be too old or not suited for emigration for other reasons. For the German authorities, the advantage of the plan lay in the alleged increase of their exports and the possibility of promoting the emigration of poor Jews. Although both sides agreed upon the main points of the plan they did not sign an agreement. The Germans did not want it to become publicly known that they had negotiated with the IGC at all; while the IGC met strong reservations in Jewish circles. They feared that the setting up of the above-mentioned corporation and the pre-financing of emigration by Jewish bankers would reinforce the antisemitic claim that there was such thing as 'international Jewry'. Therefore two different memoranda were signed independent from one another, and each party declared itself willing just to fulfil its part of the verbal agreement.

Despite the successful negotiations, the plan was never carried out. The reason for this is not completely clear. It seems likely that the reservations on the Jewish side were too strong. According to Yehuda Bauer, relief organisations like the Joint were not able to come up with further large sums for the intended Settlement Corporation.[104] This institution was established only after lengthy discussions a few weeks before the outbreak of war made every effort towards an orderly emigration fruitless.[105] Another reason for the failure of the Schacht–Rublee Plan was the fact that the IGC had major problems in finding places of resettlement for the Jewish emigrants.

Apart from the Evian Conference there were some minor attempts at international cooperation, but not on the scale of Roosevelt's far more ambitious initiative. The European governments involved did not try to solve the refugee crisis but just to coordinate their immigration policy. This was a matter to be dealt with by police and security experts or, at best, low-ranking diplomats, and no Jewish or refugee institutions were involved. Norway, Sweden, and Denmark cooperated on a limited scale. After the *Anschluss* the three countries had made an entry visa obligatory for Austrians.[106] Although the Scandinavians had decided to coordinate their refugee policies, techniques of identification implemented by the Norwegian border police[107] had not apparently been adopted by Denmark or Sweden.[108] In May 1938, the Danish border authorities were instructed to reject refugees who were not able to return to their country of origin and had no permission to enter Denmark. Exemptions were to be made for political refugees – a term which explicitly excluded Jews.

In the spring of 1939, when the Schacht–Rublee Plan had already run aground, representatives of Belgium, Luxemburg, the Netherlands and Switzerland met in Brussels for a confidential conference.[109] All of them described the situation in similar ways, complaining about an allegedly unbearable influx of refugees since the *Anschluss* and especially since the Munich agreement and the annexation of the Sudetenland. The measures taken to manage the problem were more or less the same, although Switzerland, represented by Heinrich Rothmund, proved to be the most inventive in relation to the deterrence of the refugees: Swiss authorities threatened to detain the refugees who did not obey an order to leave the country in a 'concentration camp'. All participants at the meeting agreed that the problem of illegal immigration should be combated by the expulsion of the illegal immigrants. The Dutch authorities had even expelled children and complained about the convoys of hundreds of refugees systematically organised by German agencies. According to the Dutch representative at the conference even the Jewish community in Amsterdam reacted with hostility towards the unwanted immigrants. Meanwhile the government regarded them as 'undesirable aliens' who could be expelled irrespective of their nationality.[110] The conference obviously did not have significant consequences, not to mention any influence on the practical controls at the borders, which were in any case very strict. The main effect was the mutual assurance that such practices were common and a means of guaranteeing national security.

The German authorities had drawn their own consequences from the failure of the Evian Conference and the increasing difficulties of getting rid of the Jews. They intensified the pressure on the Jews to leave the country and the Gestapo sometimes even supported their flight. After the November pogrom, the elimination of Jews from the German economy proceeded even more rigorously than before. Göring, as head of the Four Year Plan, declared that his office would now coordinate the process. As the 'good side' of the pogrom, he mentioned that it had become absolutely clear that 'the Jew can't live in Germany'.[111] On 1 February 1939, the *Reichszentrale für jüdische Auswanderung* was established in Berlin to accelerate Jewish emigration. Despite the centralisation of emigration bureaucracy under one roof, emigration after the pogrom became more and more chaotic. In the aftermath of the *Anschluss*, the Gestapo increasingly resorted to the illegal expulsion of Jews, pushing them over the border to Switzerland, Luxembourg or France, or shipping them to the Netherlands or Lithuania.[112] As a reaction to this practice, border controls across Europe were strengthened and from January 1939 on, Jewish passports were stamped with a red 'J' which made emigration much more difficult. The German policy of forced emigration thus had shaped the policy of democratic states and made the Jews into what they had been for the Gestapo anyway: namely a police problem.[113]

The growing pressure to leave the country forced the Jews to find new ways out and often made them victims of blackmail.[114] About 30,000 Jewish men had been arrested after the pogrom. To get them released from concentration camps, their wives had to prove that they had concrete plans to emigrate. Thus the black market for passports, visas, steamship tickets and landing permits flourished. In order to leave the country Jews had to learn where the borders were loosely controlled, how to bribe Gestapo men, consuls or travel agents or where to buy a forged passport.[115] As is typical for these kinds of deals there was no chance to call swindlers to account when they sold invalid tickets or visas, or stole the money they had promised to bring abroad illegally. Moreover, the representatives of German Jewry had also stopped believing in an organised, orderly emigration programme, much to the dismay of the international community that sought just such a solution. Robert T. Pell, an officer of the State Department, who, as George Rublee's deputy, took part in the negotiations with Schacht and Wohlthat, visited Germany in the spring of 1939 and met the representatives of German Jewry. His report, which was forwarded to President Roosevelt, indicates how frustrated German Jews were about the poor results of international refugee policy and that for them the time to cooperate in the organisation of orderly emigration was over:

[The leaders of the Reichsvereinigung] were quite frank about the shiploads of their co-religionists which are heading in various directions such as Shanghai, the Mediterranean and the Caribbean. They said that they had to get their people out, whether there was an easing of the tension or not. At any moment an incident might occur which would endanger the very lives of their people. They could not afford to take chances, with the consequence that they were very ready to yield to the pressure of the secret police and the enticement of the shipping companies and to emigrate their people without papers and without a fixed destination. ... I pleaded with them that they were doing more harm than good by this way of proceeding, that they were defeating our efforts to open up places in Latin America, but they laughed in my face. After six years of dealing with this problem they are very hard. They do not believe in promises. Too many promises have been broken.[116]

Conclusion

From the very beginning of Nazi rule in Germany it became obvious that the old system of refugee management was untenable; and even the newly founded High Commissioner was unable to provide a substitute. Subsequently the countries of refuge reacted according to their perceived national interests and tried to set up immigration barriers. Although not coordinated, these reactions were related to each other in a negative way: none of the governments concerned wanted to lag behind in respect to immigration restrictions in order not to make the country the last accessible haven for refugees who had been rejected everywhere else.

After a chaotic start, German authorities focused on the promotion of Jewish emigration, but through dispossessing the Jews they rendered their emigration even more difficult, especially for those groups the SD most urgently wanted to get rid of – the elderly and the poor. They tried to overcome this self-inflicted contradiction in their policy by increasing the pressure on the Jews through various forms of harassment. The German government denied any responsibility for the refugee crisis and refused to participate in any search for international solutions.

The Jewish non-Zionist organisations in Nazi Germany only reluctantly gave up their reservations against emigration, but the rapidly deteriorating situation for the Jews led to a large scale restructuring of Jewish community life and the foundation of a variety of new institutions for economic support and professional retraining. However, many Jewish refugees left the country on their own and without major institutional support. They had to rely on their own family networks, their ingenuity and luck to establish a new life abroad. The receiving countries, the German authorities, the German and international Jewish organisations and the individual Jewish refugees all reacted in their own ways to the refugee crisis initiated by German anti-Jewish policy. None of these agencies was completely independent and they even cooperated with each other on a limited scale. The efforts of the High Commissioner turned out to be of no particular relevance for the refugees in this early stage of Nazi rule.

In the two conferences of 1936 and 1938, the receiving countries tried to fix the status of refugees formally, but in the end they achieved only what had already been guaranteed to the Russian refugees in 1933. Apart from deficits in the refugees' protection, both international agreements reaffirmed the view of the refugee as a victim of adverse circumstances, who might deserve preferential treatment, but had no right to claim it. The contracting parties restated the principle of non-intervention in allegedly internal (German) affairs and explicitly insisted on the states' 'power to regulate the right of residence' – although they slightly limited the states' rights to expel refugees.

The Evian Conference embraced much higher aims – but failed in its main ambitions. Nevertheless Rublee as head of the Intergovernmental Committee had achieved more than the two High Commissioners who had never been received by any high-ranking German representative.[117] The Schacht–Rublee Plan was the first attempt at a compromise which would have included at least limited German obligations. It is probably no accident that Göring ordered the establishment of the *Zentralstelle für jüdische Auswanderung* – a key institution of the SD policy to force the Jews out of Germany – at the same time as his representative Wohlthat was negotiating with the IGC about a well-defined emigration programme

While still negotiating with the IGC the Germans increasingly cut the ground from under any consensus in international refugee policy, however limited. The SD policy of hounding the Jews out of the country in complete disregard of the diplomatic consequences was, in the end, much more 'efficient' than the talks Wohthat held with the IGC at the same time. Both strings in emigration policy came together in Göring's office and the policy of brutal expulsion prevailed. As a consequence of the closure of international borders, the Gestapo pushed Jews into neighbouring countries illegally, or supported Jewish agencies in organizing clandestine or badly equipped transports to Palestine and other destinations, often under terrible conditions. The relief organisations that, in the first years of Nazi rule, had guaranteed the financial support of the refugees, now reached their limits. They tried to cushion the most brutal effects of states' refugee policy but also played an ambivalent role by cooperating in a more and more rigid selection of refugees and by suggesting that they be housed in camps – a plan whose long-term consequences after the war began were hardly foreseeable and certainly not intended. After the November pogrom the refugees were more than ever left to their own devices, dependent on family and community relations and good luck in trying to find a way out of Germany and a refuge in a neighbouring country or overseas.

Notes

*   I am grateful to Frank Caestecker, Ahlrich Meyer and Bob Moore for advice and comments on the manuscript of this article.

1. D. Gosewinkel, *Einbürgern und Ausschließen. Die Nationalisierung der Staatsangehörigkeit vom Deutschen Bund bis zur Bundesrepublik Deutschland*, Göttingen 2001, p.371.
2. C. Skran, *Refugees in Inter-War Europe: The Emergence of a Regime*, New York 1995.
3. M.R. Marrus, *The Unwanted. European Refugees in the Twentieth Century*, New York 1985; H. Walter, *Deutsche Exilliteratur 1933–1950, Bd. 2: Europäisches Asylrecht und überseeische Asylpraxis*, Stuttgart 1984; A. Tartakower and K. Grossmann, *The Jewish Refuge*, New York 1944; Y. Bauer, *My Brother's Keeper. A History of the American Jewish Joint Distribution Committee 1929–1939*, Philadelphia 1974; W. von Glahn, *Der Kompetenzwandel internationaler Flüchtlingshilfsorganisationen - vom Völkerbund bis zu den Vereinten Nationen*, Baden-Baden 1992; T. Sjöberg, *The Powers and the Persecuted: The Refugee Problem and the Intergovernmental Committee on Refugees (IGCR), 1938–1947*, Lund 1991; R. Weingarten, *Die Hilfeleistung der westlichen Welt bei der Endlösung der deutschen Judenfrage. Das Intergovernmental Committee on Political Refugees (IGC) 1939-1939*, Bern 1981.
4. A. Thomas, 'International Migration and its Control', in Margaret Sanger (ed.), *Proceedings of the World Population Conference*, London 1927, pp.257–65.
5. v. Trendelenburg to Gaus, 4.8.1933, PA AA R 49411.
6. B. McDonald Stewart, *United States Government Policy on Refugees from Nazism 1933–1940*, New York and London 1982, p.97.
7. Gaus to Trendelenburg, 4.9.1933, PA AA R 49411. Vermerk Dieckhoff, 30.8.1933, PA AA R 49411.
8. Vermerk Bülow (German Delegation at the League of Nations), 26.9.1933, PA AA R 49411. Similar: Vermerk Dieckhoff, 30.8.1933, ibid.
9. McDonald Stewart, *United States Government Policy*, p.125.
10. James Barros, *Betrayal from within: Joseph Avenol, Secretary-General of the League of Nations, 1933–1940*, New Haven 1969, p.26.
11. R. Breitman and A. Kraut, *American Refugee Policy and European Jewry 1933–1945*, Bloomington 1987, p.36.
12. Sjöberg, *The Powers and the Persecuted*, p.35; McDonald Stewart, *United States Government Policy*, p.115.
13. H. Genizi, 'James G. McDonald: High Commissioner for Refugees, 1933–1935', *The Wiener Library Bulletin* 30, 1977 (New Series Nos. 43/44), pp.40–52, here p.47.
14. Quoted after McDonald Stewart, *United States Government Policy*, p.133.
15. For the full text of McDonald's letter of resignation and the appendices see K.J. Greenberg (ed.), *The James G. McDonald Papers* (Archives of the Holocaust, vol. 7), New York 1990, pp.237–78.
16. Genizi, 'James G. McDonald', p.46f.
17. Ibid.
18. For more details see the national case studies and the comparative article in this volume.
19. Memorandum from André Wurfbain, Executive Secretary of the High Commission for Refugees, to James G. McDonald, 31 December 1934; published in Greenberg (ed.), *The James G. McDonald Papers*, p.144f, here p.144.
20. Ibid., p.145.

21. Notes of a meeting between Norman Bentwich, Deputy High Commissioner for Refugees, and representatives of the Danish government, 21 April 1934, in ibid., pp.140f.
22. Report of a Visit to Austria, submitted by Walter M. Kotschnig, staff member of the High Commission for Refugees, 5 and 6 February 1935, in ibid., pp.152–56, here p.153.
23. V. Caron, 'Loyalties in Conflict: French Jewry and the Refugee Crisis, 1933–1935', *LBIYB* 36, 1991, pp.305–38.
24. Memorandum des SD-Amtes IV/2 an Heydrich, 24.5.1934, Rossijskij Gosudarstvennyj Voennyj Archiv (RGVA) 501/1/18, published in M. Wildt (ed.), *Die Judenpolitik des SD 1935 bis 1938. Eine Dokumentation*, München 1995, pp.66–69, here p.67 (translation S.H).
25. H. Strauss, 'Jewish Emigration from Germany. Nazi Policies and Jewish Responses', *LBIYB* 25, 1980, pp 313–61, here pp.341f.
26. D.Mußgnug, *Die Reichsfluchtsteuer 1931–1953*, Berlin 1993, p.39; McDonald Stewart, *United States Government Policy*, p.128.
27. Strauss, 'Jewish Emigration from Germany', p.344.
28. A. Prinz, 'The Role of the Gestapo in Obstructing and Promoting Jewish Emigration', *Yad Vashem Studies* 2, 1958, pp.205–18; F. Nicosia, *The Third Reich and the Palestinian Question*, London 1985; S.Heim, '"Deutschland muß ihnen ein Land ohne Zukunft sein." Die Zwangsemigration der Juden aus Deutschland 1933–1938', in C. Dieckmann et al. (eds), *Arbeitsmigration und Flucht. Vertreibung und Arbeitskräfteregulierung im Zwischenkriegseuropa*, Beiträge zur nationalsozialistischen Gesundheits- und Sozialpolitik Bd. 11, Berlin 1993, pp.48–81, here pp.54–56.
29. Instructions for the Department II 112, RGVA 500/1/506, published in Wildt, *Judenpolitik*, pp.156–60.
30. W. Feilchenfeld, D. Michaelis, L. Pinner, *Haavara-Transfer nach Palästina und Einwanderung deutscher Juden 1933–1939*, Tübingen 1972; Avraham Barkai, 'Das deutsche Interesse am Haavara-Transfer 1933–1939', in *Hoffnung und Untergang. Studien zur deutsch-jüdischen Geschichte des 19. und 20. Jahrhunderts*, ed. A.Barkai, Hamburg,1998, pp.167–95.
31. Y. Weiss, 'The Transfer Agreement and the Boycott Movement: A Jewish Dilemma on the Eve of the Holocaust', *Yad Vashem Studies* 26, 1998, pp.129–71. F. Kieffer, *Judenverfolgung in Deutschland – eine innere Angelegenheit? Internationale Reaktionen auf die Flüchtlingsproblematik 1933–1939*, Stuttgart 2002, pp.132ff.
32. S.Friedländer, *Nazi Germany and the Jews, vol. 1. The Years of Persecution, 1933–1939*, New York 1997, p.63. On the Ha'avarah Agreement see also the article of Aviva Halamish in this volume.
33. About the Warburg Plan see Greenberg (ed.), *The James G. McDonald Papers*, pp.106–14.
34. Kieffer, *Judenverfolgung in Deutschland*, p.99.
35. According to the New York Times, Schacht was believed to be the real author of the Warburg Plan: 'Nazis lay Ground for Refugee Plan', *New York Times*, 20 December 1938.
36. Barkai, 'Das deutsche Interesse', p.182.
37. Kieffer, *Judenverfolgung in Deutschland*, p.127.
38. Friedländer, *Nazi Germany and the Jews*, vol I, p.70.
39. Kieffer, *Judenverfolgung in Deutschland*, p.126 sees the dispossession of German Jews through the flight tax as 'realities which could not be ignored'.

40. Barkai, 'Das deutsche Interesse', p.182
41. Kieffer, *Judenverfolgung in Deutschland*, p.122.
42. High Commissioner of the League of Nations, James McDonald in his report to the Governing Body, 11.1.1934, PA AA R 49414; Letter of Chamberlain to McDonald, 10.29.1934, McDonald Papers, Columbia University, Herbert Lehman Suite: D 361: General Correspondence.
43. Kieffer, *Judenverfolgung in Deutschland*, p.48; Bauer, *My Brother's Keeper*, p.126.
44. According to this agreement the Jewish parents could deposit the school fees for their children abroad in Germany. The foreign aid organisations paid the equivalent of the related sum to the Jewish youngsters in schools and Hachsharah camps abroad, while the money in Germany was used to help Jews in Germany. Thus the Jewish organisations in Germany and abroad and the children's parents 'were able to finance their respective activities without providing the German government with hard currency' (A. Gottlieb, *Men of Vision: Anglo-Jewry's Aid to Victims of the Nazi regime 1933–1945*, London 1998, p.99). According to Gottlieb, this agreement was established already in 1934. S. Adler-Rudel, *Jüdische Selbsthilfe unter dem Naziregime 1933–1939. Im Spiegel der Berichte der Reichsvertretung der Juden in Deutschland*, Tübingen 1974 gives two different dates for the introduction of the education clearing: 1935 (p.70) and 1937 (p.101); Kieffer, *Judenverfolgung in Deutschland*, p. 131.
45. 'Ortsgruppenrundbrief Nr. 4', 15.4.1935, quoted in J. Matthäus, 'Abwehr, Ausharren, Flucht. Der Centralverein deutscher Staatsbürger jüdischen Glaubens und die Emigration bis zur "Reichskristallnacht"', *Exilforschung* 19, 2001, pp.18–49, here p.29 (translation S.H.).
46. Bauer, *My Brother's Keeper*, p.106.
47. Deutsche Bibliothek Frankfurt (ed.), *Die jüdische Emigration aus Deutschland 1939–1941. Die Geschichte einer Austreibung*, Frankfurt 1985, p.155f; Susanne Heim, 'Immigration Policy and Forced Emigration from Germany: The Situation of Jewish Children (1933–1945)', in *Children and the Holocaust. Symposium Presentations*, ed. United States Holocaust Memorial Museum, Center for Advanced Holocaust Studies, Washington D.C. 2004, pp.1–18.
48. Up to then the representation of German Jewry was organised according to the federal principle. In the new Reichsvertretung, apart from the regional Jewish associations the main political forces were represented. O.D. Kulka (ed.), *Deutsches Judentum unter dem Nationalsozialismus*, Tübingen 1997, vol. 1, pp.9–14.
49. H. Lavsky, *Before Catastrophe: The Distinctive Path of German Zionism*, Detroit 1996, pp.242ff.
50. This is one of the main reasons why emigration numbers are no more than estimates because only those who were supported by the rescue institutions were registered as emigrants.
51. In memoir literature vivid descriptions are given of the emigration bureaucracy to be managed before leaving the country; see for instance W. Benz (ed.), *Das Tagebuch der Hertha Nathorff, Berlin–New York. Aufzeichnungen 1933–1945*, Frankfurt 1988; A. Heller, *Dr. Seligman's Auswanderung, München–Israel*, München 1990.
52. Note about the citation of Hirsch, Stahl and Eppstein to the Gestapo, 16.12.1938, CJA 2B1, no. 1, pp.255–57.

53. Marion Berghahn, 'Women Emigrés in England' in *Between Sorrow and Strength: Women Refugees of the Nazi Period*, ed. Sibylle Quack, Washington 1995, pp.69–80, here p.78.
54. In the Australian refugee community there existed an 'unwritten agreement' to trade and shop and use health services exclusively within the community. A. Silbermann, *Vewandlungen. Eine Autobiographie*, Bergisch-Gladbach 1992, p.201.
55. The European meeting of Jewish refugee aid organisations held in London in autumn 1933 can be seen as a coordination of national and international attempts to regularise Jewish emigration; see Caestecker and Moore in this volume.
56. Martin Rosenblueth to Bernhard Kahn, 17.1.1936, CZA S7/362.
57. K. Grossmann, *Emigration. Geschichte der Hitler-Flüchtlinge 1933–1945*, Frankfurt 1969, p.57.
58. For the criticism of Jewish refugee aid organisations against Malcolm see Senator to Goldmann, 23.2.36, CZA S7/362.
59. Report by Myron C. Taylor at the Evian conference pertaining to American emigration policy, 29 June 1938, published in John Mendelsohn (ed.), *Jewish Emigration from 1933 to the Evian Conference of 1938*, The Holocaust: Selected documents in Eighteen Volumes, vol. 5, New York 1982, pp.245–64, here p.258f.
60. Rupprecht v. Keller, Aufzeichnung II über die Entwicklung und den gegenwärtigen Stand der Behandlung des deutschen Flüchtlingswesens durch internationale Organisationen, 31.10.36, PA AA R 49417.
61. 'Provisional Arrangement of 4th July 1936 concerning the Status of Refugees coming from Germany; League of Nationals Treaty Series, Vol. CLXXI, No. 3952, Article 1', cited in Office of the United Nations High Commissioner for Refugees, *Conventions, Agreements and Arrangements Concerning Refugees Adopted Before the Second World War* (HCR/120/34/80), pp.33–38, here p.35.
62. Ibid, p.33.
63. See Caestecker and Moore this volume.
64. F. Caestecker, *Ongewenste gasten. Joodse vluchtelingen en migranten in de dertiger jaren in Belgie*, Brussels 1993, p.80f.
65. 'Provisional Arrangement of 4th July 1936', p.35.
66. Ibid, p.34.
67. Ibid, p.35.
68. Peter Heumos, 'Tschechoslowakei', in *Handbuch der deutschsprachigen Emigration 1933–1945*, eds. C. Krohn, P. von zur Mühlen, G. Paul, L. Winckler, Darmstadt 1998, pp.411–26, here p.416.
69. Grossmann, *Emigration*, p.59.
70. Jacob B. Lightman, Confidential memorandum 'Some analytical notes on second revised text of 'Provisional Arrangement concerning the status of German Refugees' as agreed upon by the League of Nations Intergovernmental Conference for the adoption of the Statute of the Refugees coming from Germany', JDC 252.
71. 'Memorandum der Zentralvereinigung der deutschen Emigration zur Beratung des Völkerbunds über die Fragen, die die Flüchtlinge aus Deutschland betreffen, August 1936', League of Nations Archives, R 5720 5/25570/7100 and IfZ ED 201/5. See also 'Memorandum des Comité National Tchéco-Slovaque pour les Réfugiés provenant d'Allemagne', IfZ ED 201/4, p.10.

72. In France after the Agreement had been signed on August 4, 1936 refugee organisations and immigration authorities cooperated in respect of the admission/recognition of foreigners as 'refugees coming from Germany': C. Eggers, *Unverwünschte Ausländer. Juden aus Deutschland und Mitteleuropa in französischen Internierungslagern 1940–1942*, Berlin 2002, p.23.
73. 'Flüchtlingsstatut nach den Beschlüssen der internationalen Konferenz für Asylrecht, Paris, 20. und 21. Juni 1936', IfZ ED 201/5, p.2. See also: Barbara Vormeier, 'Die Schaffung eines internationalen Flüchtlingsstatus und die Rolle der Pariser Asylrechts- und Flüchtlingskomitees', in *Fluchtziel Paris. Die deutschsprachige Emigration 1933–1940*, ed. A. Saint Sauveur-Henn, Berlin 2002, pp.41–50, here p.48.
74. Rupprecht v. Keller, Aufzeichnung II über die Entwicklung und den gegenwärtigen Stand der Behandlung des deutschen Flüchtlingswesens durch internationale Organisationen, 31.10.36, PA AA R 49417. Similar: German Consulate, Geneva, to German Foreign Office, 23.6.1936, PA AA R 49415.
75. Office of the UNHCR, 'Conventions, Agreements and Arrangements Concerning Refugees Adopted Before the Second World War', HCR/120/34/80, pp.39–52. J. Simpson, *The Refugee Problem*, Oxford 1939, p.228; O. Kimmnich, *Der internationale Rechtsstatus des Flüchtlings*, Köln 1962, p.239.
76. H. Bekaert, *Le Statut des étrangers en Belgique*, Bruxelles 1940, pp.369–71.
77. In 1942 Riegner took the initiative to inform the Western Allies about the systematic murder of the Jews of Europe. R. Cohen, 'Das Riegner-Telegramm – Text, Kontext, und Zwischentext', *TAJB* 33, 1994, pp.301–24; Christopher Browning, 'Hitlers endgültige Entscheidung zur "Endlösung"? Riegners Telegramm in neuem Licht', in *Der Weg zur "Endlösung": Entscheidungen und Täter*, ed. C. Browning, Bonn1998, pp.149–59.
78. Gerhart Riegner, Bericht über die Staatenkonferenz zur Annahme eines endgültigen Statuts für die deutschen Flüchtlinge, 14.2.1938, American Jewish Archives, The World Jewish Congress Collection, Series A, Subseries1, Box A8, File 5, pp.1–9, here p.5.
79. Riegner, Bericht, p.8.
80. Article 5, paragraph 3a, quoted according to Office of the UNHCR, *Conventions*, p.43. For the reservations made by the contracting parties see ibid., pp.50–52.
81. Riegner, Bericht, p.6.
82. Ibid., p.7.
83. Kimmnich, *Der internationale Rechtsstatus*, p.241.
84. France ratified the Convention only on 23 March 1945: United Nations Department of Social Affairs, *A Study of Statelessness*, New York 1949, p.114; Denmark ratified the Convention in 1946: H. Kirchhoff, *Et menneske uden pas er ikke noget menneske*, Odense 2005, pp.124ff.
85. H. Petersen,'Viel Papier aber wenig Erfolg', *Exil. Forschung Erkenntnisse Ergebnisse* 2, 1985, pp.60–84, here p.73 (translation S.H.).
86. Office of the UNHCR, *Conventions*, p.51
87. World Jewish Congress, Paris, Circular No. 2, 16.10.1938, CZA A138/81/1.
88. Tartakower and Grossmann, *The Jewish Refugee*, p.407; slightly different: Kimmnich, *Der internationale Rechtsstatus*, p.241.
89. V. Caron, *Uneasy Asylum: France and the Jewish refugee crisis, 1933–1942*, Stanford 1999, p.139. As can be seen from Caestecker and Moore in

this volume immigration practice at least in Belgium was less restrictive concerning refugees immigrating after the fixed date.
90. L. London, *Whitehall and the Jews, 1933–1948: British immigration policy, Jewish refugees and the Holocaust*, Cambridge 2000, p.91.
91. Bekaert, *Le Statut des étrangers*, p.373.
92. Tartakower and Grossmann, *The Jewish Refugee*, p.411.
93. Claudena Skran, *Refugees in Inter-War Europe*, p.137f.
94. Ibid., p.282.
95. Ibid., p.145.
96. Petersen, 'Viel Papier', p.74.
97. Die Menschenjagd. Zur Flüchtlingskonferenz von Evian, IfZ ED 201/4. Unfortunately the available copy does not show the title of the newsletter but only the address of the publisher: Ellen Hörup, 19, rue Henri Mussard, Genf and the fact that the circular was edited in the 3rd year and the edition on hand of July 1938 was No. 5.
98. For more details see the national case studies and the comparative article in this volume.
99. This point is discussed extensively in Sjöberg, *The Powers and the Persecuted*.
100. 'The 1937 German trade surplus had, by 1938, been converted into a 413,000,000-reichsmark deficit', H.L. Feingold, *The Politics of Rescue: The Roosevelt Administration and the Holocaust, 1939–1945*, New York 1970, p.40. See also: Nordamerikanische Presse, Bericht (des Auswärtigen Amts) Nr. 42, 3.3.1939, 'Annahme des deutschen Vorschlages durch das Evian-Komité'. There the assessment is made that the negative results of the pogroms on German export had made the Germans change their mind: LBI-NY, Max Kreutzberger Collection, AR 7/83, Box 17, Folder 7.
101. A.J. van der Leeuw, 'Der Griff des Reiches nach dem Judenvermögen', *Rechtsprechung zum Wiedergutmachungsrecht* 21, no.9, 1970, pp.383–92. See also: Avraham Barkai, '"Schicksalsjahr 1938". Kontinuität und Verschärfung der wirtschaftlichen Ausplünderung der deutschen Juden', in *Der Judenpogrom 1938. Von der "Reichskristallnacht" zum Völkermord*, ed. W. Pehle, Frankfurt 1988, pp.94–117.
102. Feingold, *The Politics of Rescue*, p.58; M. Brechtken, *"Madagaskar für die Juden". Antisemitische Idee und politische Praxis 1885–1945*, München 1997, p.264.
103. Undated Memorandum (29 April 1939) written for the meeting of Myron Taylor with the U.S. President on 4 May 1939, Roosevelt Archive, OF 3186, Box 2.
104. Bauer, *My Brother's Keeper*, pp.273–85. Bauer among other things refers to the enormous amount of money the AJDC had to spend to meet the demands of corrupt bureaucracies who tried to make a bargain out of immigration. He hints at the example of the St. Louis, a German ship with nearly 1,000 emigrants whose Cuban visas were declared invalid while they were already on their trip to the Caribbean Island. The Cuban government asked for more than the US$500,000 offered by the Joint to let the refugees in. The deal did not work out and thus the ship had to return to Europe. Only at the very last moment Holland, Britain, Belgium and France agreed to share the refugees and thus saved them from going back to Germany; see recently: Diane Afoumado, *L'exile impossible. L'errance des Juifs du paquebot St Louis*, Paris 2005; see also Caestecker and Moore in this volume.
105. Draft Report of the General Council for Jewish Refugees, The Jewish People from Holocaust to Nationhood: Archives of the Central British Fund

for German Jewry, 1933–1960, Part 1, Files 4–8, reel 002, YV JM/11389, p.29f.

106. Petersen,'Viel Papier', p.76f.
107. Even before the new peak of refugee influx after the *Anschluss* Norwegian police had started to take photographs and fingerprints of refugees and to measure their ears: E.Lorenz, *Exil in Norwegen. Lebensbedingungen und Arbeit deutschsprachiger Flüchtlinge 1933–1943*, Baden-Baden 1992, p.55.
108. About the coordination of Scandinavian refugee policy see H. Petersen, 'Die Zusammenarbeit der nordischen Länder in der Flüchtlingsfrage', in *Ein sehr trübes Kapitel? Hitlerflüchtlinge im nordeuropäischen Exil 1933 bis 1950*, eds E.Lorenz et al., Hamburg 1998, pp.69–85. The first joint conference of Denmark, Sweden and Norway on refugee policy took place in June 1938 – when Sweden and Norway had already made visas obligatory for Austrians without discussing this decision with their neighbours. Denmark introduced visa obligations two days after the conference: ibid, p.80.
109. 'Réunion du 3 avril 1939 tenue à la Sûreté publique, en vue d'examiner le problème de l'afflux clandestine de réfugiés d'Allemagne, en Belgique, dans le Grand-Duché de Luxembourg, aux Pays-Bas et en Suisse', AAD 37Cl, Gotz Aly, Susanne Heim et al (eds) *Die Verfolgung und Ermordung der europäischen Juden durch das nationalsozialistische Deutschland 1933-1945*, Bd 2: Deutsches Reich 1938–August 1939, Munich 2009, pp.726–732.
110. J. van Merrienboer, 'Hitlerflüchtlinge in den Niederlanden unerwünscht. Die Politik der niederländischen Regierung gegenüber deutschen Flüchtlingen 1933–1940', in *Flüchtlingspolitik und Fluchthilfe*, eds S. Heim, I. Meinen, A. Meyer and H. Kahrs, Beiträge zur nationalsozialistischen Gesundheits- und Sozialpolitik vol. 15, Berlin and Göttingen 1999, pp.91–107, here p.100; Moore, *Refugees from Nazi Germany in the Netherlands 1933–1940*, p.79f. Although Rothmund did not mention this in the conference the Swiss Jewish community too regarded the 'pouring in' of refugees from Germany as threat to the Jewish institutions in Switzerland. Sally Meyer, on the Conference on German situation and Emigration, 14 and 15.12.1938 held at the offices of the AJDC in Paris, 15.12.1938, JDC 363. I'm grateful to Frank Caestecker for bringing this document to my attention.
111. Protocol of the meeting in the Reich Ministry of Aviation under the direction of Göring, 12.11.1938, IMG 28, pp.499–540.
112. Friedländer, *Nazi Germany and the Jews*, vol. I, p.266.
113. See Ludi and Caestecker and Moore in this volume.
114. Susanne Heim, 'Vertreibung, Raub und Umverteilung. Die jüdischen Flüchtlinge aus Deutschland und die Vermehrung des "Volksvermögens"', in *Flüchtlingspolitik und Fluchthilfe*, pp.107–38, here p.126f.
115. S.Heim, 'Emigration and Jewish Identity – "An Enormous Heartbreak"', *The Journal of Holocaust Education* 10, no. 1, 2001, pp.21–33, here p.31.
116. Robert Pell, Assistant Chief of the Division on European Affairs in the State Department, to Pierrepont Moffat, Chief of the Division, 8.3.1939, NA College Park, MD, RG 59: State Department Office or Lot Files (NA Publication M-1284, roll 25) 840.48 Refugees/1538; see also Jürgen Rohwer, 'Jüdische Flüchtlingsschiffe im Schwarzen Meer – 1934 bis 1944', in *Das Unrechtsregime. Internationale Forschung über den Nationalsozialismus, Verfolgung - Exil - Belasteter Neubeginn* (vol. 2), ed. U.Büttner, Hamburg 1986, pp.197–248.

117. In fact, there was kind of a competition between the High Commissioner and the IGC, as Rublee had taken over the tasks originally designed for the High Commissioner, and on behalf of Roosevelt instead of the League of Nations. The conflict was solved when in 1939 Sir Herbert Emerson assumed office as the third High Commissioner and also became director of the Intergovernmental Committee after Rublee's resignation.

Chapter I.2

The Danish Immigration Authorities and the Issue of *Rassenschande*

Lone Rünitz

The German Jew Alfred L fled to Denmark in April 1937 because of the ongoing persecution in Germany and the fact that he was engaged to an 'Aryan' woman whom he wanted to marry.[1] They had been employed by the same firm and their relationship had lasted since the summer of 1935. On account of the Nuremberg Laws they officially broke off the engagement, but nevertheless secretly continued the relationship. This was brought to the attention of Gestapo and they lost their jobs. When a friend told Alfred L that he was about to be arrested, he decided to leave Germany, and chose Denmark as a refuge because his fiancée had Danish relatives.

Immediately after his arrival, Alfred L went to the police and asked for asylum. At the same time he explained that his fiancée would follow shortly and that they intended to marry as soon as possible. The Ministry of Justice turned down the request, and he was informed that he had to leave Denmark within three months.[2] In June Alfred L was offered a job in Copenhagen and applied for a work permit but the Ministry of Justice upheld the previous decision and he was told to leave within the stipulated time limit. A few weeks later the couple married thereby making it impossible for them to return to Germany. The fact that Alfred L had married in spite of the Ministry's rejection of his asylum and work permit applications aggravated the authorities. The Ministry stressed that he could not be recognised as a *political refugee* but he was given two months respite to find ways of re-emigrating.[3] Distinguished citizens tried to intervene on his behalf but to no avail. The decision was final. The Ministry's resolution was supported by the private relief committees, since the marriage had taken place *after* he had been refused residence permit[4] and in September the couple had to leave Denmark and try their luck in Sweden. It can be assumed that it was this particular case that led to a circular from the Ministry of Justice of October 1937 advising the relevant authorities to abstain from performing marriage ceremonies between German nationals if such a marriage was prohibited by German law.[5] To reinforce the point, the circular specifically quoted excerpts of the marriage stipulations in the Nuremberg Laws.

Through the Foreign Office and the local press the Danish authorities were fully aware that a violation of the Nuremberg Laws was severely punished in Germany.[6] Furthermore the Ministry of Justice and the State Police had copies of the Laws and the decrees that implemented them.[7] Ostensibly, people fleeing from Germany because they had fallen foul of the *Rassenschande* laws fell under the definition of a refugee introduced by the Social Democratic Minister of Justice, K.K. Steincke, early in 1937.[8] At that time, he defined a refugee as a person able to substantiate that, due to his political beliefs, religion, race or ideology, he was subject to the threat of considerable punishment or internment in a concentration camp by returning to Germany. However, this definition was not intended to set a precedent, but rather to explain the circumstances whereby a certain number of such refugees had already obtained asylum in Denmark. In a radio speech in April concerning 'the Emigrant Problem' Steincke explained the *Rassenschande* question in the Nuremberg Laws to the public.[9] 'Aryans' marrying Jews were no better off than political refugees, the sanctions against such a 'crime' being annulment and imprisonment. Extramarital relations between Jews and Aryans were also punishable by a term of imprisonment. In spite of this, Steinecke expressed strong reservations as to Denmark's position on German nationals trying to avoid this legislation and other German laws by emigrating. In his opinion Denmark had neither a legal nor a moral obligation to grant them asylum. To take on such a commitment would be impossible for a small country. According to the State Police there were at that time 845 Jewish refugees in Denmark[10] and the total number of refugees from Germany was 1,512.[11] This first official statement about the refugee question arose from mounting public dissatisfaction with the secrecy surrounding administrative practices and the number of refugees in Denmark. On the one hand the left wing, that is the Danish communists, attacked the Social-Democratic/Social Liberal coalition government for its inhumanity, primarily in relation to communist refugees, and on the other hand the right wing, the small and insignificant number of Danish Nazis, and sections of the opposition press accused the government and the minister of too much leniency – allowing thousands upon thousands of Jews and communists to settle in Denmark.

In a parliamentary statement in November, Steincke once again emphasised that a violation of the Nuremberg Laws did not constitute grounds for asylum in Denmark.[12] The implication being that Denmark would otherwise have to grant asylum to everybody who left Germany because of the sterilisation laws or because they were (considered) Jewish. The fact that one state's common laws were considered unreasonable by a number of its inhabitants could not lead to the assumption that another state should grant them privileges as political refugees because they had broken such laws. The government tried to take humanitarian considerations into account, but such considerations had to be weighed against Denmark's special location, size and the consequences of establishing a precedent. No one contested this statement.

It was, however, an indirect answer to the chairman of the Jewish relief organisation, Karl Lachmann, who had requested a negotiation with the Ministry of Justice regarding the government's position to the victims of the Nuremberg Laws a few weeks before.[13] Subsequently the Cooperating Refugee Committees were asked to submit a proposal. The result was a recommendation that German nationals should be put on equal footing with political refugees if they violated the Nuremberg Laws by marrying in Denmark.[14] This was nevertheless conditional on their not having been explicitly refused a residence permit prior to the wedding ceremony (as had been the case with Alfred L). Furthermore it was proposed that German nationals who had been in a steady relationship prior to 15 September 1935, and had continued that relationship in spite of the Nuremberg Laws should be regarded as political refugees. The conditions in such instances being that they were able to substantiate the duration of the relationship and that they had left Germany because of serious threats to their safety. These proposals were a result of a compromise between the relief organisations and the Ministry of Justice after private discussions on the matter.[15] Originally Karl Lachmann had wanted to include members of mixed marriages who had been harassed and harboured serious fear for their continued livelihood in Germany. This was far too far-reaching for the Ministry and the proposal was withdrawn.

The compromise suggestions were more acceptable, especially since they implied that the couples in question should have obtained residence permits prior to the wedding in order to be recognised as political refugees. Since the question of equality between the victims of the Nuremberg Laws and political refugees was raised because Jewish refugees had severe difficulties in obtaining residence permits, and considering that such marriages were effectively prohibited by the Ministry's recent circular, the chosen wording was rather surprising. It shows, however, that the relief organisations did not agree among themselves as to whether violators of the Nuremberg Laws should be given status as political refugees. The second suggestion, relating to couples in a longstanding relationship, did not cause the Ministry any problems. As one official stated, the difficulties in upholding such relationships in Germany meant that there would be few such cases. In the end the Ministry very characteristically decided not to make any binding commitments.[16] Each case would have to be considered on its own merits.

Johannes F ('Aryan') and Auguste E (Jewish) fell within the terms of the second recommendation.[17] They had lived together since 1929 and had two children to document the fact. The reason that they had not married was that Johannes F's wife would not consent to a divorce. In the summer of 1938 their relationship was brought to the attention of the German authorities and Johannes F received summons to report to the *Arbeitsfront*. The very same day the family illegally crossed the Danish border. Since Johannes F was a former member of the Social Democratic party he immediately contacted the Social Democratic relief committee in Copenhagen and asked to be recognized as a political refugee, but was turned down as the committee did not acknowledge violation of the Nuremberg Laws as grounds for asylum! Johannes F then contacted the relief committee for non-Aryan Christians, but the committee told him it was unable to assist the family unless they obtained residence permits. A visit to the Jewish committee went no better, since Johannes F was a gentile. Following this discouraging news, the family succeeded in entering Sweden but was immediately returned to Denmark and held by the Aliens Police. During his interrogation by the police, Johannes F asked to be allowed to apply for a preliminary residence permit until he and his family found a way of emigrating to South America. He stated in the strongest possible terms that he would not return to Germany alive. Without any means and without any help or support from a refugee committee, the fate of the family was quickly decided. Less than two weeks after crossing the border, they were sent back to Germany.

Notwithstanding the Ministry of Justice's circular, a few *Rassenschande* refugees obtained permission to reside in Denmark so that they were able to marry in Denmark if immigration was conditional on marriage.[18] In November 1938 a couple submitted a marriage application to the Ministry.[19] Simon B (Jewish) and Gretchen H (gentile) had met in 1930, and became engaged in 1933. They had plans to marry shortly afterwards, but due to a death in the family, the wedding was postponed. They continued the relationship after the Nuremberg Laws but were arrested in 1936 and accused of *Rassenschande*. Gretchen H spent only three days in jail, while Simon B was jailed for two months. During their trial they both had to swear that they had not had intercourse since the implementation of the racial laws and were thus acquitted. A few months later they were arrested again but released after three days due to lack of proof. In November 1936 the couple were arrested for the third time. In order to be released they had to sign declarations that they would break off the relationship. After the release Gretchen went to the Netherlands. Simon B stayed in Germany but visited her several times. He was continuously harassed by the Gestapo and interrogated again and again. In August 1938, he was once more summoned by the authorities. Due to the many arrests of Jews at that time, he chose to leave his home and sought refuge in Bremen. When he was informed that Gestapo had been at his home to pick him up, he decided to flee Germany and join Gretchen in the Netherlands. Since he was Jewish and did not carry an invitation from Dutch citizens he was denied entry. He tried Denmark instead, and on 12 August 1938 he succeeded in getting past the border controls. Ten days later Gretchen followed him and a request for temporary asylum was submitted. Both the Danish-Jewish relief committee and the Cooperating Committees were of the opinion that, due to their history of harassment, the couple were to be recognised as refugees. However, during a conversation with the Aliens Police the Committees emphasised that they should be kept unaware of that fact so that they would not attempt to settle in Denmark. Temporary protection was considered sufficient, so that the Jewish committee could assist them in their endeavours to find a country of final settlement.

Simon was lucky. He had wealthy relatives in the U.S. and shortly after his arrival he obtained an affidavit from them. Furthermore he was Dutch-born and thus able to get on the Dutch quota list for a U.S. visa. However, in order that they could both obtain visa to the U.S. they had to be married. The Ministry of Justice informed them that it would be willing to grant permission for the marriage as soon as they were able to prove that their visa was about to be issued. For good measure, the Aliens Police checked with the American Embassy to make sure that a visa would be forthcoming. The embassy was informed that the Ministry of Justice did not ordinarily permit marriages that were prohibited by national laws and it needed to be absolutely sure that nothing would prevent the emigration before granting permission. Thus the police requested that Gretchen and Simon should immediately be called up for medical examination. When the Ministry of Justice was satisfied that all the paperwork was in perfect order, Simon and Gretchen received permission to marry, and a couple of weeks later they left Denmark.

No *Rassenschande* cases were formally granted status as political refugees. Like the majority of the Jewish refugees entering Denmark in the second half of the 1930s, they were given a respite to obtain a visa to another country. The reason for the Danish reluctance to grant rights of asylum to violators of the Nuremberg Laws was obvious. Such an acknowledgment would be tantamount to sanctioning permanent settlement and furthermore attract an unknown number of new refugees. As such this reaction has to be seen within the broader context of the refugee policy at the time; the overall objective of this policy being to prevent Jewish refugees being turned into immigrants.

Like most other liberal states, Denmark distinguished between the so-called political immigrants and Jewish immigrants. In practice this meant that the latter were excluded from asylum unless they were able to convince the authorities and the relief organisations that they would be in severe personal danger if they had to return to Germany.[20] Prior to the Nuremberg Laws and the events of 1938, few Jewish refugees were able to meet these criteria. However, in 1933 and 1934 the authorities were relatively liberal in extending and prolonging residence permits, provided that the refugees were in possession of a valid passport and did not burden public funds. On the other hand work permits were extremely difficult to obtain unless the immigrant would benefit Danish interests.[21] This was not solely due to the depression and the high unemployment at the time. In the opinion of the Chief of Police, refusing work permits to Jewish refugees would lead to their voluntary re-emigration.[22] This perception was, of course, correct. The most resourceful refugees found ways to enter other countries while the borders remained open, and Denmark missed the chances of acquiring their know-how, capital and their abilities to create new job opportunities.

At the time of the Nuremberg Laws, the Danish authorities had already become markedly less generous in granting residence permits to Jewish refugees. There were several reasons for this change in policy. The growing antisemitic violence in Germany during the summer of 1935 was likely to lead to a new influx of refugees. Furthermore the Nazi threats to incarcerate in camps any refugees who returned to Germany made repatriation impossible. Finally a similar restrictiveness in other European and overseas countries meant that re-emigration became more difficult. Thus the authorities had to accept that a number of the early refugees would have to stay put, while trying to prevent any impression that newcomers would be allowed to stay on in Denmark for any length of time. To that effect an informal agreement was made with the economically hard-pressed relief organizations.[23] In order to obtain work permits for the early refugees, the committees had to accept that the issue of residence permits for new refugees would be limited. In May 1936 a ministerial official suggested that residence permits for German Jews should be refused immediately if the authorities believed that they intended to settle in Denmark.[24] Whether or not a refugee harboured such intentions was based on a more or less subjective appraisal from the Aliens Department and the State Police. This could, for instance, be the case if the plans for the future seemed vague, if a refugee applied for a work permit, made investments in Denmark or acquired real estate.

For the very same reason the authorities did not look favourably upon marriages between refugees and Danish nationals – whether mixed or wholly Jewish. It was viewed as a sure indication of an intention to settle. In accordance with the Danish nationality law, female foreigners obtained citizenship by marrying a Dane, and once the marriage had taken place the authorities were powerless. There are, however, several examples where steps were taken to prevent such marriages by denying the bride-to-be entry to Denmark.[25] There were also instances where the women were expelled when they informed the officials of their marriage plans.[26] The State Police and the Ministry of Justice made serious efforts to discourage male refugees from marrying Danish nationals by informing them that marriage did not render them any privileges in the acquisition of residence or work permits. The authorities also tried to discourage Danish women from marrying Jewish refugees. Some of the women harbouring such marriage plans were naturalized citizens and according to the nationality law they stood to lose their citizenship if they married a foreigner.[27] This was a serious threat and consequently the authorities were often able to prevent such marriages. This effectively changed administrative practice as previously foreigners marrying Danes had been granted residence and work permits.[28] According to the Minister of Justice this liberal practice had led to fraud and marriages of convenience.[29] The sources do not substantiate this suspicion, since most of the marriages in question lasted through the war and resulted in several children; at least if the refugees were able to stay on in Denmark!

Nothing in the sources indicates that the Ministry of Justice made any distinctions between mixed marriages and marriages between two Jews in its discretionary rulings. Kurt A and Hellmut W married Danish gentile women.[30] Kurt A lost his job in Germany shortly after Hitler's assumption of power and in the summer of 1935 he was offered a position in Denmark. In September 1935 he married. According to the administrative practice at that time he should have been granted a residence and work permit. However, he unknowingly failed to apply for a work permit, thereby seriously violating the Danish Aliens Act. Consequently he was denied a residence permit and received notice to leave the country. Due to his wife's pregnancy his continued residence was tolerated for a while, but in 1937 he had to leave his family. Naturally since the marriage meant a breach of the Nuremberg Laws the couple was prevented from settling in Germany. In the following years Kurt A fluctuated between the Nordic countries, staying in Denmark for three months at a time. The Ministry of Justice refused all his pleas, and in December 1939 he was forced to emigrate to the U.S. leaving his wife and child behind.

Hellmut W did not violate Danish legislation in any way. Before coming to Denmark in January 1936 he had been arrested for 'harassment of German workers' and upon his release ordered to leave Germany. Since his sister and brother-in-law were Danish nationals, he applied for a residence permit and permission to assist them in their business. The application was turned down. During a previous visit in Denmark he had met a Danish girl and in April 1936 they became engaged and a new petition was submitted and subsequently refused. Hellmut W was given one months notice to prepare for re-emigration. Notwithstanding the refusal of a residence permit, the couple married two weeks later and a third petition was submitted with the same negative result. In May the newly wed Hellmut had to leave for Spain, never to return to Denmark.

Abraham N and Richard R experienced similar difficulties with the authorities after marrying Danish Jewish women.[31] They both arrived in Denmark in 1935 and were both forced out of the country several times, notwithstanding their marriages and their wives' many pleas to the Minister of Justice. In the case of Abraham N, the reason for his harsh treatment was that he had committed some minor violations of the Aliens Act by occasionally having assisted his father-in-law in serving customers in the family business and he only had permission to do the accounts. Consequently he lost his work permit. He was informed that this offence meant that he would not receive a new permit and had to leave the country. After several futile attempts to change this decision, Abraham was forced to return to his home town of Danzig in June 1938, after more than three years stay in Denmark, leaving his wife and two children behind. He succeeded in getting past the border controls in November 1938 but was again denied a residence permit and in March 1939 he ended up in Danzig once again. In May he made a new attempt to return to Denmark but was refused entry and returned to Danzig for the third time. In March 1940 a new Minister of Justice finally granted Abraham N a preliminary residence permit in order to prepare for re-emigration. Like most of the Jewish refugees in the country at that time he became stranded because of the war and obtained citizenship only after fifteen years residence.

Richard R's offence was solely that he had married in spite of having been refused a residence permit. He was of Hungarian nationality but had been born in Germany and had never set foot in Hungary. He was not a burden on public funds, he made no attempts to acquire a work permit and he had not broken any laws or regulations. His wife was self-employed and able to support him, but the State Police and the Ministry of Justice were convinced that he intended to settle in Denmark and that he was the real driving force behind his wife's business. Even though he was kept under strict surveillance, the police never caught him at the premises. He was, however, denied an extension to his residence permit and was forced to be constantly on the move; from Hungary to Denmark, to France, back to Denmark, back to France, on to Sweden, back to France and then to Belgium until he was finally overtaken by the outbreak of war in Denmark. By that time, his many travel expenses had ruined his wife's business.

In October 1938 the borders were closed for Jews from Germany and other parts of Central Europe where antisemitic persecutions were likely to lead to widespread emigration.[32] This meant that Jews had to apply for special permission to enter Denmark and such permission was only granted if the person in question carried a visa to a third country or had very close family links to Denmark. Thus former Danish citizens were able to obtain preliminary residence permits for themselves and their children. Male spouses, however, could not obtain such a permit.[33] Before the women themselves were permitted to enter Denmark, they either had to sign declarations that they would not apply for residence permits for their husbands or were informed that their spouses could not expect to follow in their wake prior to the issuance of visa. Consequently a number of Danish-born women chose to stay on in the Third Reich with their families, with later fatal consequences. The Danish authorities undoubtedly saw their defensive refugee policy as a success. The number of Jewish refugees in Denmark never exceeded 1,000 – excluding the Hechaluz and Alijah youth in transit to Palestine.

Notes

1. Police report, 12.4.37, UDL, 58449. This article is based upon an analysis of all police files on refugees entering or trying to enter Denmark during 1933–1945, approximately 8,000 persons consisting of Jews as well as Nazi-Germany's political opponents. This thorough investigation is part of a

government-sponsored research project on Danish refugee policy during the said period, especially in regard to the victims of the antisemitic persecutions. The findings of this research have been published in L.Rünitz, *Af hensyn til konsekvenserne, Danmark og flygtningesporgsmalet 1933–1939*, Odense 2005. All sources used in this article are found in Rigsarkivet (The Danish State Archives) in Copenhagen.

2. State Police records, UDL 58449. According to the Aliens Code a foreigner could reside in Denmark for three months before he had to submit a formal request for residence permit.
3. JM to Alfred L, 21.8.37, UDL 58449.
4. The Coordinating Refugee Commitees (*De samvirkende danske Emigranthjälpekomitéer*), 28.8.37, UDL, 58449. The Coordinating Refugee Committees consisted of the Social-Democratic Matteotti Committee, the Intellectuals Assistance Committee and the Jewish Committee, The Committee of 4 May 1933.
5. JM Circular of 12.10.37, 'Love og Anordninger 1937', p.537.
6. UM to JM, 10.9.36, UM 17.T.44.
7. UDL 55173.
8. Speech in Foreign Affairs Committee, 29.1.37, UM 36.Dan.53b.
9. The speech was subsequently printed in the newspaper *Social-Demokraten*, 27 and 28 April 1937.
10. There were less than 6,000 Danish Jews.
11. JM 1936/1759.
12. Parliamentary debate, 10.11.37, Rigsdagstidende 1937/38, Folketinget, col. 899–900.
13. Letter, 15.10.37, UDL 51398, and UDL 53298.
14. The Cooperating Committees to JM, 31.12.37, UDL 53298.
15. JM Journal, UDL 51398.
16. JM Journal, 20. and 22.1.38, UDL 51398.
17. State Police reports, 29. and 30.6.38, UDL 63480.
18. UDL 51398.
19. UDL 64220.
20. Undated JM Memo concerning German refugees, JM 1935/1434.
21. Ibid.
22. Recommendations, 2.5.34, JM 1933/1206 and JM 1935/1434.
23. Statement from the chairman of the Jewish refugee committee April 1938 in the periodical *Joedisk Familieblad*, cf. JM Journal, 1.7.36, JM 1935/1434.
24. JM Journal, UDL 53048.
25. Visa File No. 95912, 100944 and UDL 37585 and UDL 65596.
26. UDL 63909 and UDL 64861.
27. For instance UDL 44569 and UDL 44917.
28. Memo, January 1936, p.11, JM 1933/1206.
29. Radio speech, April 1937, *Social-Demokraten*, 28 April 1937.
30. UDL 51324 and UDL 51108.
31. UDL 47772 and UDL 75653.
32. UM 36.Dan.53a; JM 1938/719.
33. JM 1938/34.1–34.262 and 1939/34.1–34.290.

Chapter I.3

Unwilling Refuge: France and the Dilemma of Illegal Immigration, 1933–1939

Vicki Caron

From 1933 until 1939 France's Central European refugee policy experienced a complete turnaround. In the first months after Hitler's seizure of power on 30 January 1933, French refugee policy was extraordinarily liberal. In sharp contrast to other Western European nations, France welcomed the refugees from Germany. Camille Chautemps, Minister of Interior, together with his counterpart at the Quai d'Orsay, Joseph Paul-Boncour, issued directives to the French embassy and consulates in Germany to waive visa requirements for those fleeing. Border police were instructed to allow refugees to enter freely, and it was proclaimed that the German émigrés would be granted a special status. In part, this generosity stemmed from the fact that the crisis in Germany was expected to be short-lived and that only a small proportion of Germany's 525,000 Jews would actually emigrate. But it also stemmed from diplomatic factors. In the eyes of French statesmen, Hitler's triumph and the ensuing crackdown on Jewish and political dissidents appeared to confirm the validity of the hardline stance toward Germany that France had championed, virtually alone, since 1919. Providing asylum to the martyrs of 'Teutonic barbarism' seemed but a small price to pay for the international goodwill France hoped to reap now that world opinion had to confront the Nazi threat. As a result of this liberal attitude, of the 60–65,000 refugees who fled Germany in 1933, no fewer than 25,000 came to France, and of these approximately 85 per cent were Jews.[1]

By the late 1930s, however, this liberalism had completely disappeared. In large measure this retreat was due to the Depression. As soon as the refugees began to arrive, associations representing merchants, artisans and liberal professionals – especially doctors and lawyers – in Paris as well as Alsace and Lorraine – began to raise a hue and cry that the refugees constituted 'unfair' economic competition. Sensitive to the demands of their middle-class clienteles, the French parliament and administration began to pass legislation severely limiting the right of foreigners and even naturalised citizens to work in these professions.[2] Moreover, by the late 1930s security concerns, and especially the fear that the refugees could embroil France in an undesired war with Germany, further encouraged the government to seal the borders. Despite official rhetoric that France would remain a country of asylum, the fact is that by 1938–39, just as the Central European refugee crisis was reaching acute proportions, the government enacted extremely harsh decree laws (laws promulgated by the administration as opposed to the parliament) that virtually negated the provision of asylum and mandated harsh penalties, including jail sentences, for illegal entrants.

These laws ultimately backfired, however; they failed to achieve their intended goal of closing the border. The French simply lacked the personnel to guard the entire length of their frontier, not only with Germany, but with Belgium, Luxembourg, Switzerland, and Italy, since these countries, too, were seeking to foist their refugees onto the French. And the French faced an additional crisis in early 1939, when approximately half a million additional refugees flooded across the Spanish frontier in the wake of the Republican defeat in the Spanish civil war.[3] Hence, despite increased border controls, tens of thousands of Central European refugees crossed into France in 1938–39. Indeed, by December 1938, it was estimated that France was harboring as many as 60,000 of them, nearly all illegal aliens. As one French journalist explained in May 1939: 'As a result of its geographical situation, this country is ... condemned to receive the great bulk of Central European émigrés who know that our prisons are preferable to Hitlerian concentration camps'.[4]

From Liberalism to Conservative Crackdown, 1933–1935

In order to examine the mechanisms devised by the French government to deal with the refugee crisis in 1938–39 and their tragic impact on the plight of refugees, it is useful to review the screening methods implemented by French officials in the early 1930s to determine eligibility for refugee status. By awarding refugees from Germany a special status in the spring of 1933, a situation made possible by the willingness of French Jewish organisations to pay all expenses relating to refugee settlement,[5] the French government sent a clear signal that it regarded these individuals as refugees and not economic migrants. How extraordinarily liberal these provisions were is highlighted by the directive of the French foreign minister, Joseph Paul-Boncour, to French consulates in Germany 'to welcome in the most generous manner and the most liberal spirit requests for visas presented by Jews', including Nansen refugees – Russians, Greeks, Armenians, and others who had become stateless after the First World War and were under the protection of the League of Nation's Nansen

Office, which granted them travel documents and identity papers.[6] The Minister of Interior, Camille Chautemps, also called on French border police to grant residence permits and identity cards to refugees 'without difficulties', and he went so far as to waive the normal visa regime altogether, mandating that refugees could enter France without visas as long as they reported to the police within twenty days. Indigent refugees were to be granted identity cards free of charge, and customs duties were waived for refugees who desired to transfer their property to France. The sole condition of these provisions was that refugees obey French law and abstain from political activity on French soil.[7]

The French government, however, beat a swift retreat from this liberal position in response to a mounting wave of middle-class protest regarding 'unfair competition' from German refugees, many of whom, especially in the weeks just after Hitler's seizure of power, were able to transfer their assets out of Germany and establish businesses in France. Already in July 1933, the Foreign Ministry declared that refugees could no longer be received *'en masse* in our country',[8] and in October, the liberal visa provisions were abrogated altogether. Refugees were once again requested to apply for visas at French consulates in Germany, and French consular officials were instructed to be more discerning in the delivery of visas. Indeed, it was now determined that certain categories of persons were to be excluded altogether from refugee status. First, refugees of East European origin, who constituted as many as 50–60 per cent of those entering France, were to be considered economic migrants, and they were to be repatriated to their country of origin. It was also decided in December 1933 that France would henceforth accept only refugees able to prove substantial independent means, since the Minister of Labour, notwithstanding earlier promises, now declared that work permits could not be granted to refugees under the current economic circumstances. Moreover, refugees coming from third countries were also denied visas, in an effort to dissuade France's neighbours from shoving these individuals across the border. And finally, despite numerous diplomatic reports chronicling the deteriorating situation of German Jews, French consulates in Germany as well as French border police were instructed to grant visas or identity cards only to individuals able to prove that they had been physically molested or faced imminent danger.

In addition to these 'external' screening measures, 'internal' mechanisms were beefed up as well. Police surveillance at the German border was tightened up, and refugees were barred altogether from settling in Alsace and Lorraine unless they had relatives there or were deemed non-competitive with local businesses. East European refugees from Germany already in France began to be forcibly repatriated to their countries of origin with the help of the Comité National, the Jewish refugee committee. Moreover, in late 1934–35, the conservative governments of Pierre-Etienne Flandin and Pierre Laval, in an effort to sharply reduce the number of foreign workers, initiated a harsh crackdown on all foreigners which made no provision for refugee status. The acquisition and renewal of identity cards became more difficult, and immigrants without work contracts who could not demonstrate independent financial means were rounded up on charges of vagabondage and told to leave. On 6 February 1935, the administration issued a new decree law stipulating that foreigners' identity cards would henceforth be valid only in the *département* where they had been issued, and foreigners requesting identity cards for the first time had to show proof that they had entered the country legally; a standard few refugees could meet. To ensure compliance, the government issued yet another decree law on 31 October 1935 that mandated strict prison sentences of six months to two years for failure to obey an expulsion order.[9]

Although this crackdown was not targeted specifically at refugees, they were highly vulnerable, since most of them lacked work permits and few could meet the residency requirements for renewing an identity card. In November 1934, officials of the American Jewish Joint Distribution Committee (AJDC), the principal Jewish relief organisation, noted that *refoulement* notices were being doled out to German refugees in record numbers, and they warned that 15–17,000 refugees faced 'wholesale expulsion'. Refugees flocked to the Prefecture of Police, commonly known as the 'house of tears', in an effort to secure extensions of *refoulement* or expulsion orders. These attempts generally failed, however, and thousands of refugees were ordered to leave the country. Those who refused risked arrest and imprisonment, and upon their release they faced the prospect of undergoing the entire cycle of *refoulement*, expulsion, arrest, and imprisonment again, since they had no way of legalising their status. According to one legal expert for the League for the Rights of Man and Citizen, if the decree laws were not abrogated, 'prison would become the sole asylum for political refugees in France'. Refugee organisations similarly reported a dramatic rise in the number of suicides among refugees facing expulsion orders.[10]

France did accept one further contingent of German refugees – those who fled following the Saar plebiscite of 13 January 1935, which returned the Saar, which had been under a 15-year-long League of Nation's mandate, to German sovereignty. Although France's reception of the Saar refugees has generally been described in a favourable light, this process was handled so clumsily and in a manner so insensitive to the fate of the refugees that it highlighted just how far France had retreated from its liberal stance of 1933.[11] Since many Saarlanders were either French citizens, or had worked for the French cause, and since France had enjoyed exclusive rights to the Saar coalfields under the League of Nations mandate, a deal was struck in late 1934 according to which France would offer asylum to the 6–8,000 refugees expected to flee in the event of a pro-German vote, while the League of Nations would provide financial credits for the final resettlement of these refugees, presumably in Latin America. Nevertheless, in the first days after the vote, when it appeared that the number of asylum seekers would be far greater than originally expected, the French Minister of Interior, on his own initiative and without consulting the other ministries involved, ordered the closing of the border. This action infuriated the French Foreign Minister, since it negated pledges France had made at the League of Nations to grant asylum to those Saarlanders 'who, because of their sentiments and political attitudes have reason to fear the return of the Saar to the Reich'. It also infuriated him since it 'reduced to nothing', the arduous efforts of his consular staff in Saarbrucken who were working day and night to screen refugees and deliver visas to those categories eligible for asylum,[12] since now even visa holders were being turned away at border. Worst of all, the decision had dire consequences for the refugees themselves. At the frontier, women were throwing themselves under trucks so as not to be sent back, and several police officers deserted their posts, sickened by the heartrending scenes.

Although the border was eventually reopened, border police, acting on instructions from the Minister of Interior, continued to turn away large numbers of visa holders. According to a Foreign Ministry report of 13 March 1935, 12,063 persons with visas had presented themselves at the border to date, but only 5,538 had been accepted, and of these another 586 had been *refoulés* after undergoing a screening process at one of the reception camps that had been erected near the border. Despite the relatively small size of this influx, the French government was adamant that even these refugees, aside from the few hundred who had come with independent financial means, should not be allowed to stay. As the Minister of Labour, L.-O. Frossard, explained in June 1935, 'it is important to avoid any measure that might convey the impression that the [situation of] the Saarlanders is being stabilized on our territory, in order to safeguard the rights of our country vis-à-vis the League of Nations, upon whom the definitive solution to the Saar refugee problem depends'.

The conservative administrations of Flandin and Laval even expected that the 10–12,000 German refugees who still remained on French soil would have to leave, notwithstanding the fact that French diplomats knew full well that émigrés who returned to Germany were frequently sent to concentration camps. Moreover, after the influx of Saar refugees, the government was firm that no further refugees would be accepted, regardless of the circumstances. When the Minister of Interior was alerted in 1935 to the fact that German nationals condemned to sterilisation might seek asylum in France, he directed the police and prefects 'to oppose by all means possible the entry of these individuals into our country'. And, in the aftermath of the Nuremberg Laws of September 1935, which stripped German Jews of their citizenship and defined them along racial lines, the Foreign Ministry took steps to ensure that these decrees would 'not provoke an exodus of German nationals, especially Jews, not to mention foreign Jews currently living in Germany'. Consular officials were urged to issue visas only with extreme circumspection, and border surveillance was reinforced 'to discourage any attempt at illegal immigration'. As the Foreign Ministry explained, 'It seems superfluous ... to insist on the inconveniences and risks of this new emigration following the 1933 exodus, whose repercussions we have now been able to assess completely'.[13]

The Popular Front Interregnum, 1936–1937

This hardline position was significantly alleviated under the Popular Front, which was elected to office in May 1936. The Popular Front, which included many leading pro-refugee activists from the Socialist Party, such as Marius Moutet, Jules Moch, Salomon Grumbach, and Léon Blum himself, ratified several agreements that went far toward stabilising and improving the situation of refugees already in France. In October 1936, it ratified the League of Nations Convention of 28 October 1933, which granted Nansen refugees travel and identity documents that afforded them protection against arbitrary *refoulement* and expulsion, and since France had recently agreed to treat Saar refugees on the same footing as Nansen refugees, they too were permitted to remain in France. This accord then proceeded to grant Nansen refugees far-reaching social benefits, including most-favoured nation status with regard to eligibility for social assistance (unemployment and health insurance, pensions, etc.), disability pay in case of industrial accidents, the right to attend French educational institutions, and most importantly, the right to work.[14] The Popular Front then made every effort to extend these same benefits to German refugees, in anticipation of the League of Nations' planned merger of the HCR and the Nansen Office. In early July 1936, France, together with six other nations, signed an agreement worked out by the HCR, called the 'Provisional Arrangement Concerning the Status of Refugees coming from Germany', which provided German refugees many of the same rights and social benefits as Nansen refugees, and shortly afterward the government enacted the Presidential Decree of 17 September 1936. According to this decree, refugees who had come from Germany between 30 January 1933 and 5 August 1936 were to be granted an amnesty, regardless of whether or not they had entered the country legally, and a Consultative Commission, consisting of pro-refugee activists and well-known German refugees, was constituted to screen applicants for the new refugee status.[15]

To be sure, these measures did not go as far as pro-refugee activists would have liked. Refugees of East European origin continued to be excluded, and the Popular Front proved unable to guarantee the right to work to German refugees, despite its original intention to do so, since middle-class professional organisations as well as the coalition partners of the socialists remained staunchly opposed to such a move. Nevertheless, the Popular Front did seek to deliver work permits to German refugees as liberally as possible, and it furthermore proved willing to consider for the first time alternative settlement schemes, such as steering refugees to French colonies or to under-populated regions of south western France where there was a need for agricultural labour. It also sought to accelerate the naturalisation of refugees as well as other foreigners in an attempt to increase the pool of candidates eligible for military service.

But the most serious shortcoming of these initiatives was that they failed to bind the government with respect to future refugees, and in this respect the Popular Front closely adhered to the hardline policies of its predecessors. Just prior to the signing of the Geneva Accord, Jean Longuet, France's chief delegate to the conference, declared that France's obligations toward the refugees would apply only to 'persons who are at the present moment refugees', but not to future newcomers, and in a circular of 14 August 1936, Roger Salengro, the Minister of Interior, declared that the Geneva Accord 'has as its aim to *stabilise the existing situation* of the refugees by covering and granting an amnesty for the past, but not to make any commitments with respect to the future by having to accept future immigrations'. The government's unwillingness to commit itself vis-à-vis future asylum seekers stemmed from the expectation that a renewed crackdown against German Jews would result in yet another mass exodus. Hence, in an effort to pressure the HCR to steer refugees to less 'saturated' countries, the Foreign Ministry's tough visa policy remained in place, and Salengro instructed French police to prevent 'in the most absolute manner every *new* admission of refugees who come from Germany, but whose situation is irregular [i.e., without a visa or passport]'. In reality, the Popular Front's refugee policy was predicated on a compromise: extraordinarily liberal terms of asylum, including an amnesty, were to be granted refugees already in France, but only on condition that future newcomers be excluded, regardless of the circumstances that might impel them to flee.[16]

Cracks in this compromise began to appear already in 1937 due to fears of continued illegal immigration. Although article 4 of the 6 February 1935 decree law prohibiting refugees from changing their domicile without the prefect's permission had been abrogated in October 1936, this regulation was reinstated in March 1937 for the three frontier departments of the Bas-Rhin, the Haut-Rhin, and the Moselle. As one Sûreté Nationale agent explained, German refugees posed a grave security risk, and he instructed the prefects of these departments to 'be especially severe toward German subjects [who] all too often want to settle close to their country of origin, in places where their massive settlement is dangerous in every respect'. Foreigners who had moved into the region since October 1936 were to be investigated, and those deemed 'undesirable' were to be moved to the interior. Moreover, French diplomats expected the exodus from Germany to worsen. In December 1937 the French Consul in Nuremberg noted that the increasingly strict application of the Nuremberg Laws by the Nazis 'could only precipitate the recent movement of emigration that has taken place in recent months'.[17]

But what most jeopardised the liberal aspects of the Popular Front's refugee policy was the fact that the German Jewish refugee problem became inextricably linked to the growing influx of illegal Jewish immigrants from Eastern Europe. During the summer and fall of 1937, police estimated that as many as 15,000 to 18,000 immigrants, of whom as many as 80 per cent were East European Jews, had entered the country illegally. Despite the dramatic upsurge in antisemitism in Eastern Europe in the late 1930s, the French government adamantly refused to recognise these foreigners as refugees, fearing that such recognition could trigger the emigration of hundreds of thousands and perhaps even millions of Jews. In July 1937, Minister of Interior, Marx Dormoy, railed against 'the risks of a massive immigration of undesirables', and he insisted that under no circumstances would these newcomers be eligible for political asylum. These East Europeans, he maintained, were not fleeing political persecution; rather they were seeking only to improve their economic circumstances, and in so doing they posed a competitive threat to French businesses and artisanal professions, especially in large metropolitan centres. Dormoy therefore called on border police to 'redouble their vigilance to prevent the entry of all foreigners whose status is irregular', and he instructed police to expel all immigrants who had slipped through the cracks in recent months.

To deal with the growing threat of illegal immigration, Chautemps appointed a new Undersecretary of State for Immigration, Philippe Serre, a prominent Radical deputy. The principal aim of Serre's office, officially created on 18 January 1938, was to draw up a general statute for foreigners that would distinguish between 'useful' and 'undesirable' immigrants and set up a machinery to implement these new regulations.[18] Three new councils were to be established: the Superior Council of Foreigners to coordinate the immigration policies of the various ministries and determine which immigrants were to be given permanent refugee status; the Consultative Commission of Refugees, clearly modelled on the existing Consultative Commission, to be composed of pro-refugee activists who would screen the dossiers of foreigners applying for asylum; and the Commission of Border Surveillance to coordinate immigration policies at the border.

To resolve once and for all the irritating problem of clandestine Jewish immigration, Serre, together with his chief of staff, the renowned ethnologist and immigration expert, Georges Mauco, devised a radical plan – the resettlement of the entire population of illegal East European Jewish immigrants in Paris to large-scale agricultural collectives to be created in depopulated regions of south western France.[19] While this idea appealed to the Prefect of Police for security reasons, Serre and Mauco found it attractive for its purported economic benefits. Above all, they hoped that diverting Jewish refugees to the countryside would ease competition between Jewish immigrants and French workers. Whereas in the past this problem had been addressed through expulsion, the current administration, Mauco explained, hoped to resolve it in a 'systematic and humane way'.[20]

In February and March of 1938, Serre and Mauco undertook negotiations with the French Jewish community and the AJDC to persuade them to pay for this plan. In essence, what Mauco offered Jewish leaders was an ultimatum: either they could comply with the plan and pay for the mass population transfer to the provinces, or they could finance the repatriation of these immigrants back to Eastern Europe. If Jewish leaders complied, Mauco recommended that the AJDC put up 20 million francs to launch the project. In return, he promised that all refugees sent to the agricultural centres would be granted agricultural work permits and political refugee status. Once resettled, these refugees would be prohibited from leaving the centres; otherwise, Mauco warned, they would be 'ruthlessly expelled'. Refugees who refused to leave the cities, together with those deemed unfit for agricultural work, would suffer the same fate. Finally, to ensure that this amnesty not encourage further influxes of Jews from Eastern Europe, Mauco warned that asylum henceforth would be granted only to well-known political activists and not to Jews.

The Jewish community ultimately complied with this plan, not wishing to become complicit in the repatriation of their coreligionists, and the AJDC agreed to put up some 3 million francs to finance this scheme.[21] However, the deteriorating international climate in 1938–1939, together with the collapse of the Popular Front government, with its pledge to provide a modicum of asylum, squashed any hopes that the Serre Plan would be realised. Already in March 1938 the Foreign Ministry warned that it considered any extension of refugee status to East Europeans a dangerous precedent likely to encourage further immigration. The Foreign Ministry also opposed the creation of an immigration statute, arguing that the current case by case approach was more restrictive and therefore more desirable. Finally, in the wake of the Nazi incursions into Austria and Czechoslovakia, the fierce antisemitic crackdown in Germany itself, which culminated in *Kristallnacht*, as well as the installation of antisemitic regimes in Italy, Poland, Romania and Hungary, the administration of Radical Party leader Edouard Daladier, which came to power in April 1938, abandoned the Popular Front initiatives altogether and returned to the hardline strategies of 1934–35.

Renewed Crackdown: The International Crisis of 1938–1939

Immediately after the *Anschluss* in March 1938 it seemed that France might revert to a generous asylum policy, since the government of Léon Blum, which had returned briefly to power, permitted Austrian refugees to enter solely with transit visas on condition that they register with the police within two months. This generosity completely evaporated, however, when Daladier came to power on 10 April.[22] Just two days later, Daladier's Foreign Minister, George Bonnet, ordered French consulates in Austria 'to no longer deliver visas to Austrian subjects', and French consulates throughout Central Europe were instructed to 'stop the influx of refugees of Austrian provenance into France', unless these individuals already held U.S. visas. Nor was there any question in the minds of French officials as to the refugee status of Austria's 200,000 Jews in the wake of the Nazi regime of forced expulsion and expropriation.

These harsh visa policies were complemented by an internal crackdown of unprecedented severity that culminated with the draconian decree law of 2 May 1938. In mid-April, Minister of Interior Albert Sarraut ordered police round-ups of Austrian refugees in and around Paris, and on 30 April, he issued a directive to step up police surveillance over Austrian refugees to 'avoid a massive and uncontrolled invasion by émigrés of all sorts'. Austrians who had arrived after 14 March were ordered to report to police headquarters within forty-eight hours, whether or not they held visas from French consulates. There they were required to fill out questionnaires regarding the members of their families, their financial resources, and any familial relations they might have in France, and a special stamp was placed on their passports. Austrians who arrived without papers were to be placed under heightened surveillance, and any non-Austrian refugees (i.e., those of East European background) were to be expelled in conformity with the policies hammered out in 1933.

The cornerstone of this internal crackdown was the draconian decree law of 2 May 1938. Notwithstanding Sarraut's repeated assurances that this law did 'not in the least endanger the traditional rules of French hospitality', and that the government's sole aim was to weed out criminal elements from those truly deserving of asylum, the fact is that the harsh visa policies coupled with severe internal controls completely negated the right to asylum. In an effort to force illegal aliens to leave, the decree law mandated that foreigners who lacked visas or identity cards, or those carrying false papers, would be subject to stringent fines of 100 to 1,000 francs and automatic prison sentences of one month to one year, and, for the first time, individuals who assisted illegal aliens were subject to the same sanctions. Failure to comply with an expulsion order also carried a harsher penalty than in the past. Whereas the maximum jail sentence for this infraction had been six months, the minimum sentence was now set at six months, and the maximum sentence was extended to three years. The decree law also made the renewal of residence permits and identity cards more difficult, and foreigners already in France who were unable to renew these documents faced *refoulement* and expulsion. Finally, whereas expulsion had previously been the prerogative of the Minister of Interior, that authority was now extended to the police and the prefects as well, and they were to receive additional funding to beef up border surveillance.[23]

It is true that the decree law included two articles ostensibly intended to guarantee the right of asylum for genuine refugees, but these measures either remained a dead letter or were not implemented immediately. According to article 10, newly arrived refugees had the right to file a declaration of refugee status with police within forty-eight hours of crossing the border, and article 11 stipulated that foreigners who had been expelled but were unable to depart since no country was willing to accept them, were not to be sent to prison, but to an assigned residence under police surveillance. But with respect to article 10, few refugees were prepared to declare themselves to border police for fear that their petitions would be rejected. Once they failed to comply with this forty-eight-hour requirement, they automatically became illegal aliens and lost the right to an administrative hearing if they subsequently received an expulsion order. Moreover, although the intent of article 11 was to avoid a repetition of the scenario that had emerged in 1935, when thousands of foreigners who could not be expelled landed in jail, the Minister of Interior remained deeply suspicious of alternatives to expulsion, such as internment camps, for fear that such measures might permit these individuals to remain indefinitely on French soil. Hence, it was only when the prisons were once again bursting to capacity that the Minister took measures to implement article 11.[24]

By the summer of 1938, it appeared that these harsh security measures had scored some success. Just days after the decree law went into effect, Emile Kahn, Vice-President of the League for the Rights of Man and Citizen, described the indiscriminate arrests of refugees in Paris:

> Pass by the Prefecture of Police. The unfortunates, imperiously convoked, wait trembling that someone might call them. They are shoved, in batches, before anonymous civil servants, who, with one word, will decide their fate. No discussion is allowed nor are any explanations to be given: 'So and so? Refoulement ... . So and So? Expulsion. You have 48 hours in which to leave.[25]

Moreover, due to beefed-up border security, Jewish organisations reported that refugees who lacked papers were being sent back in droves, even to Germany. As the Strasbourg Jewish committee ruefully noted, Jewish refugees now faced a painful dilemma: 'In Germany, the concentration camp awaits them; in France, they face the threat of prison for illegal entry'. And finally, France successfully staved off any further commitments to provide refugee asylum at the Evian Conference of 6–15 July 1938, which had been convened at the urging of President Franklin Delano Roosevelt in an effort to bring Austrian refugees under the juridical umbrella of the HCR to secure for them a status similar to that provided by the 1936 'Provisional Arrangement Concerning the Status of Refugees coming from Germany'. Although France had agreed to host this conference – a decision made during Blum's ministry earlier in the year – the Daladier administration had no intention of bowing to American pressure. As Jean Berthoin, the director of the Sûreté Nationale and Sarraut's chief of staff, declared at an inter-ministerial meeting to prepare for the Evian conference, France could accept no further Austrian immigration, 'no matter how minimal it might be'. Only refugees already holding visas for other countries, and especially the U.S., were to be allowed in. All others, whom he referred to as the 'waste products of the entire Austrian or German immigration', were to be *'refouler* without mercy'. France, he argued, was 'saturated', and, in an amazingly frank admission that the right to asylum no longer existed, he added that 'France under no circumstances could consent to open her borders unconditionally and without limitation to individuals solely on the basis of their claim to be refugees'. At the conference itself, Bérenger, who had been reappointed to lead the French delegation, echoed Berthoin's views almost verbatim.[26]

This effort to stave off further influxes of refugees ultimately depended on the stabilisation of the international political situation and the availability of alternative havens if the refugee crisis were to worsen. But in the fall of 1938, the international political situation sharply deteriorated, and, as the Evian Conference proved, alternative havens did not exist. Hence, as hundreds of thousands more individuals were driven from their homes in the wake of the Sudeten crisis, *Kristallnacht*, the Czech crisis of 1939, as well as the installation of antisemitic regimes in fascist Italy and Eastern Europe, these hardline policies would be put to the test by new pressures on France's frontiers.

France's initial response to this ever worsening refugee crisis was to dig in her heels and tighten existing restrictions even further. Once again, French consulates throughout Central Europe were instructed to deliver visas only with extreme circumspection. In the aftermath of the Sudeten crisis in late September, which culminated in the Munich Accords and recognised the transfer of this portion of Czech territory to Nazi control, the French offered a mere 310 visas, despite the fact that as many as 50,000 individuals were expected to flee. Moreover, the French ultimately granted only 100 visas and limited these to political as opposed to racial refugees, despite the far greater number of the latter. So niggardly was the French response that even the British complained that 'France, as Czechoslovakia's ally, might be expected to have made a rather more generous contribution to this problem than they appear to have done up to the present time'.[27]

Nor did France ease visa policies at the time of *Kristallnacht* on 9–10 November, when the Nazis launched an attack of unprecedented violence against the 350,000 Jews who had remained in Germany, to retaliate for the assassination of a German diplomat in Paris on 7 November by a seventeen-year-old refugee youth, Herschel Grynszpan.[28] Following this government-sponsored pogrom, there could be no doubt that Jews who did not flee faced the probability of incarceration in a concentration camp and even death. Aware that events had taken a dramatic turn for the worse, several French diplomats pleaded with their government to relax the stringent visa policy and border controls. As the French Consul in Nuremberg noted with regard to German Jews:

> All foreign countries are closing their borders and refusing them asylum. If the governments of the great democratic powers remain deaf to the appeals of these unfortunates and do not take immediate measures to help them, it is certain that the sole refuge of German Jews will be death, and the coming days will register a wave of mass suicides.[29]

These appeals fell on deaf ears, however. Georges Bonnet was not inclined to deviate from the hardline visa policy. Indeed, in the wake of new passport restrictions implemented by the Germans, which marked the passports of German Jews with the letter 'J' to ensure that they not return, French consulates in Germany were instructed to exercise more rigour than ever since German Jews, once allowed to enter French territory, could not be expelled. [30]

French border police, who had just received a new mandate by the decree law of 12 November 1938, were also under strict instructions to turn away all refugees without papers. Moreover, in a highly unusual move, Sarraut began to turn away even visa holders, a practice that had not been repeated since the Saar plebiscite. As he explained in a memo to border police and prefects, this measure was necessary 'to guard against the threat of a massive immigration of undesirable elements ... who believed it to be their duty to trick our consuls with regard to the duration and the true reasons for their sojourn in our country'. At the same time, Sarraut sent urgent telegrams to the prefects in the north-eastern border provinces instructing them to bar entry of German Jewish children, notwithstanding recent assurances given by Daladier that France would accept a contingent of them. As administration officials explained, if war were to break out, these children would be abandoned by their families to become wards of the state. Similarly, the government rejected a request from the Chief Rabbi to allow 200 elderly German Jews to be settled in Alsace on the grounds that such individuals constituted a security threat.[31]

Finally, this tough border policy was complemented by a renewed crackdown against refugees already in the country. Refugees were again rounded up in and around Paris at the time of the Munich mobilisation in September, and on 12 October, the Minister of Interior ordered the expulsion of all refugees without visas or passports who had not declared themselves at the border, a measure clearly aimed at ridding the country of Austrians who had not complied with the 2 May 1938 decree law. At the same time, the government extended the list of departments off limits to refugee settlement. Moreover, a new decree law of 12 November made it more difficult for foreigners to marry French citizens, an effort aimed at rooting out *mariages blancs*, and article 25 of this decree law mandated the creation of special centres where foreigners considered dangerous to national security but who could not be expelled were to be detained under heightened surveillance. Harsh penalties were also announced for those who violated yet another decree law of 17 June 1938, which imposed new restrictions, including quotas and a five-year residence requirement, on foreigners who wished to practice commerce, the sole sphere of economic activity still open to refugees. And, in yet another effort to crack down on refugees who did not possess visas to go abroad, the Minister of Interior ordered navigation companies in the spring of 1939 to sell tickets only to individuals with visas in hand since too many refugees were slipping into France on transit visas or international transit cards (documents issued by navigation companies to travellers who had to pass through third countries on their way to their final destinations).[32]

No matter how stringent these security measures, they could not dam up the frontier; nor could they force refugees already in France to leave. First, the Nazis were fiercely determined to expel the Jews of Austria and Germany, and they literally dumped them across the border, to the dismay of the Foreign Minister, who repeatedly protested such actions.[33] According to one AJDC report of July 1939, German police frequently guided refugees to the border at night and then waited until 'the guards change or when by some trickery the guards are induced to leave that part of the border without leaving any watch to replace them'. In addition, the task of expelling refugees already in the country proved no easier than policing the frontier. France's West European neighbours were similarly disinclined to accept more refugees, and whenever the French shoved refugees across the border, they simply shoved them back in what came to be called a game of international ping-pong. Finally, most refugees were so desperate that the prospect of imprisonment in France was not about to deter them. The upshot of this situation was a huge population of illegal aliens. By the end of 1938, it was estimated that 42,000 of the almost 60,000 Central and East European Jewish refugees in France had entered the country clandestinely, and among the recent arrivals, that proportion was even higher.[34]

This surge of illegal immigrants sorely strained the internal mechanisms devised to deal with this problem. The automatic jail sentences mandated by the 2 May decree law meant that thousands of refugees were again being sent to jail. According to a Ministry of Justice report delivered to the parliament on 25 January 1939, some 8,405 refugees had so far been imprisoned for some infraction of the decree laws, at a cost to taxpayers of 1,770,954 francs. At the same time, the administrative machinery for dealing with refugee matters was ill equipped to cope with this deluge. Refugees trying to regularise their legal status or obtain an extension of the standard two-week residence permit had to queue up for days at the Prefecture of Police in Paris, and as one refugee committee noted, 'The life of police employees has become an inferno, in view of the fact that each one of them has to talk to several hundred people daily, and examine their cases'.[35] Judges, too, were overwhelmed, sometimes hearing up to sixty cases per day. But what most overloaded the system was the fact that the refugees, once released from prison, were forced to return to an underground existence, since they had no means of regularising their legal status. They were therefore trapped in what critics of the decree laws called an 'infernal cycle' – repeat offenders were 'steered to the border, where they were shoved back by the neighbouring country; [and] again imprisoned'. Ironically, by sentencing the refugees to a life of perpetual criminality, the government diminished their chances of departing, since individuals with criminal records became ineligible for entry visas to other countries.

Refugees seeking escape from this 'infernal cycle' had only two options: suicide, or resorting to the burgeoning network of false passport and visa operations, an option that ultimately involved them in even more compromising criminal activities. These operations, nearly always run by other foreigners, frequently worked in tandem with corrupt Latin American consulates and extorted huge sums of money from desperate refugees for documents that usually turned out to be invalid.

Finally, the decree laws failed because law enforcement officials were beginning to balk at having to enforce measures they considered cruel and unjust. To be sure, venality played a part in motivating some officials to assist refugees. In one notorious case in southern France, a police inspector was arrested for smuggling refugees from Italy across the border allegedly in exchange for huge bribes and even sexual favours. But many police were motivated by simple humanitarian concerns. Border police, according to refugee organisations, frequently turned a blind eye when refugees sneaked over the border. According to the AJDC, 'even if the police ... saw some of these illegal entrants, they were so moved by their plight that they did not obey the orders of their superiors to send these people back, and brought them instead to the nearest Jewish refugee committee'.[36]

Judges expressed even greater frustration, especially since they were not allowed to take extenuating circumstances into account when sentencing refugees. According to a report of the Gourevitch Committee, an influential pro-refugee lobby, the president of a criminal court resigned in protest after he was forced to sentence a 72-year-old German professor to prison for some minor infraction of the decree law. In another case, when a court sentenced the renowned German Jewish lawyer, Erich Frey, to prison for having failed to comply with an expulsion order, despite the fact that Frey had applied to no fewer than eleven consulates for a visa, the magistrates reportedly hung their heads in shame. And in Nice, where thousands of refugees from Italy were being smuggled across the border, judges regularly refused to send these people to jail as long as the Jewish refugee committee guaranteed their financial support.[37]

The Amnesty Campaign of 1939

Although right-wing commentators perceived this growing incidence of refugee 'criminality' as a sign that France was being 'invaded' by the 'international underworld', others, including many moderate conservatives, were beginning to realise that most refugees were not common criminals, but had been transformed into such by the decree laws. And, while most of the critics agreed that France could not permanently absorb yet another massive influx of refugees, they nevertheless concurred with Léon Blum, who had declared in an address to the annual convention of the *Ligue Internationale contre l'Antisémitisme* (LICA), held just after *Kristallnacht*, that 'although these unfortunates cannot stay here forever', the French government, together with the French Jewish community, bore an obligation to provide them with 'asylum for one night' until they could find more permanent homes elsewhere.[38]

Inspired by this moral outrage, a broad-based coalition of groups orchestrated a campaign to reform the decree laws and reinstate the more liberal refugee policies of the Popular Front.[39] Their demands included the implementation of articles 10 and 11 of the 2 May decree law so that authentic refugees might be considered for asylum; the reconstitution of the Consultative Commission to weed out 'desirable' from 'undesirable' refugees; the creation of transit camps to provide refugees waiting to emigrate elsewhere with vocational training in agriculture and artisanry; an amnesty for refugees already in France; a provision to allow judges to consider extenuating circumstances when sentencing refugees; and automatic extensions of residence permits and identity cards as well as the creation of special travel certificates so refugees could move about freely. A revival of these Popular Front initiatives made sense not only on humanitarian grounds but on practical ones as well. As the conservative deputy, Louis Rollin, argued in a much publicised petition to the government, throwing Jewish refugees into jail was not only inhumane but counterproductive, especially since the *Comité d'Assistance aux Réfugiés* (CAR), the principal Jewish refugee committee since 1936, had agreed to support refugees willing to go to the proposed transit camps.

This campaign began to score some successes, especially after the Foreign Ministry created a new committee in December 1938 to deal with the Central European refugee crisis – the *Comité Central des Réfugiés*, also known as the Bonnet Committee. Although Bonnet's intention in creating this committee was almost certainly to deflect international criticism of France's hardline refugee policies while in reality staying the course, Louise Weiss, the prominent journalist and feminist leader whom he named as Secretary General, refused to participate in this charade. Indeed, just prior to the creation of the committee, Weiss gave an interview to the *Univers Israélite*, the principal periodical of the Jewish community, in which she publicly criticised the decree laws, and especially the practice of sending refugees to prison solely because they had 'fled with insufficient passports and visas from countries where their existence entailed the danger of death'.[40]

Due in large measure to Weiss's influence, which galvanised the pro-refugee lobby and provided it with a voice within the administration, as well as practical considerations, including the desire to reduce the cost of keeping refugees in prison and to utilise refugees either as army recruits or technical experts in the event of war, the government began to retreat from the harshest aspects of the decree laws. Already in mid-December, the administration agreed to a request from the Alliance Israélite Universelle to accept 250 refugee children, and it promised that it would accept 1,000 more on condition that they not go to Paris, but to children's homes in the provinces at the expense of the Jewish refugee committees. And, although Weiss was unable to persuade the government to grant blanket permission for elderly refugees to enter France, she did secure exceptional permission for a contingent of elderly Jews just expelled from old-age homes in the Palatinate to resettle in Lunéville and Nancy.[41] Weiss was also one of the prime movers behind another decree law passed on 21 April 1939, which was aimed at attracting refugees who possessed desirable technical or entrepreneurial skills by providing them with special terms of asylum. Finally, she joined together with Jewish organisations to lobbying for the decree law of 12 April, which allowed certain categories of refugees, especially Nansen refugees and beneficiaries of the 4 July 1936 'Provisional Arrangement', to serve in the army during wartime, and all foreigners between the ages of eighteen and forty who had resided in France more than two months to enlist for peacetime service.[42]

At the same time, the Bonnet Committee together with Jewish refugee committees also persuaded the government to revive the agricultural and colonial settlement schemes initiated under the Popular Front. By August 1939, five provincial agricultural centres had been created, which provided shelter and vocational retraining to close to 400 refugees in an effort to prepare them for eventual emigration abroad. Similarly, the suburban refugee centre in Chelles, just outside Paris, was expanded considerably; by July 1939, it was providing vocational assistance and retraining to some 800 refugees, mostly Austrians. The government also revived some of the Popular Front's colonial initiatives, albeit on a much smaller scale. In November 1938, just after *Kristallnacht*, U.S. Secretary of State Sumner Welles elicited a pledge from Bonnet and Daladier 'to conduct a study without delay of the possibilities of settling a certain number of Jewish refugees in French colonies', and privately, Daladier informed Welles that 'France was prepared to accept 40,000 Jewish refugees in Madagascar'. Although the government never delivered on this promise, it did begin to ship small contingents of refugees to French Guiana, New Caledonia and Madagascar in the spring of 1939.[43]

A full-scale campaign was soon underway to overturn the anti-immigrant decree laws of May and November 1938 altogether. Jewish organisations now had the support of influential non-sectarian groups, such as *Association des Amis de la République* and the *Centre de Liaison pour le Droit d'Asile*. In May, a delegation from the Centre de Liaison, including the prominent Socialist deputy, Pierre Bloch, as well as the Centre's director, Henri Levin, met with Sarraut and submitted a memorandum demanding a new statute for foreigners in France in view of the new decree laws mandating military service for foreigners.[44] As Bloch declared in *Fraternité*, the immigrant paper of the Confédération Générale du Travail, thousands of foreigners were waiting to enlist, but feared coming forth since they were not in compliance with the decree laws. On 9 May the *Association des Amis de la République* sponsored a rally in Paris that called for an end to the government's anti-immigrant economic policies and an amnesty for 'victims of racism'. 'It's unacceptable', declared Robert Lange, former Vice-President of the Radical Socialist Party, 'that those who will be called on to defend France, first find asylum in her prisons'. The next day, the *Association des Amis de la République* sent a delegation to meet with Sarraut.

While these delegations were petitioning the government, the Bonnet Committee was busy drafting an amnesty proposal. In April, the Committee's executive committee, working together with Alexis Léger, Secretary General of the Foreign Ministry, adopted a motion demanding 'urgent reform' of the decree laws, and on 15 May, the Committee sent a delegation – including Louise Weiss, Albert Lévy, director of the CAR, and Isaïe Schwartz, the Chief Rabbi of France – to petition the Minister of Justice to overturn the decree laws and grant an amnesty to refugees who had been arrested so they could 'reconstruct their lives on a dignified and stable foundation ... in France or elsewhere'. Prison, this petition declared, was 'neither an equitable nor a humane solution', since it rendered impossible the re-emigration of the refugees as well as their ultimate assimilation. The time had therefore come 'to show clemency and enact ... those measures that will save the ... lives of thousands of innocents and will be consistent with our generous national tradition'. In June, the *Intercomité des Oeuvres Françaises d'Assistance aux Réfugiés*, the administrative arm of the Groupement de Coordination, which served as a coordinating body for the thirty different refugee committees, including the Bonnet Committee, seconded this proposal and called on the government to extend the amnesty provisions of the September 1936 Presidential Decree to Central European refugees who had arrived after that date.

These appeals ultimately reached the highest levels of government. In the Chamber of Deputies, the conservative deputies Louis Rollin and Louis Marin, together with the powerful Foreign Affairs Commission of the Chamber of Deputies, implored Sarraut and Paul Marchandeau, the Minister of Justice, to implement the amnesty plan. The debate over amnesty came to a head on 8 June, when the Parliamentary Commission on Civil and Criminal Legislation introduced an amnesty bill in the Chamber of Deputies. Speaking on this bill's behalf, Charles Valentin, a conservative deputy, condemned the decree laws as 'cruel', 'merciless', and 'inhuman', and called on the Minister of Justice to allow judges to take extenuating circumstances into account in their sentencing. Most significantly, this proposal called for an amnesty for political and religious refugees who had committed no crime other than having violated the decree laws.[45]

Ultimately, the administration refused to overturn the decree laws, claiming that they constituted an indispensable tool in dealing with the criminal element among the foreign population. It nevertheless took steps to amend the anti-immigrant decree laws in important ways. On 24 June, it was announced that judges could henceforth take extenuating circumstances into account. Even more strikingly, the administration was prepared to consider the request of Jewish organisations and the Bonnet Committee to grant an amnesty to refugees already in France, including even those considered illegal aliens. On 29 June, the Minister of Interior convened a meeting between his Secretary General, Berthoin, and the leaders of the Groupement de Coordination, presided over by Robert de

Rothschild. The administration announced that it was once again prepared to offer an amnesty to all Central European refugees sponsored by the *Groupement de Coordination* on condition that these refugees be sent to the provinces, where they could receive vocational retraining in agriculture or artisanry to prepare for eventual re-emigration. For, as Sarraut noted in a letter of 16 July to Rothschild, the few emigration possibilities that existed were reserved exclusively for farmers and artisans. Once again, Jewish organisations were expected to pay for this scheme. Finally, Sarraut set forth one last condition: that Jewish organisations do everything within their power 'to no longer solicit the introduction of new foreigners – except for ... exceptional cases in which the life of the concerned is in question, *and to reserve possibilities for overseas settlement exclusively* for refugees who are, at this moment, benefiting from our hospitality'.[46] Despite the absurdity of this demand, given that Jewish organisations had no means to prevent refugees from entering the country, it was nevertheless in keeping with previous amnesty plans which limited their provisions exclusively to refugees already in France.

Jewish organisations, desperate to see the most severe aspects of the decree laws overturned so that they could return to 'constructive' work instead of spending all their time, energy and money on regularising the legal status of refugees and keeping them out of jail, sought to comply with the administration's demands. Every effort was made to accelerate the agricultural settlement schemes and the vocational retraining programmes. Jewish organisations even endeavoured to comply with Sarraut's request to prevent further refugees from seeking asylum in France. As Raymond-Raoul Lambert, Secretary General of the CAR, declared at a AJDC-sponsored migration conference in Paris in late August: 'Due to the international situation, to the ever growing number of attempts to enter the country clandestinely and illegally, we cannot request any new entries into France at the present moment. Jewish organisations have obtained a privileged treatment for refugees already in France on condition that they not intervene on behalf of new entries'. To be sure, he noted, the refugee committees 'would continue to do our duty and defend the refugees as energetically as possible'. But from now on, Lambert insisted, France should be considered only 'a provisional asylum', reserved exclusively for refugees already in the country.[47]

By the end of the summer a *modus vivendi* had been worked out between the refugee committees and the administration. As early as June, the AJDC noted a marked improvement in the relations between the CAR and the authorities, commenting that with regard to refugee settlement 'a more liberal regime [is] coming into effect'. At the same time, Jewish organisations observed an intensification of the police crackdown against illegal refugees at the border. In late May the CAR reported that 'following the international tension, surveillance at the French borders ... has been reinforced considerably, and as a result, illegal immigration has become increasingly difficult, if not impossible'. In June, the AJDC similarly reported that 'the police are becoming more severe and recent refugees ... were [being] arrested'. Although initially baffled by this discrepancy, the AJDC soon realised that it constituted the cornerstone of the administration's policy. While pro-refugee advocates would certainly have preferred to keep the borders open, they nevertheless recognised that Sarraut's amnesty proposal was the best deal possible under existing circumstances.[48]

From the Phony War to Vichy

The outbreak of war brought an abrupt end to this accommodation. Not only were border controls further stiffened, but the administration, inspired by fifth-column fears, resorted to a policy of mass internments. On 4 September, just a day after war had been declared, the administration, still under the premiership of Daladier, ordered the internment of all males from Greater Germany between the ages of seventeen and fifty, and this age limit was soon extended to sixty-five. As a result, some 18,000 Central European victims of the Third Reich, most of whom had enthusiastically signed up for military service in France in the wake of the April 1939 decree laws, were now declared enemy aliens and placed under strict police surveillance at one of the eighty or so internment camps scattered throughout the country. To be sure, even now, the forces pushing for liberalisation continued to operate, and by the spring of 1940, most of these internees had been released to serve either in the Foreign Legion or in some sort of *prestataire*, or civilian military service. Nevertheless, when the Nazis invaded the Low Countries in May 1940, the government re-interned these individuals, now including even women up to the age of sixty-five as well as some 10,000 additional refugees from the Low Countries who had streamed across the border in flight from Hitler's armies.[49]

Under the Vichy regime, the hardline policies toward refugees already in the country would prevail, reaching an apogee in Laval's decision to turn over Jewish refugees to the Germans in the summer of 1942. Indeed, Laval justified this decision by claiming that since the U.S. had repeatedly refused to take these refugees off France's hands, he had no choice but to turn them over to the Germans. Yet even under Vichy, at least until the summer of 1942, forces pushing for a more liberal policy continued to operate, albeit with their hands tied behind their backs.[50]

Conclusion

To conclude, French refugee policy in the 1930s was not a steady progression toward ever harsher policies. Rather, the policy fluctuated between periods of intense crackdown, such as 1934-35 and 1938-39, and periods of liberalisation, such as the early months of 1933, the Popular Front era, and to some extent the period following *Kristallnacht* until the outbreak of war. These fluctuations were due in part to the political leanings of the administration in power, with conservative administrations, including those affiliated with the Radical Party, tending to engage in crackdowns, and more left-wing administrations, such as the Popular Front, seeking to embrace a more humane policy that would allow at least a portion of the refugees to remain in France. But they were also due to the fact that even the most restrictive refugee policies could not effectively seal France's borders. With every intensification of pressure on France's borders, due to the dramatic upsurge of antisemitism throughout Central and Eastern Europe, and even Italy, tens of thousands of newly displaced persons set out to seek asylum wherever possible, legally or illegally, if need be. It is therefore not surprising that every crackdown against illegal refugees in France was followed by an amnesty – a tacit admission that the previous hardline policies had failed – and every amnesty was accompanied by a proviso that no future influxes of refugees would be tolerated, a proviso that proved impossible to enforce. Ultimately, the fact that France continued to serve as a principal haven for refugees, in spite of a fierce determination to keep these individuals at bay, was more a matter of necessity than choice. France, especially during the crackdowns of 1934–35 and 1938–39, was no more liberal than her neighbours – Switzerland, Belgium, Luxembourg and the Netherlands. Rather, due to its geography, France was simply less able to seal its borders.

But while geography was partly to blame for the problem of illegal immigration, which was clearly the most intractable aspect of the refugee crisis by the late 1930s, French administrators bore a portion of the blame as well. By declaring all refugees without exception to be illegal – which was clearly the intent of the 2 May 1938 decree law as well as the harsh visa policies in place – the administration ensured that France would be saddled with a huge population of clandestine refugees. During the 1930s, however, even the most hardline administration recognised that it had no choice but to grant refugees some sort of provisional asylum – 'asylum for one night' – even though liberals and conservatives fiercely debated what this term meant. Ultimately, however, it was left to the Vichy regime to end this tradition.[51]

Notes

1. For an overview of initial French responses to the German refugee crisis in 1933, see V. Caron, *Uneasy Asylum: France and the Jewish Refugee Crisis, 1933–1942*, Stanford 1999, pp.13–19. For the geographical distribution of refugees from Germany between 1933–1935, see C. Skran, *Refugees in Inter-War Europe: The Emergence of a Regime*, Oxford 1995, p.50.
2. See especially Caron, *Uneasy Asylum*, pp.11–42, and passim; V. Caron, 'The Antisemitic Revival in France in the 1930s: The Socioeconomic Dimension Reconsidered', *Journal of Modern History* 70, 1998, pp.22–73. For a recent essay that downplays the impact of the Depression, see G. Burgess, 'France

and the German Refugee Crisis of 1933', *French History* 16, no. 2, 2002, pp.203–29.
3. On the Spanish refugee crisis in France see L. Stein, *Beyond Death and Exile: The Spanish Republicans in France, 1939–1955*, Cambridge MA, 1979, pp.5–106; D. Wingeate Pike, *In the Service of Stalin: The Spanish Communists in Exile, 1939–1945*, Oxford 1993; M.R. Marrus, *The Unwanted: European Refugees in the Twentieth Century*, New York 1985, pp.190–94; D. Peschanski, *La France des camps: L'internement 1938–1946*, Paris 2002, pp.36–71.
4. P.Lahaspe, 'Les réfugiés au service de l'agriculture', *La Lumière*, 19 May 1939, p.2.
5. Caron, *Uneasy Asylum*, pp.16, 96–97. On the role of the Jewish community in the early 1930s, see Caron, *Uneasy Asylum*, pp.94–116; Caron, 'Loyalties in Conflict: French Jewry and the Refugee Crisis, 1933–1935', *Leo Baeck Institute Year Book* 36, 1991, pp.305–37.
6. All quotes in this paragraph are cited in Caron, *Uneasy Asylum*, p.17. On the Nansen regime, see Marrus, *The Unwanted*, pp. 51–121; Skran, *Refugees in Inter-War Europe*, pp.101–45 and M.D. Lewis, *The Boundaries of the Republic: Migrant Rights and the Limits of Universalism in France, 1918–1940*, Stanford, 2006.
7. In addition to a passport and visa, all foreigners over fifteen years of age who intended to stay in France longer than two months without a salaried job were required to apply for a *carte d'identité des étrangers sans profession* at their local police department within eight days of arrival. This card was generally valid for three years and constituted a *permis de séjour*, or residence permit.
8. Ministère des Affaires Etrangères, Paris (MAE) Z 710, Note, 18 July 1933, pp.196–97. On these increasingly restrictionist policies in late 1933, see Caron, *Uneasy Asylum*, pp.33–42, and Burgess, 'France and the German Refugee Crisis of 1933'.
9. On this retreat from earlier liberal policies, see Caron, *Uneasy Asylum*, pp.13–63; G. Cross, *Immigrant Workers in Industrial France: The Making of a New Laboring Class*, Philadelphia 1983, pp.198–200; M. Livian, *Le Parti socialiste et l'immigration*, Paris 1982, pp.49, 62–63; R. Schor, *L'Opinion française et les étrangers en France, 1919–1939*, Paris 1985, pp.577–611; R. Harouni, 'Le Débat autour du statut des étrangers dans les années 1930', *Le Mouvement Social* 188, 1999, pp.61–75, esp. pp.62–63; C. Zalc, 'Des réfugiés aux indésirables: Les pouvoirs publics français face aux émigrés du IIIe Reich entre 1933 et 1939', in *Construction des nationalités et immigration dans la France contemporaine*, ed. E. Guichard and G. Noiriel, Paris 1997, pp.259–73, esp. pp.263–64; Burgess, 'France and the German Refugee Crisis of 1933'.
10. All quotations here cited in Caron, *Uneasy Asylum*, pp.47–48, 60, 114. On the treatment of foreigners at the Préfecture, see also C. Rosenberg, *Policing Paris: The Origins of Modern Immigration Control between the Wars*, Ithaca 2006, pp.76–106.
11. For a positive view of France's reception of the Saar refugees, see Marrus, *The Unwanted*, p.133. For an overview of this question, including all quotations cited in this and the next two paragraphs, see Caron, *Uneasy Asylum*, pp.52–57.
12. The categories to be granted visas included: French passport holders, Nansen refugees, Germans who had fled to the Saar after 1933, and native Saarlanders who felt endangered by the advent of Nazi rule, a category that included the 5,000 Jews of the Saar. Excluded categories included

individuals of East European origin, who were to be repatriated to East European countries, and German refugees who had been *refoulés* or expelled from France previously.
13. All quotations cited in this paragraph are in Caron, *Uneasy Asylum*, pp.58–59. On this hardline policy after the Nuremberg Laws see also Livian, *Le Parti socialiste*, p.56; H. Schramm and B. Vormeier, *Vivre à Gurs: Un camp de concentration français, 1940–1941*, trans. Irène Petit, Paris 1979, p.205.
14. For the text of this accord see J. Simpson, *The Refugee Problem: Report of a Survey*, London 1939, pp.566–95; S. Feblowicz and P. Lamour, *Le Statut juridique des étrangers en France: Traité pratique*, Paris n.d., pp.433–41. See also Skran, *Refugees in Inter-War Europe*, pp.113, 120, 124–26, 201; Caron, *Uneasy Asylum*, pp.120–22, 137.
15. Caron, *Uneasy Asylum*, pp.120–25; Zalc, 'Des réfugiés aux indésirables', p.265. For a review of Popular Front refugee initiatives, see Caron, *Uneasy Asylum*, pp.117–70. On the debate to devise a *Statut des immigrés* during the Popular Front, see Harouni, 'Le Débat', pp.64–71.
16. All quotations in this paragraph are cited in Caron, *Uneasy Asylum*, pp.123–24. Some scholars, especially Rita Thalmann, argue that the Popular Front's Central European refugee policy did not mark a significant break with the hardline policies of preceding administrations. (R. Thalmann, 'L'Immigration allemande et l'opinion publique en France de 1933 à 1936', in n. auth., *La France et l'Allemagne, 1932–1936*, Paris 1980, pp.149–72, esp. pp.171–72). This argument, however, neglects the many positive reforms enacted by the Popular Front with respect to refugees already in the country, as well as its colonial and agricultural initiatives. On this debate, see Caron, *Uneasy Asylum*, pp.117–70.
17. All quotations in this paragraph are cited in Caron, *Uneasy Asylum*, pp.162–63.
18. The discussion here follows ibid., pp.164–70. On the Serre Plan see also M. Marrus and R.O. Paxton, *Vichy France and the Jews*, New York 1981, p.57; Schor, *L'Opinion française*, pp.645–46; Jean-Charles Bonnet, *Les Pouvoirs publics francais et l'immigration dans l'entre-deux-guerres*, Lyons 1976, pp.32–33, 328–39; Cross, *Immigrant Workers*, pp.209–10; Harouni, 'Le Débat', pp.69–71; P. Weil, 'Racisme et discrimination dans la politique française de l'immigration, 1938–1945/1974–1995', *Vingtième Siècle* 47, 1995, pp.77–102, esp. pp.78–79; P. Weil, *La France et ses étrangers: l'Aventure d'une politique de l'immigration, 1938–1991*, Paris 1991, pp.33–37.
19. Y. Bauer, *My Brother's Keeper: A History of the American Jewish Joint Distribution Committee, 1932–1939*, Philadelphia 1974, p.237, mistakenly suggests that Serre's plan was intended for German refugees. Recent French scholarship, by contrast, treats the Serre Plan as if it dealt with immigration in general. See Harouni, 'Le Débat', pp.69–71; P. Weil, 'Racisme et discrimination', p.78; P. Weil, *La France*, pp.33–37. While Serre was concerned with immigration in general, there is no doubt that his principal focus was illegal Jewish immigration from Eastern Europe.
20. All quotations in this paragraph and the next relating to the Serre Plan are cited in Caron, *Uneasy Asylum*, pp.164–69. The labour unions that complained were those dominated by East European Jews, suggesting that to some extent this conflict was an internal Jewish one.
21. Obviously, this amount fell far short of the 20 million francs recommended by Mauco, but as Bernhard Kahn of the AJDC commented, 'there can be

no question of raising fantastic sums for fantastic schemes'. 'Notes on JDC Activities during the Months of January–March, 1938', 28.3.1938, JDC No. 188, Appendix VII a.
22. All quotations in this paragraph and the next are cited in Caron, *Uneasy Asylum*, pp.172, and 179–82.
23. For the text of the 2 May 1938 decree law see *Le Temps*, 5 May 1938, p.4; Emile Kahn, 'La Police et les étrangers', *Les Cahiers des droits de l'homme* (CDH), 15 May 1938, pp.294–300; Boris Gourevitch, 'The Legal Position of the Refugees and Stateless Persons to Whom the Right of Residence is Refused in the West European Countries of Refuge', [mimeographed pamphlet], New York, 25 September 1939, in Franklin Delano Roosevelt (FDR) Library, Myron Taylor Papers, Box 9, pp.17, 97–101; Feblowicz and Lamour, *Le Statut juridique*, pp.428–32, 461–65. See also Schramm and Vormeier, *Vivre à Gurs*, pp.206–7, 223–24; Skran, *Refugees in Inter-War Europe*, p.137; Zalc, 'Des réfugiés aux indésirables', p.265. On 14 May, another decree law was declared that elaborated the legal mechanisms according to which foreigners could acquire and renew identity cards. Most of the provisions of the 6 February 1935 law remained in place. For the text of this law, see Feblowicz and Lamour, *Le Statut juridique*, pp.465–85. Several recent works accept at face value the administration's claim that the aim of these decree laws was selection. However, while the administration continued to use the language of selection, in reality it intended to close the doors altogether. For this claim, see Harouni,' Le Débat', pp.72–74; P. Weil, 'Racisme et discrimination', p.81.
24. Foreigners had to show proof that they had been rejected by at least three foreign consulates in order to be considered eligible for the 'benefits' of article 11. Sarraut instructed the prefects to intervene personally with foreign consulates to pressure them to grant visas to refugees already in France. See Caron, *Uneasy Asylum*, p.179.
25. Ibid., p.178.
26. All quotations in this paragraph are ibid., pp.181, 183–84. On the Evian Conference, see also Marrus, *The Unwanted*, pp.170–72; Skran, *Refugees in Inter-War Europe*, pp.208–14.
27. On the French response to the Sudeten refugee crisis see Caron, *Uneasy Asylum*, pp.190–91.
28. On the repercussions of *Kristallnacht* in France, see Caron, *Uneasy Asylum*, pp.187–205.
29. Cited in Caron, *Uneasy Asylum*, p.200.
30. Ibid., p.189. On the origins of the policy to mark the passports of German Jews, see Regula Ludi's chapter in this volume.
31. Caron, *Uneasy Asylum*, pp.202, 209.
32. For an overview of these policies in the fall of 1938, see ibid., pp.185–205. On the decree law of 17 June 1938 see ibid., p.176.
33. Ibid., p.181. On the Nazi practice of dumping refugees into France and Switzerland, see Skran, *Refugees in Inter-War Europe*, p.253, and Frank Caestecker and Bob Moore in this volume.
34. All quotations in this paragraph are from Caron, *Uneasy Asylum*, pp.209–10.
35. This and the subsequent three paragraphs follow ibid., pp.209–12.
36. On the ambivalent attitude of the police, see also M.B. Miller, *Shanghai on the Métro: Spies, Intrigue, and the French between the Wars*, Berkeley 1994,

pp.148–50; K. Voigt, 'Les Naufragés: L'arrivée dans les Alpes-Maritimes des réfugiés allemands et autrichiens d'Italie (septembre 1938–mai 1940)', in *Zone d'ombres, 1933–1944: Exil et internement d'Allemands et d'Autrichiens dans le sud-est de la France*, ed. J. Grandjonc and T. Grundtner, Aix-en-Provence 1990, pp.93–117.

37. The Nice courts also gave light sentences to Italian boatmen apprehended in these smuggling schemes. See Caron, *Uneasy Asylum*, p.210; P.Veziano, *Ombre di confine: L'Emigrazione clandestina degli ebrei stranieri d'alla Riviera dei Fiori verso la Costa Azzurra (1938–1940)*, Pinerolo 2001, p.201.
38. All quotations in this paragraph are from Caron, *Uneasy Asylum*, p.212.
39. This paragraph and the next follow ibid., pp.229–30.
40. On Weiss and the Bonnet Committee, see ibid., pp.213–15, 219, 223, 226, 228, 233–34, 303, 308–9.
41. Ibid., p.213.
42. Ibid., pp.224–25, 314. Skran, *Refugees in Inter-War Europe*, p.216, sees this law regarding military services as a form of discrimination, but it was hailed by both refugee organisations and the refugees themselves as a positive step leading toward an amelioration of the status of refugees.
43. Caron, *Uneasy Asylum*, pp.221–23.
44. On the protests of the Centre de Liaison des Immigrés cited in this and the next two paragraphs, see ibid., pp.229–30.
45. For the text of this debate, see *JO, Débats Parlementaires, Chambre de Députés*, 8 June 1939, pp.1524–27; Gourevitch, 'The Legal Position', pp.85–93. See also Bonnet, *Les Pouvoirs publics*, p.346; T.P. Maga, 'Closing the Door: The French Government and Refugee Policy, 1933–1939', *French Historical Studies* 12, no. 3, 1982, pp.438–39.
46. Cited in Caron, *Uneasy Asylum*, p.232.
47. Ibid. For an overview of Jewish responses to the refugee crisis in the late 1930s, see ibid., pp.302–20, Caron, 'The Politics of Frustration: French Jewry and the Refugee Crisis in the 1930's', *Journal of Modern History* 65, no. 2, June 1993, pp.311–56.
48. All quotations in this paragraph cited in Caron, *Uneasy Asylum*, pp.232–33.
49. Ibid., p.259. For an overview of French refugee policies from September 1939 through June 1940, see ibid., pp.240–67; Caron, 'The Missed Opportunity: French Refugee Policy in Wartime, 1939–1940', in *The French Defeat of 1940: Reassessments*, ed. Joel Blatt, Providence 1998, pp.126–70; Peschanski, *La France des camps*, pp.152–74.
50. One striking example of how even Vichy was susceptible to pressure to reform its policies toward foreign Jews was the appointment in April 1941 of André Jean-Faure, Prefect of the Ardèche, to serve as Inspector General of the internment camps. Although Vichy's aim in appointing Jean-Faure was to counter negative publicity from abroad regarding the camps, Jean-Faure, who was shocked by camp conditions, ultimately succeeded in carrying out important reforms. On Jean-Faure's mission see Marrus and Paxton, *Vichy France and the Jews*, pp.171–75; Caron, *Uneasy Asylum*, pp.344–45.
51. Caron, *Uneasy Asylum*, p.339; A. Grynberg, *Les Camps de la honte: Les Internés juifs des camps français, 1939–1944*, Paris 1991. On the eagerness of other Vichy officials to get rid of foreign Jews in the unoccupied zone, see also S. Zuccotti, *The Holocaust, The French and the Jews*, New York 1993, p.98; Marrus and Paxton, *Vichy France and the Jews*, p.232.

Chapter I.4

Dwindling Options: Seeking Asylum in Switzerland 1933–1939

Regula Ludi

In the past, research on Swiss refugee policy has concentrated on the period of the Second World War and paid less attention to the prewar era. The reasons for this were obvious: Switzerland was one of the few countries to remain unoccupied after most of Europe had fallen under Axis control in June of 1940. Given its strategically exposed position, it was the 'last chance' for refugees, for many the only safe haven within reach.[1] This situation became even more dramatic when the Nazi regime began to implement its extermination programme, first with a ban on Jewish emigration in late 1941, and then with mass arrests and the deportation of Jews from Western Europe to the killing centres in occupied Poland from early 1942 onwards.[2] In spite of this, the Swiss government closed the border for Jewish refugees in the summer of 1942, in direct response to the growing number of persons who tried to enter the country from France and Italy. This decision was published on 13 August, just weeks after the Vel' d'Hiv mass arrests in Paris. At first glance, its phrasing merely confirmed the previous practice of denying Jews recognition as political refugees, but at that moment in the summer of 1942, the Swiss authorities could no longer cherish the illusion that such a decision would not have deadly consequences for the affected refugees, as even their internal reports conceded.[3] Rumours about Nazi atrocities became increasingly common from the spring of that year. Information trickled in from a variety of sources, little by little confirming the apparently unbelievable suspicion that the Nazis were systematically killing the Jews. Moreover, in spite of official efforts to suppress any reference to Nazi violence in the media, news of the atrocities was commonplace by the late summer of 1942.[4]

In Switzerland, the closing of the borders in August 1942 was a rare occasion in that it incited widespread protest against official asylum policy.

At the beginning, police and border guards enforced the order relentlessly, even expelling Jews who had already spent some time in safety. Such events aroused public outrage. Upset citizens held spontaneous rallies and demanded that arrested refugees be allowed to stay. As a consequence, the border closure immediately became a symbol of official callousness toward the plight of the Jews, even though the full tragedy of those who were denied asylum would only be revealed after the war.[5] Official justifications further contributed to the emotionally charged meaning of the event. A few weeks after the decision, the Federal Councillor responsible, Eduard von Steiger used the metaphor of a 'full lifeboat' to suggest that Switzerland's capacity to absorb refugees was exhausted. The expression has since framed many debates about the moral dimensions of wartime asylum policy.[6] However, full reckoning with the consequences of this past began only in the 1990s, but then with unpredicted vehemence that led to the most comprehensive investigation into Swiss relations with the Third Reich.[7] Based on this new research, the officially appointed commission of historians has come to the conclusion that the Swiss government, in declining to accept people in mortal danger, helped the Nazi regime achieve its genocidal goals.[8]

From today's perspective, the border closure of 1942 can be interpreted as a break with humanitarian tradition, but it was nonetheless perfectly in line with previous efforts at making Switzerland unattractive for asylum seekers. It also corresponded with widespread, though largely covert, antisemitic feelings among decision makers and sections of the general public. Since the 1930s, for example, the authorities had argued that to prevent the violent anti-Jewish excesses seen in neighbouring Germany and Austria it was necessary to restrict Jewish immigration into Switzerland. Blaming an increase in antisemitism on the Jews, this rationale was not completely unrelated to Nazi speculations that expelling impoverished Jews to other countries would arouse antisemitism abroad and promote the comprehension of Nazi race policies.[9]

It would still be wrong to consider Swiss refugee policy of the 1930s as a mere prelude to these later events and their fatal consequences. Despite stunning continuity in policy as well as underlying rationale, the outcome was always contingent, the result of deliberate choices, as much as determined by the impact of routine and structures. The 1930s had witnessed various events when decision makers, not yet restrained in their actions by wartime conditions, declined to change course and prioritise rescue over keeping out foreigners. In the following chapter, I will look at some of these occasions in the prewar era. The first part will focus on the conditions found by refugees arriving in the early 1930s and raise the question about official responses to the distress of Nazi victims immediately after Hitler's rise to power. In the second part, I will discuss Swiss efforts at controlling the influx of refugees in the spring and summer of 1938, after the German 'annexation' of Austria. Eventually, as Nazi Germany intensified its efforts to expel the Jews from the territory of the Third Reich, all measures designed by the Swiss government to deter refugees were bound to fail. Expellees often had little alternative, since most countries raised entry hurdles and eventually closed their borders, including Switzerland. In this situation, the Swiss government entered into negotiations with the German authorities, seeking their guarantee to abstain from expelling Jews to Switzerland. As a result of these negotiations, the Nazi regime consented to mark the passports of German Jews with the infamous 'J'-stamp, allowing the Swiss to reintroduce the visa requirement exclusively for the Jews and with this decision shift control from the border to the desks of centralised bureaucracies. These events will be the issue of the third and last part of this article.

By the end of 1938, it is estimated that between ten and twelve thousand refugees were on Swiss territory.[10] For the entire prewar era, no reliable data exist regarding the number of refugees who crossed the borders into Switzerland, who were allowed to stay or expelled, as such statistical information was not collected systematically before the Second World War. A centralised registration only emerged after 1939. In addition, authorities changed the categorisation of refugees several times between 1933 and 1945, thus aggravating methodological problems. Finally, many of the records that would have allowed the reconstruction of data at local and cantonal levels have been lost or destroyed by the agencies responsible.[11] The figures cited in this chapter come mainly from official estimates, or from reconstructions by researchers.

1933 – Not a Place to Stay: Swiss Conditions of Exile after the Nazis' Rise to Power

In 1933, Switzerland, or to be more precise: its German speaking part, seemed the obvious destination for German emigrants, given the many cultural similarities, but also the preferential treatment that German citizens enjoyed because of a trade and residence agreement between the two countries. In the first year of Nazi rule, approximately 10,000 refugees from Germany entered Switzerland. A total of 7,631 Jewish refugees passed through the Basel train station alone in the months from March to May.[12] For most of them, Switzerland was not yet their preferred place of residence, and only a few stayed for an extended period of time. By the end of 1933, no more than 2,500 refugees were still on Swiss territory; the rest having either left for another final destination or returned to Germany, hoping that Hitler's rule would be of short duration or expecting the situation to improve once the Nazis consolidated their power. Of the Jews who sought shelter from the violence and insecurity that accompanied the Nazi boycott on 1 April 1933, 90 per cent were said to have returned to their homes in Germany after a few days or weeks, the remaining ten per cent moving on, mainly to France.[13]

At first, these emigrants encountered no major obstacles when crossing the border provided they had German documents and enough cash to pay for their accommodation. Germans were indeed welcome as long as they pretended to be visitors and brought relief to Switzerland's ailing tourist industry. In the interwar era, the Swiss government had gradually lifted the immigration restrictions that had originated from the time of the First World War and renewed bilateral agreements with neighbouring countries.[14] However, such hospitality quickly evaporated when the guests expressed their wish to stay and revealed that they were neither willing nor able to return to their country of origin. In the circle of exiled Germans, Switzerland therefore had a negative image. A wealthy German publisher concluded in the fall of 1933: 'Temporarily it seems that Switzerland, a country praised for its hospitality, makes more difficulties even regarding short-term residence permits than any other European state.'[15] A manual for emigrants that appeared in 1935 warned that in Switzerland 'the ban on the employment of foreigners is very rigorously enforced.'[16]

Despite their commitment to free trade and (relatively) free movement of persons, the Swiss authorities raised obstacles to immigration in response to the political and economic insecurities of the 1930s. Soaring unemployment advanced economic protectionism and furthered calls for stricter border controls. Thus, for poor and job-seeking foreigners it became increasingly difficult to enter the country legally.[17] At the same time, the authorities intensified measures against a wide variety of so called 'undesirable' aliens. These included traditionally unwanted groups, such as itinerant workers and beggars, Roma and Sinti, East Europeans of Jewish and non-Jewish descent. Increasingly however, they were joined by a new category of 'undesirables': the diverse and rapidly multiplying group of stateless individuals, the miserable victims of civil wars and politically motivated acts of expatriation.[18] Merely tolerated by some countries, the stateless were generally barred from regularising their residence status wherever they tried to stay. With no government to protect them, they lacked the most fundamental rights. As the economic situation worsened, most countries were eager to dispose of these groups of foreigners. It became common practice for the police to expel them secretly, often at night and in disregard of international law. For the stateless, such practices resulted in an odyssey from one country to the other, interrupted only by the weeks and months spent in detention before being deported again. Without ever committing an offence other than having no nationality, through no fault of their own they were eventually marked as 'criminals' and treated so by law enforcement officers.[19]

Following the first big wave of emigration from Germany in 1933, the Nazi regime began to revoke the citizenship of refugees or refuse to renew their passports. The mere fact that they could no longer return to their homeland made them suspicious in the eyes of Swiss immigration officers. Thus the grievances of the stateless would soon become the fate of many refugees from the Third Reich.[20] Such practices contributed to blurring the distinctions between refugees and various categories of unwanted aliens, a development reflected in the sources by the use of increasingly depreciatory language when referring to these groups: in the mid 1930s, border guards and cantonal police reports indiscriminately labelled undocumented immigrants and refugees as 'undesirable elements', 'riff-raff' and 'suspicious'.[21]

Growing hostility toward foreigners dated back to the early 1900s. Xenophobic discourses then emerged as a cipher for the elite's discomfort over modernisation, indicating a deeper cultural malaise, and easily translated into widespread obsession with national identity. The newly created catchphrase *Überfremdung*, meaning an inundation or infiltration by foreigners, was the catalyst for changing attitudes toward immigrants shortly before the First World War.[22] These discourses paved the way for an integrated Swiss migration policy that was facilitated by emergency legislation and the concentration of power during the First World War. Social unrest after the war provided the ruling class with an additional justification for keeping emergency powers in force well into the 1920s. Throughout the interwar era, Switzerland's establishment was haunted by the nightmare of a bolshevist takeover orchestrated from abroad and increasingly blind to political dangers looming on the right.[23] These circumstances furthered the creation of a powerful new bureaucratic institution, the Federal Police for Foreigners.[24] In the years that followed, this new agency found ample opportunities to enlarge its competences, skillfully playing on people's fears about economic competition and infiltration of Swiss culture by foreign customs and habits.[25]

For more than three decades, the Federal Police for Foreigners was closely identified with its chief Heinrich Rothmund, who began his career in 1917 as a young, dynamic man driven by his belief in a special mission: saving Switzerland from foreign 'overpopulation'. Rothmund became the architect of interwar migration policy and exerted considerable influence on the government's decision making throughout the Nazi era. Known for his xenophobic attitudes and feared for his autocratic conduct, he often served as the figurehead, and sometimes as the scapegoat, for repressive immigration policy in this era. In reality, however, he could count on a highly motivated bureaucracy and the support of superiors who fully shared his views, for example in underwriting the claim that refugees were not persons in need of special protection but simply 'undesirable' foreigners, whose presence embodied cultural, social and political risks for Switzerland.[26]

Thus the federal authorities responded with alarm to the mass flight from Germany. In early 1933, they declared that Switzerland would permit refugees only temporary residence, allowing them time to prepare for transmigration and resettlement in another destination country. A federal decree of 31 March 1933 specified new regulations concerning the treatment of different refugee categories from Germany. The federal government embarked on a twofold strategy based on the distinction between 'political refugees', who qualified for asylum, and 'emigrants', a new category created to encompass all those who could no longer be considered regular German citizens but at the same time were not eligible for political asylum, according to the prevailing interpretations of the regulations.[27] Two separate agencies, applying different bureaucratic mechanisms, dealt with these two groups. On the one hand, competence to grant asylum to political refugees rested with the Federal Prosecutor's Office. This was the same agency that also made arrangements for the surveillance of politically suspect persons, Swiss citizens as well as aliens, and ordered the expulsion of foreigners who were considered a security hazard. In the 1930s, these were mostly communists and other leftists charged with subversive activity.[28] As a legal term, 'political refugee' was modelled on the liberal experience of the nineteenth century. Accordingly, the ideal type underlying its definition was an individual threatened by persecution and criminal punishment in his or her home state because of his or her political activity. The term also implied that asylum seekers should endorse Switzerland's political order and dominant value system. In the nineteenth century, such conformity had been almost a matter of course since the majority of refugees were fleeing autocracy and monarchism and embraced Switzerland's liberal democracy enthusiastically. But by the 1930s this was no longer the case as by then political refugees were mostly people who suffered persecution for their leftist convictions. Many resumed their anti-fascist struggle once they were in safety, joined underground networks and participated in illegal activity, such as smuggling clandestine literature and refugees over the border to and from Nazi Germany.[29] Throughout the 1930s, German diplomats complained that the Swiss were condoning and supporting activity hostile to the new regime. Worried about diplomatic complications, the Swiss government consequently prohibited all political activity by refugees and generally did not welcome the presence of exiled anti-fascists. In the end, only very few refugees qualified for political asylum, no more than approximately 650 individuals between 1933 and 1945. However, an unknown number of communists and socialists never attempted to regularise their residence and survived underground, thanks to the support provided by Swiss comrades and solidarity networks.

According to the decree of 31 March 1933, refugees escaping racial persecution were excluded from political asylum. This was not to change until July 1944, when the federal government eventually acknowledged that all Jews were in mortal danger. Yet even before that date, the categorisation of Jewish refugees occasionally caused internal disagreement. Various government agencies considered the discriminatory treatment of the Jews in comparison with that of political refugees to be unjustifiable in the face of German realities.[30] Nonetheless, in the end, the narrow definition of the political refugee always prevailed. As a consequence, Jews were considered as 'emigrants' or refugees in transit and were only eligible for a so-called tolerance permit, a document valid for a maximum of six months and renewable only under special circumstances.[31] Emigrants were exposed to the same treatment as any other foreigner whose return was not guaranteed and their asylum applications had to be approved by the Federal Police for Foreigners, the same agency whose primary target was the prevention of Switzerland's 'inundation by foreigners' and whose procedures were not fashioned in such a way as to acknowledge the particular vulnerability of Jews or other refugees who could not produce evidence of political persecution in Nazi Germany. Nor were its officials prepared for dealing with a category of foreigners in need of special protection. An antisemitic undercurrent, intrinsic to the Swiss preoccupation with foreign infiltration from its very beginning, further diminished the chances of Jewish refugees finding an understanding of their difficult situation. In contrast to Nazi racism, Swiss antisemitism did not have biological foundations but relied on entrenched religious and cultural prejudices. It mostly denied that Jews, and especially those of Eastern European origin, had the capacity and willingness to assimilate into Swiss society.[32] Throughout the interwar era, Jewish immigrants were the primary targets of a variety of political efforts to keep foreigners at bay. At the same time they were also the objects of a policy that was fighting domestic antisemitism by enforcing anti-Jewish measures. Its paradoxical rationale stemmed from Rothmund's belief that Switzerland's 'Jewification' (meaning an excessive Jewish presence and influence) would arouse antisemitism among the Swiss themselves.[33] However, the Jewish population never exceeded 0.5 per cent of Switzerland's total inhabitants in these years.[34]

The arrival of the first wave of refugees from Germany also coincided with the implementation of federal legislation on foreigners in 1934.[35] This law, which had been enacted in 1931 and was generally known by its acronym ANAG, legalised the concentration of organisational competences, which up to that point had lacked proper legal foundations. At the same time it filled loopholes that had previously allowed for many cantonal exceptions in immigration issues and generally tightened the authorities' grip on foreigners, including refugees and emigrants. ANAG provisions were relevant for all matters of foreigners' temporary or permanent residence, including work permits and business activity. With regard to refugees, they bolstered the cornerstones of Swiss asylum policy, especially the principle that people were only admitted on the basis that they were in transit elsewhere. Their primary purpose therefore was to prevent asylum seekers from settling down and immersing themselves in Swiss society. Federal legislation, for instance, prohibited the purchase of property by emigrants and refugees. It also barred them from opening their own businesses or taking up employment. Only under very restrictive conditions and after consulting professional organisations did the authorities allow for exceptions. Organisations that were normally rather insignificant suddenly claimed considerable influence on official decision making, as illustrated by the example of the Swiss Writers Association. Exiled journalists and authors, after being banned in Nazi Germany, often sought to publish their texts in Swiss journals and magazines. For this they needed prior authorisation which depended on the opinion issued by the professional association. Eager to protect the interests of domestic authors, the Swiss Writers Association was restrictive in its recommendations and more than once denounced refugees who tried to get around the ban by using pseudonyms.[36]

Even more than other foreigners, refugees were thus exposed to exigent conformity pressure. Working without permission, engaging in political activity or helping other refugees cross the border illegally could lead to the revocation of residence permits. Expulsions were frequent in the prewar era and the grounds on which they were based were often trivial.[37] Labour market protectionism also drove refugees into dependency on relief agencies. The federal government refused financial aid for the support of refugees unless it was spent on their transmigration, while foreigners applying for public assistance risked expulsion. To spare asylum seekers such measures, relief agencies shouldered the financial responsibility for the refugees' support. As early as 1933, the authorities had imposed this obligation on Switzerland's tiny Jewish community and later also on other associations. Soon the resulting expenses surpassed the capacities of most relief agencies. In response to their chronic financial crisis, the federal authorities eventually introduced a 'solidarity tax' in 1941, a highly problematic levy on assets of wealthy refugees for the benefit of refugee organisations.[38]

Switzerland's Jews were in an especially difficult situation, with a heavy financial and moral burden resting on their shoulders. As a tiny minority striving for respectability, they were not in a position to oppose official demands, but as the number of impoverished refugees arriving in Switzerland grew and possibilities for transfering assets from Nazi Germany rapidly dwindled, community leaders faced a major dilemma: insisting on a liberal and open asylum policy to save German Jews would sooner or later risk the community's financial ruin. Declaring insolvency, however, would inevitably give the authorities a pretext to send Jewish refugees back to Nazi Germany.[39] In the face of official intransigence, there was only one solution, which was to tap into the much larger funds of the international relief organisations. From 1939 onwards, the American Jewish Joint Distribution Committee offered Switzerland's Jewish community its help, and in the following years, it provided 50 per cent or more of the funds needed to support Jewish refugees in Switzerland. Step by step, however, Switzerland's Jewish, as well as other relief agencies, had been forced into an uneasy relationship with the authorities that implied compliance with restrictive principles of federal asylum policy. In vain they hoped that such an accommodation would eventually lead to a greater degree of official benevolence for their cause.[40]

1938 – 'The Fateful Turning Point'[41]

After reaching its first peak in 1933, the mass flight from Germany to Switzerland steadily declined but changed again dramatically in the spring of 1938. Within days, the number of refugees on Swiss territory almost doubled, jumping from 5,000 to roughly 8–9,000 persons. The reason was the German *Anschluss* of Austria in March 1938, which was followed by a series of fateful events for the Jewish victims of Nazi persecution – their systematic expulsion from Austria and later also from the rest of the Third Reich, the closing of the borders by most potential countries of refuge in response to these events, and eventually the dramatic radicalisation of Nazi violence, brutality and arbitrariness during and after the *Reichkristallnacht* Pogrom in November 1938.

For Austrian Jews, legal security collapsed overnight in March 1938. Street violence and public humiliation in front of an indifferent and applauding Austrian public were only the unpleasant omen of much worse to come. Immediately, tens of thousands fled the country, often leaving behind whatever of their businesses, valuables and personal belongings had not yet been looted by Austrian and German Nazis in acts of 'wild Aryanisation'. Soon, the Nazi leadership also enacted legislation for the confiscation of Jewish property, not least to prevent private enrichment by unauthorised individuals and protect the state's share of the loot. In August 1938, Adolf Eichmann's Central Office for Jewish Emigration (*Zentralstelle für jüdische Auswanderung*) began operations in Vienna. It established a machinery to rob and expel Austria's Jews in the most systematic and organised way and even secured the consent of international Jewish organisations to meeting the costs of poor people's emigration. Stripped of all their possessions, but vested with a valid passport, exit visa, train tickets to the border and the ridiculous amount of RM 10 that they were allowed to take out of the country, Jews were told to leave the Third Reich for good.[42]

Escape from Austria can thus not to be compared to the flight from Germany in the early days of Nazi rule, when Jews could still prepare emigration, choose destination countries and transfer at least part of their assets. By 1938, the options for those having to leave the Third Reich in a hurry had been radically reduced. Most countries were no longer willing to accept impoverished refugees who would flood their labour markets and burden their welfare systems. The Evian conference of the summer of 1938 confirmed this hopeless situation with all governments speaking out against accepting Jews from the Third Reich. Its general tenor, moreover, provided many countries with the pretext to further tighten legislation.[43]

From 13 March to 1 April 1938 alone, according to official statistics that were probably inflated, three to four thousand people from Austria were said to have arrived in Switzerland.[44] For these refugees, a lack of viable alternative destinations brought Switzerland onto centre stage, not only as a transit country but, even more importantly, as a country of asylum. Like most other nations, however, the Swiss government quickly responded to this new wave of refugees with increasingly restrictive measures. As a first step, it demanded an entry visa on all Austrian passports from 1 April 1938 and advised Swiss consulates to reject 'on principle' all applications from refugees who desired to resettle in Switzerland. In addition, if they had doubts about an applicant's intentions, consular employees in Austria were required to submit visa requests to the Federal Police for Foreigners with an indication of the applicant's religion. Diplomats interpreted these instructions differently: as a general rule, they demanded that applicants provide evidence of their intention to transmigrate, by having travel tickets and entry visas for other countries. For some diplomats this was not sufficient: the Swiss consulate in Vienna also asked for a proof of 'Aryan' descent before issuing a visa, according to information of a Swiss Jewish journal.[45] In contrast, a number of consular employees in Northern Italy admitted Jewish refugees in defiance of federal instructions. In this way, 2,800 people who were theoretically barred from immigration entered Switzerland legally. When cited for non-compliance, the diplomats involved referred to heartbreaking scenes in their offices and acknowledged that they were often simply overwhelmed by the refugees' plight. One man also expressed feelings of moral obligation toward emigrants who would not be able to find shelter somewhere else. Similarly, Ernest Prodolliet, a consular employee at Bregenz (Austria) near the Swiss border helped several thousand (mainly Jewish) refugees enter Switzerland legally. Many had already been turned down by the Vienna consulate or expelled when crossing the border without permission. Mr Prodolliet openly expressed sympathy with the victims of Nazi persecution when he faced charges in Switzerland for disregarding official instructions and showing too much interest in the 'Jewish question'. He admitted that he considered assisting people in distress his first obligation.[46] The disobedience shown by these men cannot be explained by stressful circumstances alone, with dozens if not hundreds of desperate people besieging their offices and soliciting their help, but has to take account of their own perceptions that, when refusing to observe and implement federal regulations strictly, they were acting in defence of Switzerland's reputation as a humanitarian country.

While most countries raised the hurdles against Jewish asylum seekers, the methods applied by the Nazi regime became ever more brutal. Half of the refugees arriving in Zurich in the summer of 1938 reported that Gestapo agents had driven them over the border. Expulsion often was accompanied with the threat of detention in a concentration camp for those who dared to return. This was disturbing news for the Swiss government. Such practices transcended the familiar dimensions of driving unwanted aliens into neighbouring states, apart from the fact that these expellees were not foreigners with unresolved residence status but ordinary citizens of the perpetrator state. In Switzerland, this gave rise to demonstrations protesting against such violations of international law. The police chief from Zurich, for instance, demanded that refugees be sent back to German territory without mercy, to make an example and to indicate to the Gestapo that Switzerland would not tolerate such practices.[47] Some local authorities refused to admit any refugees at all, claiming that their rejection would be the 'most severe punishment' for the German authorities.[48]

In the particularly exposed border areas of St Gallen and Basel, mass flight from Austria further aggravated the conundrum of Jewish organisations. In Basel alone, thirty to fifty Jews from the Third Reich arrived every day in the first weeks of August, most of them without any further means to pay for their food and accommodation or to continue their journey. Basel was known for its liberal policy in the prewar era and refused to transport these refugees back to Germany as the federal authorities often demanded. Instead, the Basel police tolerated members of the Jewish relief organisation helping refugees to cross the border into France. Though not an officially endorsed method, this practice was nevertheless based on previous arrangements with the French Sous-Préfet at Mulhouse who would admit up to six refugees every day and grant them amnesty for illegal entry. This became impossible after France closed its borders on 18 August 1938.[49] The presence in Basel of a growing number of refugees thus soon exceeded the capacity of the Jewish community to accommodate refugees in private homes. Community leaders had to resort to local authorities for support. As a result, the city provided for mass accommodation in camps run and financed by relief agencies but formally under the control of local police authorities. A similar solution was found in St Gallen. With the Jewish community covering the expenses, cantonal authorities opened a refugee camp in an empty factory in Diepoldsau that provided shelter for up to three hundred persons. These mass accommodations and the rigid disciplinary regime that was imposed on their inhabitants became precedents for the camp system that would dominate everyday life for a majority of refugees after 1940.[50]

Growing dependence on official assent made the Jewish community vulnerable to political pressure, a situation that Heinrich Rothmund exploited without hesitation. At a meeting in August 1938, he declared to community leaders that the number of refugees to be admitted in the future depended entirely on the ability and willingness of private relief agencies to support them. In response to such pressure, the Jewish community had to organise three fund raising drives in 1938.[51] A few days after this meeting, on 19 August 1938, the federal government nevertheless closed the border and deployed troops to fend off the 'refugee invasion'.[52] Soldiers and border guards relentlessly sent back the refugees they intercepted and often turned them over to the German police, fully aware of the consequences this had for the people involved. Various reports gave evidence of a gradual dehumanisation. Border guards were said to have literally driven refugees like cattle and hit them with their rifle butts to prevent them from crossing the border. This corresponded to an ongoing desensitisation in discourse and practice, with refugees often being referred to as 'undesirable elements'.[53] In contrast, other officers who were confronted with the refugees' distress on a daily basis expressed revulsion about the increasingly brutalised methods applied on both sides of the border. They questioned whether the border closure was enforceable at all, as refugees tried to enter at any price, under conditions of mortal danger and often after being sent back up to five times. They also cited, as a reason to underline their doubts, what desperate refugees had told them in interviews: Jews from Vienna, one report stated, 'say they have only three options: leaving Germany, concentration camps, or suicide.'[54]

One of these dissenters was Paul Grüninger, the police captain of St Gallen, who had a long record of opposition to the hardline stance of the federal authorities. With some of his men, he actively assisted refugees after the border was closed in August 1938. A network of refugee helpers – many were jobless young men familiar with cross-border smuggling as a means of survival – would show refugees places where they could enter secretly. Grüninger turned a blind eye to such trafficking and fabricated records to prevent the refugees from being expelled. It is estimated that he saved up to a thousand or even more Jewish refugees from Austria. By the end of 1938, however, as rumours and accusations against him began to multiply, his superiors withdrew their protection, which cost Grüninger his job, his career and his reputation.[55]

For those responsible, these events – both the brutalised practices and the obstruction of federal instructions in favour of the refugees, raised the question about the political and human costs of the adopted policy. How much further could the authorities push the envelope in fending off the 'refugee invasion' at the border, without provoking an excess of violence or open defiance? Was it not futile to simply keep sending back refugees while the Nazi regime stayed committed to expelling Jews in a systematic way? And could Switzerland risk international damage to its reputation if it continued to send back refugees to Germany where they faced concentration camp?[56] The federal governments' dilemma was even more aggravated by rumours that Nazi Germany would soon replace Austrian passports by German ones, thus thwarting all efforts by the Swiss to prevent immigration from Austria. What would happen if 'unwanted persons' from Austria benefited from free travel between Germany and Switzerland? At that point, the federal government conceived of the only other option to control the influx of Jewish refugees: namely entering into negotiations with Germany and convincing the Nazi regime to stop expelling Jews to Switzerland.

How to Recognise Jewish Emigrants? The 'J'-Stamp and Shifting Control from the Border to the Desks

In the summer and autumn of 1938, in spite of the radicalisation of Nazi persecution in annexed Austria and the rest of the Reich and the increasingly dramatic scenes at the border and at consulates, the federal authorities remained adamant. They showed no signs of departure from their fixed priorities: the prevention of Jewish immigration and fighting 'overpopulation by foreigners'. However, the prevailing circumstances led them to the conclusion that their strategies needed revision. Refugees' chances to transmigrate had rapidly reduced and thus it no longer appeared appropriate to the authorities to let them enter the country in the first place. Instead, emphasis had shifted to controlling the influx of expellees from the Third Reich. But even with stricter regulations, more manpower and determination, conceptual problems remained.

How would it be possible to identify 'undesirable foreigners', i.e., those who were seeking asylum, once the Austrians had German passports? A circular of 7 September 1938 addressed this problem and instructed border guards to refuse entry to 'emigrants' from Germany, in spite of the fact that travel between the two countries was still unrestricted. This left the question of how to recognise an 'emigrant' among the holders of German passports. The instructions only advised officers to single out those who 'are with certainty or great possibility Jews' because 'nearly all of those who are emigrants are Jews'.[57] Other than suggesting border guards resort to cultural stereotypes and implicit assumptions about Jews, this tautological explanation was probably not much help for the everyday fulfilment of duties at the border. Still, it also demanded that the passports of emigrants who were rejected be stamped as having been 'turned back'. In the future, this would ease the border guards' dilemma and provided at least circumstantial evidence about a passport holder's identity.

In Bern, throughout the spring and summer of 1938, different agencies were tackling the problem of how to identify Jewish refugees at the border and distinguish them from other German travellers.[58] Anxious not to disturb 'normal relations' with the Third Reich, Swiss diplomats were eagerly seeking a practicable solution. In May of 1938, Rothmund was the first to propose a visa requirement for the Jews only in an internal note. While his suggestion found the approval of colleagues from other government agencies, it did not resonate well with the German authorities. Such a provision was obviously in direct contradiction to the Nazi goal of removing Jews from the Third Reich. In addition, it would require mechanisms for the identification of Jews that were not yet in place.

By the end of July 1938, Swiss worries materialised: the German government officially announced the replacement of Austrian passports by German ones.[59] Some time later in August, the idea to mark the passports of 'non-Aryan' German citizens emerged in a letter by Hans Frölicher, the Swiss ambassador to Berlin. However, the documents are not clear about whether German or Swiss negotiators first came up with this suggestion. They only testify to the persisting reluctance of the Nazi regime to agree to any solution reducing the chances of emigration for the Jews. Eventually, in August of 1938, the Swiss threatened to reintroduce a general visa requirement. As Rothmund stressed, such a step would require German applicants to 'present proof that they were Aryan', which implied additional administrative work for Swiss consulates.[60] In addition, the general visa requirement would probably have failed to find federal government approval because of its unpredictable economic repercussions and potential damage to the tourist industry. As a bluff to speed up negotiations, however, it was successful. In early September, the Swiss sensed a breakthrough as the Germans gave up their opposition and agreed to mark the passports of Jewish nationals, but they insisted on reciprocity. This entailed that the Swiss government condone discrimination against its own Jewish citizens. Rothmund objected to this compromise, even though he had been the first to propose discriminatory measures, and he warned that such a step would not only alienate Swiss Jews, but also expose Switzerland internationally to the accusation of becoming embroiled in Nazi antisemitism. As a consequence he reiterated the demand for a general visa requirement. None of these considerations eventually entered the final agreement.

The German–Swiss Protocol of 29 September 1938 included the German promise to mark the passports of its nationals belonging to the 'Jewish race', to be defined according to the Nuremberg Laws, with a distinctive mark and thus prevent their holders from entering Switzerland. The mark should be a clearly visible and indelible 'J'-stamp, as the two parties agreed. The document also included provisions that introduced discrimination against Swiss Jews. Rothmund, who was directly involved in the last rounds of negotiations, did not endorse the agreement. The Federal Council did not heed his reservations and adopted the Protocol in a meeting of 4 October 1938. Simultaneously, it introduced the visa requirement for 'Non-Aryan Germans'. It thereby allowed Nazi racial terminology and 'German racial legislation to penetrate Swiss administrative law'.[61] The federal authorities had to deal with the international and domestic protests that followed publication of the visa requirement. This decision, however, was the only part of the whole story to become publicly known in 1938, in contrast to Switzerland's active role in the preceding negotiations that only entered public knowledge through an Allied edition of German documents in 1953.[62] Within days, on 15 October 1938, Sweden followed the Swiss example and signed a similar agreement with the German government.

More than ever, the federal authorities were zealously dedicated to fighting 'foreign inundation', but by the autumn of 1938 they had dropped all pretences, leaving no doubt of whom they had in mind when talking of 'undesirable elements'. Official discourse no longer distinguished between Jewish foreigners and refugees but used the terms 'emigrant' and 'Jew' in an interchangeable way. And all those considered 'emigrants' were treated as if they were undocumented or even stateless persons. The introduction of the visa requirement for German Jews was soon followed by mandatory visa for all 'emigrants' on 20 January 1939, regardless of their country of origin and subsequently also for holders of Czechoslovakian passports on 15 March 1938. Eventually, not only German Jews, but all Jews and any potential refugee had to reckon with expulsion, even when they arrived from a country that had no travel restrictions between itself and Switzerland. As a consequence, they were trapped in a dilemma: either they risked being turned away when entering without permission or they forfeited almost any chance of acceptance when revealing their true intentions by submitting a visa application.

In addition, with the help of the 'J'-stamp and Nazi bureaucracy, federal efforts had succeeded in shifting control away from the border. In the long run, this helped neutralise both unreliable cantonal governments and individual officials who were motivated in the fulfilment of their duties by compassion rather than obedience.[63] Yet even then, a few border cantons successfully dodged federal attempts at stricter control in the months that followed. Basel for instance, let refugees enter without visas and consistently refused to implement expulsion orders issued by the federal authorities. Such practices were only interrupted by the beginning of the war when the army took over border controls and emergency powers eventually helped the Federal Police for Foreigners complete the centralisation of decision making on all issues related to asylum policy.[64] Elsewhere, cantonal leniency ended when police authorities launched criminal investigations against refugee helpers and officials who were acting in violation of their instructions. On 17 December 1938, for example, the federal authorities suspended Ernest Prodolliet, the consular employee who had issued visas to refugees from Austria. In early February of 1939, St Gallen abandoned its liberal policy and two month later, the cantonal government dismissed its police captain Paul Grüninger. Preceding investigations had involved a number of refugee helpers, leading to the arrest of policemen as well as prominent members of St Gallen's Jewish community. Recha Sternbuch, the wife of a respected orthodox businessman, spent time in prison because of her role in rescue activity. Charges against her were eventually dropped. In an act of retaliation, however, the Federal Police for Foreigners refused her parents entry visas after the German invasion of Western Europe. Switzerland had been their last chance and they died at Auschwitz.[65]

It remains difficult to assess the full impact of the 'J'-stamp on Jews who were trapped in the Third Reich by the autumn of 1938. Generally speaking it added to the accumulation of measures that had made emigration almost impossible for Jews at the time of the November pogrom: intensified spoliation by the Nazis and accelerated impoverishment made these refugees less and less attractive for receiving countries. The 'J'-stamp eventually stigmatised them, thwarting their chances to slip through borders unidentified. Based on the documents of Swiss embassies, exemplary cases of German Jews in exile can be reconstructed. As soon as the new regulations entered into force, the Swiss legation in Paris, for instance, made the 'J' stamp a prerequisite for visa requests and reminded applicants to have their passports marked at the German embassy. Usually, if German Jews could provide residence permits and tickets to other countries of exile they were given a short-term entry visa for Switzerland. In special cases, however, the applications had to be submitted to the Federal Police for Foreigners in Bern. This agency granted entry only under very restrictive conditions, if it was reassured that visitors would leave the country again. But the 'J'-stamp also became an instrument of economic protectionism. It allowed immigration authorities, in concert with private business associations, to keep away one category of foreign competitors: Jewish business people who succeeded in rebuilding their companies abroad after escaping from Germany. In the worst cases, if they depended on business contacts in Switzerland, the refusal of a visa could ruin their existence.[66] For refugees, bankruptcy did not mean economic failure, debts and loss of income alone, but it could result in the revocation of residence permits and eventually expulsion from the country of exile, especially if they became welfare dependents. At that point, Swiss policy increasingly damaged people who were not even seeking asylum in Switzerland and maybe had no other connections to the country than a stamp in their passport that was partly a Swiss invention.

Conclusions

> The Aliens Police ... though dealing with individual cases on a daily basis, always have to keep an eye on developments that are years and decades ahead ... In 1933 Jewish emigration from Germany took them by surprise. But they would not be disturbed by this event in the fulfilment of their job. The Federal Council gave them clear orders to resist emigrants' desire to settle down.[67]

In the spring of 1939, looking back on the past six years, Heinrich Rothmund believed himself to be in a situation where he could take pride in the accomplishments of his agency. Notwithstanding disturbing events abroad, he had stuck to his mission and fended off wave after wave of refugees. Statistics confirm his apparent success. They reflect a constant decrease in Switzerland's foreign population during his time in office. After peaking at almost 15 per cent of the total population in 1910, the proportion of foreigners dropped to 8.7 per cent in 1930 and 5.2 per cent in 1941.[68] Naturalisation did not contribute to this decline as standards were raised for citizenship acquisition alongside restrictions in immigration policy, with Jews facing additional discrimination, for instance through longer residence requirements than other candidates.[69]

Throughout the period under discussion, immigration policy determined the fate of refugees. Continuity in principles, goals and methods, therefore, was the most striking feature of Switzerland's prewar asylum policy. The Swiss authorities did not welcome those who were fleeing Nazi persecution in the first place. No matter what happened beyond the border, humanitarian policy remained a police affair, carefully watched by Rothmund and his staff. This institutional choice was not incidental but mirrored deeply rooted perceptions shared by policy makers, bureaucrats and the wider public as well. For them, refugees were suspicious. They embodied a source of unfathomable dangers that ranged from undermining Switzerland's political order to contaminating its morals and introducing contagious deceases. In brief, asylum seekers were not seen as people in need of protection but as undesirable foreigners.

Evidently, the police approach blinded decision makers to the human consequences of developments abroad as well as their own decisions. Moreover their remote position was such that the refugees' distress was too abstract when weighed against the presumed political and financial costs of an open door policy. In the spring of 1939, the cantonal government of Basel complained that the federal authorities did not comprehend the strain imposed on the men who had to carry out their orders. The latter, they wrote, 'have to listen every day to the grievances and solicitation of these wretched emigrants. No official can totally avoid such influence and after all, it does not seem desirable that he suppresses all his emotions.'[70] Under the extraordinary circumstances after March 1938, the daily practice of implementing instructions and regulations no longer resembled routine but confronted officials charged with the task of rejecting or admitting refugees with critical decisions. Therefore, under the level of discourse and official decision making, a complex and disparate practice had prevailed until the beginning of the Second World War, although the federal authorities had continuously curtailed cantonal room for manoeuvre. But such diversity is often poorly documented, unless it concerned extreme cases of either inhumanity or disobedience for humanitarian motives. In the end, this makes it difficult to draw a conclusive picture of Switzerland's prewar refugee policy and its outcome.

'Once again, I was filled with the wonderful sensation of hope,' the Austrian communist Karl Schiffer remembered when recounting his visit to the Swiss consulate at Bregenz in the late summer of 1938. All his previous attempts to enter Switzerland had thus far been futile. But after recounting what he had gone through in Vienna, 'I could see that the Swiss official believed me.' In violation of his instructions, the official gave him a transit visa with the remark 'Let's just try it.'[71]

Notes

1. 'The Last Chance' was the title of a movie released in 1945 and dealing with refugees' escape to Switzerland over the snow-covered Alps. Its Austrian director Leopold Lindtberg himself spent the Nazi era as a refugee in Switzerland and was in the exceptional situation to resume film making despite his emigrant status.
2. See F. Brayard, La 'solution finale de la question juive'. La technique, le temps et les catégories de la décision, Paris 2004, pp.108–50. Also S. Zuccotti, The Holocaust, the French and the Jews, Lincoln 1993.
3. See Independent Commission of Experts Switzerland – Second World War (ICE) (ed.), Switzerland and Refugees in the Nazi Era, Bern 1999, pp.85–99, henceforth ICE, Refugees. This report can be downloaded from www.uek.ch/en/index.htm. On knowledge in Switzerland of Nazi extermination policy: G. Haas, 'Wenn man gewusst hätte, was sich drüben im Reich abspielte', 1941–1943. Was man in der Schweiz von der Vernichtungspolitik wusste, Basel 1994; W. Laqueur and R. Breitman, Breaking the Silence, Hanover 1994.
4. F. Battel, 'Wo es hell ist, dort ist die Schweiz.' Flüchtlinge und Fluchthilfe an der Schaffhauser Grenze zur Zeit des Nationalsozialismus, Zurich 2000, p.137, citing the report on a local socialist meeting.
5. Critical journals published the heartbreaking stories of individuals who were expelled, see for instance National-Zeitung, 24 August 1942. On the postwar reconstruction of the history of refugees who were denied asylum see S. Friedländer, When Memory Comes, New York 1979, on the deportation of his parents; S. Mächler, 'Abgrund zwischen zwei Welten. Zwei Rückweisungen

6. jüdischer Flüchtlinge im Jahre 1942', *Studien und Quellen* 22, 1996, pp.137–232; ICE, *Refugees*, pp.127–29, 138ff.
6. See A. Häsler, *The Lifeboat Is Full. Switzerland and the Refugees 1933–1945*, New York 1969, whose German original *Das Boot ist voll* appeared in 1967. Markus Imhoof based his prize-winning film 'Das Boot ist voll', released in 1980, on this book.
7. See ICE, *Switzerland, National Socialism and the Second World War*, Zurich 2002. For the question of legal liabilities arising from the expulsion of refugees see S. Keller, *Die Rückkehr. Joseph Springs Geschichte*, Zurich 2003: F. Haldemann, 'Geschichte vor Gericht: der Fall Spring. Hintergründe und Analyse des Bundesgerichtsentscheids vom 21. Januar 2000 i.S. J. Spring gegen Schweizerische Eidgenossenschaft', *Aktuelle juristische Praxis* 8, 2002. For the wider political context of these debates see R. Ludi, 'Waging War on Wartime Memory: Recent Swiss Debates on the Legacies of the Holocaust and the Nazi Era,' *Jewish Social Studies* 10, no. 2, 2004, pp.116–52.
8. For this very controversial formulation see ICE, *Refugees*, p.271
9. J. Picard, *Die Schweiz und die Juden 1933–1945. Schweizerischer Antisemitismus, jüdische Abwehr und internationale Migrations- und Flüchtlingspolitik*, Zurich 1994; S. Mächler, 'Kampf gegen das Chaos. Die antisemitische Bevölkerungspolitik der eidgenössischen Fremdenpolizei und Polizeiabteilung 1917–1954,' in *Antisemitismus in der Schweiz 1848–1960*, ed. A. Mattioli, Zurich, 1998, pp.357–421; F. Kieffer, *Judenverfolgung in Deutschland – eine innere Angelegenheit? Internationale Reaktionen auf die Flüchtlingsproblematik 1933–1939*, Stuttgart 2002.
10. C. Hoerschelmann, *Exilland Schweiz. Lebensbedingungen und Schicksale österreichischer Flüchtlinge 1938 bis 1945*, Innsbruck 1997, p.12.
11. G. Koller, 'Entscheidungen über Leben und Tod. Die behördliche Praxis in der schweizerischen Flüchtlingspolitik während des Zweiten Weltkriegs', *Studien und Quellen* 22, 1996, on the problem of categorisation also ICE, *Refugees*, pp.130–33.
12. Juliane Wetzel, 'Auswanderung aus Deutschland', in *Die Juden in Deutschland 1933–1945. Leben unter nationalsozialistischer Herrschaft*, ed. W. Benz, Munich 1988, p.102.
13. J. Wacker, *Humaner als Bern! Schweizer und Basler Asylpraxis gegenüber den jüdischen Flüchtlingen 1933–1943 im Vergleich*, Basel 1992, p.75, citing police reports from Basel.
14. U. Gast, *Von der Kontrolle zur Abwehr. Die eidgenössische Fremdenpolizei im Spannungsfeld von Politik und Abwehr*, Zurich 1997.
15. Kurt Wolff, 29 March 1933, cited after H. Walter, *Asylpraxis und Lebensbedingungen in Europa. Deutsche Exilliteratur 1933–1950*, Darmstadt 1972, p.118 (translation RL).
16. M. Wischnitzer, *Die Juden der Welt. Gegenwart und Geschichte des Judentums in allen Ländern*, Berlin 1935, p.177 (translation RL).
17. ICE, *Refugees*, pp.105ff.
18. C. Skran, *Refugees in Inter-War Europe: The Emergence of a Regime*, Oxford 1995.
19. Hannah Arendt has dedicated a whole chapter of *The Origins of Totalitarianism* to the problem of statelessness. For Switzerland's policy toward stateless and other 'undesirable aliens' see T. Huonker and R. Ludi, *Roma, Sinti und Jenische. Schweizerische Zigeunerpolitik zur Zeit des Nationalsozialismus*, Veröffentlichungen der Unabhängigen Expertenkommission Schweiz – Zweiter

Weltkrieg, Bd. 23, Zurich 2001, pp.67–79. For an example illustrating such practice see also ICE, *Refugees*, p. 135.
20. H. Walter, *Asylpraxis und Lebensbedingungen in Europa. Deutsche Exilliteratur 1933–1950*, Darmstadt und Neuweid 1972, pp.7–21.
21. ICE, *Refugees*, p.136.
22. P. Kury, *Über Fremde reden. Überfremdungsdiskurs und Ausgrenzung in der Schweiz von 1900 bis 1945*, Zürich 2003.
23. The general strike of November 1918 overshadowed class relations for most of the interwar era. Until the early 1930s, conflicts repeatedly turned violent and more than once, the federal authorities detached troops to put down workers' demonstrations. On the general strike see W. Gautschi, *Der Landesstreik 1918*, Zurich 1968; on Swiss elites of the interwar era: A. Mattioli (ed.), *Intellektuelle von Rechts. Ideologie und Politik in der Schweiz 1918–1939*, Zurich 1995; H. Jost, *Les Avant-gardes réactionnaires: la naissance de la nouvelle droite en Suisse 1890–1914*, Lausanne 1992.
24. S. Mächler, 'Kampf gegen das Chaos. Die antisemitische Bevölkerungspolitik der eidgenössischen Fremdenpolizei und Polizeiabteilung 1917–1954,' in *Antisemitismus*, ed. Mattioli, Zurich 1998, pp.357–421; H. Wichers, *Im Kampf gegen Hitler. Deutsche Sozialisten im Schweizer Exil 1933–1940*, Zurich 1994, pp.35–45; B. Studer, 'Die "Ausländerfrage" zwischen militärischem Sicherheitsdenken und rechtsstaatlichen Garantien zu Beginn des Zweiten Weltkriegs', *Studien und Quellen* 29, 2003, pp.161–87.
25. On the institutional history see Gast, *Kontrolle*.
26. ICE, *Refugees*, pp.55ff.
27. On the decree of 31 March 1933 see C. Ludwig, *Die Flüchtlingspolitik der Schweiz in den Jahren 1933 bis 1955. Bericht an den Bundesrat zuhanden der eidgenössischen Räte*, Bern 1957, pp.52f.; for a definition of emigrant also ICE, *Refugees*, p.107.
28. Swiss Federal Archives (FA), E 4320 (B) 1991/87, Vol. 4, C. 17.3. Schweizerische Bundesanwaltschaft: Ausweisungen.
29. Wichers, *Kampf*.
30. Koller, 'Entscheidungen', pp.28f. See also 'Aide-mémoire du Chef de la Division de Police du Département de Justice et Police, H. Rothmund, 4 April 1933', in *Documents Diplomatiques Suisses* 10 (1930–1933), no. 257, pp.626–29. On categorisation see also ICE, *Refugees*, pp.56, 130-133.
31. Normally, emigrants also had to deposit a security of several thousand Swiss francs. See W. Kälin, 'Rechtliche Aspekte der schweizerischen Flüchtlingspolitik im Zweiten Weltkrieg', in *Schweiz, der Nationalsozialismus und das Recht. I. Öffentliches Recht*, ed. ICE, Zurich 2001, p.284.
32. Picard, *Die Schweiz und die Juden*; Mattioli (ed.), *Antisemitismus*; U. Altermatt, *Katholizismus und Antisemitismus. Mentalitäten, Kontinuitäten, Ambivalenzen*, Frauenfeld 1999.
33. Cited after S. Erlanger, *'Nur ein Durchgangsland'. Arbeitslager und Internierungsheime für Flüchtlinge in der Schweiz 1940-1949*, Zurich 2006, p.51. On prejudice against Jews from Eastern Europe: P. Kury, '"...die Spielverderber, die Juden aus Galizien, Polen, Ungarn und Russland... Überhaupt die Juden." Ostjudenfeindschaft und die Erstarkung des Antisemitismus', in *Antisemitismus*, ed. Mattioli.
34. ICE, *Refugees*, p.84. On Rothmund's biography and career: H. Roschewski, *Rothmund und die Juden. Eine historische Fallstudie des Antisemitismus in der*

schweizerischen Flüchtlingspolitik 1933–1957, Basel 1997. For data on the Jewish population: Picard, Die Schweiz und die Juden, p.61.
35. Bundesgesetz über Aufenthalt und Niederlassung der Ausländer vom 26. März 1931 (Federal law on the temporary and permanent residence status of foreigners)
36. H. Walter, Deutsche Exilliteratur 1933–1950. Band 2: Europäisches Appeasement und überseeische Asylpraxis, Stuttgart 1984, pp.170–73.
37. ICE, Refugees, pp.149ff.
38. ICE, Refugees, pp.59ff., 191–99, 226–30.
39. For an extensive discussion of this dilemma as well as responses of Jewish community leaders see S. Mächler, Hilfe und Ohnmacht: der schweizerische Israelitische Gemeindebund und die nationalsozialistische Verfolgung 1933–1945, Zurich 2005.
40. A. Schmidlin, Eine andere Schweiz. Helferinnen, Kriegskinder und humanitäre Politik 1933–1942, Zurich 1999; Mächler, Hilfe und Ohnmacht, see also ICE, Refugees, pp.235ff.
41. S. Friedländer, Nazi Germany and the Jews: The Years of Persecution, New York 1997, p.180.
42. H. Safrian, 'Beschleunigung der Beraubung und Vertreibung. Zur Bedeutung des "Wiener Modells" für die antijüdische Politik des "Dritten Reiches" im Jahr 1938', in 'Arisierung' und Restitution. Die Rückerstattung jüdischen Eigentums in Deutschland und Österreich nach 1945 und 1989, ed. C. Goschler and J. Lillteicher, Göttingen 2002, pp. 61–89; Friedländer, Nazi Germany and the Jews, pp.241–45.
43. Friedländer, Nazi Germany and the Jews, pp.248–52; R. Weingarten, Die Hilfeleistung der westlichen Welt bei der Endlösung der deutschen Judenfrage, Bern and New York 1982; also F. Kieffer, Judenverfolgung in Deutschland – eine innere Angelegenheit? Internationale Reaktionen auf die Flüchtlingsproblematik 1933–1939, Stuttgart 2002.
44. ICE, Refugees, p.75. Recent research has come to consider these figures inflated. See Mächler, Hilfe und Ohnmacht, p.151.
45. The federal authorities specified procedures in a circular of 29 March 1938. The weekly Israelitische Wochenblatt für die Schweiz 27, 1938 reported on the practice of the Vienna consulate. See Ludwig, Die Flüchtlingspolitik der Schweiz, pp.75ff., 83; also ICE, Refugees, p.106.
46. Protokoll der Einvernahme von Herrn Prodolliet, 20.2.1939 and Protokoll über die Einvernahme des Herrn Ernst Prodolliet, 7.12.1938, FA E 2500 (-) 1990/6, vol.141 also ICE, Refugees, pp.106f.
47. Letter by the Zurich Police Chief, 3.8.1938, FA E 4320 (B) 1991/243, Vol. 17, C.31.1. Dossier: Judenfragen. Korresp. Allgem. On the border situation see also C. Hoerschelmann, Exilland Schweiz. Lebensbedingungen und Schicksale österreichischer Flüchtlinge, Innsbruck 1997, pp.97ff.
48. Polizeidirektorenkonferenz (Minutes of the Meeting of the Cantonal Police Chiefs, 17.8.1938), FA E 4260 (C)1969/146. vol. 6. See also J. Krummenacher-Schöll, Flüchtiges Glück. Die Flüchtlinge im Grenzkanton St. Gallen zur Zeit des Nationalsozialismus, Zurich 2005, pp.116–19.
49. Wacker, Humaner als Bern!, pp.113ff.
50. Erlanger 'Nur ein Durchgangsland'; Mächler, Hilfe und Ohnmacht, p.158.
51. Mächler, Hilfe und Ohnmacht, pp.161–69.
52. Report by Robert Jezler on Border Crossing by Austrian Refugees, 16.8.1938, FA E 4300 (B) 1, vol. 12.

53. ICE, *Refugees*, pp.75f., 136f.
54. Report of a border guard officer from Chur, 22 August 1938, cited in ICE, *Refugees*, p.137.
55. S. Keller, *Grüningers Fall. Geschichten von Flucht und Hilfe*, Zurich 1994.
56. For an extensive discussion of these considerations see 'Le Chef de la Division de Police du Département de Justice et de Police, H. Rothmund, au Président de la Confédération, J. Baumann, 10 August 1938', in *Documents Diplomatiques Suisse* 12, Bern 1994. pp.817–23, no. 357.
57. Highly Confidential Directive of the Federal Police Division, 7 September 1938. Cited in ICE, *Refugees*, p.133.
58. See on the following ICE, *Refugees*, pp.75–85 ; also Daniel Bourgeois, 'La porte se ferme: la Suisse et le problème de l'immigration juive en 1938,' *Relations internationales* 54, 1988, pp.181–204.
59. S. Ferrero, 'Switzerland and the Refugees Fleeing Nazism: Documents on the German Jews Turned Back at the Basel Border in 1938–1939', *Yad Vashem Studies* 27, 1999, p.215.
60. Letter of 1 September, 1938 from Rothmund to the Foreign Affairs Division, cited in ICE, *Refugees*, p.79.
61. ICE, *Refugees*, p.82.
62. *Akten zur deutschen auswärtigen Politik 1918–1945*, Series D, vol. 5; the Swiss documents can be found in *Documents Diplomatiques Suisse*, 12, See also G. Kreis, *Die Rückkehr des J-Stempels. Zur Geschichte einer schwierigen Vergangenheitsbewältigung*, Zurich 1996.
63. On the concentration of competences see ICE, *Refugees*, pp.56f.
64. On cantonal policies in 1939 Wacker, *Humaner als Bern!*, pp.140f., also Krummenacher-Schöll, *Flüchtiges Glück*, pp.122–49. On the concentration of competences see ICE, *Refugees*, pp.56f.
65. See Krummenacher-Schöll, *Flüchtiges Glück*, pp.180ff., 194. Normally, the Federal Police for Foreigners granted entry visa to close kin of Swiss citizens. ICE, *Refugees*, pp.110f.
66. Such cases can be found in the Swiss Embassy in Paris, Vols. 103–105, Visa Applications, FA E 2200.41 (-) -/11. The Swiss foreign missions in France are the few to have preserved this type of documents.
67. Heinrich Rothmund in an address to the Swiss Jewish Community Federation, 26 March 1939, cited in S. Mächler, 'Kampf gegen das Chaos. Die antisemitische Bevölkerungspolitik der eidgenössischen Fremdenpolizei und Polizeiabteilung 1917–1954', in *Antisemitismus*, ed. Mattioli, p.390.
68. ICE, *Refugees*, p.46.
69. Since the 1910s, some cantonal and later also the federal naturalisation agencies began introducing discriminatory quota for Jewish applicants. See Picard, *Die Schweiz und die Juden*, pp.62–70.
70. Wacker, *Humaner als Bern!*, p.135.
71. Karl Schiffer, *Über die Brücke. Der Weg eines linken Sozialisten ins Schweizer Exil*, Vienna 1988, p.136.

Chapter I.5

The 1930s: The End of the Latin American Open-door Policy

Patrick von zur Mühlen

Political and Jewish refugees from Germany only considered Latin American states as possible countries of refuge and settlement in the later years of the 1930s. In 1933, most people fleeing the Nazis chose to stay nearby in the countries of Western Europe, primarily because they hoped that conditions would improve or that the Hitler regime would collapse, thus allowing them to return. However, the continuance of an increasingly brutal political system and its increasingly aggressive foreign policy after 1935 caused restrictions for immigration and asylum in the adjoining countries and diminishing international readiness to tolerate the growing immigration of émigrés. As a result countries on the periphery of the European continent and overseas achieved a growing importance for exile and asylum. In this context, 1938 was a decisive year, when after the annexation of Austria, the annexation of the Sudetenland and the noticeably more radical antisemitic policy of the Reich began a mass exodus of mostly Jewish refugees from both Germany and Austria. This resulted in a rising flood of refugees to overseas countries with the consequence that even the open-door policy of the Latin American states came to an end.

At this point it is important to note that the immigration policies of the Latin American republics were not uniform and sometimes subject to temporary modifications; from flexible to restrictive rules and vice versa. Some states never admitted more than a few refugee immigrants at any time, for example Peru, Venezuela and the Central American republics. As the refugees after 1933 perceived other states as more attractive for settlement, so they tended to attract larger numbers – like Argentina, Brazil, Chile and Uruguay. A third category consisted of those states which became important for asylum and exile after the previously mentioned countries had restricted any further immigration: Mexico, Cuba, the Dominican Republic, Colombia, Ecuador, Bolivia and Paraguay.

We can generalise that all Latin American states treated refugees as normal immigrants who came for social or economic reasons and not as victims of political or racist discrimination and harassment. In no case were they offered asylum in order to protection them against physical danger or racial and political persecution. Immigration policy was oriented to utility and the advantage of the host country. This attitude did not change after 1938. The only exception was Mexico, which offered asylum to former citizens of the defeated Spanish Republic and those foreigners who had fought in the International Brigades and in the Republican Army against fascism. In this way, about 3,000 mostly political German and Austrian refugees escaped from wartime Europe to Mexico in 1940. The Mexican authorities took this decision on humanitarian grounds, making it the only Latin American country to consider political activists fleeing Nazi Germany as refugees and not as regular immigrants. However, the problems of asylum and assistance to persecuted people were sometimes the subject of press and public debate in several Latin American states, when political parties, trade unions and aid committees urged their governments to introduce more liberal immigration rules.

Refugees who left Germany soon after January 1933 had more chance to emigrate to a country of their own choosing. The most attractive countries were those with a more European character, a moderate climate, a well-developed economy and better prospects for employment and a decent standard of living. In many cases, the refugees already had connections to the country of immigration through the presence of relatives, friends, political associations or co-religionists. The existence of political groups and Jewish communities provided an essential precondition for further immigration. Thus it is not surprising to find that Argentina – once one of the most prosperous countries of the world – and especially its capital, Buenos Aires, had a magnetic attraction for refugees from Europe. Until 1938 it was very easy to enter the country, either by tourist visa or through a request by relatives who were already living in the country – the so-called *'llamada familiar'*. Those who arrived at Buenos Aires as first-class passengers received a tourist visa without any difficulty. Less affluent passengers could make use of the badly organised Argentinian administration and obtain immigration papers through corruption or by the use of fake documents. With entry permit documents it was easy to disappear and to legalise one's residence after a certain time.[1]

Brazilian immigration rules were different. In the 1930s, immigration policy was determined by the internal politics of the regime of President Getúlio Vargas. After a putsch in 1930 he steered a constitutional course until 1934, but after the suppression of a communist insurgency in 1935 he established an authoritarian government. In 1937 he proclaimed the *'Estado Novo'*, dissolved parliament, banned all political parties and abolished basic civil rights. In so doing, he followed the example of fascist European states like Italy and Germany by proclaiming a nationalist ideology and the idea a 'Brazilian race' with xenophobic and antisemitic overtones. This policy did not prevent him from admitting a selective immigration of refugees from Germany and Austria. Well-educated engineers, scientists and wealthy people were preferred over those without such qualifications, as well as immigrants who where willing and able to develop unsettled areas for agricultural purposes.[2] However, in practice a considerable number of refugees was able to enter Brazil, mainly due to administrative incompetence, an inability to apply immigration rules and probably also through bribery. Unlike in Argentina, Uruguay and to some extent Chile, the refugees did not just settle in the capital – then Rio de Janeiro – but also in the southern urban centres of São Paulo, Curitiba and Porto Alegre as well as in agricultural areas of the states of Paraná and Santa Catarina.

In Uruguay, immigration laws allowed the entry of anybody who had a valid employment contract or capital funds of at least US$400. In Chile, immigration rules were both liberal and flexible, but their application became more restrictive as a result of the world economic depression. Other Latin American republics were also easy to enter until 1938, but only a few refugees seized the opportunity because most Latin American countries were less attractive than European and North American destinations, and trans-Atlantic passages were expensive.

As a result, the emigration of refugees from Germany to most Latin American countries was limited in the years immediately after 1933. Unfortunately statistics are not exact. It is estimated that in the years 1933–1935 about 1,500–2,000 refugees entered Argentina, 1,800–4,500 Brazil and 600–900 Chile. In the case of Uruguay we do not have any detailed information for this period. Smaller groups of refugees entered Paraguay, Ecuador and Mexico. The total number of refugees who arrived in Latin America during this period is estimated at between 6,700 and 9,100 persons.[3] The inexactness of this estimate can be explained by an application of immigration rules that did not distinguish between regular immigrants for economic reasons, tourists, commercial travellers and refugees, as the 1930s also saw a continuing, economically motivated, emigration from Germany to Latin America. For instance, in the years 1933–1936, Argentine official statistics registered more than 18,000 immigrants from Germany including all these categories.[4] If one estimates the total number of German (and after 1938 also Austrian) refugees who entered Latin American countries between 1933 and 1941/42 as at least 90,000 persons, more than 90 per cent of them were Jews (as defined in the Nuremberg racial laws of the Nazis). In the first years the percentage of (non-Jewish) political refugees was higher but after 1938, immigrants to Latin America (with the exception of Mexico) were exclusively people of Jewish descent. Less than 10 per cent of these 90,000 refugees arrived before 1938.

Local Jewish refugee aid committees and relief organisations were of great importance in facilitating this immigration. They gave financial assistance to newly arrived immigrants, cared for social and humanitarian problems, interceded with the authorities to apply for documents or for the legalisation of residence. They procured jobs and domiciles for refugees and founded a great many social institutions. A considerable percentage of their budget came from two American Jewish organisations, the American Jewish Joint Distribution Committee (AJDC) and the Hebrew Intergovernmental Committee for European Migration (HICEM); and also from local Jewish organisations already working in Latin American countries. Also for political refugees and those people of Jewish descent who no longer had connections to the Jewish faith, traditions or social networks, several relief committees were established, but their resources were very limited.

Only a very limited amount of aid was given to refugees by national governments, local governments or international organisations. One example was the emigration of exiled Saarlanders to Paraguay. When the Saarland was returned to Germany from League of Nations Administration after the plebiscite in 1935, about 8,000 political opponents of the Nazi regime and some Jewish families fled to France. Because of high levels of unemployment it was thought impossible to integrate them into French society, and Paris therefore urged the League of Nations and its High Commissioner for Refugees to care for these people. At the suggestions of the League of Nations, the International Nansen Office bought unsettled areas in Paraguay for colonisation purposes and offered homesteads to the Saarlanders. The French Government was ready to pay the transport, and in 1937 about 150 people emigrated to Paraguay.[5] There were also other organisations that initiated colonisation projects in Latin America, but the scale of these rescue operations was very limited.[6]

One can generalise that most Latin American states abandoned their liberal immigration policy and introduced increasingly restrictive rule through an insistence on entry visas. The *Anschluss* of Austria in March 1938, the unsuccessful end of the Evian conference in the summer of 1938, the secession of the Sudetenland from Czechoslovakia to Germany in the autumn of 1938 and the November pogrom prompted an enormous increase in mass emigration to Latin America. After immigration to Argentina had grown during 1937 and 1938, the government closed the border and stopped the issue of entry visas. Mass immigration of refugees nevertheless continued as a result of the ponderous nature of the ineffective Argentine bureaucracy and the lack of controls over clandestine immigration. It can be estimated that up to the beginning of the war in September 1939, at least 35,000 refugees arrived in Argentina. Thus, per capita, Argentina gave asylum to the greatest number of refugees from Nazi Germany in the world.[7]

In Uruguay, restrictions to mass immigration had already been introduced in October 1936 with the intention of stopping the entry of refugees and admitting only 'normal' immigrants. The authorities tried to achieve this aim by requesting of a certificate of good political conduct, issued by the Gestapo, and further references on the political reliability of the applicant.[8] Nevertheless a continuing clandestine or half-legal immigration remained possible. When the number of immigrants was seen to be growing again by the end of 1938, nationalist parties, groups and newspapers pressed the government for a more restrictive legislation. In May 1939 a bill was introduced which was intended to stop the immigration of people with mental or nervous diseases, heart disease, epileptics, beggars, vagabonds, and those with criminal convictions. The sum requested as 'landing money' was also increased. This new immigration policy was combined with a nationalist and antisemitic campaign, but the Uruguayan Parliament did not pass the bill until 1941.[9]

In Chile, practical immigration policy developed differently than in other Latin American countries. Until 1938, Chile introduced increasingly restrictive rules. A special quota system for Jews and people from the liberal professions that favoured agricultural immigrants was undoubtedly antisemitic in character.[10] Only the Popular Front Government of President Pedro Aguirre Cerda temporarily relaxed these immigration rules, but a further inflow of refugees initiated an anti-immigration campaign in conservative and nationalist circles with the result that the government stopped all immigration in 1940.[11] Immigration policy also became more restrictive in Brazil before the decisive year of 1938, but in that year, antisemitic tendencies became more evident in the issuing of entry visas. Brazilian embassies, missions and consulates were instructed by the Foreign Minister not to issue even those entry visas that had been officially offered by the government. When the Vatican asked President Vargas to sanction the immigration of at least 3,000 'non-Aryan' Catholics, only half of the entry visas were actually issued as a result of 'sabotage' carried out by Brazilian diplomats and consuls in Berlin and Hamburg.[12] Immigration restrictions in the most important countries of settlement, like Argentina, Brazil, Chile and Uruguay, meant that from 1938 onwards, the stream of refugees pushed to other Latin American republics increased. Thus countries such as Colombia, Ecuador, Bolivia and Paraguay, which had been perceived as less attractive before because of their climate, poverty and economic and political instability suddenly seemed to hold better prospects.[13] Like Brazil and Chile, these countries had a preference for agricultural colonists, well-educated specialists or wealthy people. In many cases, entry visas could only be obtained by the use of falsified documents or bribery. Some Caribbean countries like Cuba or the Dominican Republic were nothing other than 'waiting rooms' for the U.S. The only country of the Western hemisphere to grant generous asylum to a large number of European refugees was Mexico, which gave refuge to many thousands of republican Spaniards, and also about 3,000 Germans and Austrians.

It was a paradox that the increasing restrictions on immigration imposed in the most preferred exile countries in the years before 1938 meant that 90 per cent of all German-speaking refugees leaving after that date went to Latin America and we should keep these quantities in mind when considering the end of the open-door policy in the Latin American states.

Notes

1. C. Jackisch, *El nazismo y los refugiados alemanes en la Argentina 1933–1945*, Buenos Aires 1989, pp.254–57; E. Levin, *Historias de una emigración (1933–1939). Alemanes judíos en la Argentina*, Buenos Aires 1991; L. Senkman, 'Argentina Immigration Policy during the Holocaust (19381945)', *Yad Vashem Studies* 11, 1991, pp.155–88.
2. I. Kestler, *Exílio e Literatura: Escritores de fala alemã durante a época do nazismo*, São Paulo 2004, p.46.
3. P. von zur Mühlen, *Fluchtziel Lateinamerika. Die deutsche Emigration 1933–1945: politische Aktivitäten und soziokulturelle Integration*, Bonn 1988, pp.40–41.
4. Jackisch, *El nazismo*, p.135.
5. von zur Mühlen, *Fluchtziel Lateinamerika*, p.107.
6. Saint Sauveur-Henn, *Un siècle d'émigration allemande vers l'Argentine 1853–1945*, Köln 1995, pp.458–61; B. Breunig, *Die deutsche Rolandwanderung (1932–1980)*, München 1983; E. Kosminsky, *Rolândia, a Terra Prometida. Judeus Refuigiados do Nazismo no Norte do Paraná*, São Paulo 1985; von zur Mühlen, *Fluchtziel Lateinamerika*, pp.104–6.
7. L. Senkman, *Argentina, la Segunda Guerra Mundial y los refugiados indeseables*, Buenos Aires 1991.
8. I. Wojak, 'Deutsch-jüdisches Exil in Uruguay. Einwanderungspolitik, öffentliche Meinung und Antisemitismuserfahrung deutsch-jüdischer Flüchtlinge in Uruguay 1933–1945', *Zeitschrift für Geschichtswissenschaft* 11, 1995, p.1009.
9. Wojak, 'Deutsch-jüdisches Exil in Uruguay', p.1007; A. Milgram, *Entre la aceptación y el rechazo: América Latina y los refugiados del nazismo*, Jerusalem 2003.
10. I. Wojak, *Exil in Chile. Die deutsch-jüdische und politische Emigration während des Nationalsozialismus 1933–1945*, Berlin 1994, pp.83–85, 90.
11. Wojak, *Exil in Chile*, p.119.
12. J. Lesser, *Welcoming the Undesirables: Brazil and the Jewish Question*, Berkeley 1995, pp.184–86.
13. M. Kreuter, *Wo liegt Ecuador? Exil in einem unbekannten Land 1938 bis zum Ende der fünfziger Jahre*, Berlin 1995.

Chapter I.6

Shanghai: A Last Resort for Desperate Jews

Steve Hochstadt

Shanghai had the name, it had a bad name, it was the worst place to go to. It was sort of a hierarchy of things. If you went to the United States, that was a good thing. If you went to England that was a good thing. If you went to another European country, it was fine, to Holland, to France, all that was good. If you went to New Zealand and to Australia and then to Canada, that was good. There were countries that were considered to be okay. Brazil was okay, Argentina and Uruguay were okay, maybe Chile. There were countries that were considered to be not so okay, Paraguay and Bolivia ... because they were considered to be primitive countries in which it was difficult to make a living, where a European wouldn't be happy. Dominican Republic, Panama, certain Central American countries were considered to be ... semi-desperation countries you went to, *faute de mieux*, there was no place else. And the worst place was Shanghai. Shanghai, we heard rumors of people, you know, poverty, illness, disease, death, and these refugees being thrown in the middle of it, and so forth. And of course we, as of that time, 1938, we knew we would leave with nothing, no possessions fundamentally. So this ... was a very frightening prospect.

W. Michael Blumenthal[1]

Shanghai occupies a unique place in the sad history of Jewish escape from Nazi Germany.[2] It was both the last resort of desperate Jews seeking refuge from constantly escalating persecution and the easiest place for a foreigner to enter. It lay across the world from central Europe, yet allowed penniless refugees to step off the boat without a visa. The strongest power in Shanghai was the Japanese military, allies of the Nazis, who allowed Jews to settle in Shanghai and remain there without physical attack for the entire war. This wide open door to physical safety was finally closed in August 1939 by a series of political decisions by men of many nations. The analysis of the immigration policies which confronted potential

Jewish refugees to Shanghai takes somewhat different paths than similar discussions of European countries. Shanghai was not one city, but a series of enclaves with differing governing structures. In international Shanghai the interaction of the policies of many governments, and even private citizens, determined how refugees would be received.

Shanghai's unique openness to immigration derived from the inability of Chinese rulers to resist Western imperialism. After the British navy defeated Chinese forces in the Opium War of 1842, extraterritorial enclaves were created in Shanghai for British commercial interests and settlement. Some of the earliest British subjects in Shanghai were Jews who originated in the Middle East. Some of these Baghdadi families became enormously wealthy and joined the financial elite in Shanghai, including the Sassoons, Kadoories, and Hardoons.[3] Other Western nations joined in the scramble for special rights in China. In the 1860s, two large pieces of central Shanghai became autonomous legal entities: the International Settlement, dominated by British and American business interests and governed by the elected Shanghai Municipal Council, and the French Concession, run by the French government through its Consul General.[4] The extraterritorial governments controlled police, customs, and judicial matters in the two settlements. The British retained dominant power in the International Settlement well into the twentieth century, exercised through the Shanghai Municipal Council (SMC), which was elected by the tiny proportion of foreigners who owned substantial property. Chinese won the right to vote for the SMC only when Chiang Kai-shek and the Nationalists came to power in 1927.[5]

Although Westerners were able to protect their dominance in Shanghai politics, during the early twentieth century the Japanese became the largest foreign colony in the city. After World War I, Japanese efforts to develop their own imperial base on the Asian mainland brought them increasingly into conflict with both Chinese and Westerners. In the 1930s, Japanese military pressure on China, especially the occupation of Manchuria in 1931-1932, coincided with increasing Japanese presence in the Hongkou district of Shanghai. After the so-called Marco Polo Bridge incident in Beijing in July 1937, Japanese forces also fought against the Chinese army in Shanghai for several months, destroying large parts of Hongkou. Sporadic fighting continued until February 1938, by which time the Japanese were the dominant military power in Shanghai.[6] They controlled customs, post, and telegraph, and they took over police powers in Hongkou, officially part of the International Settlement. They demanded more voice in the SMC and its police forces.[7] Unwilling, however, to antagonise the Western powers, the Japanese did nothing to challenge the extraterritorial powers within the International Settlement. They also made no effort to restrict Jewish refugee immigration.

During the century of foreign domination, Shanghai developed into one of the world's leading commercial centres. The lack of any central Chinese government control over business interests, the unregulated competition for power among authorities of many nations, and the central role of the opium trade in Shanghai's economy led to Shanghai's reputation as a world centre for drugs, illegal weapons trade, prostitution, and corruption.[8] The lack of legal restriction on the international movement of goods, money, and people also made Shanghai into one of the world's most cosmopolitan cities. Because there was no requirement for official papers of any kind when entering the port of Shanghai, the city became a destination for refugees from twentieth-century conflicts. A significant source of refugees was Russia, and later the Soviet Union. By the 1930s two Russian communities had established themselves in Shanghai, with considerable mutual enmity. The so-called White Russians had fled from the successful Red Army after 1917, and displayed considerable antisemitism; Russian Jews were forced out by both Tsarist and Soviet antisemitic policies.[9]

For the period from the Nazi takeover in 1933 until August 1939, there were no restrictions on entry into Shanghai. The first German Jewish refugees arrived in Shanghai shortly after the Nazis came to power in 1933. For the reasons outlined by Michael Blumenthal in the quotation at the beginning of this chapter, most potential Jewish refugees sought more obvious destinations. By 1937 there were only about 300 Jewish refugees in Shanghai, mainly well educated doctors, lawyers and academics.[10] Few Jews in Germany knew anything about Shanghai, including its open immigration policies. The first discussion of Shanghai in the German Jewish press was an article in May 1936 in Berlin's *Central-Verein Zeitung*, followed in September 1937 by an article in the *Israelitische Familienblatt* in Hamburg. Only in June 1938, as the Nazi government greatly increased the pressure to emigrate, did the largest Jewish periodical in Germany, the *Gemeindeblatt der Jüdischen Gemeinde Berlin*, bring up Shanghai as a possible destination.[11] By the autumn of 1938 the German Jewish organisations which aided possible emigrants with advice and sometimes money, such as the Hilfsverein der Deutschen Juden, were advising Jews about the freedom of entry in Shanghai.[12]

By that time, the stream of refugees to Shanghai was already underway. The reluctance to see Shanghai as a possible destination was finally overcome by the rapid escalation of Nazi violence against Jews in 1938. The *Anschluss* of Austria into the Third Reich in March was accompanied by remarkable popular violence, partly encouraged by the Sturmabteilung (SA) and partly the spontaneous action of Viennese antisemites.[13] In June hundreds of German Jews with previous police records, including traffic violations, were arrested and thrown into concentration camps. Public brutality reached its peak during *Kristallnacht*, November 9–10, when the SA organised the burning of synagogues, destruction of businesses, invasions of apartments, and widespread physical violence across Germany and Austria, followed by the incarceration of about 30,000 men in Dachau, Buchenwald, and Sachsenhausen.

The illusion that Jews could somehow manage to find an accommodation with the Nazi government was destroyed in 1938. Accompanying the violence, and intimately related to it, was a more coordinated Nazi effort to organise and speed up Jewish flight.[14] The Gestapo told arrested men and their families that the only way to get out of a concentration camp was to present evidence that they would leave the country. Many Shanghai Jewish refugees have reported those conversations with the Gestapo, which took place in jails, concentration camps, and Gestapo offices.[15] Suddenly Shanghai was transformed from 'the worst place' to the best possibility. Yet even at this point, voices within the German Jewish community worried that the chances of surviving in Shanghai were no better than those in the Third Reich.[16]

Since anti-Jewish violence was first applied on a broad basis in Austria seven months before *Kristallnacht*, Viennese Jews were the first to seek out Shanghai as a destination for mass flight. No authority thought to keep count of the new arrivals. During 1938 perhaps 1,500 refugees arrived in Shanghai, two-thirds of whom were Austrian. When the families of men arrested during *Kristallnacht* began to arrive in Shanghai in large numbers in early 1939, the proportion changed to more than two-thirds from Germany, in line with the relative sizes of the Jewish populations of Germany and Austria.[17]

Because Nazi policy against Jews had focused on driving them out of the German economy, most Jewish refugees in and after 1938 arrived in Shanghai with virtually no financial resources. After April 1938 Jews had to register all private property valued over RM 5,000; in July Jews were excluded from carrying on many types of businesses, like real estate; and after *Kristallnacht*, the decree 'For the Elimination of Jews from German Economic Life' legalised the confiscation of virtually all Jewish property.[18] Government officials came into Jewish homes to observe the process of packing and certify that the rules against taking valuables were followed. A ship ticket to Shanghai was very expensive, and some companies required Jews to pay for a first-class round trip. Jews on their way to Shanghai were allowed to carry only RM 10 in cash. By the time that Jewish refugees stepped onto the pier at Shanghai, nearly all were impoverished.

As the trickle of German-speaking Jewish refugees suddenly increased during 1938, the existing Jewish communities in Shanghai expanded their efforts to alleviate their distress. Already in 1934 the earliest German refugees created a Hilfsfond to aid newcomers. By the summer of 1938, this was no longer adequate to deal with the masses of Austrians arriving on every ship. A new, broader organisation was created by wealthy Baghdadi Jews to greet the refugees, provide temporary housing, and integrate them into the Shanghai economy.[19] Soon their resources were exhausted. In October the so-called Komor Committee expressed the first negative reaction to the refugee influx into Shanghai by demanding financial help from the American Jewish Joint Distribution Committee (AJDC) in the U.S. At that point, the wealthy Shanghai Jews who were behind the Komor Committee hoped to spur American Jews to provide more financial support.[20] Over the next year intensive discussions among representatives from many nations about European Jewish refugees in Shanghai eventually resulted in the closing of this last open door. While the roles of some of the key actors have been discussed in the literature on Shanghai Jews, conclusions about the responsibility for this decision need correction. In particular, Jewish leaders in Shanghai itself have been widely blamed for helping to shut out fellow Jews in need.[21] I will argue that the responsibility in fact lay elsewhere.

In response to the reports from Shanghai, between October and December the AJDC began to advocate restricting the flow of Jewish refugees to Shanghai, in order not to overtax available resources, even as the number who had arrived only numbered in the hundreds. On 12 December, Joseph Hyman, Director of the JDC, wrote that the JDC would try to prevent more refugees from arriving.[22] Yet Nazi persecution in Germany and Austria increased the flow. The landing of the Italian ship 'Conte Verde' on 24 November nearly doubled the number of recently arrived refugees to about 400, which again doubled to about 1,000 in the middle of December.[23] Later that month, Hyman wrote that it was 'quite impossible to absorb any large number of foreign refugees'.[24] But the Shanghai Jewish leaders still perceived the flow of refugees as requiring their fraternal assistance. *Israel's Messenger*, the newspaper of the Baghdadi community, published a positive article on the refugees on 16 December.[25]

In late December, Western business interests entered the discussion. The Shanghai Municipal Council voted to halt the Jewish influx. The Chair of the SMC, Cornell S. Franklin from Great Britain, wrote a circular on 23 December to the international consular community, asking them 'to take any steps in your power to prevent any further arrival of Jewish refugees in Shanghai'.[26] A few days later Franklin repeated this demand in a letter to the Portuguese Consul General, who was also the Senior Consul of the International Settlement. Franklin's words demonstrate the causes of the Western businessmen's concern:

> There is already in Shanghai an acute refugee problem which is taxing to grave degree the resources of both the municipality and of private philanthropy. There is to be considered not only the provision of accommodation and subsistence, but the degree to which any further number of refugees could be absorbed without still further impairing the standard of living of the present community. ... [S]hould this problem increase in magnitude it would be the Council's duty to protect the community of the International Settlement by taking steps to prohibit the landing in the International Settlement of any further Jewish refugees without adequate means of subsistence or promise of employment.[27]

Although the next meeting of the consular corps was scheduled for early January, after the return of the Italian Consul General from Japan, the Consul Generals from England, France, and the U.S. felt the problem was so urgent that they met on 29 December.[28] While the letter of 23 December by Franklin stated that the SMC was 'desirous of assuming its share of the responsibility' to care for the refugees, there is no evidence that the Western business community had yet provided any funds.

The German Consul General, Bracklo, reported on the next meeting of the consular corps on 28 January 1939. The English representative demanded 'all possible measures to prevent further flow to Shanghai'. The Dutch representative suggested using the shipping lines to prevent penniless refugees from boarding. But the Japanese representative privately told Bracklo that his government was against discrimination.[29] On 30 January 1939, a leading article in the American newspaper *Shanghai Evening Post and Mercury* demanded an immediate meeting of all foreign consuls to deal with this 'alarming' problem.[30]

This united effort by self-interested non-Jewish Western businessmen soon unleashed other voices outside of Shanghai to call for a halt to Jewish refugees. While it would take further research to follow the chain of decision making outward from Shanghai, it is clear that Western governments acted quickly on behalf of their citizens in Shanghai. In early January, the French Minister of Foreign Affairs told French Consuls in Berlin, Vienna, and Prague to advise local Jewish organisations to prevent their members from going to Shanghai.[31] The British Consul in Dresden wrote to the *Israelitische Religionsgemeinde* in Leipzig in January that the financial resources of the welfare organisations in Shanghai were exhausted, and therefore they should try to stop further emigration.[32] By February the American Embassy in Berlin reported to Cordell Hull, U.S. Secretary of State, that the British were 'discouraging' the travel of Jews to Shanghai on British ships. Hull responded that the matter had already been discussed at the highest levels of the Roosevelt administration, 'in order that appropriate steps might be taken to discourage refugees from going to Shanghai'. Hull suggested to the Ambassador in Berlin that he 'mention informally to the German authorities the desirability of discouraging the travel of Jews to Shanghai on German vessels'.[33]

For whom would such a policy be desirable? Certainly not for Jews in the Third Reich, against whom most countries, like the U.S., had erected high barriers to immigration. The U.S. State Department and the British Foreign Office had already demonstrated remarkable ignorance of Nazi policy and attitudes toward Jews after the Evian Conference in July 1938, when both countries appealed to the Nazi government not to send out Jewish emigrants with no monetary resources, because this put 'great burdens on its friendly neighbours'.[34] Even after *Kristallnacht*, the American and British governments were unwilling to recognise that Jews in the Third Reich were in deadly danger. Like the members of the SMC, their diplomatic leaders saw Jewish flight from Germany primarily as a problem for themselves.

While Secretary of State Hull was organising an appeal to the Nazi government to discourage Jewish emigration to Shanghai because it inconvenienced U.S. citizens there, the Nazis were in fact stepping up their efforts to get Jews to go to Shanghai. After *Kristallnacht*, the Gestapo itself helped to organise the transport of former concentration camp inmates to Shanghai on German liners.[35] Martin Beutler met his father, who had just been released from Buchenwald, on the pier in Hamburg in April 1939, and the family travelled to Shanghai on the 'Usaramo' of the German East African Line.[36] German policy insured that more and more Jews were desperately trying to find a way out of the Third Reich and Italian steamships brought the great majority of Jews to China. In Shanghai itself, however, it was Japanese policy that was most important in maintaining the open door to refugees well into 1939.

Since the war with Russia in 1905, when the American Jewish banker Jacob Schiff had helped bankroll the Japanese war effort, the official Japanese attitude toward Jews was extremely positive. Although the Japanese belief that international Jewry possessed wide powers betrayed a willingness to accept antisemitic stereotypes, government policy was designed not to antagonise Jews. Even as the Western community in Shanghai was beginning to complain about the influx of refugees, a conference of the top five ministers in Japan on 6 December 1938 decided to erect no hurdles to further immigration. This policy served the increasingly close diplomatic relationship with Germany, since the Nazis were clearly interested in maximising the flight of Jews out of Germany. But the Japanese were not willing to accept German demands for a hostile attitude toward Jews within their sphere of control. Fearful of hurting relations with the United States, where Jews were assumed to be powerful, the ministers confirmed their policy of treating Jews like any other foreigners, in line with the traditional Japanese stress on equal treatment for all races.[37] When the SMC requested at the end of December that the Japanese help to restrict Jewish arrivals, the Foreign Ministry told its representatives in Shanghai to reject this attitude. Instead the Consulate General there should try to insure that the responsibility for any restrictions against Jewish immigration be placed on the SMC.[38] Japanese Foreign Minister Arita stood by this policy publicly several times in the first half of 1939.

But German and Japanese consular officials in Shanghai, like their Western counterparts, began to complain about the economic impact of the growing Jewish refugee stream. The German Consulate alerted the Foreign Ministry in Berlin in February 1939 to the dangers that Jews presented to German economic and political interests. In March a report of the Consulate expressed 'the greatest objections to any further immigration of Jews to Shanghai.' In particular, the heavy presence of Jewish doctors and dentists was a source of dissatisfaction among the Western medical community.[39] In May and June, the Japanese Consul Ishiguro repeatedly complained to Bracklo that Jews were taking business away from Japanese in Shanghai, and asked what the German reaction would be if the Japanese restricted Jewish entry.[40] The Japanese Foreign Ministry received early in 1939 a report from Shanghai that 1,000 more refugees could be expected, most of them in need of assistance, also noting the resulting problems for the Japanese community.[41]

The year of greatest Jewish immigration into Shanghai was 1939. Although the total number of Central European refugees cannot be stated precisely, estimates cluster around 16,000 people between 1933 and 1945. About 1,500 of these had arrived by the end of 1938. By mid 1939 well over 1,000 per month landed on the Shanghai piers.[42] Many Jews in the Third Reich were unable to buy tickets on the fully booked ships which travelled to China. This increasing stream of refugees further alarmed the business elite of Shanghai. An article summarising the economic fears of the established foreigners appeared in the *Shanghai Evening Post and Mercury* on 15 April entitled 'Economic Threat Caused by Jewish Refugee Emigrés from Europe. Soon to Form Fourth of Foreign Population'. The article argued that Jewish arrivals created 'a serious menace to part of the established western communities'.[43] On 17 February 1939 the *North China Herald* reported that the foreign communities had taken another step in their effort to end Jewish immigration. Representatives of the Jewish community, including the influential Victor Sassoon, had been contacted.[44] There is no evidence that the Jewish leaders were ready to join that chorus.

The Japanese finally moved to change their open door policy: on 9 May investigators from the Ministries of Army, Navy and Foreign Affairs met in Shanghai to consider the question of Jewish immigration. Then the three Japanese officials in charge of monitoring refugee affairs in Shanghai set up a meeting with the leading personalities among the Baghdadi Jews and the most generous contributors to the relief efforts, Sassoon and Ellis Hayim, for 25 May. The Japanese summary of this meeting places responsibility for creating restrictions on the Jews. Sassoon and Hayim supposedly complained of the inadequacy of their resources to deal with the constantly increasing numbers of refugees and asked for help in stemming the flow. They offered assurance that such restrictions would not meet with opposition from Jews outside Shanghai, nor would the local Committee object. In their later public pronouncements, the Japanese asserted that restrictions had been considered 'at the request of the Jewish Refugee Committee itself which fears a new influx of refugees'. But the next day the Japanese already had a draft plan for restricting entry. On 11 June, a revised plan was sent to Tokyo, including the following provisions: restrictions against new immigrants except those already underway on ships, and negotiations with German and Italian representatives to seek their help.[45]

The Japanese now moved quickly to put these restrictions into effect. Foreign Minister Arita asked the German government to prevent further Jewish emigration to Shanghai, and informed them that further Jewish entry into Japanese-controlled China would not be permitted. Berlin responded positively.[46] On 9 August the Naval Landing Party, the highest Japanese military authority in Shanghai, sent a letter to the Jewish relief committee announcing that no further refugees would be admitted to Hongkou after 21 August. The SMC followed on 14 August with a similar announcement that European refugees would no longer be permitted to enter the International Settlement. Over the next few days steamship companies and Jewish agencies in Europe and the United States were notified that all emigration to Shanghai must end.[47] Although none of these new regulations specifically mentioned Jews, it was clear to all concerned that only refugees with a 'J' stamped into their passports would be affected.

Not all Westerners were in favour of closing this unique refuge for persecuted Jews. The Consul Generals of Italy and Portugal argued that the SMC decision had no value unless the full consular corps agreed. Bracklo from the German Consulate brought up the problem of emigrants already on ships steaming toward Shanghai, and requested the SMC to allow them to land.[48] Most telling, Paul Komor, head of one of the Jewish relief committees, wrote to Ellis Hayim on 15 August protesting against the SMC decision on the basis that they did not have proper authority. Komor essentially worked for Sassoon and Hayim, transforming their donations into relief programs for new arrivals. It is unlikely that he would contradict their opinion on restricting immigration.[49]

The closing of this unique open door was not so simple. The complete prohibition of further entry was soon revised to allow exceptions. First, those who had already embarked before 21 August were allowed to land. Then in October new regulations were announced by the SMC, allowing immigration to those who could fulfil any of the following conditions: they had an immediate relative or intended to marry someone already in Shanghai; they had a contract for a job in Shanghai; or they possessed US$400 as so-called 'guarantee money'. The French lowered the demand to US$300 for entry into the French Concession, but the Japanese did not employ such a clause at all.[50]

Thus by September 1939, the Shanghai door was effectively closed for the tens of thousands of Jews remaining in the Third Reich. After 21 August, 1,100 more refugees arrived on boats which were already underway or about to leave. About 14,000 Central European refugees had arrived in less than a year and a half. The flow of about 1,000 per month dwindled immediately to a few hundred over the next year, although again exact statistics are not available.[51] Only a handful of refugees managed to get Japanese permission to land directly in Hongkou. Most who entered Shanghai after the restrictions went into effect received an entry permit from the SMC. According to a report from Shanghai published in the New York emigrant newspaper *Aufbau* in January 1940, most of the successful applications came from parents of residents. A much smaller number were able to show US$400.[52] The Jewish relief agency HIAS (or HICEM) supplied some refugees with cheques to cover this amount. Both Jewish and non-Jewish businesses in Shanghai offered fictitious job contracts to refugees to help them get out of Europe.[53] The trickle of successful applicants for entry permits suddenly ended on 10 June 1940, when Italy entered the war and closed the Mediterranean. After that it was still possible to reach Shanghai but only by crossing the Soviet Union.

One more sizable group of eastern European Jews was still able to make these arrangements.[54] After the German and Soviet armies divided up Poland in 1939 and the Soviets began to move into the small Baltic countries, Jews in Lithuania discovered that the Japanese Consul, Chiune Sugihara, and the Dutch Consul, Jan Zwartendijk, were willing to issue visas for Japan and Curacao. Brandishing these papers, at least 2,000 Jews were able to cross the Soviet Union in 1940 and 1941, and land in Kobe, Japan. Eventually they were sent to Shanghai and allowed to settle in Hongkou.[55] The German invasion of the Soviet Union in June 1941 cut off the final means of escape.

The multiplicity of governmental authorities who played a role in the closing of Shanghai's open door offers some insight into the attitudes toward Jewish refugees from the Third Reich. The arrival of the first few hundred penniless refugees in Shanghai disturbed the Western residents, who enjoyed power and a standard of living far in excess of what they could have expected in their home countries. They immediately tried to close the door, and eventually succeeded. Western governments showed little understanding of the real plight of Jews in Nazi Germany, although they were quite well informed. British and American authorities did not hesitate to try to prevent Jews from getting to Shanghai, a city in which their residents represented a tiny minority. The Japanese, allies of the Nazis, despite the discomfort of some of their Shanghai citizens, did hesitate, and continued to show hospitality to Jewish refugees until the Pacific War broke out. The local Jewish communities were the only ones who actually offered financial help to the refugees out of their own pockets, and they defended the need to allow desperate Jews to leave Europe.

Life in Shanghai for a Jewish refugee was not easy. Many lived in barracks housing and ate at soup kitchens for the entire war. Undernourishment left them more susceptible to tropical diseases. Perhaps 10 per cent among the thousands died before 1945.[56] Meanwhile only a few of their relatives and friends who were forced to stay behind in Europe survived.

Notes

1. Interview with W. Michael Blumenthal, Shanghai Jewish Community Oral History Project, Berlin, 3 February 1995, pp.4–5.
2. The standard work on the Jewish refugees in Shanghai is D. Kranzler, *Japanese, Nazis and Jews: The Jewish Refugee Community of Shanghai, 1938–1945*, Hoboken (NJ) 1988, first published in 1976. The best memoir by an eyewitness is by the late E. Heppner, *Shanghai Refuge: A Memoir of the World War II Jewish Ghetto*, Lincoln 1994.
3. On the Baghdadi, or sometimes Sephardic, community, see M. Meyer, *From the Rivers of Babylon to the Whangpoo: A Century of Sephardi Jewish Life in Shanghai*, Lanham 2003.
4. Betty Peh-T'i Wei, *Shanghai: Crucible of Modern China*, Hong Kong 1987, pp.62–76.

5. Wei, *Shanghai*, p.205; A. Freyeisen, *Shanghai und die Politik des Dritten Reiches*, Würzburg 2000, p.19.
6. F. Wakeman, Jr., *Policing Shanghai 1927–1937*, Berkeley 1995.
7. Barbara Geldermann, 'Shanghai a City of Immigrants: Shanghai und die Gründer der ersten jüdischen Gemeinde, die bagdadischen Juden', in *Exil Shanghai 1938–1947: Jüdisches Leben in der Emigration*, ed. G. Armbrüster, M. Kohlstruck and S. Mühlberger, Teetz 2000, p.48.
8. On the intermingling of policing, criminal gangs, opium trade and politics, see Wakeman, *Policing Shanghai*.
9. On the Russian Jews, see the interesting memoir by R. Krasno, *Strangers Always: A Jewish Family in Wartime Shanghai*, Berkeley 1992. A scholarly study of both Russian communities is M. Renders Ristaino, *Port of Last Resort: The Diaspora Communities of Shanghai*, Stanford 2004.
10. J. Ross, *Escape to Shanghai: A Jewish Community in China*, New York 1994, pp.24–25, describes some of the early refugees.
11. Freyeisen, *Politik des Dritten Reiches*, pp.390–95.
12. A. Finnane, *Far From Where? Jewish Journeys From Shanghai to Australia*, Melbourne 1999, pp.21–23, on Horst Eisfelder.
13. On the violence that accompanied the *Anschluss*, see E. Burr Bukey, *Hitler's Austria: Popular Sentiment in the Nazi Era, 1938–1945*, Chapel Hill 2000.
14. The words used to characterise the physical movement of Jews out of the Third Reich inevitably contain judgments about the nature and causes of that movement. 'Emigration' is most often used, both by scholars and by Jewish survivors themselves (e.g., '*Wir gingen in die Emigration.*'), to denote the act of leaving Nazi Germany. Many writers employ 'exile', especially in the description of the experiences of intellectuals. Although it is not easy to find alternatives in the English language, I find these words inappropriate in marking the violent coercion applied by the Nazis to force Jews to leave.
15. For example, interview with Hans Eisenstaedt, Shanghai Jewish Community Oral History Project, Berlin, 12–13 August 1991, pp.14–15; interview with Ilse Krips, Shanghai Jewish Community Oral History Project, Potsdam, 28 February 1995, pp.2–3; Ross, *Escape to Shanghai*, p.35, on Horst Levin.
16. In early 1939, Dr Julius Seligsohn, one of the directors of the *Reichsvereinigung der Juden in Deutschland* and of the *Hilfsverein*, wrote a report in which he stressed how undesirable Shanghai was as a destination, comparing it to a transit camp. His report demonstrates that at least some of the organisers within Germany of Jewish flight tried to discourage travel to Shanghai. The report is reproduced by M. Avalon, '"Gegenwaertige Situation": Report on the Living Conditions of the Jews in Germany. A Document and Commentary', *LBIYB*, 1998, pp.271–85.
17. These estimates come from the careful analysis by Christiane Hoss of the registration of Jewish refugees with the German Consulate in Shanghai, reported in 'Abenteuerer: Wer waren die Shanghai-Flüchtlinge aus Mitteleuropa?', in *Exil Shanghai*, ed. Armbrüster, Kohlstruck and Mühlberger, p.107.
18. A discussion of how well this policy had operated through the end of 1938 is contained in a letter of 25 January 1939 from the German Foreign Ministry to all embassies. This document is Nürnberg document NG-1793, translated in Steve Hochstadt, *Sources of the Holocaust*, Houndmills and New York 2004, pp.79–82.

19. Freyeisen, *Politik des Dritten Reiches*, p.403; Kranzler, *Japanese, Nazis and Jews*, pp.91–92.
20. Ross, *Escape to Shanghai*, p.53.
21. Those who have written about this decision have said that Shanghai's Jewish leaders were responsible for the final Japanese decision to prevent further immigration: Kranzler, *Japanese, Nazis and Jews*, pp.158–61, 236, 268; Heppner, *Shanghai Refuge*, pp.44–45; Geldermann, 'Shanghai a City of Immigrants', p.55; Ross, *Escape to Shanghai*, p.60.
22. Kranzler, *Japanese, Nazis and Jews*, pp.166–68, n. 37–39.
23. *North China Daily News*, 25 November 1938; *The Shanghai Times*, 24 December 1938.
24. Ross, *Escape to Shanghai*, p.52.
25. Geldermann, 'Shanghai a City of Immigrants', p.54.
26. Freyeisen, *Politik des Dritten Reiches*, p.93. A copy of this letter can be found in BABL R9208/2329.
27. The letter is quoted in Kranzler, *Japanese, Nazis and Jews*, pp.164–65, n.18.
28. Report by Traut to German Foreign Ministry, 29.12.1938, BABL R9208/2329, on a conversation with the Portuguese Consul General Dr Alves, who also attended that meeting, but did not agree that there was an urgent problem.
29. Telegram from Bracklo to Foreign Ministry Berlin, 28.1.1939, BABL R9208/2329.
30. Freyeisen, *Politik des Dritten Reiches*, p.420.
31. Communication of Minister of Foreign Affairs to Minister of the Interior, 11.1.1939, AN F7/16072.
32. United States Holocaust Memorial Museum, RG 19 'Rescue, refugees, and displaced persons', Sub-group 001M.01, Reel 9, p.676.
33. Cordell Hull's instruction to U.S. Embassy in Berlin, archived in United States National Archives, file number NA 893.55J/4, microfilm publication LM63, roll 143. I am grateful to the late David S. Wyman for alerting me to this document. Hull's telegram is reprinted in Hochstadt, *Sources of the Holocaust*, p.83.
34. See British memorandum from their Embassy in Berlin and the German reply in John Mendelsohn, ed., *Jewish Emigration from 1933 to the Evian Conference of 1938*, The Holocaust: Selected Documents in Eighteen Volumes, vol. 5, New York 1982, pp.141–48; also reprinted in Hochstadt, *Sources of the Holocaust*, pp.67–68.
35. Freyeisen, *Politik des Dritten Reiches*, p.397.
36. Interview with Martin Beutler, Shanghai Jewish Community Oral History Project, Berlin, 29 June 1995, pp.3–4. I am indebted to Mr Beutler for his research about the voyage of the 'Usaramo' and about Shanghai more generally.
37. Kranzler, *Japanese, Nazis and Jews*, pp.232–33, quotes from the declaration.
38. Gerhard Krebs, 'Antisemitismus und Judenpolitik der Japaner', in *Exil Shanghai*, ed. Armbrüster, Kohlstruck and Mühlberger, pp.65–66.
39. Report of Bracklo to Foreign Ministry Berlin, 24.2.1939; report of German Consul General to German Embassy Shanghai, 20.3.1939; report of German Consul General to Foreign Ministry Berlin, 27.3.1939; all in BABL R9208/2329.
40. Reports of Bracklo to German Embassy Shanghai, 24.5.1939 and 30.6.1939, BABL R9208/2329.
41. Kranzler, *Japanese, Nazis and Jews*, ch. 7, especially p.234, and pp.267–68.

42. The German Consulate processed official *Meldeblätter* filled out by incoming refugees. Statistics compiled by Hoss, 'Abenteuerer', p.107, show that between June 1938 and February 1939, about 200 a month registered, which jumped to nearly 1,000 a month from March to June 1939, when the records ended.
43. Geldermann, 'Shanghai a City of Immigrants', pp.55–57.
44. Cited in Geldermann, 'Shanghai a City of Immigrants', p.55.
45. Kranzler, *Japanese, Nazis and Jews*, pp.268–72; a translation of the Japanese summary of this meeting is on p.609. Because our understanding of what transpired at this meeting comes from this Japanese source, and the Japanese were especially interested that they not be given responsibility for creating restrictions, it is not credible evidence that Sassoon and Hayim argued in favor of restrictions. The preface of the later 'Joint Report of Investigations on Jewish Problems' of 7 July offers a version of how the key 25 May meeting came about which might indicate more Japanese initiative: 'First they successfully approached the leading characters among the Jewish people in Shanghai. Subsequently, when they grasped a general picture of the Jewish situation in Shanghai, they mapped out a plan on the disposition of future Jewish refugees.' This 'Joint Report' is excerpted in Kranzler, *Japanese, Nazis and Jews*, pp.269–70.
46. Krebs, 'Antisemitismus und Judenpolitik der Japaner', p.67.
47. Kranzler, *Japanese, Nazis and Jews*, pp.271–72; Freyeisen, *Politik des Dritten Reiches*, p.421.
48. Letter of Italian Consul General, Brigidi, to Senior Consul Scheel of Denmark, 16.8.1939; letter of Portuguese Consul General, Alves, to Senior Consul Scheel of Denmark, 18.8.1939; letter of Bracklo to SMC, 14.8.1939; all BABL R9208/2330. No other direct evidence from the Baghdadi elite is available.
49. Letter of Komor to Hayim, 15.8.1939, BABL R9208/2330.
50. Kranzler, *Japanese, Nazis and Jews*, pp.272–73, 279 n. 31.
51. Ross, *Escape to Shanghai*, pp.104–5, says that 460 more arrived by early 1940. The *Shanghai Jewish Chronicle*, 6 March 1940, reported that the impending arrival of the Italian 'Conte Rosso' with 150 Jewish refugees would be the first mass arrival since the new regulations.
52. 'Brief aus Shanghai', *Aufbau*, 12 January 1940.
53. Kranzler, *Japanese, Nazis and Jews*, pp.273–76; Ross, *Escape to Shanghai*, p.105.
54. The difficulties are illustrated by the experiences of the Adler family. Ilse Adler reported that her grandparents sent them a landing permit for the French Concession after Italy had entered the war. It had to be used within four months. They were able to get a transit visa through the Soviet Union only after they first received a transit visa through Japan, which they got in Prague from the Japanese Consul. Then they travelled via the Trans-Siberian Railroad. See Finnane, *Far From Where?*, pp.35–36.
55. The story of Sugihara has been told a number of times in print, often with exaggerated figures of the numbers of Jews saved. An example is Hillel Levine, *In Search of Sugihara: The Elusive Japanese Diplomat Who Risked his Life to Rescue 10,000 Jews From the Holocaust*, New York 1996. Nothing extensive has yet been written about Zwartendÿk.
56. Kranzler, *Japanese, Nazis and Jews*, p.605, provides demographic statistics.

Chapter I.7

Palestine as a Destination for Jewish Immigrants and Refugees from Nazi Germany

Aviva Halamish

Palestine was one of the main destinations for Jews fleeing Nazi Germany in the 1930s. Though compared to the magnitude of the refugee crisis, the number of immigrants and refugees from Nazi-ruled countries who settled there between 1933 and 1940 was small, nonetheless, with about 60,000 immigrants, it was second only to the United States as a country of refuge.[1] The number of Jewish immigrants and refugees from Nazi Germany who found asylum in Palestine was principally determined by the policy and attitudes of Britain – the Mandatory power that ruled the country – and to a much lesser extent by those of the Zionist Organisation, which was entrusted with partial responsibility for Jewish immigration into the country. The developments in Germany were not the sole or even the main factor in shaping these policies and attitudes, which were moulded first and foremost by Britain's overall considerations and by the unique status of the Zionist Organisation and the complexity of its obligations.

To understand the role of Palestine as a destination for Jews from the Third Reich, we must first introduce the main actors in the Palestinian arena and the rules regulating immigration into the country. The article will then portray and analyse the reactions of Britain and of the Zionist Organisation to the deteriorating situation of the Jews in Germany after 1933 and in Austria after 1938 until the beginning of the Second World War. It should be borne in mind that Palestine did not constitute a typical destination for immigrants, being small, poor, lacking in natural resources, most of whose area could not be cultivated using the available methods of the time, and with a majority of its population, the Arabs, opposing Jewish immigration. On the other hand, the Yishuv (the Jewish community in Palestine) had an inherent interest in immigration. The Yishuv was an immigrant society, the majority of whose members were first generation immigrants themselves, many with relatives abroad whom they were eager to bring to Palestine. In addition, Zionist ideology had conditioned the Yishuv to adopt a favourable attitude towards further Jewish immigration into Palestine, and made it an integral component of the Zionist ethos. Ideological commitment and personal obligation towards immigration prevailed even when – at least in the short run – the flow of newcomers harmed the (Jewish) 'natives' and countered their immediate interests. Unlike other countries, where, in times of economic depression, trade unions were among the leading 'restrictionist' forces, the General Federation of Jewish Labour (Histadrut) favoured large-scale Jewish immigration even when unemployment was high.

A brief clarification regarding the use of the terms 'immigrant' and 'refugee' also needs to be made. Rules in the British Mandate regulating immigration into Palestine assumed all incoming Jews (except tourists) to be permanent 'immigrants'. A few months before the Second World War, a special quota for 'refugees' was established for the purpose of allowing persecuted Jews to enter Palestine as a final destination. From the Zionist point of view, immigration to Palestine was the ultimate realisation of Zionist ideology and every Jew was welcome to settle in Palestine no matter how he or she arrived there, with whatever motivation and for whatever reason or purpose. Once a Jew had entered Palestine, he or she was no longer considered a refugee but rather an equal member of the existing community. A more suitable term might be 'repatriate', even if the label 'refugee' conforms to international law and universal tradition. As for German Jews who moved to Palestine after Hitler's rise to power, there is no way of knowing whether the immigrant was a long-time Zionist who had intended to immigrate to Palestine at some point anyway, and the new situation only hastened his departure; or whether he had been forced out of Germany, but once he had to emigrate, Palestine was his first choice; or whether Palestine was just the most available destination and a staging post for the first opportunity to move on to another destination. Therefore, unless the reference is to a legal definition or to a case in which either the term 'immigrant' or 'refugee' is the unequivocally suitable definition, those terms are used interchangeably. Finally, the main focus of the chapter is Zionist activity in relation to the immigration of Jews from Nazi Germany to Palestine, and it is in this field that the chapter puts forward new empirical elements and interpretations. The policies, attitudes and motivations of the British and the German authorities are brought out as essential components of presenting the issue and analysing it, as well as a background to the Zionist policy.

Immigration Policy and Regulation in the Palestine Mandate

In 1922, the League of Nations entrusted Britain with 'full powers of legislation and of administration' over Palestine, and made her 'responsible for placing the country under such political, administrative and economic conditions as will secure the establishment of the Jewish national home'. At the same time, Britain proclaimed that 'for the fulfilment of this policy it is necessary that the Jewish community in Palestine should be able to increase its numbers by immigration', but went on to say that 'it is essential to ensure that the immigrants should not be a burden upon the people of Palestine as a whole, and that they should not deprive any section of the present population of their employment'.[2] From the outset, Britain detached its Palestinian policy from the situation of the Jews in Europe, and insisted that immigration to Palestine was not to be expected to supply the solution for deprived or persecuted Jews.[3]

Until 1937, immigration to Palestine was officially regulated in accordance with the economic absorptive capacity of the country. However, in the 1930s, immigration was in fact primarily governed by political rather than economic considerations.[4] The main concern of the British authorities was to ensure law and order in the country, and they were attuned to the complaints of the Arabs that Jewish immigration harmed them economically and threatened their status as the majority in the country. In 1934, when Jewish immigration grew rapidly and substantially, Britain came to the conclusion not to allow the Jews to become the majority group in the country.[5] In the second half of the decade, following the Arab Revolt that broke out in 1936 and continued until late 1939, Britain acted to maintain the existing demographic composition of Palestine (about one-third Jews and two-thirds Arabs). In July 1937, it formally abandoned the principle of economic absorptive capacity as the yardstick for Jewish immigration, replacing it with the 'political high level' principle aimed at preventing the growth of the Jewish population beyond the one-third limit. This 'political high level' principle fixed a ceiling on Jewish immigration of all types, ages and sexes, determined by political and demographic considerations, regardless of the country's economic ability to absorb immigrants. In 1937, it was set at 12,000 immigrants per year;[6] in the May 1939 White Paper, the number was raised to 15,000,[7] reflecting the rapid natural growth of the Arab population in Palestine.

Immigration regulations in the Mandate divided immigrants into four groups: Persons of independent means (Category A, 'Capitalists'); Students and persons of religious occupations whose maintenance is assured (Category B); Persons who have a definite prospect of employment (Category C, 'Labour'); Dependants of permanent residents of Palestine or of immigrants in other categories (Category D). Only category C immigrants were subject to the economic absorptive capacity principle, as the immigrants of categories A, B and D were not expected to join the labour market. Therefore, until 1937, there was no limit on the number of immigrants in these categories, and most importantly on that of persons of independent means. A special quota for 'refugees' was established only as late as May 1939.[8] Britain alone regulated the immigration of categories A, B and D, granting the Zionist Organisation partial authority over the issue of category C certificates in return for its undertaking to guarantee the maintenance of the immigrants during their first year in Palestine.

The Zionist Organisation and Its Role in Immigration to Palestine

The Zionist Organisation was founded in 1897 for the purpose of establishing an independent Jewish political entity in Palestine. It functioned as a Parliamentary Democracy, its constituency composed of all those who paid membership dues (The Zionist Shekel). Elections to the Zionist Congress (the Parliament or the legislator) were held every other year. A newly elected congress, convened only once, voted on an Executive formed by coalition agreements. The Zionist Organisation was a voluntary association lacking any attributes of a sovereign state and its leadership barely had the means to enforce its decisions.

The Zionist Organisation's limited authority over some immigration matters constituted one of the few bases of power held by its leadership. The labour certificates were the most precious resource that the Zionist Organisation controlled and could dispense among its 'citizens'. In the 1930s, the certificates were distributed first and foremost on political grounds: the various Zionist parties would make promises regarding immigration prospects and then competed in providing this benefit to their members. Prospects of receiving a labour certificate were a weighty incentive for joining the Zionist Organisation, and calculation, even speculation, as to the probability of getting one had some bearing on the decision of which party to join. To sum up, the distribution of the certificates had some effect on determining the balance of power in Zionist institutions. Furthermore, since immigration was the main source of growth for the Yishuv, distribution of the certificates also played a role in shaping its political structure.

From its inception, the Zionist organisation was caught in an inextricable tension between the devastating and oppressive conditions in which masses of Jews lived in various countries, and the limited and gradual solution that Zionism was able to offer. After the First World War, the League of Nations recognised the Zionist Organisation as the representative of the Jewish people in all matters concerning Palestine,[9] and the Mandatory power granted it limited authority to regulate some immigration matters.[10] However, the latitude in decision making that the Zionist Organisation had in general, and in immigration matters in particular, was so limited that it is doubtful whether is it appropriate to speak of Zionist immigration 'policy' in the sense of exploring alternatives and then choosing a course of action. The Zionist Organisation had no influence over the volume of immigration, and it was Britain that determined the rules of the game and always had the final say. The small number of immigration certificates given to the Zionist Executive in the two years preceding the outbreak of the Second World War made the administration of Zionist immigration policy a matter of theory and left the Zionist Organisation with almost no room to manoeuvre, to apply discretion or to offer substantial solutions to the plight of the Jews of the Third Reich. In the 1930s, the Zionist Organisation encompassed a relatively small proportion of the Jewish people, and it neither considered itself, nor was it regarded by most Jews, as representing the interests of the entire Jewish people. Consequently, it was not held solely responsible for the fate of the Jewish people, nor was it expected to provide an overall solution to the refugee crisis.

The Reaction of Britain, the Mandatory Power, to the Refugee Crisis 1933–1939

From 1933 on, Britain granted Jews from Germany (and in 1938–9 from Austria as well) a preferential status in immigration into Palestine. On almost every schedule of type C certificates (published twice a year), the Mandate Government allotted a specific number of certificates to Germany, or directed the Zionist Executive to do so. It also allotted a certain percentage (5 to 10 per cent) of the labour schedule to male immigrants from Germany aged 36–45, while the maximum age for labour immigrants from other countries was 35. Another affirmative step in favour of German Jews was qualifying professionals from Germany who had only one year's experience to receive certificates as skilled experts, instead of the eight years demanded of candidates from other countries.

Britain did not supplement this favouritism towards German Jews with an increase in the total number of certificates, but rather made a change in the apportioning of the cake. In other words, the generosity of Britain toward German Jews in immigration to Palestine resulted in diminished immigration opportunities for Jews from other countries. This was also the case when in May 1939 the MacDonald White Paper set up a special quota for refugees. First, Britain decided that in the following five years, 75,000 Jews would be allowed to enter Palestine, 'a rate which ... will bring the Jewish population up to approximately one third of the total population of the country', and then it announced that:

> [T]hese immigrants [will] ... be admitted as follows:
>
> For each of the next five years a quota of 10,000 Jewish immigrants will be allowed ...
>
> In addition, as a contribution towards the solution of the Jewish refugee problem, 25,000 refugees will be admitted ... special consideration being given to refugee children and dependants.[11]

The May 1939 White Paper was formulated under the shadow of an imminent world war, with the purpose of placating the Arabs in Palestine and in neighbouring countries in order to ensure their support for Britain should war break out. It was clear to the British policy makers that the most important measure that could be taken to achieve this goal was to meet the Arab demands concerning immigration.[12] However, as stated in paragraph 14 of the White Paper, an abrupt stop to further Jewish immigration into Palestine:

> would damage the whole of the financial and economic system of Palestine and thus affect adversely the interests of Arabs and Jews alike. Moreover, [it] would be unjust to the Jewish National Home. But, above all, His Majesty's Government are conscious of the present unhappy plight of large numbers of Jews who seek a refuge from certain European countries, and they believe that Palestine can and should make a further contribution to the solution of this pressing world problem.

The White Paper clearly reflects the fluctuation of the British between their various obligations and interests. Thus it also stated that 'after the period of five years no further Jewish immigration will be permitted unless the Arabs of Palestine are prepared to acquiesce in it', and went on to declare in paragraph 15 that 'His Majesty's Government are satisfied that, when the immigration over five years which is now contemplated has taken place, they will not be justified in facilitating, nor will they be under any obligation to facilitate, the further development of the Jewish National Home by immigration regardless of the wishes of the Arab population'. Shortly after that, following the outbreak of the Second World War, Britain prohibited people from Germany or from German-occupied territory from entering Palestine, and thus the effect of the refugee clause almost totally lapsed.[13]

The Zionist Reaction to the German Crisis

The German crisis of 1933 placed the Zionist Organisation in an unprecedented situation. For the first time in history, an entire Jewish community was confronted with aggressive antisemitism when hardly any immigration destinations were available. The crisis put Zionism to the test, and Zionist leaders were concerned lest their failure to provide meaningful solutions would prove their ideology to be obsolete and their cause irrelevant. The Zionist response to the German crisis evolved as a series of reactions to the unpredictable but constant changes in the German policy towards the Jews.[14] Zionist leaders were puzzled as periods of intensive persecution were followed by interludes of eased tension, when it seemed that the threat was over. As a rule, until November 1938, they widely conceived the situation of the Jews of Eastern Europe and particularly of Poland, as worse than that of their brethren in Germany.

From the very beginning of the crisis the Zionist Executive aspired to turn the plight of Germany's Jews into a lever for increasing Jewish immigration into Palestine. One of its first reactions was an appeal to the British High Commissioner to grant special quotas of Labour certificates for German Jews. He agreed to do so but only by taking the special allotment for German Jews from the general pool of certificates.[15] This course of action posed moral dilemmas for the Zionist Organisation, since it was a matter of a zero-sum game, and organisational difficulties as well. Membership of the Zionist Organisation or affiliation with a Zionist movement, party or association was generally a prerequisite for receiving a category C (Labour) immigration certificate. German Jews constituted a relatively small fraction of the Jewish population in Europe and an even smaller proportion of the Zionist Organisation membership. Internal political calculations, feelings of obligation towards veteran members of the Organisation in East European countries and estimations of the relative danger and distress of the various Jewish communities, all provided apparently insoluble problems for the Zionist leadership when they had to distribute the labour certificates.

From the beginning, some Zionist leaders and functionaries anticipated that granting a significant portion of the certificates to German Jews would diminish the immigration prospects of Polish Jews, a situation which in its turn would cause desperation among Jewish youth and push them into the arms of Communism.[16] At the eighteenth Zionist Congress (August 1933), the first to convene after Hitler's rise to power, one of the experts on the resettlement of German Jews, himself of German descent, warned of focusing the entire Zionist and Jewish efforts on bringing German Jews to Palestine because it would hurt potential immigrants from other countries. 'Palestine does not exist only for German Jews. ... Its gates have to be open to Jews from other countries as well'.[17]

The number of members of Zionist pioneer organisations in Germany, which served as vehicles for immigration to Palestine of young men and women under the labour schedule, grew rapidly from about 500 in April 1933 to 2,800 in May and reached 14,000 by the end of that year.[18] An emissary of the Histadrut to Germany reported mass enrolment in the pioneer organisations since Hitler's rise to power, and warned that 'the quality of this material is doubtful. ... From the Zionist point of view it is very questionable material'.[19] The term 'Hitler-Zionist' was in common use as an expression to describe what was generally conceived to be the motivation of German Jews in joining the Zionist Organisation.

Another measure that turned the plight of Germany's Jews into a lever for increasing Jewish immigration into Palestine was the establishment of numerous funds and institutions dedicated to aiding them to leave Germany and to be resettled in Palestine.[20] Monies raised by the special funds for the migration of German Jews to Palestine were earmarked, and could not be spent for any other purpose, not even for the absorption of Jews from other countries. The Zionists worried that if they did not make good use of the money, donors would divert their funds to the relocation of German Jews elsewhere.

As early as 1933, the urge to increase the number of wealthy immigrants from Germany under Category A (Persons of independent means, or 'Capitalists'), led to the signing of the so-called Ha'avara Agreements with German authorities, allowing Jews to take a larger proportion of their money and property out of Germany than the existing regulations allowed. The results of this scheme will be discussed below.

An Interlude: 1934–1935

In the summer of 1933, after the first wave of persecution against Jews in Germany had subsided, criticism over the changes in the geographical allocation of the certificates was publicly expressed. 'How come ... it is the German [Jews] who became privileged', argued a member of the Zionist Executive, known as an advocate of Polish Jews' rights in immigration.[21] In April 1935 the Histadrut resolutely demanded an increase in the number of certificates designated for members of the pioneer movements in Poland by reducing the allotment to Germany.[22] So numerous were the complaints about the favourable status given to Germany and the inequity towards other countries in the distribution of certificates that the Immigration Department of the Jewish Agency pleaded for a cessation of the protest letters or telegrams regarding the number of certificates allocated to each country. It went on to explain that its course of action had been taken because of the explicit dictate of the government to grant one-third of the certificates to immigrants from Germany.[23]

The Zionist Executive, which had actually initiated the affirmative action in favour of German Jews, eventually found itself trying to curtail the preference given them by the government. For example: in the spring of 1934, the government demanded that 50 per cent of the certificates be granted to Germany (including German refugees in neighbouring countries), while the Zionist Executive wanted to give them only 33 per cent and at most 40 per cent, claiming that at that time there were not that many qualified persons in Germany who had completed their term of training for agricultural work in Palestine, while thousands of trained young people were waiting their turn to immigrate in Austria, Czechoslovakia, Poland, and other countries.[24]

The conjuncture of an extended relatively calm period in Germany with the easing of the government requirement to grant Germany a substantial number of certificates, caused a decline in Germany's share in the labour schedules (see Table I.7.6), and it was the turn of the German Jews to complain. In May 1935, the Association of Immigrants from Germany (Hit'ahdut Oley Germania) protested the Executive's allocation of certificates for immigrants from Germany, and presented absolute and relative numbers to show that Germany's share in the labour schedules had declined from 33 per cent in 1933 to 24 per cent in 1934 and to 17.7 per cent in 1935.[25]

The Nuremberg Laws, September 1935

The reaction of the Zionist Organisation to the Nuremberg Laws of September 1935 was shaped by two concurrent developments. One was deterioration of the situation of the Jews in Poland after the death of Polish President Pilsudsky in May, and the other was the drastic reduction in the number of labour certificates (the schedule for the autumn 1935 season was 3,250 compared to 8,000 in the spring of that year). In an attempt to utilise the renewed interest in the fate of German Jews following the adoption of the Nuremberg Laws in its struggle to prevent the drastic cut in labour immigration, the Zionist Executive asked the government for an advance of 2,000 certificates, half for trained young persons who had been living for a long time in training institutions in Germany and were ready for immediate immigration. The government granted the Executive only 1,000 certificates of which 750 were given to Germany.[26] As had previously been the case, the special allotment of certificates to Germany automatically reduced the quantity given to other countries.

The preference given to German Jews was not limited to the allocation of certificates but was evident in the absorption process as well, and complaints were voiced over inequality in the treatment of new immigrants from different countries of origin.[27] The absorption of German Jews was not financed solely by the special funds earmarked for them but also by the regular Zionist budget. For instance: the British Council for German Jewry allotted one hundred pounds for every German Jew who joined an agricultural settlement in Palestine; however this amount did not cover the full cost of absorption and the Jewish Agency had to supplement it with much higher sums, taken from other parts of the Zionist budget.[28]

The *Anschluss*, March 1938

The annexation of Austria to the Reich in mid March 1938 struck a severe blow to about 182,000 Jews living in Austria, mostly of the lower-middle class, and endangered their very existence.[29] At the time of the *Anschluss* there was little the Zionist Executive could do right away, since it had only 153 certificates at its disposal (of the 8,000 allotted for all the immigration categories for the period August 1937 to March 1938). For the next six months the Executive received one thousand labour certificates, of which it gave 170 to Austria, most originally designated for other countries including Germany.[30] The Zionist leadership was well aware that this was like a drop in the ocean, but they also knew there was no chance to get special certificates for Austria, beyond the fixed general quota.[31] The *Anschluss* aroused feelings of emergency similar to those experienced after

Hitler's ascent to power five years earlier. However, in 1938 the situation was considerably worse than in 1933. Not only did the Jews of Austria experience in a few weeks what the Jews of Germany had gradually suffered over five years, but at that time the capability of Palestine to absorb newcomers was much lower, due to poor economic conditions and the curb on immigration imposed by Britain a few months earlier.

Since at that time immigration was not regulated on the basis of economic considerations, there was no point in trying to increase the labour schedule, and therefore the Zionists focused on the categories of immigration which were not subject, at least in the short term, to the ceiling imposed by the British Mandate authorities, mainly youth immigration (Youth Aliya) and the arrival of dependants. When dependants were again included in the total numbers, the Executive endeavoured both to have them excluded from it and to extend the definition of eligibility for this category so that it would include not only minors under 18 of age and elderly parents over 55, but also, in the case of Austria, brothers and sisters. Additionally, the President of the Zionist Organisation, Chaim Weizmann, tried to convince the British government to issue 1,000 special immigration certificates for Austrian Jews; 400 for refugees based on the readiness of agricultural settlements to cover their maintenance and to employ them; 300 for members of pioneer organisations whose absorption would be financed by the Council for German Jews; 200 for experts invited by factories and manufacturers; and 100 for persecuted Zionists.[32]

Very little materialised from those efforts and they are depicted here not only for historical reasons but also to illustrate both the futility of the Zionist endeavours and the marginal role that Palestine could have played in solving the refugee problem, even had the British met the Zionist requests. After all, the numbers requested by the Zionists and turned down by the British were pitifully small.

The Evian Conference (6–15 July 1938)

A few days after the *Anschluss*, the American President, Franklin D. Roosevelt invited European and South American states to a conference on the issue of German refugees, assuring the participants that 'no country would be expected or asked to receive a greater number of immigrants than is permitted by its existing legislation'. The Zionist Executive was not aware of the silent Anglo-American understanding that Palestine would not be raised at the conference as a potential destination for the refugees, though they suspected this might be the case.[33] The discussion held at a meeting of the Zionist Executive prior to the Evian conference sheds light on the ideas and considerations that existed and evolved within the Zionist leadership.[34] The discussion reveals a clear awareness of the limited potential of Palestine as a destination for German Jews. Having admitted that Palestine was unable to solve the problem of the Third Reich's Jews, some members of the Executive were willing to have the

Jewish Agency be involved in non-Zionist solutions, and proposed to ask the conference to work out an agreement with Germany on the orderly exit of the Jews with some of their property over a period of ten years. One third of these would emigrate to Palestine, one third to the U.S. and the rest to other countries. Most of the members, however, insisted on limiting Jewish Agency involvement to Palestine, leaving other agencies to deal with other destinations.

The discussion also exposes the concerns about the irrelevancy of Palestine as a solution to the crisis of German Jews, not only because of the political restrictions imposed by the British and the severe economic situation, but also because of the Arab Revolt, which had then reached its peak. The chairperson of the Zionist Executive, David Ben-Gurion, phrased it thus: 'In the eyes of the world the situation in Palestine seems similar to that of Spain [afflicted by civil war]. A country experiencing riots, where bombs are thrown every day, people are killed and unemployment and economic stagnation prevail – a country like that is no place for solving the refugee question.' Knowing that Palestine could not provide a meaningful answer to the plight of the Jews of the Reich, members of the Executive worried lest the conference might totally eliminate Palestine from the list of immigration destinations, with the result that Jewish organisations would divert the contributions for aiding their refugee brethren to other countries.

The deliberations preceding the Evian conference mark the beginning of a change, which was to continue after *Kristallnacht*, towards perceiving the German crisis as being a massive refugee crisis rather than a matter of orderly immigration and, as such, calling for a whole new approach. This change of attitude was apparent in the plans contemplated to erect huge labour camps and employ newcomers in public works and private enterprises. However, most members of the Executive thought it was inconceivable to launch such a project when thousands in the country were unemployed.

The Zionist Executive also debated whether to send delegates to the Evian conference. Ben-Gurion recommended sending high-level officials, headed by the Organisation's President, Weizmann, to make sure that the conference would not detach the problem of European Jews from Palestine. When it became clear that the Jewish case would be presented before a sub-committee and not in the plenary, that the Jewish Agency would not enjoy any official status, and that its representatives would appear before the sub-committee with a similar status to that of many other Jewish delegations, Zionist officials already in Evian advised Weizmann to stay at home.[35]

In the final analysis, the Zionists had no impact on either the proceedings of the conference or its outcome. The conference, attended by delegates of twenty-nine nations and representatives of thirty-nine private organisations, made no contribution to solving the problem of Jewish refugees from the Third Reich and did not ease their plight. Palestine was not considered as a possible destination, taking the British line that economic and political reasons meant it could not be opened to refugees, and therefore that it could not be considered as a country of settlement.[36] All in all the conference realised the pessimistic predictions of the Zionists, namely that the removal of Palestine from the list of destinations would not result in opening other countries' gates to Jewish immigration.[37]

The *Kristallnacht* Pogrom of 9–10 November 1938

In a coincidence that history produces every so often, two events which dramatically influenced the Zionist immigration policy took place within two days (9–10 November 1938): The *Kristallnacht* pogrom and the release of the Woodhead Commission report stating that the partition of Palestine and the establishment of a Jewish State in part of it, which had been proposed about a year and a half before by a British Royal Commission (better known as the Peel Commission),[38] were not practical.[39] Zionist reaction to *Kristallnacht* was therefore formulated under the shadow of the disturbing change – from the Zionist point of view – of Britain's Palestine policy. The combination in *Kristallnacht* of aggressive antisemitic policy initiated by the authorities, which had been the fate of Germany's Jews in various degrees of intensity since 1933, with the physical attack on their lives and property by violent crowds acting in accordance with instructions by the authority, in a mode typical of East European countries, led the Zionist leadership to realise that the Jews of the Reich were doomed and that they had to get out of Germany and Austria, and the sooner the better. *Kristallnacht* had a decisive impact on the transformation of the Zionist approach to the German crisis from conceiving it as being an immigration issue to constituting a refugee problem requiring emergency action. The Woodhead Report was also influential in forging a line of political action linking the refugee crisis with the establishment of a Jewish State in Palestine, and ruling out other ideas that would only divert attention from Palestine as a destination for the refugees without offering other feasible alternatives.

The idea of erecting temporary camps for young people from Germany financed by the Jewish people that had been raised prior to the Evian conference by junior members of the Zionist establishment was now expressed by the chairperson of the Zionist Executive himself: 'We will put up camps for hundreds of thousands. They will be better off here than in detention camps in Germany, and the Jewish people will take care of them after they get to Palestine'.[40] The feeling of emergency brought to the fore other, non-Zionist ideas. Werner (David) Senator, a representative of the non-Zionist wing of the Jewish Agency, put it bluntly: 'Since I do not see the likelihood of rescuing the Jewish people in Palestine alone, I cannot reject proposals aimed at rescuing some of the people in other countries'.[41] But the unequivocal stand of the two prominent Zionist leaders – Ben-Gurion and Weizmann – was to focus exclusively on solutions connected to Palestine.

There was an obvious discrepancy between the Zionists' lofty public declarations and the modest actual plans they proposed. For instance, in late 1938, the Zionists demanded that 100,000 Jews from Germany be allowed to enter Palestine,[42] while in concrete negotiations the numbers added up to less than a quarter of this figure (22,500).[43] Moreover, a comparison of the solutions that Palestine was able to provide to the grandiose plans of the British Council for German Jewry may help to illustrate how modest the former were. In mid November 1938, when members of the Council asked the British Prime Minister that Britain take part in financing the emigration of 300,000 German Jews to various destinations, Weizmann asked him to open the gates of Palestine – in spite of the severe economic situation there – to 6,000 youngsters detained in concentration camps and 1,500 children, to be absorbed by monies of the British Council for German Jewry.[44] The National Council (ha-Va'ad ha'Le'umi) announced that the Yishuv would absorb 5,000 children from Germany in foster families and educational institutions, expecting, in this case as well, that world Jewry would shoulder the financing of the rescue operation.[45] A few days later the number was doubled;[46] however, both figures were more declarative than actual and the project never really materialised.[47]

At the same time Britain announced its intention to grant entrance to child refugees, whose maintenance would be financed either by their relatives or by other financial sources.[48] In reaction to this proposal Ben-Gurion made on 7 December 1938 a statement that turned out to be one of his most frequently cited quotations:

> The demand to bring to Palestine children from Germany does not originate in our case only from feeling of pity for those children. Were I to know that all Germany's [Jewish] children could be rescued by bringing them over to England, and only half by transporting them to Palestine, I would opt for the latter, because our concern is not only the personal interests of these children, but the historic interest of the Jewish people.[49]

When this contentious saying was made, the Jewish Agency presented the demand to let the children enter Palestine as an ultimate condition for its participation in a conference Britain was about to convene to deal with the future of Palestine. The British pretext for refusing the arrival of the children to Palestine was that it would cause Arab boycott of the conference, and an infuriated Ben-Gurion said at the same meeting, that 'even immigration of children is subject to the good grace of the Arabs'.[50] Britain's policy on Palestine in general and its immigration policy in particular were conceived by Ben-Gurion and other Zionist leaders as meant to placate the Arabs in Palestine and neighbouring countries and was depicted as component of the appeasement policy towards Nazi Germany prevailing at the time, especially after the Munich Agreement of September 1938. To put this controversial saying in context, it should also be noted that the word 'rescue' was not charged at the time with the fateful meanings of life and death it received during the Holocaust.[51]

The fate of Ben-Gurion's controversial stand in the matter of rescuing the children from Germany was similar to that of the Zionist position regarding the Evian conference: neither had an impact on the path of history, one way or the other. Nevertheless both have been subject to endless discussions and accusations and are often carelessly used as anti-Zionist ammunition.[52] For instance, a book criticizing the Zionist policy during the Holocaust counts the Zionist stand at the Evian conference as one of 'the mistakes made by the Zionist movement during the Holocaust', deploring Zionism for having 'crucial influence in determining the course events took' in that conference.[53] Ben-Gurion's remark regarding the transfer of children was presented in another book as an example of Zionist betrayal of German Jewry, of Zionism turning its back on them.[54] Other scholars blame the accusers of Ben-Gurion and of Zionism of manipulative and insincere use of the quotation, though their own arguments in defending Ben-Gurion tend to be somewhat apologetic. But even those scholars, who do analyse the remark in its historical context, do not refrain from labelling it 'unfortunate', 'brutal', 'stark' or 'bold'.[55]

Attempts to Increase the Flow of German Jews to Palestine

Encountering the German crisis generated some creative ideas and intensified some modes of operation that had already existed before, all intended to increase the flow of German Jews to Palestine beyond the limited quotas of the labour schedules. This was done either in cooperation with the relevant Governments – the German and the British – or illegally.

The Ha'avara Transfer Agreements[56]

In 1931, at the height of the world economic crisis, the German Government introduced the Reich Flight Tax, aimed to prevent the flight of capital abroad.[57] Whoever wished to leave the country or to transfer money to other countries, though relinquishing a considerable portion of his assets, could do so. At the turn of 1933–4, money could be taken out of Germany by handing over 23 per cent of its value; in 1936 the loss of value reached 70 per cent and in 1939 until the outbreak of the war, it reached 95 per cent.[58] Wishing to get the utmost number of Jews out of Germany, the Nazi Government granted Palestine special status, allowing those emigrating there to take with them the minimum of £1,000 sterling required for the 'Capitalist' visa (category A) with almost no financial loss.[59] On 1 January 1935 the Germans limited the number of the people entitled to do so to only twenty per month,[60] and in April 1936 the special status was cancelled altogether.[61]

In 1933 Zionist institutions signed a series of agreements with the German Government intended to facilitate the accelerated transfer of Jewish property from Germany to Palestine (the Ha'avara Transfer Agreements). From the outset the Ha'avara was aimed at wealthy Jews who did not wish to leave a considerable portion of their property behind in Germany, as those who were willing to take only £1,000 sterling could have done so anyway in the first years of Nazi rule.[62] The initial Ha'avara Agreements set two channels of transferring money to Palestine. 'Account A' was destined for transferring money by immigrants. The potential immigrant deposited Reichsmarks in a special account in Germany used for the purchase of German goods to be exported to Palestine. After the goods were sold in Palestine, the Ha'avara company refunded the immigrant in Palestine, paying him in Palestine pounds, minus a commission.[63] 'Account B', opened at the request of the Jewish side, was intended to transfer money by Jews who wanted to invest in Palestine while remaining, at least for the time being, in Germany. Strange as it may sound, in the years from 1933 until late 1935 Palestine was an island of economic prosperity in a world struck by economic depression, and was considered an attractive destination for investment. 'Account B' was also intended for transferring contributions to Zionist funds.[64]

The changes Germany made in the Ha'avara Agreements and the more severe rules it applied on exporting foreign currency, on one hand, and the limited ability of the Jewish market in Palestine to absorb German products on the other, caused a bottleneck in the Ha'avara pipeline. The amount of money deposited in the special accounts in Germany far exceeded the demand for German goods in Palestine, and the waiting line of potential immigrants grew longer and longer. In the second half of 1935 there were over 1,000 people on the waiting list,[65] and in November the number rose to 1,300.[66] In order to accelerate Jewish emigration by speeding up the use of the monies in 'Account A', the Germans blocked 'Account B' in April 1936, and the Ha'avara stopped being used as a vehicle for transferring monies other than that of immigrants. Nevertheless, at the end of August 1938 there was a total amount of about RM 83 million deposited in the Ha'avara account whereas in that entire year only RM19 million had been approved for transfer.[67]

In the first two years of its operation, the Ha'avara served mainly the following purposes: transferring money of wealthy immigrants who wished to bring substantial amounts of money to Palestine, well above the minimal £1,000 sterling; transferring investments of wealthy Jews who remained in Germany; and transferring contributions to Zionist funds and investments in private and public companies. After the Germans limited the number of Jews entitled to take out of the country the £1,000 sterling needed for the category A visa with no loss of money to only twenty a month (at the beginning of 1935), the Ha'avara became virtually the only avenue of immigration for wealthy German Jews to Palestine. This amendment of policy generated a change in the composition of Ha'avara users, increasing the absolute and relative numbers of those using it to transfer the minimal amount of money needed for immigration as a person of independent means.

In the early phases of the Ha'avara Agreement a decisive factor in motivating the German authorities to give preference to emigration to Palestine was the fear of a reduced level of German exports due to a world-wide boycott of German goods. They found the Ha'avara particularly attractive since it served their goal of pushing Jews out of Germany while it could also be utilised to promote another goal, that of increasing German exports to Palestine and the Middle East. A circular issued by the Ministry of Economics in August 1933 stated clearly that the agreement was concluded 'in order to promote the emigration of German Jews to Palestine through the allocation of the necessary amounts without excessive strain on the currency holdings of the Reichsbank, and at the same time to increase German exports to Palestine'.[68] Four years later the Nazis still found the Ha'avara to be 'the cheapest way – in respect to foreign exchange – to facilitate Jewish emigration'.[69] However, in later phases, the crucial factor in giving continued preference to emigration to Palestine was the diminishing availability of destinations allowing the immigration of German Jews. The Nazis wanted the Jews out of the country, and Palestine, even given the restrictions of the Mandate government, appeared to be almost the only country open for organised large-scale absorption of Jewish immigrants, with the Zionist Organisation being the only Jewish organ capable of implementing and spurring emigration on such scale to Palestine. However, by the end of 1938, after *Kristallnacht*, it was clear to the Nazis that the Jews were sufficiently motivated to emigrate that they would do so even if they had to leave their possessions behind, and thus there was no longer need to promote Jewish emigration to Palestine (and elsewhere) by easing and facilitating the transfer of assets.[70]

All in all the Ha'avara served as vehicle for transferring £8,100,000 (Palestine sterling) from Germany to Palestine.[71] This was equivalent to RM140 million, which constituted only about 1–1.5 per cent of Jewish property in Germany.[72] Only 30 per cent of the Ha'avara monies (about £2.5 million Palestine sterling) were used to cover the £1,000 needed for category A visas,[73] bringing the number of immigrants who got their visas through this arrangement, and could not have acquired them in any other way, to about 2,500. An immigrant coming to Palestine with category A visa brought along with him, on average, slightly over one dependant,[74] thus the Ha'avara directly facilitated the immigration to Palestine of about 5,000 Jews from the Third Reich, mostly from Germany. The advantages of the Ha'avara were, however, even more profound. The money brought in by category A immigrants, in particular by those who brought in sums well above the minimum; and the money invested in public and private companies and enterprises, as well as contributions to the Zionist funds, all contributed to the development of the Jewish economy in Palestine, increased its absorptive capacity and thus, directly and indirectly, facilitated the immigration to Palestine of thousands of more Jews from Germany and other countries.

Though fully aware of the economic potential of the Ha'avara, the Zionist Organisation was at first hesitant about conducting direct and open negotiations with the Nazi authorities, out of concern about the negative reaction of Zionist, Jewish and world public opinion at a time when Jewish and other organisations were advocating the boycott of German products.[75] Therefore, in the first two years, negotiations on the Jewish side were mainly conducted by representatives of private enterprises, by semi-official Zionist delegates and by the Anglo-Palestine Bank. Only in 1935, after the situation of Germany's Jews had deteriorated and more severe obstacles were placed on exporting foreign currency, did the Zionist Organisation openly deal with the Ha'avara and officially adopt it and put it under the supervision of the Zionist Executive.[76] In this way, the Ha'avara also strengthened the Zionist Organisation's control over the flow of money to Palestine and rendered it more influential as to how it was invested.[77]

Youth Immigration (Youth Aliya)

Youth Aliya, the organized immigration to Palestine of Jewish teenagers, first from Nazi Germany and then from other countries, was founded in 1933 and its first group arrived in Palestine in February 1934.[78] Financed by the Zionist Organisation and other Jewish funds, Youth Aliya entailed preparing teenagers in Germany to live in Palestine by teaching them Hebrew, Jewish studies and Zionist history, literature and songs, and training them for agricultural work; secured their visas and transportation to Palestine; and ensured their education in Jewish agricultural settlements, mostly kibbutzim (communal settlements) and in boarding schools. Some 5,000 Youth Aliya teenagers came to Palestine before the Second World War.

Most Youth Aliya youngsters came from Germany for three main reasons. The emergency situation in Germany prompted parents to send their children on their own to a distant Asiatic country. Next, a large proportion of the funds financing the project were earmarked only for the absorption of German youth. And finally, Britain made it implicitly clear to the Zionist Organisation that Youth Aliya should be limited to candidates from Germany (and from March 1938 to Austria as well), otherwise this type of immigration would also be put under the quota system.[79]

Youth Aliya's immigrants, aged from 14 to 17, came under Category B, which was not subject to quotas or numerical restrictions, thus leading to a net increase in the number of immigrants to Palestine. However when the first youngsters graduated from educational programs and were about to join the labour market in 1936, the government included their number in the calculation of the economic absorptive capacity of the country, so eventually, the Youth Aliya immigrants from Germany did affect the number of permits issued under the labour schedules.[80]

Another project, similar in some respects to Youth Aliya but on a much smaller scale, was 'Training in Palestine', initiated in 1936 by Sir Herbert Samuel, the first British High Commissioner for Palestine. The idea was that since it had become more and more difficult to run training programs in Germany, young people would be brought to Palestine, beyond the labour quota, for the purpose of training them there for agricultural work. The Council for German Jewry financed the maintenance and training of the newcomers in their first year in Palestine, but once they joined the labour market, the number of participants, 200, was deducted from the labour schedule.[81]

After the *Anschluss*, the Zionist Organisation asked that in the case of Austria the age ceiling for eligibility to Youth Aliya be raised in order to bring to Palestine 800 youngsters over the age of 18 outside of the labour quota to be trained for agricultural work.[82] Like many other efforts and experiments, this one too was futile, exemplifying once again how ineffectual and frustrating the activity of the Zionist Organisation was in the face of the accelerating German crisis, and how modest even their unfulfilled plans were.

Illegal Immigration

From 1932 on, the demand for immigration to Palestine exceeded the supply of labour certificates. This situation not only generated competition over the certificates but also increased the volume of illegal immigrants into Palestine. Illegal immigration existed from the very beginning of the Mandate period, carried out through three main methods: smuggling immigrants across land and sea borders, entering Palestine as tourists and remaining in the country after the tourist visa had expired, and fictitious marriage. At the beginning of the 1930s, organized illegal immigration of 'tourists' was added, and in 1934 the first ships carrying illegal immigrants approached the shores of Palestine, a method fully-developed several years later. All in all, more than 20,000 immigrants attempted to make their way to Palestine on illegal ships in the years 1937–9. Some of these were intercepted, but others did manage to put their passengers ashore.[83]

Until 1937, German Jews seldom used these methods, as the legal routes were more available for them than for Jews from other countries. However, in 1937, when the total number of immigrants was drastically reduced and the number of immigrants of independent means (category A) allowed to enter Palestine also lessened, a new method was soon to develop: wealthy Jews from Germany entered Palestine with a tourist visa and after a while applied for permanent residency as category A immigrants. This practice became widespread after *Kristallnacht*, when the demand for type A certificates much exceeded the supply. As a rule, tourists wishing to register as permanent residents had to leave Palestine, return to their country of origin and apply there for the visa. Until the spring of 1939 tourists from the Third Reich and Italy, considered 'countries of persecution', were exempt from this demand.[84] In June 1939 the government applied the rule to all, with no exceptions, notifying the Jewish Agency that people already in Palestine would be legalized but no new applications would be handled.[85] On the eve of the war, the government announced that its Immigration Department would not register any more tourists as immigrants.[86] The new regulations meant that Jews from the Third Reich who entered Palestine without an immigrant visa could not get one at all, as returning to their countries of origin was out of the question, certainly after war broke out.

In the last year before the war (after *Kristallnacht*), illegal immigrants from Germany and Austria (and after March 1939 from Czechoslovakia as well) were, for all practical purposes, refugees, as was the case with many of the legal immigrants arriving from those countries. The adjective 'legal' or 'illegal' refers to whether they possessed a legal visa to enter Palestine, but all were fleeing their country of origin not of their own free will and were stripped of almost all their property and financial means. Well-to-do people, who had no way of getting their money out of Germany and no legal permit to enter Palestine used the last of their resources to get on rickety boats and begin a dangerous voyage across the Mediterranean Sea to enter Palestine clandestinely.

In 1937–8 the British authorities were not yet prepared to block the ships loaded with illegal immigrants and they did not intercept even one. In 1939 many ships were captured and their passengers either detained in Palestine or deported. Another measure employed by the government was the deduction of the number of illegal immigrants, either accurate or assumed, from the immigration quotas. In the Spring of 1939, the government deducted the number of illegal immigrants not only from the yearly quota of 10,000 immigrants fixed by the MacDonald white paper but also from the refugee quota (of 25,000 for the next five years), claiming that some of the illegal immigrants came from countries for which that quota was originally intended. The government informed the Zionist Executive that its records showed that the number of illegal immigrants was even higher but for lack of hard evidence it only deducted 1,300 certificates. It warned the Executive that should illegal immigration continue at the same pace, the government would consider giving no certificates at all either to immigrants or to refugees for the season beginning October 31.[87] In July 1939 it carried out the warning,[88] and in fifteen of the first thirty-nine months of the war the Mandate Government did not issue any schedules for legal immigration,[89] while emigration of Jews from the Reich and from certain occupied areas was not only possible, but also favoured, encouraged and promoted by the Germans. Only in late October 1941 was emigration of Jews from the Reich banned by the Nazi regime.[90] Due to the immigration policy pursued by the British in Palestine, including prohibiting people from Germany or from German-occupied territory from entering Palestine (mentioned above) in those crucial months, the only possible way for Jews from the Reich to enter Palestine was through illegal immigration.

From 1938 until early 1941 Nazi officials and Jewish individuals representing various elements of Zionism (and sometimes themselves) had contacts whose aim was to further Jewish emigration from the Reich and immigration into Palestine.[91] The most prominent person involved in those contacts from the German side was Adolf Eichmann, who arrived in Vienna in March 1938 as the Gestapo delegate in charge of emigrating Jews, and established there the Central Office for Jewish Emigration in August. From then onwards, both before and after *Kristallnacht*, various organisers of illegal immigration to Palestine – either affiliated with the Zionist organisation, belonging to the dissenting Revisionist Party or private organisers – turned to Eichmann's office in Vienna for assistance in getting Jews out through neighbouring states to a port where they could board boats taking them clandestinely to Palestine. It was only the Gestapo that could, and was willing to help, with all the technical, financial and bureaucratic red tape involved in such complex operations. In addition to providing Jews exit permits against the surrender of all their property, Eichmann's Central Office in Vienna assisted in releasing from concentration camps individuals who were promised to have places on illegal immigration transports heading to Palestine. At the beginning of 1939 a Central Office was established in Berlin and Eichmann soon became responsible for Jewish immigration from the whole Reich. In this capacity he had contacts with the various organisers of illegal immigration mentioned above, but they did not lead to any actual transports taking place.

In early 1939 Eichmann, probably in order to weaken the Zionists, nominated his own Jewish agent to coordinate illegal immigration matters, and a year later he nominated him to be the sole agent in charge of Jewish immigration, both legal and illegal. The coordinator, Berthold Storfer, had become active in Jewish affairs only after the *Anschluss*, and in his role as member of the Austrian Jewish leadership he had contacts with Eichmann with the aim of facilitating more Jewish emigration. Zionist emissaries in the Reich were reluctant to cooperate with Storfer, whom they considered a traitor collaborating with the devil. Storfer's ventures were funded to a great extent by the American Jewish Joint Distribution Committee (AJDC), a non-Zionist organisation. His plans to send illegal ships to Palestine did not materialise before the war, and it was exactly a year after the war broke out that about 3,600 refugees left Vienna and Bratislava (Slovakia) on their way to Palestine on a transport he had organised. They arrived in Palestine on three boats in late November 1940, but were not allowed into the country. The British announced they would be deported to Mauritius, an island in the Indian Ocean and never will be permitted to enter Palestine. The passengers of two boats were already transferred to a deportation ship, *Patria*, when the Haganah, the military arm of the Yishuv, blew it up in what had been planned to be a limited scale sabotage intended only to disable the ship from sailing to Mauritius. Close to three hundred people died, and those who survived the sunken ship were allowed to remain in Palestine. The approximately 1,600 passengers of the third boat were deported to Mauritius and brought back to Palestine only after the war was over.[92]

The purpose of organised illegal immigration in 1938–9 was not limited to the rescue of Jews fleeing from Nazi ruled areas but also to serve as a component of Zionist policy. The arrival of the ships and the protest activity of the Yishuv over the detention and deportation of the immigrants aimed at mass communication, public opinion and policy makers, with the ultimate purpose of creating a linkage between the solution to the problem of Jewish refugees in Europe and the establishment of a Jewish state in Palestine. Neither aim – the humanitarian nor the political – was achieved by the time the Second World War broke out.

Conclusions

Three cardinal factors were involved in turning Palestine into one of the major destinations for immigrants and refugees from Nazi Germany – British policy, Jewish philanthropy, and Zionist activity, each having an inconsistent impact on the final outcome. The basic, and negative, feature of Britain's role was its restrictive immigration policy, particularly from 1937 on. Next in importance, and a positive feature, was the preference that Britain gave to German Jews in immigration to Palestine over their brethren from other countries. However, negatively again, Britain never devised special allotments for German Jews beyond the regular quotas, and from the end of 1935, when the situation of the Jews in Germany steadily worsened, Britain consistently cut down on the overall number of Jewish immigrants allowed to enter Palestine and reduced the special benefits granted to German Jews.

Jewish organisations and individuals launched philanthropic campaigns to assist the immigration and resettlement of German Jews more than for other Jewish communities before and during the German crisis. They did so, to a large extent, because they felt more akin to German Jews than to other distressed Jewish communities in terms of their lifestyle and status in the general community. To put it in familial phrasing, our rich cousin, the post-Emancipation, educated and affluent German Jew who suddenly became ill, deserved better treatment than our poor and chronically ill cousin (the Polish Jew).[93] Contributions for the relocation of German immigrants in Palestine were destined for them only, and, combined with the affirmative policy of the Mandate Government, their chances both to get certificates and to be properly resettled were much greater than of Jews from other countries. In 1936, a German Jew's chances of receiving a certificate were four times greater than those of a Polish Jew (see Table I.7.5).

The good will of the Zionist Organisation towards immigrants was fundamental, not only as an act of national solidarity but also as a means to increase the Jewish population of Palestine as a step in achieving sovereignty. However, more than anything else, Zionist activity regarding the German crisis was a reaction to and the result of the first two factors – British dictates and Jewish philanthropic preferences. The Zionist Organisation's receptive attitude towards immigrants from Germany was curtailed by considerations stemming from its accountability to its members in other countries and concern for other Jewish communities in distress as well as by the raison d'être of its very existence as an organisation. The Zionist Executive was walking a narrow path. On the one hand it needed to continue helping German Jews because, among other factors, the flow of money into Palestine was dependent on the continuation of immigration from Germany. On the other hand, it had to be loyal to its members in countries with larger Zionist constituencies. Decision making was even more difficult because conflicting data and predictions ruled out a rational evaluation of the relative danger facing the various European Jewish communities.

Until 1938 the tension between the Zionists and other Jewish organisations focused on matters of fund raising and distribution. At the Evian conference there was a dispute over the question of who should present the Jewish cause and who should represent the Jews. Later on, after *Kristallnacht*, the Zionists were worried that ideas for solving the German refugee crisis, other than Palestine, would only divert attention from Palestine without suggesting feasible alternatives. Though the Jewish front was divided, it is difficult to point to the negative impact this had on the flow of German Jews to Palestine in particular, or on the handling of the crisis in general.

Finally, let the figures again speak for themselves. The Jewish population of Palestine at the beginning of the German crisis was approximately 200,000 and reached about 450,000 at the outbreak of the Second World War. In about seven years, the Yishuv absorbed almost 60,000 Jews from the Third Reich. Without going into the detailed annual ratio of immigrants from Germany, it is sufficient to conclude that Palestine, which was second only to the United States in the absolute number of immigrants from Germany, was by far the first in terms of German Jewish immigrants and refugees in proportion to its existing population.

Tables

General note to the tables: The figures in the following tables are based on official Government data, which does not include unregistered illegal immigrants.

Table I.7.1: Palestine's Contribution to the Absorption of Jewish Immigrants (1932–1939)

Year	Total Jewish migration	Immigration into Palestine	
		Total *	% of total Jewish migration
1932	20,683	9,553	46.2
1933	71,095	30,327	42.7
1934	61,384	42,359	69.1
1935	78,021	61,854	79.3
1936	55,300	29,727	53.8
1937	35,143	10,536	30.0
1938	54,534	12,868	23.6
1939	96,000 **	27,561	28.7

* Official (government) figures
** In round figures

Source: David Gurevich and Aaron Gertz, *Statistical Handbook of Jewish Palestine 1947*, Jerusalem: Department of Statistics, The Jewish Agency for Palestine, 1947, p.116.

Table I.7.2: Jewish Immigration to Palestine, 1932–1938 (from selected countries)

Year	Germany and Austria*	Czechoslovakia	Poland	Total no. of immigrants to Palestine
1932	334	88	3,299	9,553
1933	6,515	380	13,251	30,327
1934	8,885	858	17,723	42,359
1935	7,277	1,415	33,204	61,854
1936	7,468	505	14,210	29,727
1937	3,328	181	4,449	10,536
1938	5,154	421	4,986	12,868
1939	8,114	1,648	4,082	27,561

* including refugees in neighbouring countries.

Sources: Moshe Sikron, *Ha-Aliya l'Israel 1948–1953: Tosefet Statistit*, Jerusalem: Central Bureau of Statistics, 1957, p.7, Table 10A; various government reports.

Palestine as a Destination for Jewish Immigrants

Table I.7.3: Percentage of Immigrants from Germany in Jewish Immigration to Palestine, 1932–1938

Percentage	Year
3.7	1932
18	1933
16	1934
11	1935
27	1936
34	1937
52 *	1938

Sources: My calculations, based on: Great Britain, Colonial Office, *Report by His Majesty's Government in the United Kingdom of Great Britain and Northern Ireland to the Council of the League of Nations on the Administration of Palestine and Trans-Jordan, 1932–1938.*

No report was submitted for 1939.

* Including Austria

Table I.7.4: Summary of Jewish Immigration into Palestine, 1932–1938 (from selected countries)

Total number of immigrants = 197,236

Country	Number	Percentage
Poland	91,122	46.2
Germany	34,768	17.6
Austria	4,193	2.1
Czechoslovakia	3,848	1.95

Sources: Figures – Sikron, *Ha-Aliya l'Israel 1948–1953*, p.6, Table 8A; percentages – my calculations (which are somewhat different from ibid., p.7, Table 9A).

Table I.7.5: Comparison of Immigration into Palestine from Germany and Poland, 1936

Category	No. of immigrants		No. of immigrants per 10,000 Jews *	
	Germany	Poland	Germany	Poland
Capitalists A	2,985	722	75	3
Labour C	2,386	4,488	59	14
Other categories	2,809	6,386	70	20
Total	8,180	11,596	204	37

* The calculations are based on the estimated number of Jews in the respective countries in 1936: Germany – 400,000; Poland – 3,150,000.

Note: Only the line 'Labour C' reflects Zionist immigration policy. The figures here are the number of persons arriving in Palestine (certificate-holders and their dependants). By isolating the number of certificates allotted to each country, the outcome is as follows: 8 certificates per 10,000 Jews in Poland compared to 45 certificates per 10,000 Jews in Germany.

Source: Halamish, *Mediniyut ha-Aliya*, p.275.

Table I.7.6: Germany's Share in Labour Certificates, 1933–1937

Period	Total Number of certificates	Number of certificates for Germany	Percentage of certificates to Germany
April–Sept. 1933	5,500	1,300	24
Oct. 1933–March 1934	5,500	1,741	32
April–Sept. 1934	6,800	2,093	31
Oct. 1934–March 1935	7,500	1,361	18
April–Sept. 1935	7,600	1,350	18
Oct. 1935–March 1936	3,250	874	27
April–Sept. 1936	4,500	1,473	33
Oct. 1936–March 1937	1,300	295	23

Source: Halamish, *Mediniyut ha-Aliya*, pp.415–21.

Notes

1. Aviva Halamish, 'Refugees', in *Holocaust Encyclopedia*, ed. Walter Laqueur, New Haven 2000, p.522; see also Tables 1 and 2.
2. The Council of the League of Nations, 'The Palestine Mandate', 24 July 1922, articles 1 and 2.
3. G. Sheffer, 'Political Considerations in Determining Britain's Policy on Immigration of Jews to Palestine' [Hebrew], *Ha-Tziyonut* 5, 1978, pp.182–226.
4. Aviva Halamish, 'Immigration According to the Economic Absorptive Capacity: The Guiding Principles, the Implementation and the Demographic Ramifications of the British and the Zionist Immigration Policy in Palestine between the World Wars' [Hebrew], in *Iyunim bi-Tkumat Israel / Thematic Series: Economy and Society in Mandatory Palestine 1918–1948*, ed. A. Bareli and N. Karlinsky, Sde Boker 2003, pp.179–216.
5. Cabinet 14 (34), 11.4.1934, PRO Cab. 23/78; 'Some Factors in Our Present Immigration Policy', signed: Arthur Wauchope, C.P. 209 (34), PRO Cab 24/250 [August 1934].
6. Cmd. 5513. Great Britain, Colonial Office, *Palestine: Statement by His Majesty Government*, London, July 1937, par. 6.
7. Cmd. 6019. Great Britain, Colonial Office, *Palestine: Statement of Policy by His Majesty's Government*, London, 1939, par. 14 (1).
8. Cmd. 6019, par. 14 (1) [b].
9. The Council of the League of Nations, 'The Palestine Mandate', 24 July 1922, article 4. The document recognised a 'Jewish Agency' for that purpose, but stated that, 'The Zionist Organization, so long as its organization and constitution are in the opinion of the Mandatory appropriate, shall be recognized as such agency.' The Jewish Agency was established in 1929,

composed of Zionist and non-Zionist members on a parity basis. The terms 'Zionist Organisation' and 'Jewish Agency' are synonymous throughout this article.
10. M. Mossek, *Palestine Immigration Policy under Sir Herbert Samuel*, London 1987, pp.123–24.
11. Cmd. 6019, par. 14.
12. Ronald W. Zweig, 'The Palestine Problem in the Context of Colonial Policy on the Eve of the Second World War', in *Britain and the Middle East in the 1930s: Security Problems, 1935–39*, ed. Michael J. Cohen and Martin Kolinsky, London 1992, pp.206–16. On the Palestine British policy in the late 1930s see also: M.J. Cohen, *Palestine, Retreat from the Mandate: The Making of British policy, 1936–45*, New York 1978, in particular pp.66–87; and the groundbreaking book by J.C. Hurewitz, *The Struggle for Palestine*, New York 1968[1950], where the 1939 White Paper is discussed in pp.94–111.
13. Bernard Wasserstein, *Britain and the Jews of Europe 1939–1945*, Oxford 1979, pp.51–52. As a result of Zionist pressure the Colonial Office allowed persons in enemy territory who already held immigration certificates to Palestine to proceed.
14. For a comprehensive discussion of the Nazi Policy towards German Jews prior to the Second World War see S. Friedländer, *Nazi Germany and the Jews: The Years of Persecution*, New York 1997.
15. ZE meeting, 19.4.1933, CZA S/100.
16. Aviva Halamish, 'Mediniyut ha-Aliya v'ha-Kelita shel ha-Histadrut ha-Tziyonit 1931–1937', Ph.D. diss., Tel Aviv 1995, p.267.
17. A. Ruppin, S*hloshim Shnot Binyan b'Eretz-Yisrael*, Jerusalem 1937, p.270.
18. D. Frankel, *Al Pi T'hom: Ha-Mediniyut ha-Tziyonit u'She'elat Yehudey Germania 1933–1938*, Jerusalem 1994, p.132.
19. D.Ben-Gurion, *Zikhronot*, vol.1, Tel Aviv 1973, p.606.
20. For details on the various funds see A.J. Edelheit, *The Yishuv in the Shadow of the Holocaust : Zionist Politics and Rescue Aliya, 1933–1939*, Boulder1996, pp.33–40.
21. ZE meeting, 14.7.1933, CZA S/100.
22. ZE meeting, 30.4.1935, ibid.
23. 'Immigration Department Circular', no. 167, 19.6.1934, CZA S6/5361.
24. D. Ben-Gurion to E. Mills, 23.7.1934, CZA S25/2415.
25. Letters from the Association of Immigrants from Germany to the Jewish Agency Executive 5.5.1935, CZA S25/2519 and 13.5.1935, CZA S25/2482.
26. M. Shertok at a meeting of Mapai's [Jewish-Palestine Workers Party] political committee, 8.10.1935, LPA 23/35.
27. ZE meeting, 21.12.1934, CZA S/100.
28. ZE meeting, 27.12.1936, ibid.
29. The official periodical of the Zionist Organisation reported that 60,000 of Vienna's Jews were in need of food and basic supplies, 25,000 Jews in remote locations were under threat of death, many had been arrested and 30,000 Jews had applied for Hungarian citizenship. *Ha-Olam*, 24 March 1938.
30. ZE meetings 8.5.1938 and 7.6.1938, CZA S/100.
31. ZE meeting, 7.6.1938, ibid.
32. Cable from M. Shertok to Ch. Weizmann, 21.6.1938, CZA S25/2479.
33. H. Feingold, *The Politics of Rescue: The Roosevelt Administration and the Holocaust, 1938–1945*, New Brunswick 1970, p.26.
34. ZE meeting 26.6.1938, CZA S/100.

35. ZE meeting, 21.8.1938, ibid.
36. Feingold, *The Politics of Rescue*, p.33.
37. On the Evian conference in general and how it was perceived by the Germans in particular, see Y. Bauer, *Jews for Sale?: Nazi-Jewish Negotiations, 1933–1945*, New Haven 1994, pp.30–43.
38. Cmd. 5479, *Report of the Palestine Royal Commission*, Presented by the Secretary of State for the Colonies to the United Kingdom Parliament by Command of His Britannic Majesty, July 1937.
39. Cmd. 5893, Great Britain, Colonial Office, *Palestine: Statement by His Majesty Government*, London, November 1938.
40. D. Ben-Gurion at the ZE meeting, 11.12.1938, CZA S/100.
41. ZE meeting, 11.12.1938, ibid.
42. *Ha-Olam*, 4 December 1938.
43. 7,500 young people from the training institutions in Germany; 2,500 Youth Aliya teenagers; 2,500 family relatives (under category D – dependants); and 10,000 children. 'Statement by the Jewish Agency for Palestine', 22.11.1938, CZA S7/756; M. Shertok to M. MacDonald, 23.11.1938, ibid.
44. A. Sherman, *Island Refuge :Britain and Refugees from the Third Reich 1933–1939*, London 1973, pp.171–72.
45. *Davar*, 20 November 1938.
46. Yitzhak Ben-Zvi, chairperson of the National Council in a public assembly in Tel Aviv, 30 November 1938, *Davar*, 1 December 1938.
47. Frankel, *Al Pi T'hom*, p.292.
48. Sherman, *Island Refuge*, pp.178–79.
49. D. Ben-Gurion, *Zikhronot*, vol.5, Tel Aviv 1982, p.398.
50. Ben-Gurion at a meeting of Mapai's central committee, 7.12.1938, LPA 23/38 and see Shabtai Teveth, *Ben-Gurion and the Holocaust*, New York 1996, pp.47–49.
51. See Teveth, ibid; Toviyah Friling, *Hets ba-'Arafel : David Ben-Guryon, Hanhagat ha-Yishuv ve-Nisyonot Hatsalah ba-Sho'ah*, Kiryat Sedeh-Boker 1998, pp.156–57.
52. See T. Segev, *The Seventh Million : The Israelis and the Holocaust*, New York 1993, p.28.
53. S.B. Beit Zvi, *Post-Ugandan Zionism on Trial: A Study of the Factors that Caused the Mistakes Made by the Zionist Movement during the Holocaust*, vol.1, Tel-Aviv 1991, p.199.
54. L. Brenner, *Zionism in the Age of the Dictators*, Westport 1983, pp.148–50.
55. Teveth, *Ben-Gurion*, pp.47–49; idem, 'The Dark Hole' [Hebrew], *Alpayim* 10, 1994, pp.156–57; Friling, *Hets ba-'Arafel*, pp.156–57.
56. A great number of books and articles deal with the Ha'avara Transfer Agreement. For relatively update discussion and references see Edelheit, *The Yishuv in the Shadow of the Holocaust*, pp.73–92 and Halamish, 'Mediniyut ha-Aliya', p.294 note 95. For a concise summary and evaluation, see Leni Yahil, *The Holocaust : The Fate of European Jewry, 1932–1945*, New York 1990, pp.100–104. The German angel is presented in: Bauer, *Jews for Sale?*, pp.5–29; A. Barkai, *From Boycott to Annihilation: The Economic Struggle of German Jews, 1933–1943*, Hanover 1989, pp.51–53, 76, 80, 100–104, 144; F.R. Nicosia, *The Third Reich and the Palestine Question*, London 1985, pp.29–49. It should be noted that the Hebrew word for 'transfer' – *ha'avara* – was also the official term in German documents, Barkai, *From Boycott*, p.194, note 91.
57. Barkai, *From Boycott*, p.99.

58. Frankel, *Al Pi T'hom*, p.122; Barkai, *From Boycott*, p.100 presents somewhat different figures.
59. Y. Gelber, *Moledet Hadasha: Aliyat Yehudey Merkaz Eiropa u'Kelitatam 1933–1948*, Jerusalem 1990, p.153.
60. Ibid., p.168.
61. Frankel, *Al Pi T'hom*, p.122.
62. The initial Ha'avara Agreements specified that the arrangement was meant for 'Jewish emigrants who desire to build a new life in Palestine through the transfer of a portion of their assets over and above the letter of credit required by immigration authorities – 1,000 £Pal ...', Nicosia, *The Third Reich*, pp.45–46.
63. The Palestine pound was roughly equivalent in value to the pound sterling.
64. Frankel, *Al Pi T'hom*, pp.121–22.
65. Gelber, *Moledet Hadasha*, p.169.
66. ZE meeting, 11.11.1935, CZA S/100.
67. Barkai, *From Boycott*, p.144; Werner Feilchenfeld, 'Die Durchführung des Ha'avara-Transfer', in *Ha'avara-Transfer nach Palästina und Einwanderung deutscher Juden, 1933–1939*, ed. W. Feilchenfeld, D. Michaelis and L. Pinner, Tübingen 1972, pp.45 and 75.
68. Nicosia, *The Third Reich*, pp.46–47. See also Barkai, *From Boycott*, p.52 and Feilchenfeld, 'Die Durchführung des Ha'avara-Transfer', p.26.
69. German inter-governmental discussion, 18 October 1937, Barkai, *From Boycott*, pp.101–2.
70. Barkai, *From Boycott*, p.144.
71. Feilchenfeld, 'Die Durchführung des Ha'avara-Transfer', p.75.
72. Avraham Barkai, 'German Interests in the Ha'avara-Transfer Agreement 1933–1939', *LBIYB* 35, 1990, p.266.
73. Frankel, *Al Pi T'hom*, p.126.
74. Halamish, *Mediniyut ha-Aliya*, appendix V.
75. Sha'ul Esh, 'Ha-Ha'avara', *Iyunim be-Heker ha-Sho'ah ve-Yahadut Zemanenu*, Jerusalem: The Institute of Contemporary Jewry, The Hebrew University, 1973, pp.82–90.
76. Halamish, *Mediniyut ha-Aliya*, pp.295–99.
77. Ibid., p.300.
78. Yoav Gelber, 'The Origins of Youth Aliya', *Studies in Zionism* 9, no. 2, 1988, pp.142–72.
79. Aviva Halamish, 'The Double Jeopardy of Polish Jewry, 1933–1939' [Hebrew], *Divrei ha-Kongress ha-Olami ha-Ahad Asar l'Madaey ha-Yahadut*, Section B, vol. II, Jerusalem 1994, p.291.
80. Cmd. 5479, chap. X, pars. 48(5) and 58–60.
81. From G. Landauer to M. Shertok, 13.9.1936, CZA S25/2463; Gelber, *Moledet Hadasha*, pp.113–14; Halamish, *Mediniyut ha-Aliya*, Annex II, table 12.
82. From M. Shertok to Ch. Weizman, 21.6.1938, CZA S25/2479.
83. For a concise survey of illegal immigration prior to the Second World War see Dalia Ofer, *Escaping the Holocaust: Illegal Immigration to the Land of Israel, 1939–1944*, New York 1990, pp.3–20.
84. A meeting between E. Dobkin and J. Bachar (the Jewish Agency) and E. Samuel (deputy Immigration Commissioner), 1.6.1939, CZA S6/4269. The exemption was short lived. There was no need for it at all before the end of 1937 and it was only at the end of 1938 when the practice became so obvious

that some official act was really needed. The label 'country of persecution' was used for all kinds of exceptions in immigration regulation.

85. A meeting between M. Shertok and E. Dobkin (the Jewish Agency) and E. Mills, Immigration Commissioner and his deputy, E. Samuel, 9.6.1939, ibid.
86. *The Palestine Gazette*, 24 August 1939, Supplement No. 2.
87. A meeting between M. Shertok and E. Dobkin (the Jewish Agency) and E. Mills, Immigration Commissioner and his deputy, E. Samuel, 9.6.1939, ibid.
88. Wasserstein, *Britain and the Jews*, p.51.
89. Ibid., p.52.
90. Ibid., p.45; Bauer, *Jews for Sale?*, p.53.
91. Bauer, *Jews for Sale?*, pp.44–54. The chapter dealing with the contacts between the Nazis and the Zionists between 1938 and 1941 is entitled 'Enemies with a Common Interest'.
92. On Berthold Storfer's activity in organizing illegal immigration to Palestine see Ofer, *Escaping the Holocaust*; Bauer, *Jews for Sale?*, pp.50–53; Ruth Zariz, 'Berthold Storfer and His Part in Rescuing Jews from Germany' [Hebrew], in *Ha'apalah: Me'asef le-2Toldot ha-Hatsalah, ha-Berihah, ha-Ha'apalah u-She'erit ha-Pelitah*, ed. A. Shapira, Tel Aviv 1990, pp.124–42.
93. Similar phrasing was used by Chaim Arlosoroff, the head of the Jewish Agency's Political Department in a speech given in Warsaw in June 1933, *Ha-Po'el Ha-Tza'ir*, 23 June 1933.

Chapter I.8

American Refugee Policy in the 1930s*

Bat-Ami Zucker

This chapter aims to expose the contrast between America's long accepted image as a haven for the oppressed, and its apathetic attitude towards refugees from Germany, and especially Jews, desperately seeking refuge in the 1930s. For the United States the plight of many thousands of innocent refugees constituted a serious moral dilemma, as well as a test of its basic beliefs. Moreover, its restrictive refugee policy in the 1930s challenged the country's professed commitment to freedom and democracy. In fact, by denying this commitment America was effectively compromising its own raison d'etre. Thus the United States' attitude towards German refugees may serve as a test case, not only for American immigration policy, but also for a study of the role of humanitarian considerations in the political decision-making process. Essentially, an immigration policy that reflected national and international interests was faced with a situation where thousands of refugees were in search of a safe haven.

At the height of the Great Depression, with its unprecedented levels of unemployment and the country's overall mood of despondency, President Roosevelt promised in his first 'Inauguration Address', to remember the forgotten men, to revive prosperity, and to act according to American 'precious moral values'.[1] Unfortunately, Hitler's accession to power in Germany in January 1933 served to distort American global considerations. The brutal persecution of German Jews and opposition groups that followed prompted a large-scale emigration from the Reich. Although Western Europe was the preferred destination for many in 1933, a more permanent move to the United States increasingly became the most sought-after refuge as Nazism tightened it hold. For many German refugees, who were subject to physical attacks by Nazi stormtroopers, and had been gradually stripped of their civil rights by the dictatorial Nazi regime, the United States stood for freedom and democracy. The American credo, with its emphasis on providing asylum to the needy, held firm promises for liberty, safety and well-being. However, the misfortune of these refugees was the coincidence between the tragic events in Germany and grave domestic problems in the United States, together with a public opinion that was, at best, largely indifferent to international problems.

American Immigration Policy

In contrast to the years preceding the 1880s, when practically all who sought entry to the United States were welcomed,[2] the period from 1880 to 1930, though permitting entry to over twenty million immigrants, was marked by the beginning of a more restrictive immigration policy. The new immigrants, predominantly from Southern, Central and Eastern Europe, were considered so different in composition, religion and culture from earlier immigrants as to trigger a xenophobic reaction that served to generate more restrictive immigration laws.[3] An analysis of the debates in Congress on immigrants and refugees indicates that there was 'a general feeling of dissatisfaction with the newer immigrants as contrasted with the old, a belief that immigration would increase unemployment ... and depress labor standards, [as well as] a growing feeling that American social and political institutions must be protected', among other measures, by the removal of special exemptions from political and/or religious refugees.[4]

The ability of Congress to dictate a new and restrictive immigration policy was a clear indication that the tide was turning. There is no doubt that its attitude reflected the country's mood by favouring a reversal of the open-door policy on immigration. In addition to economic considerations, openly expressed racist opinions soon dominated the formulation of legislation on immigration. Nativist theories were widespread in many intellectual, scientific and political circles, and these unleashed a new torrent of interest in restrictive immigration legislation. Notwithstanding restrictionist groups,[5] Democratic and Republican Party platforms both called for effective limits on immigration. Even the liberal *New Republic* mused that unrestricted immigration was an element of nineteenth-century liberalism which was doomed to extinction and that a progressive society could not allow social ills to be aggravated by excessive immigration.[6] The widespread popularity of racist ideas[7] was also reflected in heated Congressional debates and, eventually, contributed to the decision to base attacks on immigration on 'ethnic' arguments. As a result, racial purity replaced the idea of the 'melting pot' as the ideal for American society, and traditional liberal policy was overturned in favour of avowed restrictionism.[8]

The legal basis for immigration policy was defined by two acts, which effectively overturned the traditional open-door policy and essentially closed the gates to all but a favoured few. The first was the act 'Regulating Immigration of Aliens to, and Residence of Aliens in, the United States' of 5 February 1917 that listed the basic restrictions on immigration and specified the various categories of aliens to be excluded. Previously, only those deemed mentally defective had been kept out. After 1917, however, immigrants could be excluded on grounds of physical, mental or moral defects, or for political and economic reasons. The last category, which was to have its greatest impact in the Depression decade of the 1930s, included contract labourers, unaccompanied children under sixteen, and what would turn out to be the most difficult hurdle to overcome for German refugees in the 1930s – those 'likely to become a public charge'. The 1917 act was considered the cornerstone of the new American immigration policy. It reflected the need to adapt to the economic pressures created by a changing world and was an expression of the desire to keep America free of outside influence. Although the United States emerged from the First World War as a world power, its disillusionment with the economic and political outcome of the war had an impact on both foreign and domestic policies. America in the 1920s and 1930s retreated into isolation. At home, the national mood was intensely patriotic and unity and conformity became the ideal. Conversely, the country's new position as a major world power was liable to bring a flood of undesired immigrants, and this provided the basic justification for a more restrictive policy.

With regard to immigration policy, a new system – the quota system – based on nationality seemed the logical answer to these needs. Dr Sidney Gulick first introduced the principle of allocating quotas to the various nationalities in 1914.[9] He suggested that each nationality be assigned a quota proportionate to the number of naturalised citizens and their U.S.-born children already drawn from that nationality. The 'percentage quota principle', as it became known, was soon the centrepiece of all immigration laws passed in the 1920s. The advocates of this idea, accepting in full the logic behind racial purity, differed only on the question of precisely how to distribute such quotas among the various countries of Europe. The most prominent Congressional advocates of these racial theories were in the House Committee on Immigration. Indeed, by 1921, it was stressing a racial theory as the fundamental justification for restriction. The Senate led the way with a bill designed to reduce total immigration and to change the composition of immigration. The Quota Act of 1921, which took effect in June of that year and remained in force until 30 June 1922, was designed to ensure access for immigrants from North Western Europe while restricting those from Southern, Central and Eastern Europe. Although adopted as provisional legislation, the 1921 law came to be regarded as 'the most important turning-point in American immigration policy'.[10] The act limited the number of aliens who were admitted to the United States to 3 per cent of the number of foreign-born persons of the same nationality residing in the country. Initially the quotas were based on the United States census of 1910 but this was later changed to the 1890 census. In the final debate over the bill, and the subsequent congressional battles in 1923 and 1924, the main support for the bill came from the American Federation of Labor, the American Legion, the Immigration Restriction League, the Ku Klux Klan, the Patriotic Order of the Sons of America and the Daughters of the American Revolution, which apart from the American Federation of Labor, were known for their outspoken nativist views. The major opponents of the bill included spokespersons for various Jewish, foreign-language and other ethnic groups that would be adversely affected by the 1890 base-year criterion.[11]

The Emergency Immigration Restriction Act of 1921 was the first to establish the quota system, which was weighted heavily in favour of people from North Western Europe, and set the total quota at 357,803. The central most important criterion for determining each country's quota was the foreign-born population currently in the United States according to the 1910 data which would form the base figure from which the 3 per cent quota would be established. However, it was soon realised that to take 1910 as a starting point would permit the entry of too many immigrants from Southern and Eastern Europe. The advocates of Anglo-Saxon superiority pressured Congress into passing another immigration law, the 1924 Johnson–Reed Act, lowering the quota to 2 per cent and amending the base year to 1890. This satisfied restrictionist views on racial qualities since it mostly affected the Jews, the Italians and the Slavs, all of whom the restrictionists perceived as undesirable immigrants.

The quota provision did not take effect until 1 July 1929, on account of the difficulty of arriving at a definitive basis for determining national origins. Once the formula was established, the quota system was the sole guideline for immigration policy. It was the National Origins Immigration Act of 1924 – also known as the Johnson–Reed Act or the National Origin Act – that established the permanent administrative machinery that was to shape immigration policy in the United States for decades to come. It provided for an annual limit of 150,000 on Europeans, a total ban on Japanese, the issuance of visas against set quotas by the consul abroad rather than on arrival, and the formulation of quotas based on the contribution of each nationality to the overall U.S. population, rather than on the foreign-born population. The quota allotments as finally determined in 1929 revealed as much about the racist thinking of the period as they did about the national origins of the American people in 1890 upon which they were based. 31.9 per cent of the quota was assigned to Northern and Western European countries and 54 per cent to Great Britain and Ireland alone, indicating once more its Anglo-Saxon bias. The act, no doubt, reflected a general public consensus. It passed the House by a vote of 323 to 71 and 62 to 6 in the Senate. What public opposition there was in the country at large was confined to a few 'hyphenate-American' groups, mostly from Eastern Europe, and a handful of liberals and professionals who were concerned with immigrant groups.[12]

Playing on racist prejudices and in compliance with its title, the new law did prove to be more restrictive. Whereas the 1917 Immigration Act professed to 'regulate' immigration, the Immigration Act of 1924 proclaimed that it aimed to 'limit the immigration of aliens into the United States'. It marked the final abandonment of the open-door tradition, replacing it with the 'America for Americans' concept. The conviction that racial homogeneity was essential for the national unity of the American people was to remain the fundamental principle underlying American immigration policy throughout the 1930s and 1940s.[13]

Two new factors were specified in the 1924 act. The first was the use of ethnicity as the main criteria for establishing the quota assigned to national groups eligible for immigration. The second, and no less important than the quota system, was the provision that the visa-granting process would be subject solely to the judgment of the U.S. consuls abroad. The new role of the consul to examine and decide whether the applicant was eligible for admission into the United States put him in a critical position, and burdened him with the extra responsibility of recommending the issuance of visas and for the administrative screening of immigrants prior to their entry. The previous policy, which placed the main examination of an applicant at the point of entry, was replaced by a strict examination by the U.S. consul of the candidate's moral and financial qualification at the place of application.

The assignment of exclusive responsibility for the issuance of immigration visas to the consular officer abroad had a significant impact on the balance of power between Congress and the executive bodies with regard to immigration policy. The 1924 act enabled the executive branch of the government to encroach on congressional control of immigration policy. Until 1930, Congress had enjoyed a monopoly over formulation of immigration policy but in the 1930s the roles were reversed. This trend toward executive dominance in immigration matters, initiated by President Hoover in 1930, was developed to the full under a strong-willed Department of State during the Roosevelt administration. By the end of the 1930s it was the executive, and not Congress, which in fact controlled the formulation of immigration policy.

With unemployment rising as a consequence of the economic depression, President Hoover asked the Department of State at the end of April 1930 if there were any administrative means for further reducing immigration.[14] It recommended stricter interpretation of the 'likely to become a public charge' clause of the 1917 Immigration Act (hereafter LPC). It seemed a very useful instrument for achieving by administrative means what could not be achieved through legislation. On 13 September 1930 the Department of State, on President Hoover's directive, published a further restrictive gloss on of the LPC clause:

> The consular officer ... will, before issuing a visa have to pass judgment *with particular care* on whether the applicant *may become a public charge*; and if the applicant cannot convince the officer that *it is not probable*, the visa will be refused ... If the consular officer believes that the applicant *may probably be a public charge at any* time ... he must refuse the visa.[15]

The Department then sent detailed instructions to all American diplomatic and consular officers clarifying that the object of the new policy was to '[slacken] labour immigration from all parts of the world to the United States', urging the consuls to examine each case with great care.[16]

Thus, by purely administrative means, the Department of State was able to introduce a far more restrictive policy within the existing legal framework. As the new rules laid down only broad general principles, much was left to consuls' individual discretion and to political considerations. In the 1930s, interpretation of existing legislation proved a most efficient tool for preventing the entrance of refugees without the need for legislative action. Many of the difficulties the refugees encountered could be attributed to the biases of consular officers and to red tape.[17] In 1937 Visa Division Officer John Farr Simmons notified Pierrepiont Moffat, Chief of the Division of Western European Affairs at the State Department, that those administrative measures had resulted in 'an immediate and considerable reduction in immigration'. He estimated that 'during the past seven years approximately one million aliens who might have been admitted during normal times did not enter the United States to add to the ranks of the unemployed'.[18] Because of the predominance of the executive in this sphere, it was the decisions taken by the State Department and its representatives abroad – the consuls – that had the greatest impact. The consuls were responsible for implementing the law and for putting into effect the regulations that governed the admission of immigrants. Within the bounds of both the law and public opinion, the career diplomats, and most importantly the consuls themselves, took thousands of individual decisions, the sum total of which formed the American government's policy on immigration. What seems obvious is that although the framework was fixed by legislation in Congress and by regulations issued by the Department of State, much was left to the discretion of the consul abroad. It was he, and he alone, who determined who would be admitted to the United States and who would be excluded.

Refugees and the American Immigration Policy

George Messersmith, Consul-General in Berlin and Vienna in the early 1930s, suggested to the Secretary of State the circulation of a guide to all U.S. consuls explaining that consuls should not aim 'to maintain the United States as an asylum or refuge for dissatisfied and oppressed [people] in other parts of the world', but rather and more importantly, to protect the interests of the country and the American people.[19] Indeed, whereas the asylum ideal was an American tradition, it had not been written into the immigration laws. Refugees were not distinguished from other immigrants in existing legislation with one major exception – the exemption from the illiteracy test required by law for those seeking admission to the United States.[20] All persons, including refugees, seeking entry into the United States were classified as immigrants.[21] Under the immigration laws, refugees were accorded no special treatment. They had to wait their turn under the quota and were obliged to measure up to the usual requirements for admission. Thus in spite of the grave situation in Germany and the persecution faced by certain groups – especially

Jews – the absence of special considerations for refugees and the strict examination of applicants by the consuls in the 1930s affected thousands of innocent victims of the Nazi regime.

This lack of special consideration notwithstanding, even in 1933 Assistant- Secretary of the State Department Carr found himself facing demands for the preferential treatment of refugees from Germany – and rejecting them. He pointed out that the fact that exemption from illiteracy tests was the only reference made to refugees in the immigration laws 'would indicate that Congress did not intend to make any other provision for this special class of persons'. Therefore, 'the question of asylum', he stated, 'is removed from the problem, and no action would be deemed necessary'.[22] In the case of German refugees the exemption from illiteracy tests eventually proved irrelevant. Reporting from Hamburg in 1934, the American vice-consul stated that 'German refugees ... are probably 99% literate'.[23] Aside from this, refugees continued to face the same barriers that obstructed the path of every other would-be immigrant.[24]

As refugees came under the immigration laws it is important to single out the requirements for each applicant. Immigration laws divided all aliens coming to the United States into two categories: non-immigrants and immigrants. The immigration Act of 1924 defined the following groups as non-immigrants: government officials, temporary visitors, aliens in transit, bona fide alien seamen, and aliens entering to carry out trade. All other aliens destined for the United States were defined as immigrants and were divided into two classes: non-quota immigrants and quota immigrants. Non-quota immigrants were not subject to numerical limitation. They had to qualify within one of the following six categories: (a) close relatives of American citizens, their wife/ husband and their unmarried children under twenty-one years of age; (b) returning resident aliens; (c) natives of Western-hemisphere countries, their wives and unmarried children; (d) ministers and professors, their wives and unmarried children under eighteen years of age; (e) bona fide students; and (f) American women who had lost their United States citizenship by marrying aliens. In addition to establishing their admissibility under the excluding provisions of the law, applicants for non-quota immigration visas were required to produce satisfactory proof that they were properly classified within the category before they could be granted non-quota visas.[25]

Refugees as Visitors

Among the class of non-immigrants, the category of visitors is most striking because it proves that had the United States acted differently with regard to refugees more German victims might have been saved. Since an applicant for a visitor's visa was not screened in the same scrupulous manner as were applicants for immigration, it was much easier to obtain a visa. The U.S. authorities usually accepted at face value statements that aliens were bona fide non-immigrants. In the eighteen months following

Hitler's rise to power, there was only a very slight increase in the number of applications for temporary visitors' visas from Germany. The situation, however, changed dramatically with the intensification of anti-Jewish violence in German cities in the summer of 1935 and especially after the promulgation of the Nuremberg Laws in September the same year. Victims of Nazi persecution facing the difficulties of obtaining an immigration visa looked for another way out of Germany. Applications for visitors' visas should have been easier to obtain, not least because of the middle-class backgrounds of many who sought them. However, once in the United States on visitors' visas they had to apply for a change of status, but according to the immigration laws, aliens who wished to apply for an immigration visa were required to leave the U.S. and to make their application from adjoining countries, which added yet another difficulty to the applicant trying to use this means to obtain some temporary shelter from Nazi persecution.

Frances Perkins, the Secretary of Labor and a considerate voice in the administration, looking for means to assist German refugees, had consulted Commissioner MacCormack as early as spring 1933 with a plan to use temporary status for the refugees. MacCormack was concerned that such temporary admission would eventually be converted into a permanent stay. He argued that after granting admission to the refugees on the grounds of racial or religious persecution, the United States could hardly force them to return to the oppressive land from which they had fled. 'Temporary refugee means in effect permanent admission', he argued.[26] The Secretary of Labor opted to set aside the idea while looking for other options. Later that summer, however, MacCormack informed Dr Isador Lubin, Chief of the Bureau of Labor Statistics, that the Department of Labor had adopted a liberal policy with reference to extending the visitors' permits of German refugees already in the United States and would continue to do so, probably without seeking a legal opinion.[27] However, even at the beginning of 1938, the practice was to extend visitors' visas for one to two months only in special cases.

By 1938 the plight of European refugees was back in the headlines. The German annexation of Austria (*Anschluss*) in March and the nationwide *Kristallnacht* pogrom in November shocked American public opinion. Perkins, again defying the furious opposition of the State Department, proposed that American consuls abroad adopt a more flexible approach in granting visitors' visas to people who could not meet the requirement of returning to Germany and that the President should extend the stay of such visitors in the United States until the situation in Germany improved. Officials in the Department of State were appalled at the possibility of the 'complete breakdown of our whole visa practice' and warned that 'if German refugees should be permitted to come to the United States as non-immigrants ... the quota restriction would become a farce'.[28] However, the atrocities of *Kristallnacht* convinced the President to take at least some limited action to aid the refugees, despite the objections by the State Department. Since it was highly undesirable from a political point of view to tamper with immigration laws, and since he held legal authority with regard to visitors who were already in the United States, he accepted Perkins's recommendations to extend the stay of visitors and to display greater flexibility in the granting of visitor's visas.

At a press conference on 18 November 1938, the President announced that 12,000 to 15,000 visitor's visas already granted to German visitors would be extended for at least six months.[29] Since the law did not specify how many six-month extensions could be granted, there was ostensibly no limit to the number of times such visitors' visas could be extended. The President explained that since Germany had cancelled the visitors' passports as of 30 December 1938,[30] and in view of the dangers awaiting the returning visitors in Germany, 'it could be a cruel and inhumane thing to compel them to leave here in time to get back to Germany ... I cannot, in any decent humanity, throw them out.'[31] The Department of Labor 'continued to permit refugees who entered the country on visitors' visas to apply for further extensions and ... permission has been granted where a showing was made that the visitor would be subject to prosecution if compelled to return to Germany'.[32] The exact number of refugees who entered the United State between 1933 and 1940 on a visitors permit was never confirmed officially.[33]

Refugees as Immigrants

Quota immigrants were subject to the numerical limitation specified by law. The total number of immigrants allowed to enter annually under the quota for Germany was 25,957 and for Austria 1,413. Quota nationality was determined by country of birth; yet, in order to prevent separation of families, the law provided that the quota nationality of a child under twenty-one years of age was to be determined by the country of birth of his/her accompanying parent. A wife could be charged to the quota of her husband's native country when he was of different quota nationality and the quota of her country had been exhausted. All aliens, whether immigrants or non-immigrants, required a visa issued by a United States consul.[34] In order to obtain a visa, the potential immigrant had to present an valid passport, a police certificate attesting to his previous good conduct, a certificate from a public health official, duplicate records of all pertinent personal data and a thorough financial statement, as well as an affidavit filed by relatives or a friend – but preferably close family – listing the complete assets of the immigrant's guarantor and the specific percentage of support that he might expect to receive from this affiant.[35] The laws specified several conditions that an alien must meet in order to gain entry. They provided that certain classes should be excluded from admission to the United States, among them 'persons likely to become a public charge'; and persons who had been induced, assisted, encouraged or solicited to migrate by offers or promises of employment. In addition the laws excluded persons whose tickets or passage was paid for with the money of another or who were assisted by others to come, as well as persons whose tickets or passage was paid for either directly or indirectly by any corporation, association, society, municipality or foreign government. Applicants were also required to present to the consul such documentary proof as was necessary to establish their admissibility into the United States under the provisions of the law. If and when the records were obtained, one improper entry among fifty or more pages of the documents required could result in rejection of the application or further delays at a time when each day might prove vital.

Notwithstanding the requirements stated in the immigration laws, the main obstacles facing refugees in the 1930s were embodied in the consuls' implementation of the laws, especially with regard to two provisions: the necessity to produce all the required documents and the provision included in section 3(f) of the 1924 Act[36] forbidding the entrance of a person who might become a public charge (LPC). As for documents, although in January 1934 the Department of State had reluctantly agreed to allow consuls to waive the requirement for documents if these could be obtained only with 'serious inconvenience',[37] in practice, consuls continued to demand all documents. They kept delaying the applicants, sending them on wild goose chases, indifferent to 'serious inconveniences', and used all kinds of ludicrous excuses, such as the need to prevent people with serious criminal records from slipping through and entering the United States.[38] However, it was the LPC provision that proved to be the main obstacle for refugees attempting to acquire an immigration visa. As neither the law nor the State Department's instructions provided a precise definition or a clear-cut formula, it was the consul who determined whether the applicant was liable to become a public charge. The vagueness of the clause led to different interpretations by various consuls, at times even at the same consulate. Even after the war in Europe had begun, Breckinridge Long insisted that '[a] rule of thumb for determining an alien's admissibility under the public charge clause is neither practicable nor desirable for the reason that the circumstances of no two persons are alike'.[39] Indeed, it was the very ambiguity of the clause that served to cause the confusion that contributed in turn to the consuls making arbitrary decisions, which ended, more often than not, in refusal. From the early 1930s onwards, the Department of State had urged the consuls to check evidence very carefully to determine the 'true facts essential to a proper decision in the case and to make sure that each case should be considered entirely in the light of its particular facts'.[40] Nevertheless, the consul was left to make his own decisions with regard to each applicant, and since he was instructed to be particularly cautious and strict in requesting proof that a potential immigrant would not become a public charge, he chose to enforce the LPC firmly.[41]

With regard to refugees, the core of the problem emerged from the refusal by the Roosevelt administration – and particularly the Department of State – to acknowledge refugees as a separate class entitled to preferential treatment. Since 1933, the administration had argued emphatically in favour of continuing to treat refugees as immigrants, insinuating that the reports of persecution in Germany were exaggerated.[42] To thousands of requests asking for the establishment of a special status for refugees, the Department of State responded uniformly that U.S. Immigration laws had deliberately omitted such a category, and only Congress could amend the law.[43] The same year, Assistant-Secretary Carr stated that 'there was definitely no basis under law for the issuing of instruction undertaking to provide special treatment for the class of aliens known as refugees.'[44] On the contrary, consuls were instructed to treat refugees 'in the same manner as in cases of aliens of other classes'.[45] Although in private correspondence and among themselves, visa officials often referred to German refugees as 'refugees', the term was invariably omitted in official documents. Thus the State Department never formally recognised the particular situation of refugees from Germany in relation to its immigration laws. Moreover, consuls were advised categorically to avoid any reference to refugees when dealing with German authorities. To acknowledge German applicants as 'refugees' was tantamount to official U.S. condemnation of the situation in Germany and this definitely contradicted the policy of the State Department, which saw the persecution of German citizens as a purely domestic issue. Any intervention would cause undesirable tension in American–German relations.[46] As early as January 1934, Visa Division official Eliot B. Coulter had recommended to Assistant-Secretary Carr that it might be 'preferable to avoid any reference to "refugees" in the regulations' for two main reasons. It would eliminate the need for consuls to determine whether applicants were indeed refugees and thereby give them greater leeway. More importantly, it might lead the German authorities to infer that an American consul 'has found that the German authorities are threatening harm to the visa applicant or his family' – meaning that the U.S. was interfering in domestic German affairs. Another official warned against turning the United States into an asylum for so-called political and religious refugees, since this would 'produce untoward international repercussions ... [and] would not be aimed to promote international good will.'[47]

Correspondence between American consuls and the State Department indicates that the refusal to recognise refugees as a separate class was customary. Malcolm Burke, the vice-consul in Hamburg, stated emphatically in 1934 that 'refugees and victims of persecution are not entitled to any kind of preference by law:

> Any systematic attempt to erect a pseudo-preference group
> to expedite the admission of this group in advance of other
> immigrants, who are legally of the same classification,
> would ultimately be held to conflict with the provisions of
> the Immigration Act of 1924.[48]

It should, however, be noted that after the *Anschluss*, the President initiated a plan to present the refugee problem as a world issue. An international conference to discuss the refugee crisis was convened in July 1938 in

Evian, France. However, the outcome of the conference was clearly signposted in the invitation,[49] which read: 'No country would be expected to receive greater number of emigrants than is permitted by its existing legislation'.[50] On the face of it, the presidential initiative had pointed to official United States' recognition of the refugee problem for the first time, but there is no documentary evidence that there was any intention to take account of it in United States' legislation. On the contrary, the specific instructions given to the American delegation suggest that the United States was adhering to its former policy. Myron C. Taylor, the chairman of the American delegation to the conference, received clear instructions that '[n]o preferential treatment may be accorded to so-called political refugees as such, as distinguished from other immigrants'.[51] That said, the foreign policy consideration of 1933–1934, invoked as reasons not to intervene on behalf of refugees, were no longer applicable by 1938 and opened the door for a slightly less restrictionist policy. The liberal policy towards German refugees who managed to enter as visitors is a case in point, but also the increasing quota fulfilment can be seen as a sign of a changing policy. The quota assigned to Germany and Austria (27,370) was insufficient to meet the increasing demand for visas during the 1930s but, in practice, only a small percentage of the quota was filled before 1939, due to the strict controls imposed by U.S. consuls. During this period, quota fulfilment ranged from a low of 5.3 per cent in 1933 to a high of 100 per cent in 1939, with an average for the entire period of 32.7 per cent.[52]

American Restrictionism and the Failure of Human Rights' Activists

In this way, the long established belief in America's mission to provide a haven for the oppressed was sacrificed in favour of policies designed to meet the demands of domestic politics and the economy. This included, among other measures, strict limitations on mass immigration. Since the term 'refugee' was not written into immigration law it was easy for the administration to ignore its moral responsibility to assist refugees from Germany. The most common practice was, insofar as this was possible, to deny their existence altogether and to hoodwink the individuals and charitable groups that tried to help them.[53]

Given the fact that American Jews played a role in Roosevelt's political calculations and since the majority of the German refugees were Jewish, one wonders why and how the pro-refugee lobby – both Jewish and liberals – failed to achieve political leverage. The sources point at two main reasons. Firstly it should be emphasised that despite the fact that Jews in America enjoyed civil and political rights, they were well aware that they were suspected of dual loyalty. Their collective memory made them constantly aware that a national crisis could undermine their political and civil status by arousing the issue of double loyalty. The memories of European pogroms were fresh in their minds. Their sense of weakness urged them to prove their American patriotism again and again.[54] This was especially the case during the times of social and economic unrest that prevailed during the 1930s. This insecurity undoubtedly made American Jewish leaders reluctant to exert pressure on the administration to open the quota to more Jewish refugees.[55]

For too many Americans, complained James McDonald's daughter, 'a refugee meant a mouth to feed, an unemployed worker to locate, a source of antisemitic irritation, a potential harbinger of alien ideologies, or a break in the immigration dykes.'[56] Even if we accept the view that the administration and the consuls believed they were protecting U.S. interests and security, it is hard to assume that they viewed policy towards the refugees as a test of the United States' commitment to freedom and democracy. Throughout that period the refugee issue remained the tragic and fatal concern of the refugees alone. Although there can hardly be any doubt that American Jews felt deeply for Jewish misery in Nazi Germany, their priority, nevertheless, was to ensure their own safety. The fear that their efforts to bring Jewish refugees into the country in the midst of the depression could cause antisemitism, and thereby jeopardise their well-being, resulted in cautious behaviour.[57] According to Gulie Ne'eman Arad in her thoroughly researched analysis of Jewish behaviour during that period, American Jews found themselves tangled between their desire for acceptance by American society on the one hand, and their commitment to community solidarity on the other. What prevailed eventually was their desire to prove without doubt their patriotism.[58] The second reason for the failure of the pro-refugee lobby lies in the relative powerlessness of the 'Jewish lobby' in the 1930s. While its influence may have been exaggerated for other periods in American history, the conclusion here has to be that there was very little more it could have done in the face of overwhelming public support for restriction.

For their part, liberal circles continued to voice their abhorrence of Nazi atrocities toward the Jews and others. The liberal *Nation* and *New Republic* kept criticising the government and especially the Department of State for abandoning the American traditional credo, and called for an immediate change to a more lenient refugee policy. In a series of articles they bluntly accused the State Department and some of U.S. consuls in Germany of holding antisemitic views that were hindering the immigration of refugees. Using forceful language, an editorial of 18 August 1941 in *New Republic* charged the Visa Division and its head, Avra Warren, with fighting on the side of Hitler. An editorial in *The Nation* followed the same line and labelled Warren 'one of the most reactionary, fascist-minded members of the Department.'[59] However, condemnation was not forceful enough to bring about a change in the immigration laws or to support a movement for a more lenient interpretation of the existing laws.[60]

Conclusion

Hitler's rise to power in 1933 triggered a cruel and brutal pursuit of elements within Germany perceived as inimical to Nazism – especially Jews – who found themselves disowned by their own country. For them, it ultimately became clear that emigration was the only way out of danger. As the United States had historically committed itself to the principles of freedom and democracy, it was one of the most popular countries in which to find shelter. As a result, it soon found itself facing numerous desperate pleas for visas. Unfortunately for the refugees, America in the 1930s was wrestling with unprecedented economic problems, rampant xenophobia or at least indifference to what happened outside the country. Opening the door to the mass immigration of refugees was definitely not at the forefront of the American list of priorities. Still the radicalisation of Nazi antisemitism meant that Roosevelt became willing to use his administrative powers on behalf of refugees from Germany. The transfer to a permanent residency status of German refugees who had posed as visitors to be able to enter the U.S., but also a higher quota fulfilment were the concessions. Roosevelt however refused to go beyond that. He considered, for electoral reasons, tampering with existing legislation out of the question. This implied that the State Department, in which protectionism had held sway, kept a hold on the reins of immigration policy. In the years before 1939 the phenomenon of the unfulfilled quota can be largely attributed to the consuls' strict interpretation of the regulations.

Notes

*The article is based upon research done for my book, *In Search of Refuge: Jews and US Consuls in Nazi Germany 1933–1941*, London and Portland 2001.

1. F.D. Roosevelt, 'First Inaugural Address', 4 March 1933, Washington: Government Printing Office, 1953
2. It should, however, be noted that a strong movement to restrict immigration was under way by the mid 1870s. The first targets of the restrictionist movement, and their first national legislative success, concerned the Chinese. The Chinese Exclusion Act (May 1882), and The Immigration Act of 1882 (22 Stat. 214) excluded Chinese from entry because 'the coming of Chinese laborers to this country endangers the good order of certain localities.' For more details see A. Zolberg, *A Nation by Design: Immigration Policy in the Fashioning of America*, Harvard 2006.
3. For the development of xenophobic sentiments which were reflected in immigration laws, see, J. Higham, *Strangers in the Land: Patterns of American Nativism, 1860–1925*, New Brunswick 1955; M.C. LeMay, *From Open Door to Dutch Door: An Analysis of US Immigration Policy since 1820*, New York 1987; R. Divine, *American Immigration Policy, 1924–1952*, New Haven 1957.
4. C. Wittke, *We who Built America*, New York 1968, p.39.

5. The main groups – organised labour and a group known as the '100 Percenters' – called for the suspension of all immigration. While the labour view was grounded in fear that newcomers would compete for jobs which were becoming scarcer in the postwar economy, the '100 Percenters' were nativists who feared that European ideas, notably the menace of bolshevism, would contaminate United State institutions, customs and society.
6. Cited in Higham, *Strangers in the Land*, p.302.
7. Among the leading upholders of racist ideas were Carl Brigham, the Princeton psychologist famous for developing the IQ test; William MacDougal of Harvard, who proposed a 'Nordic Race' superiority theory; and Dr Harry Laughlin, the prominent eugenist and 'biological expert' of the House Immigration committee, who went so far as to advocate the sterilisation of all inmates of mental institutions. The main inspiration of the racial writings was Madison Grant with his highly influential book, *The Passing of the Great Race*, New York 1916.
8. 5.W.S. Bernard, (ed.), *Immigration Policy: A Reappraisal*, New York 1950, p.19.
9. Dr Gulick, a former missionary in Asia, formed the National Committee on Constructive Immigration Legislation in 1918.
10. Higham, *Strangers in the Land*, p.311.
11. M.J. Kohler, *Immigration and Aliens in the United States: Studies of American Immigration Laws and Legal Status of Aliens in the United States*, New York 1936; M. Bennett, *American Immigration Policy: A History*, Washington 1963, pp.52–53.
12. B. McDonald Stewart, *United States Policy on Refugees from Nazism, 1933–1940*, New York and London 1982, pp.14–15.
13. Divine, *American Immigration Policy*, p.18 and 49.
14. The President asked congress to halve the quotas for the duration of the depression but congress adjourned before passing any law. See *Interpreter Release*, New York, Foreign Language Information Service, 11 September 1930, p.217.
15. U.S. Department of State, 'Press Release', 13 September 1930, emphasis in original. State Department Press Releases Collection, New York University Library.
16. Acting Secretary of State J.P. Cotton to American Diplomatic and Consular Officer 17 September 1930, RG 59 150.062 Public Charges.
17. D. Wyman, *Paper Walls, America and the Refugee Crisis, 1938–1941*, New York 1968. It is interesting to note that what had been practiced by the consuls without an official directive up to 1940 was confirmed in writing in the summer of 1940 by Assistant-Secretary Breckinridge Long, who instructed the consuls to use delays deliberately as an instrument to reject applicants: 'We could do this by simply advising our consuls to put every obstacle in the way and to require additional evidence and to resort to various administrative devices which would postpone and postpone and postpone the granting of the visas' (Long to Berle, 26.6.1940, Long Papers, Library of Congress, Manuscript Division, File 212, Subject file: State Department, 1939–1944).
18. John Farr Simmons to Pierrepont Moffat, chief Division of Western European Affairs, 2.9.1937, RG 59 150.01/2552.
19. 'Some Observations on Visa Practice', written by George Messersmith for the guidance of his staff in Vienna and transmitted to the Secretary of State

with the suggestion that it be circulated to the Foreign Service, Vienna, 13.11.1936, RG59 150.01/2458, p.3.
20. Immigration Act of 1917, first provision of section 3.
21. Immigrant here is defined as a person, who seeks to enter the United State for the purpose of establishing permanent residence. People who come to the United States on a temporary basis such as visitors, students or tradesmen are defined as non-immigrants.
22. Assistant-Secretary of State Carr, 'The Problem of Aliens Seeking Relief from Persecution in Germany', 20.4.1933, RG 59 150.01/2110, pp.1,7. See also 'Memorandum' by the Legal Adviser of the State Department, 5.10.1933, RG 59 150.01/2151 1/2, p.15.
23. Malcolm Burke, American Vice-Consul, Hamburg, 'Memorandum Regarding the Immigration Situation as Discussed in an Article in the weekly *Today*', 20.1.1934, RG59 150.626 J/93.
24. H. Fields, *The Refugee in the United States*, New York 1938, pp.8–9.
25. To mention one example, ministers or professors had to establish that they had worked continuously at their profession in a college, academy, seminary, or university for at least two years preceding the time of their admission into the United States, and that they intended to continue their professions in the United States. Such a person had to establish that he had been offered a permanent position in an American institute of education. In addition he had to prove that he woouldn't become a public charge.
26. Commissioner MacCormack to the Secretary of Labor, 3.6.1933, Perkins Papers, File: Immigration Bureau III B/1 29, PP-CC.
27. MacCormack to Isador Lubin, 23.8.1933, Perkins Papers, File: Immigration Bureau III B/1 18, PP-CC.
28. Unidentified signature, Visa Division, 'Does the President Have Authority to Abolish or Waive the Requirement of Passports and Visas in the Cases of German Religious, Racial or Political Refugees?' 24.10.1938, RG 59 811.111 Regulations/2176 1/2.
29. Roosevelt press conference, 18 November 1938, in *Franklin D. Roosevelt and Foreign Affairs: September 1938–November 1938*, ed. D.B. Schewe, vol.7, New York 1979, document 1418.
30. Roosevelt was referring to the cancellation of all Austrian passports and the passports of German Jews which did not carry the 'J'-stamp, see Caestecker and Moore, this volume.
31. Roosevelt press conference, 18 November 1938, in *Franklin D. Roosevelt*, ed. D.B. Schewe, document 1418.
32. Frances Perkins to Archbishop J.D. Rummel, Archdiocese of New Orleans, 3.7.1939. Perkins Papers, File: Immigration Bureau III B/1 29, PP-CC.
33. However, given that the movement of aliens, including refugees arriving on visitor's permits seeking permanent residence, grew from 1936 onwards, a reasonable estimate of the overall number of such aliens for the years 1933 to 1940 would be between 20,000 and 30,000. Wyman, *Paper Walls*, p.169.
34. There were thirty American consular offices scattered throughout Germany. Only three of them – Berlin, Hamburg, Stuttgart and, after the *Anschluss* in 1938, Vienna – were authorised to issue immigration visas. All posts were authorised to issue visitors' visas, though the final responsibility rested with the consul-general in Berlin.
35. Section 7, Immigration Act, 1924.

36. This clause was incorporated first in section 3(f) of the 1917 Immigration Act and again in section 3(f) of the 1924 Act. It was intended, from the outset, to reduce immigration but it was President Hoover's Executive Order in 1930 that created its detrimental impact.
37. 'Special Instructions in Regard to aliens obliged to Leave the Country of their Regular Residence and who Seek Escape from Conditions in that Country', 5.9.1933, RG 59 811.111 Regulations/1662.
38. Consul Geist to Secretary of State, 5.3.1934, RG 59 150.826J/74.
39. Long to Berle, 7.2.1941, Long's Papers, Library of Congress, Manuscript division, File 211: Visa Division, 1940–1941.
40. Assistant-Secretary Wilbur J. Carr to American Diplomatic and Consular Officers, 'Examination of Alien Relatives', 12 April 1932, RG 59 150.062 Public Charge/399.
41. Cited in Secretary of State to Miss Carrie Chapman Catt, Chairwoman, Committee of Ten, 12.3.1934, Yivo Archives New York, Morris Waldman Papers, Box 19: Aliens, Folder 9: Immigration – Refugees 1933–1935, 1938–1939.
42. Dana Hodgdon, Visa Division, 'Memo' to Carr, 22.6.1933, RG 59 150.01/2129.
43. See, for example, Secretary Hull to Senator Phillips Lee Goldsborough, 29.5.1933, RG 59 150.626.
44. Carr, 'Memo of a conversation with S. Dingol, Managing Editor *The Day*', 26.4.1933, RG 59 150.01/2102.
45. Wilbur J. Carr to American Diplomatic and Consular Officers, 'Special Instructions in regard to Aliens Obliged to Leave the Country of their Regular Residence and who Seek Escape from Conditions in that Country', 5.9.1933, RG 59 811/111 Regulations/1662.
46. Coulter, Visa Division to Carr, 3.1.1934, RG 59 150.01/2168.
47. Letter to Car, 3.1.1934, RG59 150.01/2168; Wilkinson to Hodgdon, 3.1.1934, RG 59 150.01/2168.
48. Vice-consul in Hamburg, Malcolm Burke to Secretary of State, 'Memorandum Regarding the Immigration situation as Discussed in an Article in the Weekly *Today*', 20.1.1934, RG 59 150.626 J/9.
49. On 25 March the President issued an invitation to thirty-two nations to send representatives to a conference in Evian to discuss the refugee crisis.
50. *Foreign Relations of the United States (FRUS)*, 1938, vol. 1, Washington 1950, pp.740–41.
51. 'Statements on Immigration into the United States for Evian Conference', 29 June 1938.
52. M.R. Davie, *Refugees in America. Report of the Committee for the Study of Recent Immigration from Europe*, New York 1947, p.29.
53. 'Report of Quaker Commissioners', 1.7.1939, American Friends Service Committee Archives, General Files, 1939, Folder: Foreign Service European Commissioners.
54. See, for example, 'American Jewish Congress in Rosh Hashanah Message: Answer Charles A. Lindberg', For release Monday, 22.9.1941. Stephen Wise Papers, Box 54, American Jewish Historical Society Archives: 'Surely it is needless to state that we [Jews] are of and for America as truly as any other group within the nation.'
55. See, for example, G. Ne'eman Arad, *America, Its Jews, and the Rise of Nazism*, Bloomington 2000, pp.209–24. See also E. Zuroff, 'Rescue Priority and

Fund Raising as Issues during the Holocaust: A Case Study of the Relations between the *Vaad Ha-Atzala* and the Joint, 1939–1941', *American Jewish History*, 68, no. 3, 1979, pp.312–13.
56. B. McDonald Stewart, *United States Government Policy on Refugees*, p.553.
57. See, for example, Rabbi Stephen Wise's letter to Professor Otto Nathan in September 1940, with regard to Roosevelt's re-election: 'With regard to the political refugees ... [Roosevelt's] re-election is much more important for everything that is worthwhile and that counts than the admission of a few people, however imminent be their peril.' Cited in G.Ne'eman Arad, *America, Its Jews, and the Rise of Nazis*, pp.211–12.
58. Ne'eman Arad, *America, Its Jews, and the Rise of Nazism*.
59. To mention only a few, see Alfred Wagg III, 'Washington Stepchild: The Refugee', *The New Republic*, 28 April 1941, p.594; 'Fresh Hope for the Refugee', ibid., 16 June 1941, pp.816–17; Editorial, 'Don't Appease Japan', ibid., 23 June 1941, p.843; Editorial, 'Persecuting the Refugee', ibid., 18 August 1941, p.208. See also Freda Kirchwey, 'A Scandal in the State Department', *The Nation*, 19 July 1941, pp.45–46.
60. See also R. Breitman and A. Kraut, *American Refugee Policy and European Jewry, 1933-1945*, Bloomington 1987.

Chapter I.9

Were Unaccompanied Child Refugees a Privileged Class of Refugees in the Liberal States of Europe?

Claudia Curio

The decline in the number of Jews in Germany between 1933 and 1939 was primarily the result of emigration, but there were some important differences between generations – most notably in relation to children and adolescents. During these years the number of Jews in Germany over the age of 60 declined by only 27 per cent, while the generation between the ages of 25 and 39 declined by 80 per cent.[1] However, the largest reduction in Jewish population – 83 per cent – occurred in the age group between 16 and 24, closely followed by the group under the age of 16, which declined by 82 per cent.

Many of these children left Germany with their parents, but thousands left alone or with siblings, mostly as a result of organised rescue activities. By the end of 1939, 18,149 unaccompanied Jewish children and young people had fled from Germany to European countries, Palestine, the United States, Canada and Australia, approximately two thirds of them with the support of Jewish aid organisations.[2] Great Britain was by far the most important country of refuge for minors within Europe and nearly 10,000, predominantly Jewish, children and adolescents found a new home there.

Given that there were such great discrepancies between the percentages of different age groups leaving Germany, it might be appropriate to consider the meaning of the age factor in the emigration from Nazi Germany and to introduce age as a category into the analysis. Three main contributing factors have to be taken into account: the fluctuating propensity to emigrate on the part of the persecuted, even though Jewish emigration from Nazi Germany was forced migration, government immigration policies and, last but not least, the aid policy of private organisations.[3]

In the following analysis, the term 'children' will be used for those who fell into this age category in immigration practice of the countries of immigration. The age limit for this category was not identical to the age of majority in the countries in question, but was far below and ranged between 14/15 years for Belgium,[4] 17 years for Great Britain,[5] 14 years for Switzerland[6] and 15/17 for the Netherlands[7] respectively. A group within the group consisted of infants, toddlers and other very young children who received even more 'privileges' than older children. The upper age limit for this group varied between 3 years (Belgium 1939, see below) and 6 years (Switzerland 1942, see below). These ad hoc demarcations were nevertheless rather arbitrary.

The primary focus here is on the period between the November 1938 pogroms and the outbreak of the Second World War in September 1939. In these few months, far more unaccompanied children left Greater Germany as a result of rescue schemes than in all the preceding years from 1933 on.[8] Firstly, I will examine the disposition of Jews in Germany to send their children abroad and the activities of German Jewish agencies in expediting this; then the focus will shift to Great Britain. Subsequently I will refer briefly to the policies of three continental countries of refuge – Switzerland, Belgium, and the Netherlands – where the focus will be mainly on admission policy for children in the context of general refugee policy and public opinion.

The Search for Child Emigration Opportunities by the German and Austrian Jewish Population

Even though sending unaccompanied children abroad had been part of organised emigration efforts from Germany since 1933, before 1938 very few Jewish parents in Germany were prepared to part company with their children. In the vast majority of cases families emigrated together and to places where other relatives had already settled.[9] Thus the number of unaccompanied children who emigrated with the help of Jewish agencies remained rather low during this period. Most of them were sent either to Great Britain (400) or to the United States (500). The numbers emigrating to other countries were miniscule: only 6 to the Netherlands, 3 to Canada and 45 to Australia, and up to November 1938 no children at all had been sent to Switzerland or Belgium.[10]

It was not until the events of the year 1938 that large numbers of parents were ready to send their children abroad alone. The situation had to be perceived by parents as extremely threatening before family cohesion was abandoned and children were sent into an uncertain future abroad. Bertha Bracey, an English Quaker who travelled to Germany and Austria shortly after *Kristallnacht*, wrote of her impressions in a report: 'Since they [the parents] realised how great the need was, and how limited the resources, and the possibilities of reception in other countries, parents pleaded that at least as many children as possible should be brought out.'[11] In Austria, antisemitic atrocities set in immediately after the annexation, and the anti-Jewish legislation that had been introduced in Germany over several years was implemented overnight. Jewish parents became eager to enrol their little ones in a child emigration scheme as soon as possible. There was no time for arguing over the pros and cons of staying or leaving the country as there had been for Jews in Germany, where the situation had worsened gradually over years.[12] Just a few weeks after the *Anschluss*, the child emigration department of the Israelitische Kultusgemeinde Vienna had already received about 10,000 applications for the *Kindertransporte*.[13] In Germany the run on the child emigration departments of Jewish agencies began only after *Kristallnacht*.

It was after *Kristallnacht* that an opportunity to rescue a larger number of children abroad arose with the *Kindertransporte* to Great Britain. At the end of 1938, the British authorities gave an open-ended commitment to admit children, an offer that depended solely on the financial guarantees to be provided by aid committees. This contrasts very favourably with the small quota granted to refugee aid organisations in Switzerland (300), Belgium (250) and the Netherlands (1,500). Admission of children to other European countries thus took place in far smaller numbers, although the original quota numbers were considerably enlarged during the course of 1939. By September 1939, Belgium had finally accepted close to 1,000 children[14] and the Netherlands had taken in nearly 2,000 unaccompanied children (including 1,850 from Germany and 147 from Austria).[15] Continental European countries were also confronted with a rising level of illegal immigration over the green frontiers. This was a direct result of the lack of legal emigration prospects coupled with the increasing levels of persecution inside Germany. In their distress, even more parents sent their children alone over the border, hoping that the border authorities would treat them more favourably than they did adults. The question remains as to the reasons behind the decisions of governments and refugee aid organisations to adopt a policy that privileged child refugees. Did children enjoy privileges that were withheld from adult refugees and, if so, why? If one accepts the proposition that governments always acted out of self-interest and never out of altruism, the question is what did states gain from admitting children?[16]

The Facilitation of Immigration for Children to Great Britain after *Kristallnacht*

About 10,000 children, 80 per cent of them Jewish, immigrated to Great Britain between December 1938 and the outbreak of the Second World War in September 1939.[17] Most came as a direct result of the rescue scheme known as the *Kindertransporte*, which was facilitated by simplified immigration procedures for unaccompanied children up to the age of

17. This meant that individual children did not need to apply for a visa but were admitted through a special group visa procedure.[18] This had become possible through private committees and individuals who lobbied and sponsored the whole endeavour. The concessions to the children did not go beyond some easing of bureaucratic process, and the conditions of pre-1933 alien legislation, still central to the immigration laws in the 1930s, was also applied to this group of immigrants. Those arriving had to meet at least one of three criteria: a valid work permit, issued by the Ministry of Labour; an undertaking that entry was only for the purposes of transmigration; or a financial guarantee. The reasons for the government's decision to admit children lay in domestic as well as foreign policy considerations. In the former as well as the latter, the government's position was determined by contradictions, if not dilemmas. On one side there was the commitment to humanitarian engagement, on the other side the desire to protect national interests in domestic and foreign policy. In the following I will show that unaccompanied children – similar to persons admitted on a domestic permit – were a group of refugees whose admission managed to meet both these criteria.

As the mandatory power in Palestine, Great Britain had a special responsibility for the fate of the German Jews in the eyes of international public opinion. Whitehall refused to extend immigration to Palestine despite the fact that Britain had promised in 1917 in the first Balfour Declaration to create a 'Jewish National Home'. The primary reason was fear of conflicts with the Arab population that would threaten the sensitive power balance in the Middle East. In the White Paper of May 1939, the number of Jewish immigrants to be admitted without special Arab consent was limited to 75,000 for a period of ten years. Shortly before the children of the *Kindertransporte* began to be admitted to the United Kingdom in November 1938, a proposal to accept 10,000 German Jewish children to Palestine had been rejected by the British government.[19] Another reason for British generosity can be seen in the outcome of the long-cherished policy of appeasement. Thus there was some special provision made for emigrants from the Sudetenland and later for those from Bohemia-Moravia when the Munich agreement was broken by the Germans in March 1939. Against this generosity there was the strong anti-immigration lobby that argued that the admission of a larger number of persecuted would send a signal to the German government that their extortionate expulsion policy had been successful. However, Britain could not shirk its duties as a member of the League of Nations and as signatory of the 1933 League of Nations Conventions regarding the international status of refugees. She had participated in the Evian conference in 1938, but only under the precondition that there would be no discussion of British policies in Palestine. Not only was British rule in Palestine obstructive towards Jews seeking refuge; admission policies towards adults coming to Britain itself underwent restrictions after the *Anschluss*. Visa requirements, abolished in the 1920s, were reintroduced for German and Austrian citizens, a fact that fatally delayed the flight of many persecuted. Nevertheless, admission of children was in line with the 'non-intervention policy', since accepting children could be presented as a purely humanitarian activity without any political connotation.[20]

The position of the Home Office in the refugee question was also framed by contradictions: humanitarian commitment on one hand, anti-refugee fears on the other. During the 1930s, Britain had suffered from the aftermath of the Great Depression. Unemployment was high. Restricting immigration was considered necessary to protect the domestic labour market. There was also a fear that high numbers of refugees would trigger a wave of antisemitism.[21] One of Britain's representatives at Evian, Lord Winterton, had already addressed the possibility that antisemitism would rise with the opening of the country to refugees in May 1938.[22] Home Secretary Samuel Hoare warned in November 1938: 'I have to be careful to avoid anything in the nature of a mass immigration, which, in my view, would lead to the growth of a movement [antisemitism] which we all wish to see suppressed'.[23] Against this were ranged the public voices in press and in parliament that called for more commitment to the case of the persecuted.[24] However, the balance between humanitarian commitment and obstruction did not tilt in favour of the former until after the *Kristallnacht* pogroms. Even advocates of an anti-refugee policy could no longer deny that German Jewry needed help. Seventy per cent of all those who found refuge from the Third Reich in Britain reached the island in the few months between November 1938 and the outbreak of war in September 1939.[25] Red tape was now removed for certain groups of German Jews. The majority of those who came now were admitted with a domestic service permit, or were unaccompanied minors arriving on the *Kindertransporte*. Both groups had one characteristic in common: they could be made 'invisible',[26] a feature that the private aid organisations preferred in the refugees.

The Role of British Private Aid Organisations in Organising the Kindertransporte

The private aid organisations, mostly rooted in the established, liberal Anglo-Jewish community, played a crucial role in financing and selecting the refugees coming to Britain, whereupon their policies were rather obstructive. From April 1933 up to the summer of 1939, aid for refugees in Britain was entirely privately funded.[27] It was not until these resources were exhausted that the British government stepped in with financial support. In enforcement, finance and accomplishment of the *Kindertransporte*, privately funded aid was vital too. This rescue scheme is a good example of the cooperation between the Home Office and refugee aid organisations. It is quite clear that there were intensive interactions between them and that governmental and non-governmental institutions shared many of the same intentions regarding the refugees.

On 15 November, a few days after the 1938 pogroms, Prime Minister Chamberlain received a deputation from the Council of German Jewry to discuss the refugee problem. The Council deputies urged Chamberlain to support the admission of an unlimited number of Jewish refugee children from Germany. Viscount Herbert Louis Samuel, Chairman of the Council for German Jewry, guaranteed that the children would not be a burden on public funds and that they would re-emigrate eventually.[28] Two days later a subcommittee of the council was founded under the chairmanship of Samuel to expedite admission of the children. Deputies of this subcommittee met with Home Secretary Hoare on 21 November. They succeeded in convincing him of the urgency of the affair. On the same day, Hoare campaigned successfully in the House of Commons and it was decided that unaccompanied children from Germany would be admitted to Britain with a collective visa. All children whose maintenance could be guaranteed would receive permission to enter. There was no quota set by the authorities, but the Council for German Jewry limited the number of young refugees to be admitted to 5,000 since it was assumed that a higher number would overstrain the Council's funds. Later the number was raised to 10,000[29] and it is possible that the Council would have offered to support even more, had the outbreak of war not ended the rescue scheme.

The government's decision was announced on the 23 November and it was added that the children would be admitted as transmigrants only. It was decided that they would be required to re-emigrate before they were eighteen or upon completion of training which the aid organisation promised to provide.[30] Now that the legal basis had been arranged, the immigration and reception of the children had to be prepared in a hurry. For this task the Movement for the Care of Children from Germany (Refugee Children's Movement, RCM) was created. Even before the parliamentary approval, Dennis Cohen, member of the Jewish Refugees Council, and Helen Bentwich, of the London County Council Education Committee, had drafted a plan for the rescue and care of approximately 5,000 children. Some elements of the plan were implemented in the first weeks of the transports, including the temporary accommodation in holiday camps along the coastline and the transport of young refugees in groups up to 500.[31] The Refugee Children's Movement appealed to the British public for guarantees and accommodation.[32] During the first weeks of the transports the organisation provided unlimited guarantees for the most urgent cases. In the final analysis, of the children admitted under this scheme 7,482 were Jewish by religion, the other ones of Jewish descent.[33]

The Selection of Child Refugees in Britain

Those who came were carefully selected by the aid organisations involved in Germany and Britain. The selections were made according to certain criteria of suitability and urgency.[34] As long as it was guaranteed that none of the children would become a public charge, selection was entirely at the discretion of the private aid organisations. In memoirs and historiography, the *Kindertransporte* have been portrayed as an ad hoc rescue operation, carried out to save children without judging their individual suitability as immigrants.[35] This would have been a remarkable privilege granted to the children, because the normal procedure for refugee admission involved careful screening by the British refugee aid organisations that financed the rescue operation. However, an examination of the procedures prior to a child's arrival in Britain reveals that this age-defined group of refugees were only partly free of some form of pre-selection. Exemption from normal procedures was granted only in the initial phase of the transports, when the agencies temporarily reduced the routines of screening and selection to save time and to rescue the most desperate cases first. This also happened in Britain, where temporary reception camps and a group guarantee were provided. In this way, a large number of children could be transferred into safety without their 'suitability' being considered. But this initial phase was short. From March 1939 at the latest onwards, all candidates underwent a thorough examination regarding their suitability. The number of children to be accepted under the group guarantee was now limited, whereas before there had been no limits placed on the number of children that could be admitted without an individual guarantee. As a result a far smaller number of children could enter England from then on. The selection criteria to which the children had to conform had to do with their potential to adapt socially and psychologically, to fit in without trouble. This potential was measured by means of school and kindergarten reports, information about social background and physical appearance.[36] The criteria were set by potential foster parents and private guarantors – who could choose a child from a card index in the RCM offices in Britain – but also by the aid organisations.

The ideal candidates were little girls, preferably blond. Children of 'Aryan' appearance had better chances to be selected than 'Jewish-looking' ones. Potential foster parents preferred children without family attachments in order to be able to raise them as their own children. At the same time the children had to be from solid middle-class homes. Few children could meet all these criteria: Children from orphanages and children's homes often came from the lower classes or were born out of wedlock; others had a middle-class background, but were only temporarily separated from their parents – because they had been arrested or were already abroad – and who intended a family reunion in exile.

There was thus a discrepancy between 'supply' and 'demand': whereas it was mostly teenage boys who applied for places on *Kindertransporte* – since they were particularly prone to detention and antisemitic violence and parents considered them old and mature enough to go abroad by themselves – it was hard to find foster homes and private guarantees for them. On the other hand, there were not enough very young children, especially girls, 'offered', since, for obvious reasons, parents were particularly reluctant to send them abroad alone.[37] Both foster parents and aid organisations expected the children to be socially and psychologically adjustable and able to keep a low profile; preconditions for a fast and complete assimilation into host family and host society. Expectations of this kind had a long tradition in Anglo-Jewish refugee aid. The refugee aid organisations in Britain were generally anxious about their clienteles' image in public and they preferred a fast Anglicisation of the arrivals from the continent in order to avoid unnecessary furore.[38] This had already been the case with pre-1933 immigrants. Whenever a wave of immigrants arrived, the Anglo-Jewish establishment feared that their ambitions for assimilation – in their eyes the only protection against antisemitism – would suffer a setback.[39]

Immigrant children had always been regarded as particularly easy targets of Anglicisation measures through the provision of appropriate schooling and welfare services.[40] This assumption influenced the decision to lobby for the admission of minors as well as the selection strategies for the children. After the arrival of the successful candidates it also determined an extremely assimilationist welfare policy by the Refugee Children's Movement. The aim was to spread the children over the country to avoid clusters and to make them 'invisible'. The best means to achieve this was the accommodation in private – and not necessarily Jewish – foster homes. Moreover, the loss of the children's identity as Jews, and as Germans and Austrians, was accepted and even promoted by neglecting religious, cultural and language bonds. Many children were accommodated in Christian homes, thus losing the opportunity to take part in Jewish life and religion. There were quite a few cases of attempted Christian conversion, a fact that aroused worry and anger among the orthodox Jewish community in Britain, which went so far as to attack the Refugee Children's Movement as a 'Child Estranging Movement' in 1944.[41] When compulsory schooling ended at the age of fourteen, the young refugees' vocational and educational choices were directed by the RCM towards integration into the realms of the labour market that were seen as suitable for refugees. Higher education was discouraged due to lack of funding but also to avoid professional jealousy of the British.[42]

As can be seen from the information presented in this chapter, the British government, as well as the private, mostly Anglo-Jewish aid organisations, considered the admission of unaccompanied children as a suitable way to meet humanitarian commitments on the one hand and to minimise the risks associated with the admission of refugees on the other. Admitting this age-defined group of refugees was in accordance with the integration concepts of both the British government and an Anglo-Jewish community that favoured 'invisibility' and quick assimilation of the refugees. The fact that the rescue operation enjoyed great popularity also served to distract public attention from restrictive immigration politics in Palestine and the reluctance of Britain to act on behalf of the refugees in general.

Admission Policies for Child Refugees in Continental Europe 1938–1939

Belgium, Switzerland and the Netherlands are but three examples of European countries that accepted far fewer children than Britain. Nevertheless, we will see that the logic that led Britain to admit the *Kindertransporte* children was active in these countries too – but to a much lesser extent. The factors that obstructed the admission of more children were stronger here than in Britain. Another vital aspect that made these countries' positions in the refugee crisis of 1938 and 1939 entirely different from that of Britain was the fact that, due to geography, illegal immigration was a significant factor, but one that hardly played a role in Britain. Therefore the aspect of illegal immigration of children also will be presented in the following analysis. In all three countries after *Kristallnacht*, private aid organisations approached their respective governments to lobby for the admission of unaccompanied children.[43] At the same time governments and administration had to take a position on the increasing illegal immigration of children, which was a result of the intensifying expulsion policy of the German authorities.

The Limited Privileges for Child Refugees in Switzerland

The admission of 300 children to Switzerland was promoted by the *Schweizer Hilfswerk für Emigrantenkinder* (Swiss Agency for Refugee Children, SHEK), which had been active in facilitating temporary holiday stays for refugee children since 1933.[44] The SHEK had claimed an upper age limit of 16 for its applicants – knowing that adolescents were the most endangered age group among the Jewish youth in Germany – but authorities lowered the limit to 14.[45] The additional admission criteria for the children were also strict: they had to be orphans or children of mothers who had lost their homes as a result of political circumstances, or children with fathers who were in concentration camps. The children were admitted as transmigrants, and only German nationals were accepted.[46] Even though the Swiss federal alien police issued visas for the children, in some cases the cantonal authorities – being more obstructive than the federal alien police – refused residence permits. Therefore only 260 children actually came to Switzerland under this scheme.[47]

Clearly the official admission policy could not meet the growing demand of German and Austrian Jews for a refuge. Illegal border crossing became an issue soon after the *Anschluss* in March 1938. Admission of illegal immigrants by border guards was prohibited from 1 August 1938 onwards,[48] but it is known that individual border guards occasionally did not send refugees back,[49] the most well-known of them being Paul Grüninger in St Gallen.[50] Such border guards were individually responsible for their actions and risked sanctions from their state authorities.

On the issue of illegal border crossing of children, it is hard to judge whether children were treated more generously since there is no written evidence about incidents at the border. However, some former guards later recalled that they generally let in unaccompanied children on humanitarian grounds. Others followed orders and rejected children against their own humanitarian judgement.[51] Children were not only rejected at the borders but were also expelled after they had already managed to enter the country. The policies towards illegal child immigrants who reported at the cantonal alien police differed from canton to canton. Alien policy in St Gallen was rather liberal. As a rule, individuals with relatives already in the country, prominent people, and children were tolerated.[52] In contrast, the strict expulsion policy of the Zurich police authorities made no distinction between children and adults.[53] On the federal level, in the Alien Police Department of the Eidgenössische Justiz- und Polizeidepartment (EJPD) – which was headed by notorious Heinrich Rothmund[54] – the same strict measures were applied to children as to all illegal immigrants. It is highly likely that antisemitism and the fear of *Überfremdung* were too fierce at this administrative level to leave much space for humanitarian considerations. Rothmund expressed his point of view in January 1939 as follows:

> We haven't struggled against the increasing influence of the Jews (*Verjudung*) in Switzerland for the last twenty years with all the resources of the Aliens Police to have these emigrants forced upon us now. We must ... move on all emigrants, for example also the children and young people who are remaining here in markedly greater numbers.[55]

The children were, in Rothmund's eyes, a Jewish rather than a humanitarian 'problem'.

Clearly before the outbreak of the war xenophobic and antisemitic elements dominated decision making in the EJPD.[56] Moreover, due to lack of public protests at this stage of the refugee tragedy, there was no reason for authorities to demur from the general tightening of refugee policy by humanitarian concessions beyond the official admission of 300 children. The Swiss Jewish community, represented by the Schweizer Israelitische Gemeindebund (SIG), feared the growth of antisemitism and *Überfremdungsangst* generally, and was therefore rather reserved in its discussion of German Jewish refugees with the authorities. However, it fully supported the admission of children, as they were less likely to arouse such anxieties in the Swiss society. This attitude paralleled that of the British case. In Switzerland the financial aspect also played a role in the supportive position taken by Jewish community leaders. Admitting Jewish children, as opposed to adults, did not cost the SIG anything since financial and organisational responsibility for minors were carried by the *Schweizer Hilfswerk für Emigrantenkinder*.[57]

It was not until 1942 – when the illegal immigration of Jews, many unaccompanied children among them, from the unoccupied part of France was at its peak – that the police department of the EJPD decreed that certain groups of particularly vulnerable illegal immigrants should be excepted from expulsion. This applied to those over 65 years old, those who were ill, pregnant women and children below the age of 16 as well as parents with children under 16.[58] The decision to privilege these cases of hardship was a token gesture, especially in the light of the fact that the measures against illegal immigrants had been drastically tightened shortly beforehand. In contrast to the anti-refugee measures in 1938, which the Swiss public had hardly noticed, there were now intense protests. The authorities hoped to calm them by granting privileges to cases of hardship,[59] but having implemented these measures, they considered their humanitarian duty fulfilled. At the same time the Kinderhilfe of the Swiss Red Cross proposed two measures to save Jewish children: one was to admit 500 children permanently, the other one was to accept some thousand temporarily until they could re-emigrate to the United States. Both proposals were rejected by the Bundesrat in September 1942.[60]

Public Protests in Belgium and the Humane Treatment of Child Refugees

At the end of 1938, representatives of the Belgian Jewish community approached the government on behalf of these youngest refugees and obtained permission from the conservative Catholic Minister of Justice, Joseph Pholien, for the admission of 250 children up to 15 years old on condition that Jewish agencies would care for them until they either reached the age of majority or they completed their professional training. The interrelation between tightening regulations for refugees in general and opening the border for children is obvious in the Belgian case too: Pholien's decision was an immediate reaction to public protests against the expulsion of Jews living in Brussels who had entered the country illegally.[61]

Children below 15 were allowed to enter Belgium without a passport – only a *Kinderausweis* was required – and with this German identity card they could move freely over the German–Belgian border. Numerous Jewish refugees who had fled to Belgium used this provision to facilitate their children joining them in exile. When these children travelled alone by train, they mostly had a tag around their neck that stated that they had a relative waiting for them at the station. Sometimes an adult who was engaged to help the children to join his or her parents accompanied the children. Early in 1939 the number of unaccompanied child refugees increased due to the expulsion policies of German authorities, but maybe also on the expectation that all children who crossed the frontier would be cared for by the Belgian child refugee committees that had been set up to receive the official *Kindertransporte*.

When seven unaccompanied and undocumented children arrived at the checkpoint in Lontzen-Herbesthal in early January 1939, the Belgian border police received an order from the alien police that undocumented children should not be treated differently from adults without papers, thus they were refused entry.[62] At this stage even toddlers – like two-year-old Emil Imbermann from Vienna, who had been on his way to his father in Antwerp – were sent back to Germany.[63] This expulsion of children by the border guards quickly became public knowledge. A local newspaper published an account that was taken up by the national papers and caused a public outcry. Nevertheless, the practice was maintained and the authorities made only two concessions. First of all, the quota of refugee children to be admitted was raised from 250 to 750. In the wake of the public protest, new refugee organisations besides the Jewish ones had expressed their willingness to take care of refugee children. A Committee of Lawyers, a Christian-dominated, but officially neutral organisation and also a Protestant organisation undertook to take care of a number of non-Aryan Christian refugee children. The authorities had asked for a guarantee of their upkeep until their majority, but finally a guarantee until they finished their professional training was considered sufficient.[64] Secondly the border authorities were instructed that children accompanied by properly documented adults and children under the age of three years were to be admitted to Belgium. Moreover, the procedure was humanised by commissioning the Belgian Red Cross to undertake the repatriation of the children refused entry. This meant that after their return to Germany such children were usually handed over to the Jewish communities of Cologne or Aachen, where care workers saw to it that the children would travel back to their home towns.[65]

The organised emigration of unaccompanied children to Belgium in the first eight months of 1939 rose to 800 children from Germany[66] and 164 from Austria.[67] The strict conditions as far as age were concerned were not always enforced, so that some children older than 15 were sometimes admitted. In addition, in the course of 1939, a total of 181 unaccompanied children managed to reach Belgian territory without the proper authorisation and were received by the refugee aid committees. They probably included undocumented children who had been accompanied by properly documented adults, and children under the age of three years who had been admitted by the border authorities. Other children had probably arrived in the country by evading border controls altogether; maybe on their own, but also possibly with the help of other refugees and smugglers. Some of them had been put on trains by their parents to mix with children who had officially been granted a stay in Belgium.[68]

Once these Jewish refugees had entered Belgian territory they – children as well as adults – were no longer at risk of expulsion or deportation, a policy that was much more generous that in Switzerland, where children and adults alike were often deported back to Germany even after they had succeeded in entering the country. The Belgian authorities passed those child refugees who had entered illegally on to the refugee committees as part of their quota.[69] Although it does not seem that the Belgian authorities exerted any pressure on the refugee committees to make the children leave Belgium for a final destination, the refugee committees themselves were eager to find a country of settlement overseas as this would alleviate their expenses and enable them to let more children leave Nazi Germany.[70]

Again, it can be argued that in Belgium, the admission of children in the context of privately initiated rescue schemes was a strategy of the authorities to distract public attention from worsening conditions for adult refugees and to calm public protests. However, in the end the most influential voices within the administration and government and in the Catholic conservative public – such as Robert de Foy and Joseph Pholien – were those that considered the refugee children the vanguard of a Jewish invasion and their admission as a concession to German expulsion policy.[71] Advocates of this view even argued in a perversion of humanitarian principles that it was in the children's best interest to be prevented from coming to Belgium. As Pholien was quoted as saying, the children would inevitably be exposed to cold and starvation after their arrival in Belgium since nobody would care for them.[72] It is unknown how many children fell victim to the merciless border policy of Belgian authorities. Many of them were probably, like Emil Imbermann, later deported and killed in the Holocaust.

The Netherlands: Transit Children not to be Assimilated

In the Netherlands too a tightening of general refugee policy was accompanied by certain privileges being granted to children. About 2,000 children came to the Netherlands with the *Kindertransporte* between December 1938 and August 1939, whereas for adult Jews it became increasingly difficult to find refuge in the Netherlands. Moreover, illegal child refugees were – to some degree – accepted to the country at a time when all but a few adults were sent back to Germany.

In March 1938, the Dutch closed their borders to refugees except those who were in 'imminent mortal danger'. After the November pogrom the Ministry of Justice issued an instruction that limited the categories of refugees to be admitted even more: to those who were in imminent mortal danger *and* lived near the Dutch border. These strict measures went along with the definition of three groups that still were to be admitted: individuals with relatives in the Netherlands, people who were in immediate danger and could make out a special case for temporary residence in the Netherlands, and – not surprisingly – children.[73]

After the November pogrom, the inter-denominational Children's Committee (Het Kinder Comité) and the finance organisation known as the Central Relief Fund for Exiled Children were founded to support children that came with the *Kindertransporte*, those in transit to England and children who arrived without permits at the borders.[74] Children on the *Kindertransporte* were admitted by the Dutch government on condition that they would leave the Netherlands upon completion of their education and that they would never take up work in the country.[75] The children were selected by the Children's Committee on the basis of the urgency of their case.[76] Moreover, the authorities insisted on checking the children's health and their parents' place of abode.[77] Meanwhile, the illegal immigration of children continued. Children who arrived at the borders without entry papers were relatively generously treated in accordance with a decree of the Ministry of Justice,[78] as long as they did not arrive in groups. Groups of children were generally returned to Germany, as the Dutch authorities were afraid of encouraging organised German dumping practices by accepting them. Fears that Germans would 'exploit' a 'too humanitarian' policy with regard to illegal Jewish refugees were also evident from the Belgian case. The decree was enforced by the Children's Committee, which had a representative at Nijmegen railway station to interrogate arriving children and to negotiate their stay with the authorities.[79] In January 1939 there were already 500 child refugees whose illegal immigration had been legalised through the mediation of the Committee. These children were deducted from the official quota.

A typical feature of Dutch refugee policy was the fact that refugees were mostly accommodated in camps, as this was seen as the most appropriate measure to avoid assimilation of the refugees that were generally regarded as transmigrants. The principle of group accommodation was applied to the children too. In spite of thousands of offers from Dutch families that were prepared to take in a refugee child after the November pogrom the authorities did not permit private accommodation for children except with relatives[80] since it was feared that they would assimilate and the danger would increase that sooner or later they would enter the labour market. The driving force opposing accommodation with families was the Ministry of Justice. Another argument that was used against individual placements was that existing vacancies needed to be filled because otherwise they would be used to lobby for the admission of even more refugee children.[81] The Ministry of Interior, on the other hand, was in favour of family placements because of the financial benefits to the state.[82]

Even though discussion about the best form of accommodation for the unaccompanied children was clearly determined by political and economic arguments rather than by considerations about the best interest of the children, it was accepted that camp accommodation was hardly a suitable way to care for them, and therefore they were mainly housed in orphanages and other similar institutions all over the country.[83] In April 1939 the government decided that all boys above 14 should be placed in Westerbork camp. Only the intervention of the Children's Committee prevented this decision from being implemented.[84] It was not until August 1939 that government permission was given for children up to the age of 14 to be placed with families.[85] At the time of German occupation in May 1940 there were still 1,350 children in the Netherlands, of whom about 450 were in private homes.[86]

Conclusion

In all countries analysed, the admission of children was utilised to cushion the inhumanity of policies towards alien immigration, to distract domestic and international public from humanitarian shortcomings, and to do justice to the nation's humanitarian self-image with the least possible risk. The rescue of children could count on more public support than rescue of adults. On the premise that refugees were always considered ambiguously – as victims and as threats – child refugees were definitely perceived more as victims than as threats. They aroused compassion and much favourable public attention. Children were the most apolitical of all refugees; their admission could be presented as purely humanitarian without any political connotation. Children were no threat, or no immediate threat, to the labour market and they were less vulnerable to antisemitic and xenophobic projections. If they stayed in the country for longer, it was safe to assume that they would soon be entirely assimilated, since they came without their families and at an age when environmental influences were at their most powerful. An exception in this respect is the Dutch governmental attitude that attempted to prevent assimilation by all means, even in the case of the refugee children. In all the countries examined here, the children's stay was theoretically regarded as temporary, but only in the Netherlands was this enforced through a deliberately anti-assimilationist welfare policy. Nevertheless, this policy was only pursued until the summer of 1939.

Even though children were granted certain privileges in all the countries, the scale of the rescue of children was far larger in Britain than elsewhere. There are various reasons for this difference. Besides the obvious fact that the three continental countries were much smaller in terms of population and territory, it was certainly a determining factor in the Belgian and Swiss case that the indigenous Jewish communities were less extensive and influential than in Britain and therefore did not campaign as successfully on behalf of children as did their British brethren. Apparently the Dutch Jewish community and their representative bodies – even though their fear of antisemitism prevented them from lobbying too hard for the adult refugees – were quite successful in making a case of the persecuted children, as the comparably high number of minors admitted shows.

In the British case it can be clearly stated that even though private organisations put special effort into lobbying for child refugees, this preferential treatment did not go so far as to exempt the child refugees from pre-selection by these agencies. Moreover, after their arrival they were subject to a welfare policy that did not give first priority to the best interest of the child but to more general considerations of refugee and integration policy. In the Netherlands, private aid committees did not have much influence on the integration policy towards the children, as the type of accommodation used for them was entirely at the discretion of governmental bodies.

Public awareness of state refugee policies and, last but not least, the attitudes of influential individuals in the administrations were also factors that determined the policy towards child refugees. In Switzerland public attention to the illegal border crossings and the administration's fierce reaction to it in 1938 and 1939 remained relatively modest. As a result, there was little reason for the authorities to make humanitarian concessions. Moreover it is likely that the antisemitism of individual high-level bureaucrats – and primarily Heinrich Rothmund – was responsible for the fact that Jewish children received almost no privileges. It was probably the case that public opinion considered that its humanitarian duties had been fulfilled with the admission of 300 Jewish children in 1938–39 and with the ongoing support given for children in distress who were admitted for temporary holidays.

In Belgium, the public was far more aware of the refugee problem before the outbreak of the war, and maltreatment of refugees did cause public protests. But in Belgium too, the upper strata of administration were dominated by anti-refugee and antisemitic attitudes, and generosity towards refugee children therefore remained limited.

In the Netherlands, after the November pogrom, the public was generally very welcoming towards child refugees, as the high number of offers from families indicates. Even though these offers could not be accepted due to the governmental attitudes, this demonstration of pro-refugee feeling among the Dutch population might have had a positive impact on the authorities' decision making. Nevertheless, the number of children admitted was far fewer than the number in desperate need for a refuge, and the government did not extend its hospitality to Austrian children (as Austria was not a neighbouring country). Thus of the 2,000 refugee children involved, only 147 were from Austria.

Conversely in Britain, the higher levels of administration were not so dominated by such obstructive forces, even though there is no doubt that they existed. Last but not least, it was undoubtedly Britain's international position as a world power and as holders of the Palestine Mandate that necessitated a greater humanitarian gesture from Britain than from other European countries, which might have seen themselves in a liberal humanitarian tradition but lacked worldwide political influence and the commitment to serve as ethical role models for other nations. In the end, child refugees were granted privileged admission only when it served the self interest of governments, and this meant that concessions were not made according to the children's actual distress but to the opportunity to utilise their admission to enforce a stricter general refugee policy at the same time.

Notes

1. H. Strauss, 'Jewish Emigration from Germany – Nazi Policies and Jewish Responses' I', *Leo Baeck Institute Yearbook (LBIY)*, 25, 1980, pp.313–61, here p.318.

2. S. Adler-Rudel, *Jüdische Selbsthilfe unter dem Naziregime 1933–39*, Tübingen 1974, pp.217–18, does not give information about how many of them emigrated with the *Kindertransporte* and how many arrived individually. In the following, 'Austria' will be used for the territory of annexed Austria, and 'Germany' for the territory that was German before the occupations and annexations of 1938 and 1939 only. There are no reliable data about child and youth migration from annexed Austria. Youth Aliyah, in terms of extent the most important youth migration scheme, is a special case due to the fact that it was defined by its organisers as a Zionist settlement scheme rather than as a rescue operation: S. Kadosh, 'Ideology vs. Reality: Youth Aliyah and the Rescue of Jewish Children during the Holocaust Era 1933–1945', PhD thesis, Columbia University, New York 1995. Approximately 12,000 young Jews emigrated to Palestine with a Youth Aliyah certificate up to 1945. Even though the final destination for Youth Aliyah candidates was Palestine, from 1938 on youths were sent to Hachscharah camps in European countries, where they were prepared for their life in Palestine. Some hundred were sent to camps in Great Britain, using the simplified immigration requirements for minors.
3. Juliane Wetzel, 'Auswanderung aus Deutschland', in *Die Juden in Deutschland 1933–45. Leben unter nationalsozialistischer Herrschaft*, ed. Wolfgang Benz, München 1988, p.417f.
4. Fourteen was the age limit for the *Kindertransporte* to Belgium. Children up to 15 years were excluded from passport requirements and could enter Belgium with a *Kinderausweis*: F. Caestecker, 'Onverbiddelijk, maar ook clement. Het Belgische immigratiebeleid en de joodse vlucht uit nazi-Duitsland, maart 1938–augustus 1939', *Bijdragen tot de Eigentijdse Geschiedenis*, 2004, vol. 13–14, p.118.
5. That was the age limit for children to be accepted for *Kindertransporte*.
6. Children to be considered for the '300-Kinder-Aktion' were supposed to be no older than 14: N. Sutro, *Jugend auf der Flucht 1933–1948. Fünfzehn Jahre im Spiegel des Schweizer Hilfswerks für Emigrantenkinder*, Zürich 1952, p.70.
7. The upper age limit was 17 until December 1938, after which it was lowered to 15: Conference on German situation and emigration, 14–15 December 1938, held at the offices of the AJDC in Paris, statement made by Mrs Van Tijn, JDC 363.
8. Adler-Rudel, *Jüdische Selbsthilfe*, p.217.
9. Strauss, 'Jewish Emigration from Germany', p.338.
10. Adler-Rudel, *Jüdische Selbsthilfe*, p.217. There were always children who were sent abroad by their parents without support of Jewish institutions: to be educated abroad or to join family members. Apart from the cases where the Reichsvertretung der Juden facilitated schooling abroad by an 'Erziehungsclearing' scheme, there is no record of this kind of child migration. In 1937, 915 persons benefited from this scheme, in 1938, 796: Adler-Rudel, *Jüdische Selbsthilfe*, pp.101–2.
11. Bertha Bracey, *A Ten Years Survey*, p.10, in Society of Friends, Files of the Friends Committee for Refugees and Aliens, 3.
12. Konrad Kwiet, 'Gehen oder Bleiben? Die deutschen Juden am Wendepunkt', in *Der Judenpogrom 1938. Von der „Reichskristallnacht" zum Völkermord*, ed. Walter H. Pehle, Frankfurt 1988, pp.132–45. Abraham Margaliot, 'The Problem of the Rescue of German Jewry during the Years 1933–1939: The Reason for the Delay in their Emigration from the Third Reich', in *Rescue*

Attempts during the Holocaust, ed. I. Gutman and E. Zuroff, Jerusalem 1977, pp.247–65.
13. Rosa Rachel Schwarz, 'Zwei Jahre Fürsorge der Gemeinde Wien unter Hitler' (1938/40), Yad Vashem Archives 01/73.
14. Eight hundred children were sent to Belgium by the Reichsvertretung der Juden in Deutschland (Adler-Rudel, *Jüdische Selbsthilfe*, p.217) and 163 by the Viennese Jewish Community, which was in charge of emigration work for all Jews in annexed Austria: 'Aufstellung über alle von der Kultusgemeinde abgefertigten Kindertransporte in der Zeit vom 10 December 1938 bis 22 August 1939', Central Archives for the History of the Jewish People, files of the Viennese Jewish Community, (hereafter A/W) A/W 1864,1; Caestecker, 'Onverbiddelijk, maar clement', pp.126–27.
15. For the figures on Germany and Austria respectively: Adler-Rudel, *Jüdische Selbsthilfe*, p.217; and 'Stand über die in der Zeit von Ende Dezember 1938 bis August 1939 ausgereisten Kinder', A/W 2000. This figure does not include children that travelled to Belgium before December 1938: for this time span there are no figures given.
16. C. Skran, *Refugees in Inter-War Europe. The Emergence of a Regime*, Oxford 1995, p.88.
17. Rebekka Göpfert, *Der jüdische Kindertransport von Deutschland nach England 1938/39*, Frankfurt and New York 1999; W. Benz, C. Curio and A. Hammel, (eds.), *Die Kindertransporte 1938/39. Rettung und Integration*, Frankfurt 2003; C. Curio, *Flucht und Fürsorge. Die Kindertransporte 1938/39 nach Großbritannien*, Berlin 2006.
18. L. London, *Whitehall and the Jews, 1933–1948: British Immigration Policy, Jewish Refugees and the Holocaust*, Cambridge 2000, p.114.
19. Paul R. Bartrop, 'The British Colonial Empire and Jewish Refugees during the Holocaust Period: An Overview', in *False Havens: The British Empire and the Holocaust*, ed. P.R. Bartrop, Lanham 1995, pp.7–8.
20. London, *Whitehall and the Jews*, pp.91 and 113.
21. A.J. Sherman, *Island Refuge: Britain and Refugees from the Third Reich 1933–45*, 2nd edn, Ilford 1994, p.15.
22. T. Kushner and K. Knox, *Refugees in an Age of Genocide: Global, National and Local Perspectives During the Twentieth Century*, London 1999, p.140.
23. M.R. Ford, 'The Arrival of Jewish Refugee Children in England 1938–39', *Immigrants and Minorities* 2, no.2, 1983, p.146.
24. A. Sharf, *The British Press and Jews under Nazi Rule*, London 1964, pp.173, 81, 160, 170.
25. Waltraud Strickhausen, 'Großbritannien', in *Handbuch der deutschsprachigen Emigration 1933–1945*, ed. Claus Dieter Krohn, Patrik von zur Mühlen, Gerhard Paul and Lutz Winckler, Darmstadt 1998, p.253.
26. Kushner and Knox, *Refugees in an Age of Genocide*, p.208.
27. Ford, 'The Arrival of Jewish Refugee Children', p.195.
28. London, *Whitehall and the Jews*, pp.111–12
29. Council for German Jewry, Minutes of Meetings of the Executive Committee, 18.5.1939, Central British Fund Archive 2/353.
30. A. Zahl Gottlieb, *Men of Vision. Anglo-Jewry's Aid to Victims of the Nazi Regime*, London 1998, p.108. In fact it was never seriously demanded by either the authorities or by the private organisations that children should re-emigrate.
31. Gottlieb, *Men of Vision*, p.103.

32. Movement for the Care of Children from Germany, First Annual Report, November 1938 – December 1939, Central British Fund Archive 153/12.
33. Ibid.
34. Claudia Curio, '"Unsichtbare" Kinder. Auswahl- und Eingliederungsstrategien der Hilfsorganisationen', in *Die Kindertransporte 1938/39*, ed. Benz, Curio and Hammel, pp.67ff; Curio, *Flucht und Fürsorge*.
35. B. Leverton and S. Lowensohn (eds.), *I Came Alone: The Stories of the Kindertransports*, Lewes 1990; B.Turner, *...and the Policeman Smiled: 10,000 Children escape from Nazi Germany*, London 1990.
36. Curio, '"Unsichtbare" Kinder', pp.67ff; Curio, *Flucht und Fürsorge*.
37. Curio, '"Unsichtbare" Kinder', pp.70–72.
38. Louise London, 'Jewish Refugees, Anglo-Jewry and British Government Policy 1930–40', in *The Making of Modern Anglo-Jewry*, ed. David Cesarani, Oxford 1990, p.189.
39. M. Rozin, *The Rich and the Poor: Jewish Philanthropy and Social Control in Nineteenth-Century London*, Brighton 1999, p.57.
40. Rozin, *The Rich and the Poor*, pp.220–41; S. Tananbaum, 'Making Good Little English Children: Infant Welfare and Anglicisation among Jewish Immigrants in London, 1880–1939', *Immigrants and Minorities* 12, no.2, 1993, pp.176–99; Rosalyn Livshin, 'The Acculturation of the Children of Immigrant Jews in Manchester, 1890–1930', in *The Making of Modern Anglo-Jewry*, ed. Cesarani, pp.79–96.
41. Union of Orthodox Hebrew Congregations, *The Child Estranging Movement: An Exposé on the Alienation of Jewish Refugee Children in Great Britain from Judaism*, Jan. 1944.
42. C. Curio, 'Die Fürsorgepolitik des Refugee Children's Movement. Ein Instrument der Integration deutsch-jüdischer Flüchtlingskinder in die britische Gesellschaft', *Jahrbuch für Antisemitismusforschung* 10, 2001, pp.287–308.
43. Mordechai Ansbacher, 'Rescue and Return: Post-*Kristallnacht* German Jewish Refugee Children in Belgium and Their Return to Germany in 1941', in *Belgium and the Holocaust. Jews – Belgians – Germans*, ed. Dan Michman, Jerusalem 1998, p.438; Sutro, *Jugend auf der Flucht*, p.69; A. Schmidlin, *Eine andere Schweiz. Helferinnen, Kriegskinder und humanitäre Politik 1933–1942*, Zürich 1999, pp.48–53. In the Netherlands, private aid committees seem to have successfully lobbied legalisation of the status of illegal child immigrants. These numbers were deducted from the official quota granted to them: Report of the conversation of a attaché of the Belgian embassy with Tenkink, quoted in Belgian Ambassador in Den Haag to Belgian Minister of Foreign Affairs, 20.1.1939, AAD 143.
44. Sutro, *Jugend auf der Flucht*, p.69; Schmidlin, *Eine andere Schweiz*. About 60,000 war-affected children could stay in Switzerland for vacations of up to three months during the war. But from 1941 on Jewish children – except those with French citizenship – were generally excluded from this scheme since the EJPD feared that the return of Jewish children would be impossible: Unabhängige Expertenkommission Schweiz-Zweiter Weltkrieg, *Die Schweiz, der Nationalsozialismus und der Zweite Weltkrieg. Schlussbericht*, Bern 2002, p.135.
45. Sutro, *Jugend auf der Flucht*, p.70.
46. Helga Krohn, '"Holt sie raus, bevor es zu spät ist!" Hilfsaktionen zur Rettung jüdischer Kinder zwischen 1938 und 1940', in *"Nach der Kristallnacht"*.

Jüdisches Leben und antijüdische Politik in Frankfurt am Main 1938–1945, ed. Monica Kingreen, Frankfurt and New York 1999, p.100.
47. Ibid., p.101.
48. Unabhängige Expertenkommission Schweiz-Zweiter Weltkrieg, *Die Schweiz, der Nationalsozialismus*, p.110.
49. F. Battel, *"Wo es hell ist, dort ist die Schweiz". Flüchtlinge und Fluchthilfe an der Schaffhauser Grenze zur Zeit des Nationalsozialismus*, Zürich 2001, p.143; L. Seiler and J. Wacker, *"Fast täglich kamen Flüchtlinge", Riehen und Bettingen – zwei Schweizer Dörfer in der Kriegszeit. Erinnerungen an die Jahre 1933–1948*, Riehen 1996.
50. S. Keller, *Grüningers Fall. Geschichten von Flucht und Hilfe*, Zürich 1993; J.P icard, *Die Schweiz und die Juden 1933–45. Schweizerischer Antisemitismus, jüdische Abwehr und internationale Migrations- und Flüchtlingspolitik*, Zürich 1994, pp.301–2. For more details on Swiss immigration policy see the article of Regula Ludi in this volume.
51. Keller, *Grüningers Fall*, pp.121f.; Seiler and Wacker, *"Fast täglich kamen Flüchtlinge"*, pp.74–76 and 89–90.
52. Keller, *Grüningers Fall*, pp.121f.
53. Keller, *Grüningers Fall*, p.126.
54. Heinz Roschewski, *Rothmund und die Juden. Eine historische Fallstudie des Antisemitismus in der schweizerischen Flüchtlingspolitik 1933–1957*, Basel 1997.
55. Seiler and Wacker. *"Fast täglich kamen Flüchtlinge"*, p.34.
56. Roschewski, *Rothmund und die Juden*.
57. S. Mächler, *Hilfe und Ohnmacht. Der Schweizerische Israelitische Gemeindebund und die nationalsozialistische Verfolgung 1933–1945*, Zürich 2005, p.195.
58. Unabhängige Expertenkommission Schweiz-Zweiter Weltkrieg, *Die Schweiz, der Nationalsozialismus*, p.117.
59. Ibid.; Battel, *"Wo es hell ist, dort ist die Schweiz"*, pp.145f.
60. Unabhängige Expertenkommission Schweiz-Zweiter Weltkrieg, *Die Schweiz, der Nationalsozialismus*, p.135.
61. F. Caestecker, *Ongewenste gasten, joodse vluchtelingen en migranten in de dertiger jaren*, Brussel 1993, p.211; AAD 793 (37 C1/3).
62. Caestecker, 'Onverbiddelijk, maar clement', pp.121–26.
63. Emil Imbermann had been found in a train bound for Antwerp. A note around his neck stated that he was on his way to his father. He was handed over to the Jewish community in Cologne where he was cared for until his return to Vienna was facilitated: Jugendfürsorgeangelegenheiten Varia, 1938–42, correspondence between Jewish Communities of Vienna and Cologne, January 1939, A/W 3017. According to the Central Database of Shoa Victims' Names (www.yadvashem.org) Emil was later deported to Theresienstadt and killed.
64. AAD 793–794.
65. Caestecker, 'Onverbiddelijk, maar clement', pp.126f.; Caestecker, *Ongewenste gasten*, p.215.
66. Adler-Rudel, *Jüdische Selbsthilfe*, p.217.
67. 'Stand über die in der Zeit von Ende Dezember 1938 bis August 1939 ausgereisten Kinder', A/W 2000. This figure includes the 'non-Aryan' Christian children that were brought over by the Quakers, but it does not include the few children that could travel to Belgium between the annexation of Austria and December 1938.

68. S. Collignon, 'Le Comité d'assistance aux Enfants Juifs Réfugiés. Les homes Général Bernheim et Herbert Speyer (Bruxelles, 1938–1940)', Mémoire de licence inédit, histoire contemporaine, Université Libre de Bruxelles, Bruxelles 2004, pp.43–50.
69. Caestecker, 'Onverbiddelijk, maar clement', p.126.
70. By April 1941, 292 of these children had left Belgium: Collignon, 'Le Comité d'assistance', p.121.
71. Caestecker, 'Onverbiddelijk, maar clement', pp.123–25.
72. Ibid., pp.124–25.
73. B. Moore, *Refugees from Nazi Germany in the Netherlands 1933–40*, Dordrecht/Boston/Lancaster 1986, pp.82ff.
74. Interview with Adolphine Bernstein, *Project 27: The Saving of Children and Youths from Germany, Austria and Czechoslovakia through the Western Countries before World War II*, The Avraham Harman Institute of Contemporary Jewry, Jerusalem, Oral History Division, p.3.
75. Conference on German situation and emigration, 14 and 15.12.1938, held at the offices of the AJDC in Paris, statement of Mrs Van Tijn, JDC 363.
76. Interview with Adolphine Bernstein, p.4. Due to lack of archival evidence it is impossible to state if on the side of the committee there were also criteria of suitability (as in the British case) adapted.
77. Internal note Ministry of Justice, 21.11.1938, quoted in Corrie K. Berghuis, *Joodse vluchtelingen in Nederland, 1938–1940: documenten betreffende de toelating, uitleiding en kampopname*, Kampen 1990, p.34.
78. On 17 December the Ministry of Justice decreed total closing of the borders except for people with a permit or those who were in transit, and children. Moore, *Refugees*, p.87. Also before 18 December, unaccompanied children who had immigrated illegally were granted access to the country. Berghuis, *Joodse vluchtelingen*, p.34.
79. Berghuis, *Joodse Vluchtelingen*, p.43; Report of the conversation of an attaché of the Belgian embassy with Tenkink quoted in Belgian ambassador in Den Haag to Belgian Minister of Foreign Affairs, 20.12.1939, AAD 143.
80. Interview with Adolphine Bernstein, p.5.
81. Berghuis, *Joodse Vluchtelingen*, p.41.
82. Berghuis, *Joodse Vluchtelingen*, p.41.
83. There were twenty-four institutions for child refugees in the Netherlands in May 1939: Moore, *Refugees*, p.90.
84. Interview with Adolphine Bernstein, p.10.
85. Interview with Adolphine Bernstein, p.5f.
86. Interview with Adolphine Bernstein, p.7.

Part II

A Comparative Analysis of Immigration Policies of Liberal States in Western Europe and the Flight from Nazi Germany

Chapter II.1

The Legal Construction of Policy towards Aliens prior to 1933

Frank Caestecker and Bob Moore

Liberalism was the dominant ideology of the nineteenth century. It decreed that from the middle of the century to the beginning of the First World War, the movement of people across national frontiers in Western Europe was relatively unfettered. Moreover, the liberal political culture also dictated that the coercive powers of the state had to be restricted to prevent the violation of individual liberties. Laws existed that executive action against any individual person, even one of foreign nationality, could always be challenged in a court of law. Judicial power was thus employed to check the executive in those countries where the protection of aliens was written into the law. In the same way, the basic constitutional principles of liberal regimes such as equality before the law and basic rights could also be used to defend aliens.

Nineteenth-century Liberalism and Aliens Policy

In Continental Europe, aliens policy was a specific branch of state policy, whereas in Britain there was no perceived need for exceptional legislation. In Britain it was considered unnecessary to acquire powers to deny either admission or extensions of residence to aliens and normal controls were considered sufficient for dealing with troublesome individuals. In Continental Europe each liberal state assigned rights to foreigners on the basis of the length of their stay on its soil and/or their ties with the nation. This protection was sometimes written into aliens legislation, or merely formed part of administrative custom and practice. In Belgium, once an alien had been in the country for four months after registering his or her presence to the authorities, he or she was granted fully fledged residency status. In effect, this provided almost the same rights as those afforded to Belgian citizens. In Denmark, the law stipulated that an alien could not be expelled for any reason once they had been in the country for two years.[1] This liberal political culture and its antipathy to a strong state was also reflected in the division of power between agencies dealing with aliens policy within the various states of Continental Europe. In the Netherlands, Denmark and Switzerland, aliens policy was a matter for local authorities, and central government had only very limited powers.[2] In Belgium, France and Luxemburg it was heavily centralised with a specific department within the Ministry of Justice or the Ministry of Interior that decided on policy. In the interests of efficiency, France supplemented its centralised decision-making process by granting the préfets of frontier départements – préfets nominated by those same central authorities – considerable powers over immigration policy.[3] Yet even in these centralised systems, local authorities continued to have considerable influence, as central government remained largely dependent on them for the implementation of its decisions.[4]

Whether aliens policy was managed in a decentralised or centralised manner it had limited functions. Aliens policy was primarily formulated to exclude those considered a danger to public order or liable to become a public charge. Subversive political activists or those who were convicted of a crime were thus liable for deportation. In order to persuade undesirable aliens to leave these countries permanently, legislation was enacted which punished non-compliance with an expulsion order. In France, the law of 1849 provided for prison terms of between one and six months for *rupture de ban d'expulsion*, and was very similar to the Belgian law of 1835 and the Dutch law of 1849.[5] Numerically however, the most important group expellees were destitute immigrants or aliens who had no 'honest' means of earning a living. Although the liberal political regimes offered protection to aliens against an all-intrusive state, in practice these 'dangerous' lower classes were largely excluded from the protection afforded by such laws as their provisions were really only meant for 'respectable' aliens.

Liberalism also had an effect on the manner in which foreigners were expelled by states in Continental Europe. The police generally escorted undesirables to the border, but liberal regimes often granted expellees a choice of which border they were taken to. This was explicitly mentioned in the Dutch aliens law of 1849. The Belgian aliens law of 1839 had stipulated that this had to be offered to resident aliens, but from 1850 onwards border choice was systematically offered to all expellees. Belgium did this in order to respect its extradition procedures that stipulated that an alien could only be extradited if the crime he had committed was also considered a crime under Belgian law. Deporting unwanted aliens, even if the expelling state ignored the fact that the person was fleeing persecution in his or her country, was seen as the equivalent of extradition. This provision was the result of a liberal ideology that acknowledged the existence of non-liberal regimes in Europe that criminalised many acts that were perfectly legal elsewhere. Providing expellees with a choice of border was also a pragmatic decision in order to circumvent the cumbersome task of deciding to which state a person belonged. Assigning citizenship was not yet a matter of routine as the direct relationship between state and citizen had little importance for the majority of people and formal identity papers were the exception rather than the rule.[6] This meant that throughout most of the nineteenth century, refugees, when expelled from their first country of asylum, could try their luck in a country other than their country of origin.

By the end of the century, expulsion policies in Continental Europe had changed dramatically. In 1884, the German authorities unilaterally decided to send back most of the aliens expelled into the German Reich by neighbouring countries. Only German nationals and those of other countries who could prove that they had to travel through the German Empire to return to their country of origin and who had money for their fare, were not returned. This effort to rationalise the removal of undesirable aliens on a national basis was sealed with diplomatic agreements which stipulated that every country had to accept its own nationals who had emigrated or give free passage to those who had to pass through their territory. The agreements made it impossible for the expelling state to force third-country nationals onto the territory of neighbouring states without the consent of that state. Expulsions were no longer merely a unilateral affair. Providing undesirable aliens with documents and the means to travel in order to meet the formal requirements of the neighbouring state became an essential element in being able to get rid of them. Expellees could only 'voluntarily' be made to cross the border of a neighbouring country of which they were not a citizen. They could still be returned to the expelling state, but because their entry was voluntary, the expelling state could no longer be accused of breaching the bilateral agreement.[7]

Because of its long frontier and strong economic links with Germany, the Netherlands had to take full account of the new policies pursued by the Kaiserreich. This led to a radical change in expulsion policy after the German–Dutch treaty (*vestigingsverdrag*) of 1906. This regulated expulsions from the Netherlands into Germany (and vice versa). From then onwards the Dutch authorities only expelled German citizens into the German Empire after showing documentary proof of their nationality to the German border officials. This agreement also stipulated that the Dutch authorities would formally hand over the expellees and their documents to the German authorities at agreed times and places. However, faced with the costs of supporting these Germans waiting to be returned, Dutch local authorities put pressure on 'undesirable' Germans to return 'voluntarily'. This forced the Dutch central government to keep issuing reminders that the formal mechanism for expulsions had to be followed and that circumventing this procedure was not permitted.[8] This contrasted with Belgium and France, where undesirable aliens were also no longer offered a choice of border by which to leave the country, but were not handed over to the German authorities either. In Belgium, they were invariably conducted to the border, in France only those considered dangerous were still treated in this way. Other undesirable aliens were simply summoned to the préfecture to be legally notified of their expulsion and given a week to leave the country. If they did not do so, they could be taken to the courts for non-compliance (*rupture de ban*). This change was motivated by a number of factors; the high costs of transporting expellees to the borders, together with the necessity of depriving them of their liberty during the journey (and sometimes without any legal grounds for so doing), and the limited efficacy of this policy as a great many of these expellees returned to France anyway.[9]

This important change in expulsion policy, where expellees were returned to their country of origin and given no choice of border crossing meant that refugee policy soon became a distinct area within immigration policy. Liberal regimes such as Belgium and France, and to a lesser extent, the Netherlands, immediately and explicitly forbade the expulsion of the (politically) persecuted. All aliens who were to be expelled had to be questioned about whether they had been pursued for political reasons. If they made this claim, their allegations had to be investigated and genuine refugees were then excluded from deportation.[10] However, not all those fleeing politically motivated persecution were considered as 'refugees'.[11] For the liberal states, 'refugees' were the political opponents of authoritarian regimes, and thus mostly of liberal persuasion. These individuals trickled into the countries of Western Europe, which then protected them against their autocratic persecutors. 'Refugee' was thus a category within immigration policy for aliens whose situation was highly exceptional. The few who qualified found the borders of liberal states open to them, or were at least protected against *refoulement*. This exceptional provision was either written into the statute books of liberal countries or became part of administrative custom and practice.

By the end of the nineteenth century, anti-alien sentiment had become a part of a process of structural transformation that took place as democratic nation-states and concepts of national identity were established throughout Western Europe. As the numbers and varieties of resident aliens increased, they became more visible, in part because of stricter police supervision of aliens. Surveillance became commonplace in several Western European countries as foreigners were increasingly seen as carriers of dangerous ideologies such as communism and anarchism. In France in 1888, Luxemburg in 1892 and in the Netherlands in 1899, it became mandatory for all aliens to identify themselves in the municipality where they were resident. This more comprehensive administrative regulation of aliens also introduced a strengthening of controls over immigration; considered necessary to protect both the middle and working classes from economic competition.[12]

This combination of cultural and economic worries leading to a stricter aliens policy could be seen all over Europe. In Britain, the considerable public opposition to the arrival of unprecedented numbers of Russian Jews in the two last decades of the nineteenth century caused a drastic change to the law. The Aliens Act of 1905 served to strengthen the hand of the authorities against foreign criminals already residing in Britain. Their expulsion was made possible, but only with a recommendation from the judiciary. The Secretary of State could order foreign criminals convicted of crimes meriting sentences of imprisonment to leave the country, provided that the judge passing sentence had recommended an expulsion order. More importantly, the Act empowered immigration officers to sift out unsuitable immigrants on entry. Undesirable aliens, i.e., those who could not show that they were capable of 'decently' supporting themselves and their dependants, could be refused permission to land. Reception areas for aliens awaiting inspection were established at ports, but they were sometimes detained on board ships. Britain, which was unique by not having any immigration controls before 1905, still remained unique after the Aliens Act as it relied almost exclusively on external controls to restrict immigration.[13] The British measures that controlled entry before arrival nonetheless made an exception for 'refugees'. The new law stipulated that leave to land was not to be refused to an immigrant who could prove that he was seeking admission to avoid political or religious persecution. This policy, based on giving substantial discretionary powers to the administration, proved generous in practice. Most undesirable immigrants who claimed to be refugees and came from regions where human rights' abuses were well known were given the benefit of the doubt. Transmigrants were another exception. Shipping lines were keen not to impede the flow of transit passengers and a system of bonding was instituted in 1905 that exempted transmigrants from inspection.[14]

Aliens Policy during the 1920s

Immediately after the First World War, wartime regulations were rescinded throughout Europe, but external immigration controls were strengthened. Border controls became the main instrument in controlling immigration, and visa requirements were introduced as a means of remote control. These were seen more as a diplomatic tool than a means of regulating the movement of people. For example, in most belligerent countries, subjects of former enemy countries had to have a visa before entry, while citizens from former allies were granted free access without any consideration of their economic utility. Thus German citizens could only enter Belgium, Britain and France with a visa, while most other nationalities could arrive in these countries without any preliminary formalities.

The Netherlands, Denmark and Switzerland – neutral countries during the First World War – took an even more restrictive line on alien immigration than their neighbours in this postwar era. All imposed a general visa requirement and the central authorities took over the task of controlling immigration and the settlement of aliens. In the Netherlands, the Central Passport Office and in Switzerland the Central Office of the Aliens Police were established to fulfil this task.[15] Swiss, Danish and Dutch political elites had been traumatised by revolutionary events elsewhere in Europe and also saw their authority being undermined at home. Food shortages in the immediate aftermath of the war also played a role in the decision of all three countries to stem the arrival of subversive aliens. There was little need for foreign labour at the time. Population growth and the large number of returnee nationals from other countries, especially Germany, were more than sufficient to meet the needs of the economy. In Switzerland, with its linguistic divisions, the experience of war and class antagonism had underlined the fragility of its national identity. Immigration became the issue around which a (re-)construction of the Swiss national identity crystallised. To ward off the fear of so-called *Überfremdung*, the specific Swiss notion of a social, economic and cultural threat to the national character of the country, federal control over aliens became an openly acceptable and even desirable step for the government to take. The number of immigrants had to be curtailed. Above all, federal immigration policy had to prevent the 'infiltration' of communists and Jews, elements deemed foreign to the presumed Swiss national character.[16] In Denmark and the Netherlands, restricting immigration was also mainly to prevent 'contamination' by subversive ideologies. This anxiety led the Dutch executive authorities to obtain powers in June 1918 to intern dangerous aliens, those who threatened public order and security (*openbare orde en veiligheid*). This extension of administrative power over aliens was directed mainly at deserters from foreign armies and communists whom the Dutch authorities could not get rid of because of the war or because they had no papers.[17] In Denmark the protection of aliens, typical of the liberal era, was also curtailed. Foreigners resident in Denmark for more than two years were no longer protected against deportation and were henceforward liable to internment.[18] In Switzerland the interests of tourism, together with employers' wishes for particular forms of seasonal foreign labour and federalists' interests, ensured that central control over aliens was relaxed by 1919. Immigration remained under the aegis of the Central Office of the Aliens Police, but control over the settlement and expulsion of aliens already in the country was returned to the cantons, with the central authorities retaining a veto over decisions of the cantonal authorities. Likewise the Dutch centralisition of aliens policy lost its momentum and local authorities regained their influence.[19] Thereafter, immigration control in the Netherlands, Switzerland and Denmark remained decentralised. This gave a degree of latitude to the border and municipal authorities charged with executing policy, albeit within limits set by legislation and supplementary decrees. In practice, this meant that there were variations between one area and another, with different interpretations of directives being made by local mayors, police chiefs and, in the Netherlands, by the regional procureur-generalen.

In Britain, the executive was granted sweeping powers to restrict immigration and also to deport any alien resident in the country.[20] Policing operations at ports aimed to limit settlement to those aliens 'whose presence offered some benefit to the country or people with strong personal or compassionate grounds'.[21] In order to ensure that the alien would be of benefit to the country, the immigration officer could, on granting leave to land, mark the alien's passport with certain restrictions – such as a time limit or stipulations on the types of employment he or she could engage in. Although the enforcement of these restrictions required some system of internal control, this was much less developed in Britain than in Continental Europe. Nevertheless, the powers available to the executive authorities to deport an alien residing in the country were extensive and overrode the intervention of the judiciary.[22]

In the 1920s it was economic factors rather than fears of political subversion that dominated changes in immigration policy. By the mid 1920s, the visa requirement to enter Switzerland, Denmark, Luxemburg and the Netherlands had been overridden by reciprocal treaties with most major European states, but it remained in force for Germans until 1926–1927. Governments remained worried about undesirable political elements entering their countries, but the wrecked postwar German economy was a more important concern as the authorities wanted to protect the domestic labour market from the huge numbers of Germans looking to earn hard currency during the inflation period. By 1926, when the German economy had undergone a considerable recovery and there was more to be gained by these neighbouring countries from a freer movement of labour and enterprise, this policy was rescinded with appropriate bilateral treaties.[23] Henceforward, the only requirement for German immigrants in these countries was to register with the local police on arrival and obtain a renewable residence permit. Vagrancy or unacceptable political behaviour were the only likely grounds for non-renewal, except for Denmark where a work permit was necessary.[24] By 1928, Britain had also abolished its visa requirement for German citizens and it remained compulsory only for travel to Belgium and France. This was mainly a function of continued distrust and the fact that trade with Germany was of less importance to their respective economies.[25]

The abolition of the visa obligation for Germans meant that most neighbouring countries reduced their reliance on external controls, but in contrast, Britain continued to use them and made only limited recourse to internal controls although it had extensive powers to do so. British control of foreign labour was also largely based on external control. All aliens looking for employment, whether or not they needed visas, had to apply in advance for a permit from the Ministry of Labour. The Ministry's primary concern was the protection of the indigenous workforce, but once in Britain most foreigners were considered to be on an equal footing with nationals and only small numbers of foreign immigrants had conditions attached to their employment or length of stay.[26]

Most Continental European countries supplemented their external controls with internal controls. This was particularly true of Luxemburg, Denmark and France during the 1920s. Although the visa requirement for Germans wanting to enter Luxemburg and Denmark had been abolished, this did not signal the free movement of labour. In contrast to Switzerland and the Netherlands, organised labour acquired an immediate influence in political affairs in Denmark after the war. This had important repercussions on social policy, with the rise of the Danish welfare state, but also on immigration policy. From 1926 onwards it was mandatory for all foreign workers in Denmark to apply for a work permit that was only granted if no indigenous labour was available. The views of trade unions and professional bodies were heard in each case. Permits were temporary (six months) and limited to a specific employment. The self employed also required a work permit and this would only be granted if the business concerned, in the opinion of the Ministry of Trade or other government departments, did not compete with existing Danish business and furthermore could benefit the Danish export trade. Violations were penalised with fines and could in severe cases lead to the expulsion of the individuals concerned.[27] Likewise in Luxemburg, although the labour movement was less powerful, it was nevertheless seemingly able to insist that from 1929 foreign workers had to apply for a permission to work in the country.[28]

In contrast, the labour movements in Belgium, Switzerland and the Netherlands had no real influence over immigration policy. The main workers' party in Belgium, the Socialists, had a voice in nearly all cabinets until 1927 but from then until 1935 their lack of ministerial posts meant that direct representation of workers' interests was restricted to the more moderate and much smaller Christian Democratic Party. Labour's influence was never sufficient to sway other elements within the government to regulate labour migration, and immigration policy remained centred on considerations of public order. In Switzerland and the Netherlands, protecting local labour from foreign labour was perceived as less of a problem. In this context, it is worth noting that in both countries, neither organised labour nor social democratic political movements had any direct influence over the decision-making process. Social democracy was first represented in Swiss government in 1937 and in the Netherlands only in 1939.

In France, all aliens were subject to regulation through controls on the labour market. During the First World War, the economy had relied on the recruitment of foreign labour, and from 1917 onwards all such workers were obliged to carry a work permit which enabled the authorities to ensure that they were employed to serve the needs of the war effort. After the war, neither heavy industry nor agriculture wanted a return to a free labour market on account of their mutual shortage of labour. They embraced government intervention as a solution to their continuing needs for foreign manpower and insisted that foreign workers were tied to the segments of the labour market they had been recruited into. For its part, the state attempted to protect the interests of the labour-recruiting industries, in particular mining, against other industries that wanted to procure cheap foreign labour by poaching immigrant workers from the mines. Organised labour also pressed for the regulation of migration in order to protect French workers, but its role in the new regulatory mechanism was mainly informal. Aliens who earned their livelihood independently had to apply for identity cards through the Ministry of Justice. In practice, the civil servants did not monitor the economic activities of these aliens, and the issue of residence permits to the self-employed was based entirely on law and order considerations, while foreign workers were subject to an economically based administrative control of their access to the country and mobility within the French labour market. However, there appear to have been few difficulties in obtaining a workers' identity card, and even the control of aliens by the police was lenient. Moreover, supervision of foreign workers by a poorly staffed labour inspectorate was equally ineffective.[29]

In practice, increasing state intervention in the settlement of aliens and their occupational opportunities in these liberal West European countries was limited mainly to new arrivals. The liberal states exempted aliens from the stipulations of immigration legislation after a few years on a temporary residence permit. They were then granted a permanent residence permit, a type of fully fledged residency status, placing foreigners legally almost on the same footing as nationals.[30]

Economic Nationalism and the Depression, 1930–1932

By 1930, policies towards German migrants had stabilised in all Western European states and their numbers in these countries increased. Dutch policy was most favourable to this immigration. The importance of an economically resurgent Germany to the well-being of the Dutch economy dictated the free movement of labour across the frontier. This was reinforced by a further agreement of 17 October 1930 wherein both governments agreed not to obstruct the employment of each other's nationals in their respective countries.[31]

Once the economic recession began to bite and unemployment rose across Europe, protests against foreigners in the labour market became commonplace everywhere. In 1931 a Swiss and Belgian statute restricted immigrants' occupational rights and in Switzerland foreign workers' residence became dependent on the possession of a work permit. These were often limited to a year or less, and extensions were not automatic. In 1932, Luxemburg required both workers and the self-employed to apply for permits to continue their livelihoods and in France, concern about the numbers of foreign workers provoked a law under which the Minister of Labour was empowered to set quota limits to the proportion of foreigners employed in specific sectors of the economy.[32] Careful lobbying by the liberal professions in Belgium and France, and especially by the medical profession, succeeded in acquiring almost complete protection against foreign 'colleagues', even when they had acquired their qualifications at universities in that country.[33]

The Netherlands remained largely detached from this increasing restrictionism, and although the Belgian introduction of work permit requirements created frictions, the Dutch refused to be drawn into direct retaliation or legislation of its own, mindful of the numbers of Dutch men and women still employed in both Belgium and Germany. The Dutch authorities were also keen to retain normal relations with two of her major trading partners. In spite of some protests from inside the country, the government did not believe that wholesale dismissals of foreigners would bring about commensurate gains for Dutch workers.[34] However, controls on new foreign workers were sharpened from 1931 onwards. For example, domestic servants were asked to produce an offer of work from an employer. This was first enforced on the main railway routes from Germany but was soon extended to all other crossing points, and after March 1933, the employer's offer had to bear the stamp of the relevant local police chief to ensure its authenticity and the integrity of the signatory.[35]

Refugee Policy before 1933

During the 1920s, the largest group of refugees in Western Europe were the approximately one million subjects of the former Russian empire who had fled abroad in the years during and after the Russian Civil War. Political considerations – the international sympathy for these refugees and the expected role they would play once 'legality' was restored in Russia and a feeling of responsibility for the remnants of the armies once supported by the West – meant that France in particular was prepared to admit Russian refugees, thus allowing them to leave the precarious asylum they had found in the countries bordering Bolshevik Russia. There was also an important economic dimension to this generous attitude. Thousands of Russian refugees in Balkan and Turkish camps had signed up to help repair the devastated regions of north-eastern France, thereby becoming an important addition to a depleted labour force. Throughout the 1920s, France was generally far more welcoming than other countries to refugees from Russia. After the collapse of the German currency in 1923, Russian émigrés fled en masse from Germany (their first country of asylum) to settle in France.[36] By 1930, 65,000 Russian and 63,000 Armenian refugees were registered as living there.[37] Smaller number of Russians and Armenians could also be found in Great Britain, Belgium and Switzerland, and handfuls in the Netherlands, Luxemburg and Denmark.[38]

The numbers of other identifiable political refugees in Europe during the 1920s were relatively small. Italians fleeing fascism found a refuge in France, Belgium and Switzerland. There was also a trickle of Hungarians, Spaniards, and Poles, but as most were left-wing political exiles they were not especially welcome. However, the need for labour in Western Europe during most of the 1920s meant that those forced to flee their own country because of their political views could find a safe haven without too much difficulty. In all seven countries, those who might have been deemed to be refugees were in practice treated according to legislation on aliens. For the most part, this legislation was only used to keep out those deemed politically undesirable or indigent and vagrant.[39] Up to this point, there had been no justification or need to consider the principle of asylum separately from the construction of the laws on aliens.

In Britain, where destitute 'refugees' had been explicitly exempted from exclusion in the 1905 Aliens Act, this provision had been overturned by the draconian wartime Aliens Restriction Act of 1914 that continued in amended form into peacetime. It gave the Home Office enormous powers to regulate the admission and residence of foreigners, and also removed any implicit protection for 'refugees'.[40] Thus after the First World War nowhere a statutory protection for refugees was provided. Asylum was only a privilege conferred by sovereign states, and they had no legal obligations to applicants. Nevertheless, a European tradition of asylum still counted for something. Refugees could appeal to administrative discretion for a humanitarian exemption to immigration rules. In some countries, the forms that they completed on arrival at the frontier even provided space for individuals to explain their particular situation. In line with nineteenth-century policy, 'refugees' were perceived as specific and limited categories of persons whose fate could be dealt with by a minor provision in immigration policy.

In the Netherlands, however, the authorities sought to discourage both immigration and requests for asylum, not least because these came almost exclusively from left-wing elements whom successive governments found objectionable.[41] In any case, the difficulty of finding suitable jobs in the Netherlands, the absence of migrants' or exile communities, and the marginal nature of the political left meant that the Netherlands exerted little attraction to such refugees. The combination of the change in Comintern policy in 1928 to an attack on social democracy as 'social fascism', and the emergence of increasingly right-wing governments in Continental Europe meant that communists and others seen as left-wing became the targets for state repression elsewhere too. The British security services advised the immigration authorities on keeping Bolshevik agents at bay.[42] By 1926, France and Luxemburg became more restrictive towards Italian and other left-wing refugees, and in 1928 Belgium followed suit. The Swiss federal authorities also wanted to expel (mainly Italian) left-wing refugees, but encountered some opposition from cantons with strong socialist representations, who used their powers to grant residence permits and thereby undermined the wishes of the federal government.[43] Although expulsions remained common, repatriations were rare. The French and Swiss authorities had traditionally been reluctant to send politically active Italians over the Italian frontier and showed a preference for dumping them at the border of another neighbouring country.[44]

As the recession bit deeper, not only those without papers, but all aliens without visible means of support were denied access to the countries of Western Europe. This made it harder for refugees, especially where countries shared frontiers with non-democratic regimes and the systems in place were often tested to the limit. Thus when Swiss border guards returned some anti-fascist political activists back across the Italian border, special instructions were issued to the police in 1932 not to expel those destitute or undocumented Italian immigrants who claimed to be refugees. Their stories were then checked by the federal authorities and, if found to be genuine, they were granted a residence permit. 'Refugees' became a privileged category within Swiss immigration policy as even without means or without papers, they were allowed into the country and granted short-term residence permits that could be extended provided the holders refrained from political activities.[45]

Notes

1. A. Desjardins, 'La loi de 1849 et l'expulsion des étrangers', *Revue des deux mondes*, 1882, p.674; B. Porter, *The Refugee Question in Mid-Victorian Politics*, Cambridge 1979 ; F. Caestecker, *Alien Policy in Belgium, 1840–1940: The Creation of Guest workers, Refugees and Illegal Aliens*, Oxford 2000, p.10f.
2. A. Kamis-Müller, *Antisemitismus in der Schweiz, 1900–1930*, Zürich 1990; C. Van Eijl, *Al te goed is buurmans gek. Het Nederlandse vreemdelingenbeleid 1840–1940*, Amsterdam 2005; M. Leenders, *Ongenode gasten. Het vluchtelingenbeleid in Nederland, 1815–1938*, Hilversum 1993.
3. D.A. Gordon, 'The Back Door of the Nation State: Expulsions of Foreigners and Continuity in Twentieth-Century France', *Past and Present* 186, no. 1, 2005, pp.201–32.
4. L. Keunings, 'Geheime politie en politieke politie in België van 1830 tot 1914', *Panopticon 9*, no. 2, 1980, pp.128–58.
5. Gordon, 'The Back Door'; Leenders, *Ongenode Gasten*.
6. F. Caestecker, 'The Transformation of Nineteenth-Century West European Expulsion Policy, 1880–1914', in *Migration Control in the North Atlantic World: The Evolution of State Practices in Europe and the United States from the French Revolution to the Inter-War Period*, ed. A. Fahrmeier, O. Faron and P. Weil, New York and Oxford 2003, pp.120–23.
7. Caestecker, 'Transformation', pp.123–32.
8. Van Eijl, *Al te goed*, p.80–89 and 94; Caestecker, 'Transformation'.
9. Cabinet de Commissaire General to Prefect, 14.6.1912, AN F7 14711; X. Barthélemy, *Des infractions aux arrêtés d'expulsion et d'interdiction de séjour*, Paris 1936, pp.124, 174; Gordon, 'The Back Door', pp.227f.
10. Caestecker, *Alien Policy*, p.40f.; A. Martini, *Les expulsions des étrangers*, Paris 1909, p.137; J. Krabbe, *Toelating en uitzetting van vreemdelingen*, Leiden 1912, p.110; Kamis-Müller, *Antisemitismus in der Schweiz*, p.83.
11. We use the word refugees for referring to the sociological reality of migration of persons whose departure was not voluntary and politically induced. The word used in inverted commas refers to those people who were recognised by receiving countries as eligible for the status of refugee. Thus the term 'refugee' has no pejorative meaning in this context, but refers only to the political confirmation that the receiving state clearly accepts that the aliens concerned were fleeing persecution and deserved asylum.
12. Mémorial du Grand-Duché de Luxemburg, 1894, 1; F. Caestecker, 'Het Belgische management van immigratie: veranderende doelstelling, resultaten en statistische presentaties (1840-2000)', in : I.Devos, T.Eggerickx, P.Servais and E.Vilquin (eds.), *Histoire de la population de la Belgique et de ses territoires*, Louvain-la-Neuve, in press; G. Noiriel, *Le Creuset Français, histoire de l'immigration XIX–XXe siècles*, Paris 1988.

13. Social scientists and in particular Aristide Zolberg, but also Grete Brochmann and Thomas Hammar with their publication *Mechanisms of Immigration Control: A Comparative Analysis of European Regulation Policies*, Oxford 1999, have been helpful in providing an analytical framework which structures this analysis.
14. B. Gainer, *The Alien Invasion: The Origins of the Aliens Act of 1905*, London 1972; J. Pellew, 'The Home Office and the Aliens Act, 1905', *The Historical Journal* 32, no. 2, 1989, pp.369–85.
15. B. Moore, *Refugees from Nazi Germany in the Netherlands 1933–1940*, Dordrecht 1986, p.142f.; U. Gast, *Von der Kontrolle zur Abwehr. Die eidgenössische Fremdenpolizei im Spannungsfeld von Politik und Wirtschaft 1915–1933*, Zürich 1997.
16. G. and S. Arlettaz, *La Suisse et les étrangers. Immigration et formation nationale (1948–1933)*, Lausanne 2004; P. Kury, *Man akzeptiere uns nicht, man toleriere uns. Ostjudenmigration nach Basel, 1890–1930*, Basel 1998; see also the article of Regula Ludi in this volume.
17. Leenders, *Ongenode gasten*, pp.173–76.
18. The Danish authorities wanted greater power over the immigrants in their country as they feared that immigration would aggravate the (German) minority issue in Denmark. L. Rünitz, *Af hensyn til konsekvenserne, Danmark og flygtningesporgsmalet 1933–1939*, Odense 2005, p.22f.
19. G. Meershoek, *Dienaren van het gezag. De Amsterdamse politie tijdens de bezetting*, Amsterdam 1999, p.62f.
20. The Aliens law had to be extended on an annual basis. An attempt to make these powers permanent was rejected by Parliament: R. Cohen, 'Shaping the Nation, Excluding the Other: The Deportation of Migrants from Britain', in *Migration, Migration History, History. Old Paradigms and New Perspectives*, ed. J. Lucassen and L. Lucassen, Bern 1997, p.362.
21. L. London, *Whitehall and the Jews, 1933–1948: British Immigration Policy and the Holocaust*, Cambridge 2000, p.18; C. Holmes, *John Bull's Island: Immigration and British Society, 1871–1971*, London 1988, pp.154–55.
22. Cohen, 'Shaping the Nation', p.361f.
23. Moore, *Refugees*, p.55; Van Eijl, *Al te goed*, pp.111–42; J. Oltmer, *Migration und Politik in der Weimarer Republik*, Göttingen 2005, pp.428–32; Gast, *Kontrolle*, pp.239–59; D. Bourgeois, 'La porte se ferme: la Suisse et le problème de l'immigration juive en 1938', *Relations Internationales* 54, 1988, p.199; Rünitz, *Af hensyn*, p.23.
24. For further details, see section on control of the labour market below.
25. For respectively the Netherlands, Denmark and Switzerland, the trade with Germany was, in 1930, 32, 36 and 28 per cent of total import and 21, 17 and 16 per cent of total export. For Belgium, France and Great Britain it was 17, 15 and 6 per cent of imports and 11, 10 and 5 per cent of exports: B.R. Mitchell, *European Historical Statistics*, London 1980, pp.513ff and London 1998, pp.571ff.
26. London, *Whitehall*, p.20; L. London, 'British Immigration Control Procedures and Jewish Refugees, 1933–1939', in *Second Change: Two Centuries of German-Speaking Jew in the United Kingdom*, ed. Mosse Werner, Tübingen 1991, p.191f.
27. Rünitz, *Af hensyn*, p.22ff.

28. M. Gloden, *Die Asylpolitik Luxemburgs von 1933 bis 1940. Der Anspruch auf Kontrolle*, Wissenschaftliche Arbeit zur Erlangung des akademischen Titels eines Magister, Universität Trier, Fachbereich III. Geschichte, 2001, p.20.
29. J.C. Bonnet, *Les Pouvoirs publics français et l'immigration dans l'entre-deux-guerres*, Lyon 1976, p.48.
30. In France, identity cards were automatically renewed every five years, in Belgium after four months an alien acquired an unconditional leave to remain. In Switzerland, the cantonal authorities were responsible for granting full residency status from 1921 onwards and agreed in 1929 to grant aliens the status of *Niedergelassene* after three years. The small numbers of foreign immigrants who had entered the United Kingdom as foreign workers in areas of labour shortage were required to stay in that employment for four years and acquired thereafter an unconditional leave to remain: Gast, *Kontrolle*, p.328; Caestecker, *Alien Policy in Belgium*, p.56; T. Kushner, 'An Alien Occupation: Domestic Service and the Jewish Crisis, 1933 to 1939', in *The Holocaust and the Liberal Imagination: A Social and Cultural History*, Oxford 1994, pp.96–97.
31. Moore, *Refugees*, p.55f.; Gast, *Kontrolle*, pp.249f., 273–77, 325; M. Pauly, 'L'immigration dans la longue durée', in *Lëtzebuerg de Lëtzebuerger? Le Luxembourg face à l'immigration*, ed. M. Pauly, Luxembourg 1984, p.13; B. Vormeier et H. Schramm, *Vivre à Gurs. Un Camp de Concentration français 1940–1941*, Paris 1977, p.210.
32. J. Simpson, *The Refugee Problem, Report of a Survey*, London, New York and Toronto 1939, p.275; Gloden, 'Die Asylpolitik Luxemburgs', p.20; Caestecker, *Alien Policy*, pp.143ff.
33. G. Noiriel, *Le Creuset Français*, p.57; Caestecker, *Alien Policy*, p.143.
34. Moore, *Refugees*, pp.57f.; Van Eijl, *Al te goed*, pp.150–52.
35. Henkes, *Heimat in Holland*, pp.120f.; Van Eijl, *Al te goed*, pp.151f.
36. Simpson, *The Refugee Problem*, p.274; Noiriel, *Le Creuset*, p.107.
37. J. Vernant, *Les réfugiés dans l'après-guerre*, Monaco 1953, p.257.
38. M. Leenders and W. Van Meurs, 'Nederland en het Nansen-paspoort. De houding van de Nederlandse regering tegenover statenloze vluchtelingen', in *Geschiedenis van de mensenrechten*, ed. M. Kuitenbrouwer and M. Leenders, Hilversum 1996, pp.114ff.; Simpson, *The Refugee Problem*, pp.339f.
39. Simpson, *The Refugee Problem*, p.252.
40. London, *Whitehall*, p.17.
41. Leenders, *Ongenode gasten*, pp.199–234.
42. A.W. Brian Simpson, *In the Highest Degree Odious: Detention Without Trial in Wartime Britain*, Oxford 1992, pp.35–36; London, *Whitehall*, p.21.
43. M. Cerutti, 'La Suisse et les réfugiés antifascistes italiens', in *L'émigration politique en Europe aux XIXe et XXe siècles*, ed. Ecole francaise de Rome, Rome 1991, pp.305–26.
44. R. Schor, *L'opinion française et les étrangers en France, 1919–1939*, Paris 1985, p.302.
45. Gast, *Kontrolle*, pp.311–16; UEK, p.177.

Chapter II.2

Refugees from Nazi Germany and the Development of Refugee Policies, 1933–1937

Frank Caestecker and Bob Moore

Immediately after Hitler had been appointed chancellor of Germany on 30 January 1933 the flight of Jews and left-wing political opponents of Nazism began. The number of potential victims of the new regime was substantial. The SPD (about 1 million members) and KPD (360,000 members) were themselves very large organisations with many full-time employees and the Jewish population of Germany at the June 1933 census was 499,682.[1] Of the Jews in Germany, 80.2 per cent were German nationals and the remaining 19.2 per cent or 98,747 were either citizens of other countries, mostly Poles (56,480) or de facto stateless. The vast majority of these latter groups were the so-called *Ost-Juden* who had fled or emigrated from Eastern Europe in the previous half century.

The formation of a largely non-Nazi cabinet was supposed to act as a guarantee, but the euphoria of success brought a wave of unprovoked and unbridled attacks by the Nazis across the country against those perceived as their political or racial opponents. Initially it was the KPD and SPD functionaries who became prime targets as law and order broke down in an environment where the forces charged with protecting the individual came under Nazi control. Also the first Jewish targets of Nazi terror were those who had a high political profile – politicians, trade union leaders and journalists. The Law for the Re-establishment of a Professional Civil Service, promulgated on 7 April 1933 to 'cleanse' the German civil service of politically unreliable elements, soon added many others to the list. The various decrees stipulated that all 'non-Aryans' should be forcibly retired, although it took some time for the term 'non-Aryan' to be given a formal definition and many exceptions were made, including a sizeable number of Jews.

In the first weeks of Nazi rule the preponderant view in left-wing and Jewish circles was that the crisis and disorder would eventually pass and life would return to some semblance of normality. The statistics suggest that, perhaps unsurprisingly, foreign Jews were more likely to have left Germany in early 1933, although those who were Polish or stateless were as likely to have moved westwards as back to the East. A few emigrants were prescient enough to find ways to move capital out of Germany and make it accessible elsewhere but they were hindered by the severe restrictions on the export of capital that had been introduced to protect the value of the mark after 1931.[2] Soon after Hitler's seizure of power, the regime tried to prevent political opponents leaving the country. An effective strategy was to stop the issue or renewal of passports, but the reality was that many political activists fled without the necessary travel documents. Conversely, the emigration of (non-political) Jews was actively encouraged. Their requests for German passports met with little opposition.

Leaving Germany did not necessarily mean that the refugee was freed from Nazi terror. Conscious of the need to suppress dissent fomented outside the country and keen to minimise the damage done to Germany's international reputation, consulates were asked to track the political activities of the refugees. Those not considered loyal to the new German regime were denaturalised and dispossessed and by the end of 1936, 291 well-known political opponents had suffered this fate. To silence political emigrants who had escaped from the Reich, the new German authorities were not afraid to resort to acts of terrorism such as abduction, the kidnapping of family members, or physical assaults.[3] The Nazi regime did not necessarily want the return of political emigrants, and German consulates refused to renew German passports of known political opponents.[4] From January 1935 onwards, if emigrants returned to Germany, they were liable to a period of imprisonment in a concentration camp for 're-education'. Their release depended on the one hand on the attitude they had adopted towards the new German regime in the country they had re-emigrated from, and on the other on their good behaviour during their administrative detention. Only if '[the] returnees could reintegrate without problems into the national socialist state' were they allowed to leave the *Schutzhaftlager*. In practice, therefore, a great many political opponents remained incarcerated indefinitely.

Jews in the business classes were less directly affected in the weeks and months after January 1933, largely because the Hitler regime regarded economic recovery as paramount. Such Jews could expect some protection from arbitrary measures, and indeed continued to do so up to and beyond 1935 when Hjalmar Schacht went on record to berate Nazi activists for carrying out acts of violence in major German cities. Local boycotts continued to take place, even in the major cities, but it was in the smaller towns and villages that Jews were first driven out of the economy. This led to widespread internal migration (*Binnenwanderung*) of Jews from small municipalities and villages to the larger metropolitan areas where Jewish welfare provision was better and where one could live more anonymously. One minor consequence of the *Binnenwanderung* after 1933 was that some Jews who lived in towns and cities near a foreign border took advantage of a nearby haven rather than moving within Germany.

Such a step was often based purely on proximity, and the possibility of continuing to use one's contacts and expertise in the region, or through linguistic or family ties. Emigration statistics suggest that the number of refugees leaving Germany began to recede in the autumn and winter of 1933 and that the years 1934 and early 1935 saw only smaller numbers of departures. Indeed, the Nazi regime was horrified to discover that some 15,000 Jews who had left Germany for Poland during the course of 1933 had decided to return in 1934. Yet although the period 1934–1937 may have been superficially seen as a 'grace period' where few overt official attacks were made on the Jews in Germany, the accumulation of quasi-legal and local Nazi initiatives had the effect of a slow process of attrition on Jewish economic activity. The gradual 'Aryanisation' of Jewish businesses began as professionals and businessmen were forced to sell up as a result of local harassment or administrative obstruction.[5]

The Law for the Protection of German Blood and German Honour, and the Reich Citizenship Law of September 1935, collectively known as the Nuremberg Laws, had little immediate effect on the actual situation for the Jews inside Germany.[6] Although portrayed at the time as a regularisation of their (admittedly second-class) status within the new Germany, emigration statistics suggest that it had been the outbreaks of SA violence against Jews in the late spring and summer of 1935 that had precipitated a further wave of departures from people who no longer thought they had a future in Germany. The supplementary decree to the Reich Citizenship Law of 14 November 1935 finally gave a formal definition of what the term 'Jew' actually meant in relation to the legislation. By making a distinction between 'full-Jews' and so-called *Mischlinge* (half and quarter 'Jews') and by applying the regulations only to 'full Jews', it seemed that the Nazis had limited their racial targets. However, by identifying the existence of '*Mischlinge*', they also extended the potential threat of future action to many people who often had had no connection with the Jewish faith for generations. Even 'Aryan' Germans were targeted by the Nuremberg Laws, as 'Aryans' having a sexual relationship with a 'Jew' also became liable to prosecution for *Rassenschande* (race defilement).[7]

After the initial rush of refugees in 1933, the number of Jews leaving Germany dwindled, and in the course of 1934 and early 1935 some chose to return to Germany thinking that the worst was over. To combat this, from 1935 onwards the Nazi authorities arrested all Jewish returnees. In their case, there was no question of 're-education' but only of deterrence. Jews who were by definition unwanted returnees were only liberated if they had arranged to emigrate.[8] By that time close cooperation had also been established between tax offices, currency offices and local authorities in the process of issuing of passports and this began to have a substantial impact on the ability of Jews to effect their emigration from the Third Reich.[9] As a rule, passports issued to German Jews were, like those of 'Aryan' Germans, valid for five years. A circular sent out on 12 November 1935 limited the validity of German Jews' passports to six months in order to discourage any possibility of repatriation. However, these instructions were not applied in a consistent manner. In some regions, even before 1935, Jews were given passports valid for only three or six months, whereas in other regions they were still being issued for five years in 1936. These passports could easily be prolonged in German consulates abroad unless the individual was being sought for criminal or tax offences, or if their citizenship had been withdrawn. Stateless Jews who had been under the protection of the German authorities (the holders of a German *Fremdenpass*) seem to have had no right of return and the validity of their documents was not extended.[10]

After the violence of early 1933, the situation did begin to settle down and former opponents who renounced their ideas or refrained from further political activism were left in peace. They became even the focus of a charm offensive as re-integration into the national community became the declared goal of the Nazi leadership.[11] This option of submitting to the new rulers was never an option for the Jews. They were no longer considered Germans, excluded from the *Volksgemeinschaft* and totally dependent on the whims of the new regime. Jews held in the *Schutzhaftlagern* and concentration camps were invariably worse off than the other German inmates. When newspapers in Western Europe denounced the treatment of Jewish returnees in concentration camps, this 'Jewish atrocity propaganda' infuriated the Nazis and on 22 November 1937, Himmler decreed that no Jewish prisoners could be released from the concentration camps, even for the purposes of emigration.[12] This episode is an illustration of the arbitrary treatment of Jews in Nazi Germany, but reflects also the chaotic nature of policy making where huge contradictions remained in decision making by the various agencies involved.

In 1936, the showcase of the Berlin Olympic Games (temporarily) reined in Nazi violence, but by 1937, locally prompted attacks against 'Jews' again became commonplace. In that year the Gestapo assumed the authority to rescind the German nationality of political opponents. The Nazis' use of denaturalisation as a form of persecution became more widespread. The authorities still had to prove the disloyalty of 'ordinary' emigrants, but membership of left-wing organisations and even emigration itself became considered sufficient grounds to take away their nationality. At the same time the Gestapo broadened the definition of 'behaviour hostile to the state' (*staatsfeindlichkeit*) to include currency and tax offences. This too, was to be punished with denaturalisation (and confiscation of assets) as were those convicted of race defilement and homosexuality. A standard procedure was installed by 1938, which stipulated that extending the validity of a passport had to be preceded by an investigation into the possibility of revoking German nationality. This procedure speeded up the denaturalisation of German 'Jews'. Again, an anti-regime attitude, such as the mere support of an opposition party, was usually considered enough evidence for such a step. While investigations were in progress, passports were extended, especially in cases where their expiry would result in the 'Jewish' holder being repatriated by the authorities of the country of refuge.[13]

According to the Jewish organisations promoting emigration in Germany, about 200,000 Jews left Germany between 1933 and 1937. Forty per cent of them remained in Europe; outside Europe the most common refuge throughout the whole time period was Palestine, but South America also became an important destination.[14] By the autumn of 1937 there were still 350,000 'Jews' living in Germany, but emigration continued to be the Nazi strategy for making Germany *judenfrei*. Most had neither the access to capital and assets nor the international contacts to facilitate their departure. Even many who had been relatively well off in 1933 had used their savings and the proceeds from the sale of houses and business to support themselves inside Germany either because they could not countenance leaving, or in the hope that conditions would improve. Having slowly eaten away at their capital, these people were now facing a future of penury, just as conditions were about to worsen again.

First Reactions in 1933

One of the first indicators of the Nazi persecution of political and racial opponents of Hitler's new regime was when refugees began to arrive at the frontiers of surrounding countries. In the Netherlands, Denmark, Luxemburg, Switzerland and Great Britain this initial movement of people went unhindered as German citizens did not require a visa for entry and few fell foul of the regulations on vagrancy. However, the German law of 1931 prohibiting an individual from taking more that RM 500 out of the country made it difficult to live abroad unaided for any length of time. Only those who had been resident in Germany for years but had retained Polish or Russian nationality, or had been rendered stateless, could be refused access, as they did require a visa. Nonetheless, even the East European Jews fleeing Germany seem to have had little difficulty in gaining admission to Western European countries in the early months of 1933. This leniency was short-lived. In the summer of 1933 the Dutch consular officials in Germany were told to scrutinise applications for visitor's visas from stateless and Eastern European nationals far more carefully and to weed out those considered 'undesirable'. Swiss policy on granting visas for Polish and Russian Jews also became more restrictive. A financial deposit was required for such visa applications to ensure that applicants left Switzerland after their authorised stay.[15]

The British authorities refused visas to East European or stateless Jews if they suspected them to be refugees from Germany. Here, pre-selection abroad seems to have been more effective, as Britain's geographical position, combined with effective port controls, ruled out most unauthorised immigration. German nationals could turn up at British ports and expect entry, as they were not obliged to carry a visa. The immigration authorities excluded only German nationals who could not demonstrate the ability to support themselves and their dependants. The rising influx of German immigrants, including an apparently considerable number of refugees, caused the authorities to apply tighter controls at ports from 30 March 1933 onwards. When the immigration officer granted leave to land to a newly arrived passenger from the continent who seemed to be a refugee, he would routinely attach a time limitation – usually one month – plus a condition forbidding employment. The British authorities were thus able to dictate the terms of admission. Visas were refused and refugees were turned away at the border, but others who did not qualify via the normal procedure for admission could be granted access on a discretionary basis. This generosity had its limits. Immigration Officers were able to exercise their powers to refuse leave to land to any undesirable aliens and those suspected of being communists were often victims of this policy.[16] Jews were treated more generously, as the Anglo-Jewish community agreed to guarantee the maintenance of Jewish refugees from Nazi Germany. Initially the leadership of the British Jewish community had proposed free immigration to Britain for refugees from Nazi Germany, but with the condition that leave to land in Britain would be granted only if the individuals registered immediately with the Jewish refugee organisation. The selection of those qualifying for temporary protection would thus be left in the hands of the Jewish committees.[17] British authorities rejected this system of effectively subcontracting the selection process as it represented an infringement of state sovereignty and the Home Office and its administration remained the final arbiters of who was to be considered a refugee covered by the Jewish pledge.

In France, although both Germans and East Europeans needed a visa, the refugees were initially welcomed. French consulates even gave declarations to Germans who had been denied a passport that enabled them to cross the French border.[18] In general, visas were issued generously although based primarily on financial considerations. Consular officials were charged only with preventing refugees who might become a charge on public welfare from entering.[19] Belgian consuls operated on a similar basis and visas were issued generously to refugees from Nazi Germany. However, requests from Polish citizens for Belgian visas were usually met with a refusal. From the autumn of 1933 onwards, Belgian consuls also refused visas to stateless people who had lived in Germany and were in possession of a German *Fremdenpass*.[20] Not all refugees attempting to reach France or Belgium applied for a visa; some had left Germany on the spur of the moment, others decided to make the journey in spite of the fact that their visa applications had been refused, and many others could not apply for visas as the German authorities had turned down their requests for passports. In France those refugees who managed to arrive in the country without the necessary papers were given permission to stay without undue difficulty. Préfets in the frontier départements were instructed not to expel undocumented immigrants fleeing Nazi Germany. Foreigners arriving illegally who were at 'evident, immediate risk' were not to be refused asylum. The fact that nineteen of the twenty-nine ministers in the Herriot cabinet were members of the 'League for the Rights of Man' undoubtedly had some effect on this and their liberal values played a crucial role in the development of this policy towards refugees.[21] Diplomatic issues were also a factor. For the French, the refugee crisis vindicated their anti-German policy and allowing asylum, as Vicki Caron eloquently phrases it in this volume, to victims of 'Teutonic barbarism' was seen as a way of garnering international approval and support.[22] Although there was no clear initial strategy, it seems the French authorities considered settling a considerable number of these people in France without taking into account the possible length of their stay, their skills, wealth or number. This involved granting them all refugee status and rights to a work permit. Moreover, the French authorities also put their liberal admission policy within a vision of France as the centre for an international redistribution of these refugees. Whatever the precise motivation for this policy, the practical result was that de facto refugee status was granted to more or less all those fleeing Germany into France and the country received approximately 25,000 people (or between 40 per cent and 50 per cent of the total) escaping the Nazis in 1933.[23]

In contrast, the Belgian authorities were not prepared to make allowances for those refugees from Nazi Germany who arrived at the border without the necessary papers. They were refused entry to the country. When they succeeded in outwitting the border controls and entered the country illegally, they were treated as any other immigrant who had arrived without the proper authorisation and were subject to removal. Germans who had overstayed the periods stipulated in their visas were also called upon to leave the country. Only a very few – usually the most affluent – obtained extensions to their residence permits. Although orders to leave the country were handed out to the majority, the authorities did not immediately enforce them. Nonetheless, pressure was placed on aliens without valid papers to leave Belgium and many moved on to France or the Netherlands. This policy of urging refugees onto other countries soured diplomatic relations and France protested indignantly at the actions of her neighbour. In pursuing this intransigent policy, the Belgian government showed clearly that it was not prepared to share the burden when it came to refugees. However Belgian policy soon reached a stalemate as these refugees adamantly refused to return to Nazi Germany while neighbouring countries took steps to close their borders for refugees for whom Belgium had been the first country of asylum.

The Homogenisation of European Refugee Policies

The Belgian authorities were undoubtedly concerned about the potential for diplomatic repercussions that the expulsion of refugees might create. By the end of 1933, a specific refugee policy had been formulated whereby political refugees were granted semi-official asylum; with the Minister of Justice deciding which immigrants qualified for this status. The definition of 'refugee' was restrictive: only those seeking asylum whose lives or freedom were endangered because of their political activities could remain in Belgium. However, the beneficiaries of this policy were strictly prohibited from engaging in any economic activity and had to support themselves or find aid from refugee relief organisations or other welfare organisations.[24] In practice, only German political activists, who were small in number, qualified for this informal refugee status, and Jews who had fled Nazi Germany were largely excluded, but repatriation was not forced upon them either. The authorities granted temporary protection to the German Jews in order to enable them to prepare for re-emigration. During their temporary stay in Belgium these refugees were strictly prohibited from engaging in any economic activity and the Jewish community had to shoulder all the financial responsibilities for 'their' refugees. This latter requirement had come at the request of the Belgian-Jewish organisations themselves and they had undertaken to guarantee the maintenance of Jewish refugees from Nazi Germany pending their travel to other countries. The fact that Jewish organisations undertook the management of the refugee influx and underwrote its costs became the linchpin of Belgium's policy towards Jewish refugees.[25] In this respect, the Belgian authorities operated a policy that all West European countries had adopted to some degree during the course of 1933. British policy has already been mentioned, but as early as April 1933, the Swiss authorities had also made the Jewish community responsible for maintaining all Jewish refugees whom the authorities were ready to temporarily protect until their final emigration. Under a decree of 31 March 1933 these *Emigrants* (a new legal category within Swiss alien policy) were barred from any participation in Swiss (economic) life while they prepared their further migration to a country of final destination.[26] Very soon afterwards Denmark, the Netherlands and Luxemburg adopted similar policies, but in these countries only those refugees who had to be supported financially by refugee aid organisations were told to find a final destination. All other refugees could remain in the country as regular immigrants. In most countries, once they had entered the country legally or had their stay regularised by the authorities, the immigrants could have their resident permits renewed as long as they had some means of subsistence just like any other class of immigrant.[27] In all countries concerned, permits for refugees from Nazi Germany were almost always temporary.[28]

In France, where political and racially persecuted people had been granted an informal refugee status in the spring of 1933, the pattern established in the other countries was quickly duplicated, partly because France had taken the majority of the refugee efflux in early 1933, and partly because other countries had pushed 'their' refugees from Germany into France. From the summer of 1933 onwards, French policy towards the admission of refugees from Nazi Germany gradually became much more restrictive. After August 1933, the illegal immigration of German refugees was no longer condoned and préfets in the frontier départements were again allowed to expel German refugees who did not have the necessary documents to enter France. The authorities decided also that refugees with Eastern European nationality, who constituted no less than 50 per cent of all those who came to France, were to be considered as economic, rather than political émigrés. Five thousand Polish Jews who had fled Germany were singled out for harsher treatment. They were not forcibly expelled from French territory, but as a rule the préfecture de police refused them a residence permit and ordered them to leave the country. They were excluded from the informal refugee status the French authorities had granted to refugees from Germany. They could, however, lodge an appeal with the Ministry of the Interior against the expulsion order that served to suspend it until the appeal was heard. In the meantime, their residence became legal again and shortages of staff at the Ministry ensured that applications remained pending for a considerable length of time. By January 1934, the French authorities had begun expelling refugees from Germany whose papers were not in order.[29] It is highly likely that this was the result of the Ministry of Interior having upheld expulsion orders against East Europeans who had lodged appeals. In addition, October 1933 saw the liberal regulations relating to German refugees residing in France rescinded.[30] The French authorities no longer granted the refugee status originally afforded to Jewish Germans and they were now urged to re-emigrate overseas. Individuals who could prove that they had been physically assaulted or that they faced imminent danger were the only ones still to be welcomed as refugees. Only they received visas or identity cards. This stringent procedure excluded most of those who had fled from Nazi Germany and the mayors of Paris went on record to claim that most were mere immigrants as 'most of the alleged facts have been exceptionally exaggerated and are sometimes even totally imagined as very few of them can provide any details on this persecution ... They had left Germany on a voluntary basis'.[31] In effect, the French had come into line with the policies of their neighbours.[32] As Vicki Caron explains, in the following months more and more refugees faced expulsion orders. Since most could not leave, they ended up in French jails. France had brought its immigration policy into line with those of neighbouring countries and refugees could count on only marginal concessions to a more restrictive alien policy.

As highlighted above, the Belgian authorities had introduced a privileged status for political refugees by the end of 1933. Even earlier, the Swiss authorities had adopted a policy that also differentiated between political and Jewish refugees.[33] This went as far as creating a legal procedure for the granting of 'refugee' status and the speed of its introduction was largely a result of previous experience with refugees from Italy and replicated the instructions given to officials on the Swiss-Italian border in September 1932. The granting of 'refugee' status reflected not only the humanitarian concerns of the Swiss authorities, but also their desire to control political activists and prevent them from endangering diplomatic relations or domestic order. Incoming refugees had to apply to the police for 'refugee' status within 48 hours of arrival. The request, together with an extensive information sheet, was then sent to the Federal Prosecutor's Office. If considered as refugees, they were given temporary renewable residence permits valid for between one and three months. These 'refugees' could nevertheless be obliged to reside in a specific area and remained under the strict supervision of the local police authorities.[34] Denmark developed an informal refugee policy similar to that of Belgium. The illegal immigration of political refugees without papers was pardoned if a refugee aid committee made a case for the individual and guaranteed their upkeep. This policy was mainly of help to left-wing refugees and Jewish refugees were less generously treated; at best benefiting from some temporary protection.[35]

The Refugee Relief Committees and the New Refugee Policies

All those who had fled Nazi Germany, either by entering another Western European country legally, with a visa and/or by demonstrating they had sufficient means at their disposal, or illegally, and who found the means to support themselves without employment, or had their support guaranteed by relief organisations, were temporarily protected. The latter were the beneficiaries of refugee policies that were ostensibly more liberal than regular immigration policies. Affluent refugees had no need of recognition of their need for protection. They could be treated purely as immigrants and be granted a leave to remain.[36] For the less affluent refugees, it was the relief organisations that held the key to their protection as their (financial) support allowed them to qualify for temporary protection. The role of the aid organisations in facilitating the influx was thus of critical importance. The Jewish aid committees guaranteed that the refugees would not become a public charge until their final emigration. Their financial support was the indispensable condition of official readiness to tolerate the presence of large numbers of Jewish refugees. Aid committees had limited funds and therefore had to make choices about whom they supported. Each organisation had its own selection criteria. Thus in some, a distinction was made between Germans, who had no other country of refuge, and Eastern Europeans, who, it was argued, could return to their country of origin, in spite of the fact this was often a country in which many had never set foot. Other aid committees did not use this distinction, but based their decisions on the plight of individuals or their perceived worth as respectable members of society.[37] In either case, Jews with Eastern European passports could not expect to be sympathetically treated by the authorities. The majority had some claim on Polish nationality and the authorities usually argued that such people should be repatriated, even if this was opposed by the aid organisations.[38] For their part, the Polish authorities agreed to accept the repatriants provided that they came voluntarily, although they pointed out that in 1933, about a third of the Jews who had left Germany had returned to an East European country of origin or nationality.[39] However, the *Ost-Juden* also included many stateless people, mainly individuals who had actually been born in Germany but who had never acquired German citizenship on account of restrictive naturalisation procedures. Such people were far more difficult to deal with, as they had no obvious destination they could be returned to but were nevertheless 'encouraged' to move on to other countries. Jewish refugee aid committees thus sometimes provided people whom they could not help with a train fare back to Germany.[40]

As mentioned before, Great Britain had developed a similar scheme of temporary protection for Jewish refugees, but the country's much stricter external controls meant that the Jewish committees shouldered an even greater responsibility. In contrast to the British case, the arrival of refugees from Nazi Germany in the countries of Continental Europe was much less state controlled. Numerous refugees entered without the necessary documents by evading border controls in some way. These illegal entrants needed the support of the refugee committees for any asylum request to the authorities, and it was up to the committees to undertake responsibility for them. The Jewish organisations could also cover those who had overstayed visas and those who had temporary residence permits but whose means were exhausted with their guarantees of financial support, but the Continental European Jewish refugee aid organisations were more active in deciding whom to support than their British counterparts.

The relatively generous attitude towards the refugees in 1933 was largely the result of Jewish refugee aid committees being able to provide support for 'their' refugees. Figure 1 indicates the number of refugees registered by the Jewish committees in France, Belgium, Switzerland, Denmark and the Netherlands.[41] Jewish refugees were granted temporary protection, but the financial risks of admitting these people were transferred to the relevant Jewish community organisations. In some countries, the authorities stepped in and made unused military barracks available to serve as temporary refugee shelters.[42] The financial support provided to refugees by relief organisations allowed the refugee influx to occur without threatening jobs at a time of high unemployment, and also insured public funds from any additional burden.

The only country where German refugees were able to enter the labour market without restriction was the Netherlands, where the Dutch–German treaties of 1906 and 1930 prohibited any restrictions on the free movement of labour. In other states, visas or work permits were a requirement and thus restricted the possibility of refugees being able to support themselves.[43]

The actions of the Jewish refugee relief organisations in all countries had their roots in Jewish philanthropy towards their co-religionists. Persons of Jewish origin who were Christian converts or agnostics were, notwithstanding their beliefs, categorised as Jews by the Nazis and thus persecuted as well, but they did not always qualify for help from

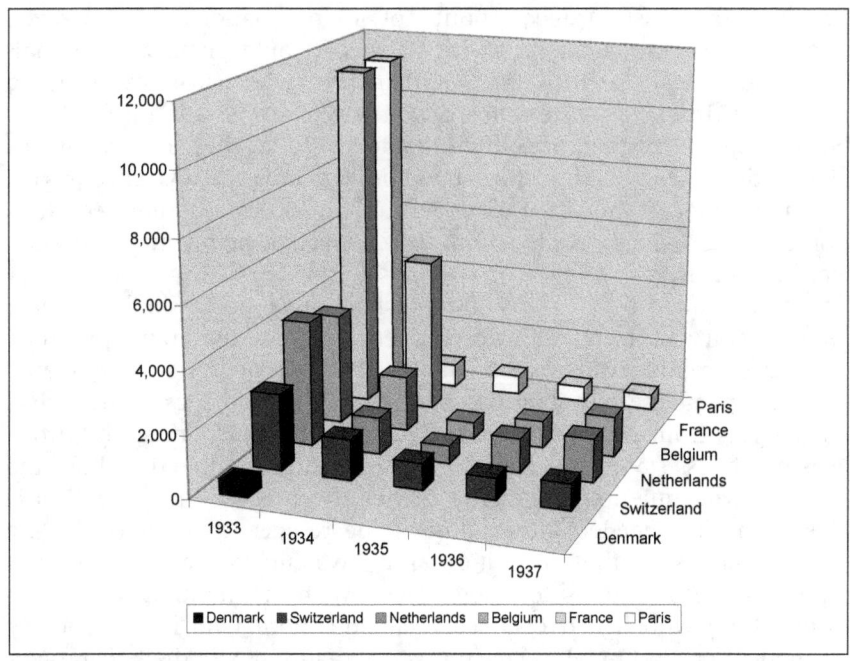

Figure 1. Refugees Newly Registered by Jewish Refugee Committees, 1933–1937

the Jewish religious communities outside Germany.[44] Many of these charitable organisations had been created at the turn of the century to help Jewish transmigrants from Tsarist Russia, and their relief strategies continued to be framed by these first experiences of helping refugees. Thus Jews fleeing Germany were only to be helped on a temporary basis and it was assumed that their stay in Europe was only until they could find a permanent destination overseas.[45] Nevertheless, even in 1933, assistance for Jews was bedevilled with considerable financial difficulties. American Jewish organisations, most notably the American Jewish Joint Distribution Committee (JDC) soon had to step in so that national committees could honour their pledges. The support of Jewish refugees also became more selective. In the autumn of 1933, a European meeting of the Jewish refugee aid organisations in London decided in favour of a more organised emigration for the Jewish refugees from Germany. The plan implied that the *Hilfsverein der deutschen Juden* would screen Jewish emigrants who applied for support from the aid committees and if these applicants turned out to be fleeing only economic hardship rather than physical danger, they would not be supported but urged to return to Germany.[46]

Activists of the German labour movement who fled Nazi Germany applied en masse for support from the socialist refugee committee, the International Matteotti fund. At the end of 1933, its various national relief committees were helping just under 10,000 refugees. Once it became clear that the Hitler regime was not about to disappear and that returning to the Reich was impossible, relief provision across Europe was reorganised out of financial necessity. A first initiative was to purge the relief lists. Support from the national Matteotti funds became centralised and all support applications were listed so that each application by German socialists was verified. This purge was in the first instance aimed at so-called parasites. All Germans who applied for help had to go through a screening process that included an interview with an exiled German socialist. As a result, those who fled their country 'merely' because of the severe economic crisis, and also communists, were removed from the relief lists, but the procedure became more severe even for bona fide social democrats. Only those who were likely to be arrested upon their return were eligible for support and all others were urged to return to Germany.[47] Despite this severe selection process, the financial resources of the social democratic movement were soon under severe strain. In every country, an urgent search for funds began. A number of public appeals for solidarity with the refugees were made, but met with little success. In April 1934, the weakest link in the socialist relief network, France, took drastic decision. All financial support was stopped.[48] In Belgium, Switzerland, Denmark and the Netherlands, refugees continued to receive (minimal) support from local Matteotti Funds, but none of these organisations had a solid financial basis and all were totally dependent on donations from local political parties and trade unions.[49] Similarly, the communist aid organisation, the International Red Help (IRH), could do little more than to give minute subsistence allowances for a short time, a huge contrast to the important structures created to help Jewish refugees.[50] The strategy and fortunes of the Red Help in the various countries of Western Europe were closely related to those of the local Communist Party. While the French Communist Party had a mass following, in the other countries the Communist parties remained very small. Each national section of the International Red Help was to large extent responsible for its own fund-raising. Subscriptions, donations and the sale of propaganda material provided the bulk of its income and any support from Moscow was not related to the financial needs of the refugees, but to the perceived political importance of the country concerned. Sometimes loyal and reliable communist refugees who continued to work for the KPD were provided with food and shelter. For their part, the KPD took the view that German communists should not stay in exile for long, but return to Germany as soon as possible to continue the struggle against fascism.[51] The need for legalising the stay of communist refugees was not that pressing, but the authorities were also not keen to protect these subversive aliens. Members of smaller German left-wing groups were even worse off. They could not count on any help from the social democrat or communist organisations in their countries of refuge, and were entirely dependent on like-minded activists who usually had no means to give these refugees even the most minimal support.[52]

Thus in the first year after the Nazis took control in Germany, the pattern of refugee policy was set for the years to come. This consisted of a two-track policy that differentiated between Jews and political refugees. The input of private initiatives – the refugee aid committees – was crucial. In most countries they selected those qualifying for protection by supporting them financially and recommending them to the authorities. The final say in refugee matters nevertheless remained the prerogative of the state in all countries. In the British case, control was exercised at the frontier, while in all countries of Continental Europe, decisions about residence were usually taken after the individual had been admitted. Policy towards refugees in Western Europe during 1933 was largely determined by domestic economic considerations. The danger of any country being seen as more sympathetic to refugees than their neighbours also became a central preoccupation of the authorities in the countries being considered here, and the French example shows that the domino effect of countries making comparisons with their neighbours created a restrictive dynamic of its own.

Developments in Policy towards Aliens, 1933–1937

In all Western European countries, the authorities continued to tighten their grip on the movement of aliens after 1933. The Flandin government in France promulgated decrees in November 1934, that all foreigners not in possession of residence permits would be expelled. The prison terms for those who did not leave France voluntarily after an order to do so, or who returned illegally, were raised to a minimum of six months and a maximum of two years in 1935. Actual expulsions remained rare, but many more aliens illegally staying in France were convicted.[53]

In Belgium, the arrival of refugees from Nazi Germany convinced the authorities to reform their legislation on aliens. According to the nineteenth-century alien legislation all immigrants acquired residency status after a few months registered stay in the country and subsequently, even if they became unemployed or destitute they could only be expelled if they disturbed public order. Government ministers were struck by the limits placed on the powers of the authorities in dealing with aliens, especially since these foreigners could make demands on public welfare. To maintain some level of control, a law of August 1933 extended the state's powers over aliens so that residence permits were made valid for a maximum of two years, with the possibility that they could be revoked at any reapplication. Luxemburg, following the Belgian example, introduced a centralised control of all foreigners with specific identity cards for aliens.[54] These profound legislative reforms were supplemented by smaller administrative changes that made it more difficult for immigrants to settle in Western Europe. For example, new arrivals were given even shorter periods to register with the authorities, and the duration of residence permits was also more limited.

In Denmark, Luxemburg and Britain, economic competition by immigrants was already fully regulated by the state – a stance supported by the trade unions.⁵⁵ Such tight domestic protectionism had been less evident in other countries, but during the depression even conservative governments enacted legislation against foreign labour as a palliative against protests about economic hardship. In France the quota system had proved to be impractical and administrative control of foreign labour through work permits was perceived to be far easier. With short-term residence and work permits, the French state tried to mould its foreign population to the needs of the economy. By February 1935 and in the face of burgeoning unemployment, the French Labour Ministry ordered that all applications for work permits from immigrants who had arrived after 1925 were to be rejected without exception.⁵⁶ The advent of the Popular Front government in France served to liberalise the state's alien policy slightly, with controls over foreign labour residing legally in the country being relaxed. However, at the same time there was considerable pressure from labour unions to stop immigration and increase controls over the unauthorised employment of foreign labour.⁵⁷ In Belgium after 1933, recent arrivals who were ostensibly competing with nationals in the labour market were refused residence. In 1935, the socialists entered the government and notwithstanding the improvement of the economic situation, they were instrumental in the introduction of comprehensive controls on foreign labour in 1936.

In the Netherlands, the authorities only began restrictions on foreign labour from 1935 onwards. The 17 October 1930 agreement with Germany on the equal treatment of Dutch and German workers was cancelled in 1934 by the Dutch government as a prerequisite for a protectionist labour market policy. A law of 16 May 1934 determined that from 1 January 1935, foreign workers in specified trades and industries were subject to government permits which would only be granted when no Dutch labour could be found to fill the vacancy. The number of economic sectors affected by the legislation was gradually increased until October 1936, when only work in the merchant marine or the Rhine barges was exempted. Certainly trades in which Jews had been prominent were included in the restrictions, but it is difficult to argue that this was the prime purpose behind the initial legislation.⁵⁸ Permits were renewable, and in practice, most of those already working in the Netherlands were allowed to continue and only new applicants were likely to be rejected. In contrast to both Belgium and France, the Netherlands had only a relatively small number of foreign students studying in Dutch universities. This did not prevent the legal profession from requesting and obtaining a Royal Decree in 1938 that denied aliens with Dutch law degrees access to the bar.⁵⁹

It was not only employees, but also the self-employed who became the subject of state control during the 1930s. This control was already well established in Britain, where a foreigner had to prove that his or her proposed undertaking did not offer serious competition to native citizens before a business could be opened.⁶⁰ Aliens, including refugees, became an easy target when economic nationalism and xenophobia became more commonplace. Within this economically motivated anti-foreigner discourse of the middle classes, Jewish refugees became a symbol. Moreover, the lack of state controls and reliable statistics allowed even their numbers to become part of the debate. The image of a refugee influx was often exaggerated to grotesque proportions. The motivation of these newcomers was often questioned and almost invariably presented in a bad light with accusations that it was 'failed entrepreneurs', criminals and paupers who were fleeing Nazi Germany. It can be argued that the increasing political power of the middle classes in Western Europe allowed them greater scope to protect themselves against local competition from foreigners. This strategy is most obvious in Belgium, the Netherlands and France, where the protests against the competition from German refugees in the trades rapidly turned into a general attack on foreign entrepreneurs. In France by 1935, foreign artisans and peddlers had to obtain a licence and the right to reside in France became linked to their right to work. In Belgium, peddlers were required to apply for permission to continue their livelihoods. In the Netherlands by 1937, the establishment of foreign-owned businesses was restricted in particular sectors of the economy.[61]

These measures were designed primarily to assuage public opinion by demonstrating that the government was *doing* something. In general, the legislation on aliens' wage labour or entrepreneurial endeavours increased state control over all immigrants, whether refugees or not. The legislation restricting the economic activities of aliens had little or no direct relationship with the increasing numbers of refugees created by the Nazi regime during and after 1933. In reality, in part due to the restrictions placed upon them, most Jewish refugees from Germany stayed only for a few months in their first (Western European) country of asylum before moving on overseas. Nonetheless, those who stayed, even if they were given residence permits, were largely excluded from national socioeconomic life. Within these restrictive policies, the period of residence required for protection against expulsion and/or restriction within the labour market was also extended in most countries. The probationary period before an immigrant could be granted the right to stay (and work) was lengthened from three to five years in Switzerland and from five years to ten years in France.[62]

All these measures were part of the internal control exercised when the aliens were already present in the country, but states also undertook measures to control entry. Visa restrictions were a means to keep unwanted immigrants out and these became increasingly difficult to obtain.[63] More resources were devoted to border control. In 1935, the French government appointed 25 new border police inspectors, and customs officers were also used to control immigration.[64] The same tightening of border controls can be seen in other countries, although there were few legislative changes. In the Netherlands, successive heads of the Border Security and Aliens Service (GVD), pressed for tighter controls, not necessarily because they saw the immigrants as inherently dangerous to Dutch interests, but primarily because they felt their resources were insufficient. This lack of means was also strongly felt in Luxemburg where the 121 km long border with Germany was only patrolled by customs officials.[65] Similarly in Belgium, the authorities felt that border control had to be tightened, especially away from the main border crossing points.[66]

The Evolution of Specific Refugee Policies, 1934–1936

In all seven Western European countries surveyed here, refugees requiring but not possessing visas who tried to enter illegally after the summer of 1933, or refugees without means apprehended by the authorities close to the frontier, were habitually expelled by border police. Even when they had succeeded in entering any of these countries, they ran the risk of being treated like any other undesirable alien. This was especially true of those who were destitute and/or undocumented and who were not given any help by refugee committees, either because they were not given the opportunity to make contact or because their application was refused. Forty Jews from Germany staying in Amsterdam were arrested in 1937. Their visible means of support was considered insufficient and they were treated just like any other alien in a similar position. The official expulsion document refers to them as 'so-called Jewish refugees'. The Dutch authorities did not acknowledge that they were refugees, and they were repatriated by the Amsterdam aliens police and handed over to the German authorities at the border.[67] Similarly in Denmark, such people were either put on the ferry to Germany or Danzig, or accompanied to the border and handed over to the German police.[68] In Belgium the authorities dumped unwanted immigrants across their side of the border with Germany and in France they were simply ordered to leave the country.[69] Only if they succeeded in contacting refugee committees and were considered as eligible for support were they then protected against deportation. Swiss law did recognise a formal refugee status but the refugee had to apply to the authorities within 48 hours of arrival. Albeit not a judicial procedure, the Swiss system had more safeguards against administrative arbitrariness than eligibility procedures in other West European countries. Even then, refugee status in Switzerland did not necessarily provide protection against expulsion. Failure to comply with the obligation to abstain from political activity was considered sufficient cause to expel a 'refugee' on public order grounds, the decision being taken by the Bundesrat. Between 1933 and 1935, the Swiss granted political refugee status to 366 persons who had fled Germany.[70] In Belgium, Denmark, France and Luxemburg an informal eligibility procedure was introduced which depended on administrative discretion. By 1935, no more than 400 refugees were considered 'refugees' in Belgium, and 450 in Denmark.[71] In France, 'refugee' became a status sanctioned by the law, as the decree law of October 1935 exempted stateless foreigners and those recognised as refugees from expulsion.[72]

In the Netherlands, the government was particularly wary of allowing entry to what they regarded as 'red elements' (which included both communists and social democrats) and such people were never considered for special status. Political refugees did enter the country and could receive residence permits, but only under the rules pertaining to all aliens. Provided that they did not engage in political activities or come to the notice of the authorities for some other reason, they were left in peace. However, even this implicit toleration was short-lived. Fuelled by fears of internal subversion and encouraged by the Germans to believe that their numbers would increase dramatically, the Dutch authorities took more direct action to identify aliens thought to be engaging in political activity during 1934. Numbers of refugees, mostly communists, were expelled. The only concession to their refugee status was that they were given a choice over which border they were sent.[73] Given the geographical position of the Netherlands the choice was between Belgium and Germany, in other words, no real choice at all. Originally, the Dutch had been content to place political refugees on trains at Roosendaal that then conveyed them into Belgium. As the Belgian authorities became aware of this, protests began to be made and a Dutch–Belgian accord on the expulsion of aliens across their respective frontiers in the autumn of 1934 meant that the Dutch abandoned the idea of giving the refugees a choice. The solution adopted late in 1934 was to take these people to the *Drielandenpunt* and put them over the German frontier, but only a few yards from where it dissected the Belgian frontier. This rather cynical policy continued to cause disputes with Belgium, but fears of an increase in numbers during 1935 and as a concession to Belgian protests, the Dutch altered their policy to re-employ the *vreemdelingenreglement* of 1918, whereby subversives could be interned. A camp for internees was set up at Fort Honswijk and only when it became apparent that the expected influx was not going to materialise was the camp closed. The few remaining inmates considered unsuitable for release or expulsion were incarcerated in civil jails.[74] This included the communist refugees whom the Dutch authorities considered a danger to public order. Their open-ended detention caused specific difficulties as some lost any hope of ever being liberated and resorted to suicide. Such act of despair did occur: in the year between July 1937 and August 1938 ten German emigrants attempted to take their own life in Dutch civil goals, of whom two died.[75]

This anti-communist bias in refugee policy was also clearly identifiable in the other countries. In Belgium, communist refugees were not eligible for informal refugee status and their expulsion was very common.[76] The French decree issued in November 1935 exempting refugees from expulsion nevertheless stipulated that those refugees who were engaged in subversive activities could still be expelled.[77] Numerous German communists were also expelled from France and a number of them had settled in the Saar, but when the territory was returned to the Reich in January 1935 and the French authorities reluctantly agreed to give asylum to refugees from the Saar, these communist refugees were denied re-entry altogether.[78] Denmark did officially consider German communists as refugees, as of the 450 recognised refugees in the country, 132 were communists, but these politically inconvenient people were kept under strict surveillance. In order to obtain a temporary residence permit, they had to comply with the so-called 'communist conditions' defined by the authorities as early as the autumn of 1933. This meant that they were obliged to reside in the Copenhagen area and had to report to the police weekly and were only granted renewable residence permits valid for two months. Finally the communists had to abstain from participating in any political activity whatsoever.[79]

Both Swiss and Danish authorities expelled communist 'refugees' who did not abide by the rules set for them, but the authorities were nevertheless reluctant to send communists back to Germany. The Swiss chose to send them over the French border, and when Paris protested, they continued the process by clandestine means.[80] In Denmark however, due to a lack of alternatives, repatriation to Germany was considered suitable for (undeserving) communists, as it would send a clear message that they had to adhere strictly to the conditions set by the Danish authorities. The authorities did not want this exemplary repatriation to be heavily publicised, but the Red Help realised this and as soon as one of its protégés was arrested, the organisation engineered widespread press coverage. In an interesting compromise, the Danish authorities encouraged the Red Help to organise the refugees' departure to the Soviet Union while they served a short prison term. This process was by no means straightforward. German communists needed authorisation from the central committee of the KPD to be able to emigrate to the USSR, and such authorisations were only sparingly granted as the USSR did not want mass immigration. Nevertheless, the Soviet Union did offer the German communists in Denmark asylum, but the threat to repatriate them never materialised. From May 1935 onwards the Soviet Union increasingly restricted access to its territory for communist refugees. This refusal to accept any more German communists was primarily the result of the increasing xenophobia within the Soviet regime itself.[81]

The changing dispersal patterns of communist refugees are shown in Table II.2.1, which documents the distribution of communist officials in Europe. This is not a clear-cut picture of asylum granted to all communist refugees as it reflects primarily the communist strategy of protecting its functionaries and the formation of communist centres for 'exile politics'. The table shows the importance of the Soviet Union as a country of asylum for German communists in 1935–1936 notwithstanding its isolationist stance. From 1936 onwards, Spain became the favoured destination for many German communists, but France remained the country of asylum par excellence for communist refugees throughout the whole period.

Table II.2.1: Country of Asylum of a Sample of 333 German Communists, 1933–1937[82]

	1933	1934	1935	1936	1937
France	90	81	89	76	78
USSR	14	19	41	56	53
Spain				18	42
Switzerland	16	24	24	21	20
Denmark	19	14	12	15	19
Saar	12	28	10	1	
Netherlands	12	15	18	16	13
Great Britain	13	1	4	8	7
Belgium	5	3	10	7	6
Luxemburg			1		

Eligibility for what was essentially only an informal refugee status in Western Europe not only excluded most communists but also most Jews fleeing Germany.[83] Traditional definitions of a refugee failed to cover the circumstances pertaining in Nazi Germany but remained largely unchanged in this period. It seems the Belgian and Danish informal refugee policy was slightly more liberal as some of those fleeing antisemitic persecution were granted an informal refugee status. Of the 400 'refugees' in Belgium, 330 were supported by the Jewish refugee aid committee, including not only political activists, but also civil servants dismissed because of their Jewish origins.[84] However, most Western European states failed to acknowledge antisemitic persecution as prima facie grounds for anything more than temporary protection. This rigidity in defining a refugee, ignoring the persecution of groups to which individuals belonged not by choice but by virtue of their parentage, was not only a feature of state attitudes but also filtered into civil society. A striking example of this is the refugee definition adopted at the International Conference on the Right of Asylum in Paris in 1936 in which the headline element was the political persecution of 'all foreigners who have been forced to migrate not only because of their political activities, but also their unionist, pacifist or scientific activities'. This gathering of human rights activists, primarily representing labour, socialist and communist movements, considered persecution for religious or racial reasons as secondary and relegated this to the third article of the Conference's adopted text.[85] This was severely criticised by the French human rights' activist Rubinstein who pointed out that this underlined the complete lack of understanding of the nature of the persecution the majority of refugees were fleeing. It supposed that the persons in danger of their life or liberty were those in an active struggle, whereas in reality the vast majority of the refugees were 'only' victims of the politics brought to bear against them. It was for this reason, he argued, that the right to asylum needed to be reconceptualised.[86]

Great Britain could stay largely aloof from these discussions as its effective external controls meant that the immigrants who arrived on British territory were pre-selected. The British could even afford a proactive refugee policy in that those selected could fit in with Britain's needs. The refugee aid organisations fostered selective refugee immigration by providing opportunities for persons of intellectual distinction, displaced scholars and scientists.[87] From 1937 onwards, refugee manufacturers were even solicited by the commercial counsellors at British embassies to set up factories in depressed areas in Britain. Government investment in factories available for rent and other financial inducements were part of an economic policy to persuade entrepreneurs in Germany who, because of their persecution as Jews, were willing to leave and to set up manufacturing firms in British regions with high unemployment.[88] This selective immigration policy meant that Britain mainly received people from the upper socioeconomic strata of Germany Jewry, while in continental Europe this was much less the case. This process can also be seen in the distribution of East European nationals. In Great Britain, Polish Jews formerly resident in Germany were a small minority among the refugees, while in France and Belgium they constituted a sizeable share.[89]

Due to the restrictive asylum policies in Continental Europe, many refugees who arrived in Western Europe during the spring and summer of 1933 re-emigrated or even returned to Germany. This was especially true of Jewish refugees who enjoyed only limited or temporary protection in their countries of refuge. Their re-emigration was often brokered by local Jewish relief agencies and financed by them in concert with the major international Jewish charities such as the HIAS-HICEM and JCA. Figures 2 and 3 (p.325) show that about 15,000 refugees in continental Europe were assisted by HICEM in their re-emigration from a country of temporary protection between 1933 and 1937.[90] These assisted refugees were mostly settled overseas with Jewish refugees mostly going to Palestine or South America.[91] Smaller numbers were actually repatriated, either to Eastern Europe or back to Germany.[92] Indeed, the German authorities noted more and more Jews returning from Western Europe during 1934. They attributed this to difficulties in earning a livelihood in these countries. According to the police authorities in Berlin, most of these returnees had left Germany *'ohne triftige Veranlassung'* (without good cause). After November 1934 the German police pointed out that the pressure on the emigrants must be considerable as some of those who returned were under investigation by the German tax authorities and even by the German courts.[93]

The Institutionalisation and Reform of Policies towards Refugees, 1936–1937

By 1936, the refugee issue had lost much of its importance and procedures had become more or less institutionalised in many Western European states. This more constructive approach to refugee matters can be partly credited to the political shift to the left evident in France, Belgium and Luxemburg in the mid 1930s and also to developments in Germany, where Nazi violence was curtailed during the Olympic year. Moreover there was a belief in early 1935 that the refugee crisis was about come to an end and the creation of an international refugee regime aimed at burden sharing diminished the risks of adopting a more liberal policy. Liberalisation of refugee policy was also facilitated by the change in communist strategy away from condemning Social Democrats as 'social fascist' and towards allying with them in a broad-based popular front.

Reformers in all countries pointed out the blatant ineffectiveness of the hard-line stance towards both communist and Jewish refugees. Refugee aid committees were forced to spend most of their time and energy on legalising the stay of refugees who had arrived since 1933 instead of focusing on their re-emigration or integration. Restrictive policies only served to force refugees to go underground or to leave for neighbouring countries where their arrival would cause diplomatic problems. They therefore advocated a new policy aimed at regularising and thus stabilising the existing refugee population by improving their legal status, and these appeals found willing ears in the new cabinets. The overtly anti-communist attitude among policy makers in Western Europe during the early years of the refugee crisis gave way to a more tolerant attitude in the middle of the decade. The communist strategy of seeking recognition by the authorities was not all that successful, as the Dutch, Swiss and Danish governments refused point blank to treat the communist refugee organisation on par with other 'respectable' refugee aid organisations, but in Belgium and France some progress was made.[94]

The Impact of Reform

In 1936, the French and Belgian governments had designed a formal refugee policy, in line with the international refugee regime they had both supported.[95] In contrast to the existing Danish and Swiss refugee policy where asylum seekers could be granted refugee status by the aliens' administration, the new French and Belgian policy was much more transparent. Asylum applications were not handled exclusively by civil servants but dealt with on a case-by-case basis in concert with an investigative commission that included people from outside the administration. In both countries an amnesty was declared for all German refugees. Their illegal immigration and residence was condoned and they were allowed to petition for asylum. The French and Belgian refugee commissions then advised their respective Ministers of Justice on whether these people should be granted refugee status and it seems that in most cases their advice was followed.[96] This introduction of a formalised procedure in both Belgium and France served to diminish administrative discretion in such matters. The new Belgian refugee policy was definitely more generous than the French one. Any refugee, irrespective of the country that had persecuted them, could petition in Belgium for asylum, while in France only those who had fled Germany before 5 August 1936 could do this. In Belgium, the engagement was an open-ended one, but France only granted an amnesty for refugees already in the country by 1936.[97] As can be seen from Table II.2.2, France received 6280 applications for refugee status (encompassing some 8,000 people) from people who had fled Nazi Germany before August 1936.

The institutionalisation of refugee policy in France and Belgium entailed new criteria for eligibility. The previous informal procedure had been dependent primarily on a recommendation from a 'respectable' refugee committee. The new accountability entailed a more bureaucratic handling of asylum cases and more concrete forms of evidence.[98] Many of the criteria used had been employed in earlier periods. Only those with German citizenship or the stateless who had been long-term residents of Germany were eligible for refugee status while Eastern Europeans and those with criminal records were excluded.[99] Belgium or France had to be the refugee's first country of asylum. Although this system had been used since 1934 there were, as yet, no internationally accepted criteria by which a country became unequivocally responsible for an asylum seeker on its territory. Even Belgium and the Netherlands, who had signed a bilateral agreement on this matter on 19 April 1937, had not done so. The foreigner who had been refused asylum in a country on these formal grounds had no guarantee whatsoever that his asylum application would be investigated properly in the country that had been considered to be his or her first country of asylum.[100] Thus while some criteria were carried forward, there were radical changes in that the definition of refugee also included those subject to anti-communist or racial persecution. The new policy extended the numbers of people entitled to claim protection as refugees.

The new refugee regime was a breakthrough for the protection of communist refugees. By 1938, when the German refugee commission in France stopped its activities, at least 400 German communists were granted refugee status and leave to remain. Even in Belgium where German communists had, before 1936, been considered as subversives rather than refugees, they became eligible for refugee status. Eligibility for refugee status implied that communists had to trust the bourgeois state as information had to be given about the whereabouts and political activities of asylum seekers. The German communist party in Belgium was not very eager to make the Belgian authorities aware of what they were doing or even divulge the addresses of refugees lest they fell into the hands of the German authorities and endanger their political work in Germany. The distrust voiced by the German communist leadership in Belgium was a great embarrassment to the local Red Help, but Moscow decided that the Popular Front policy demanded loyal cooperation with liberal regimes and the German communists were forced to acquiesce.[101]

Of the people who were considered for refugee status in France shown in Table II.2.2, most were Jews.[103] The collective persecution of Jews seems to have been acknowledged by the French asylum agency, but not by their Belgian counterparts. During the hearings of the asylum seekers, the advisory commissions had to take into account this new kind of persecution. The only victims of Nazi antisemitism to be considered eligible for protection by the Belgian refugee commission were Jews accused of *Rassenschande*. However in order to thwart 'abuses', the commission demanded proof that the relationship involved predated the Nuremberg Laws. This stipulation suggests that the commission harboured deep suspicions that immigrants would use the German laws as a means of deliberately bringing persecution on themselves. For that reason the detention of returnees in concentration camps for so-called 're-education' from 1935 onwards was not considered sufficient grounds for asylum, nor was the unlicensed export of capital, even though it carried the death penalty in Germany. Every citizen was expected to abide by their national laws and thus also to the rules pertaining to the export of capital. Only the *Rassenschande* laws were considered unacceptable and thus a ground for refugee status.[104]

Table II.2.2: The Treatment of 6,280 Asylum Applications in France, 1936–1938[102]

Decision	Eligible	Commission not competent (Saar, Nansen)	Refused	Without decision (died, emigrated)
	85%	7%	5%	3%
Citizenship	German	Stateless	Polish	Other
	84.6%	13%	1.9%	5%
Reason of flight	Political	Economic discrimination	Racial or religious motives	Other reasons
	16%	66%	9%	9%

Even in Denmark, where refugee policy operated in relative isolation and decisions remained entirely in the hands of the administration, there was some rethinking about who had to be protected. By the end of 1935, those Jewish refugees who had fled to Denmark in 1933 and who had had their temporary residence permits renewed time and again were discreetly granted the status of refugees. In April 1937, the Danish Minister of Justice, Karl Steincke, declared that the definition of a refugee had been widened for 'humane reasons' so that those who were persecuted 'due to their political beliefs, religion, race or ideology' had to be considered as genuine refugees. In particular, his reference to race as a collective category represented a change in the perception of refugees. He even explicitly mentioned internment or sterilisation on the grounds of race as justification for granting asylum.[105]

For the Netherlands and Luxemburg there is no indication that any discussions took place within the state apparatus on the need to protect certain categories of persecuted persons. In the Netherlands, even political refugees were not automatically included, mainly due to the fear of the Left. Thus the Netherlands did not formalise its refugee policy, but as a result of Belgian protests about the dumping of political refugees at or over the border and the Dutch reluctance to repatriate political refugees to Germany, a hybrid refugee policy did emerge. The bilateral agreement with Belgium on 19 April 1937 prohibited the expulsion of political refugees across their common frontier, implying that the Dutch were bound to accept political refugees for whom the Netherlands was the first country of asylum. In this way, Dutch refugee policy was not entrenched in domestic law, but based purely on this bilateral agreement. Political refugees, and especially the communists, were not granted residence permits even if they were no longer politically active but were no longer subject to expulsion. They were thus implicitly tolerated, but sometimes still interned in prisons.[106]

The status of refugees granted residence rights, but with no permission to take up paid employment, remained anomalous. In Denmark and Switzerland all refugee aid committees except the communists joined forces in 1937 and asked the authorities to grant their protégés the right to work or provide subsidies to guarantee their upkeep. In both countries the authorities remained unwilling to concede the right for refugees to work, but chose instead to make small financial allowances to the refugee committees.[107] While access to the labour market by those with only temporary protection still depended on administrative discretion, those who had received residence permits because of their formal refugee status received more benevolent treatment. The left-wing governments in 1936 made the labour market slightly more accessible for 'refugees', aided by a limited economic recovery that made this concession more politically acceptable. Nonetheless, the authorities still made sure that even 'refugees' would not threaten the livelihoods of local labour. In Denmark, the Social-Democrat/Social-Liberal coalition agreed to grant social democratic 'refugees' work permits if they had been in Denmark for 18 months and their application met with the approval of the Trade Unions.[108] Similarly in France, the Netherlands and Belgium, refugees were given more favourable treatment with regard to work permits than other immigrants.[109]

By the mid 1930s, France, Belgium, the Netherlands and Denmark had all regularised the status of the refugee population still resident in their respective countries. In the same way, the British authorities had quietly dropped conditions attached to the residence of those who had arrived in the first half of the 1930s and were still in the country in early 1938. They were no longer put under any real pressure to re-emigrate.[110] Many of those who had fled Nazi Germany in 1933 and 1934 had returned home or resettled overseas. Improving the legal status of the few remaining refugees was designed to hasten their integration into the host society and was also beneficial to the state in that it would be freed from the cumbersome task of close control and supervision.

The executive authorities in France and Belgium voluntarily limited the exercise of their powers in 1936 and 1937 by developing a formal and transparent refugee policy. This concession to humanitarianism was designed to rationalise immigration practices. This was in stark contrast to policy in the Netherlands where the authorities only made concessions under intense international pressure. The Dutch were reluctant to deport the subversive 'red elements' to Germany and had to accept that those who had arrived in the country should be allowed to remain as the only other available frontier was with Belgium, which refused to accept them. This example shows how international and domestic considerations could combine to determine the development of policies towards refugees. In all the countries considered in this survey, it seems from the actual state of research that the judiciary refrained from intervening in immigration policy and even refused to apply general legal principles (due process, proportionality) or domestic constitutional principles (equality before the law, basic rights) to such cases. Courts considered immigration issues as a matter for the executive and they set no limits to the states' capacity to deal with foreigners as they saw fit.[111]

New Arrivals and the Return to Restriction

A few political refugees continued to arrive in the liberal states of Western Europe after 1933, but by 1937 they were heavily outnumbered by Jews fleeing Nazi Germany. Solidarity with the Jewish refugees was most evident in Great Britain, where selective immigration was now encouraged. Private organisations in Great Britain chose candidates in Germany for emigration overseas. They were then admitted to training courses in Britain where they were taught skills to enhance their chances of finding a country of permanent settlement. The British authorities granted 'leave to remain' for short periods on production of proof of funds for emigration and promises of attendance on a training course. This immigration policy, which was part of the organised flight from Germany underwritten by the major international Jewish charities, carried few dangers for the British authorities. The refugee organisations were financially liable for these temporarily admitted refugees and as the authorities linked the admission of additional arrivals with the embarkation of previous entrants, there was no question of overall numbers inside the country increasing.[112]

By the end of 1937 refugee policy across continental Europe was in retreat from the liberalism of 1936. Restrictive immigration policies were reintroduced everywhere. This was the most striking in France where the cut-off date for the amnesty – 5 August 1936 – had dramatic repercussions. Although people arriving in France after 5 August could still petition the Minister of Interior at the border or inside the country itself, the advisory commission only investigated very few of these cases.[113] Once again, eligibility had become a matter of central administrative discretion and the dissolution of the advisory commission in 1938 did away with any possible uncertainty about the decision-making process.[114] Local discretion was also curtailed: préfets in frontier départements no longer decided the fate of those who requested asylum at the border, as this became the competence of the Minister of Interior. The Minister returned largely to the pre-1936 policy and ignored the broader definitions of a refugee used by the advisory commission. Only political refugees, and in particular those coming from concentration camps, could henceforward qualify for refugee status. This implied that the benevolence towards those fleeing antisemitic persecution had ended and that only political refugees could still count on some measure of protection. The Popular Front was fiercely determined to keep further unwanted (Jewish) immigrants out, even though, according to the Socialist Minister of the Interior, Marx Dormoy, this strict immigration policy did 'not affect the right of asylum' and did 'not affect authentic political refugees, who in reality are relatively few in number'.[115] As Vicki Caron explains, the arrival of the Popular Front in France did not serve to liberalise the state's policy towards *newly arriving* (Jewish) refugees.[116] Moreover, as the Popular Front coalition crumbled, the préfets in frontier départements recovered some of their powers and again took it upon themselves to deal with asylum seekers from Germany who arrived without the necessary documents. At the same time French refugee policy became generally more restrictive as refugee status became restricted to famous political personalities.[117]

One of the main reasons for the hard-line stand taken by the Popular Front towards newly arriving Jewish refugees was that the Ministry of Interior feared appearing tolerant at a time when other West European countries were strengthening their policies against Jewish refugees.[118] Even Belgium and Denmark, the only other countries in Continental Europe who had experimented with a more generous refugee policy, retreated from this policy. During 1937, the socialists remained in the Belgian government, but lost the Justice portfolio to a Catholic politician in November 1937, who lost no time in attacking the achievements of the new refugee policy. By April 1938, 320 asylum seekers had been recognised as refugees. The refugee commission still excluded most 'Jewish' refugees from refugee status, the only lasting concession remained that victims of 'race defilement' were still included.[119] 'Jewish' refugees supported by the relief committees still qualified for temporary protection, which remained a prerogative of the executive powers and in which the advisory commission had no say. 'Jews' remained still second-class refugees and dependent on administrative discretion: the recommendations of the Jewish committees were sometimes ignored and sometimes 'Jewish' refugees were ordered to leave the country. Shortly after the *Anschluss* the alien police outlined its policy in a note which stipulated that the 'harassment by the new masters of Austria of which the Jews are victims is not considered sufficient [for them] to be considered as political refugees'.[120]

Similarly in Denmark, the new definition of a refugee that included the victims of antisemitic policy had been applied to those who had arrived in 1933 or shortly thereafter, but by 1937 the Danish authorities returned to their previous definition of a refugee. This total change of course was possible because the Danish refugee policy remained an informal one, even though the country adhered to the international refugee convention of July 1936. Administrative arbitrariness remained the rule and the government made no binding commitments.[121] By 1938, Jewish refugees arriving in the Continental European countries who were supported by the refugee committees and were temporarily protected continued to be placed under great pressure by the authorities to organise their re-emigration as soon as was possible.

Notes

1. H. Strauss, 'Jewish Emigration from Germany – Nazi Policies – Jewish Responses', *LBIYB* 25, 1980 and 26, 1981: 25, p.317.
2. M. Dean, 'The Development and Implementation of Nazi Denaturalization and Confiscation Policy up to the Eleventh Decree to the Reich Citizenship Law', *Holocaust and Genocide Studies* 26, no. 2, 2002, p.221.
3. M. Hepp, *Die Ausbürgerung deutscher Staatsangehöriger 1933–45 nach den im Reichsanzeiger veröffentlichten Listen*, Munich 1985; H.E. Tutas, *National-Sozialismus und Exil. Die Politik gegenüber der deutschen politischen Emigration*, Wien 1973.
4. Note German Ministry of Foreign Affairs, 14.1.1938, Auswärtiges Amt (AA) R 48907
5. A. Barkai, *From Boycott to Annihilation: The Economic Struggle of German Jews, 1933–1943*, Hanover 1989, pp.54ff.
6. J. Noakes and G. Pridham, *Nazism 1919–1945*, vol. 2, Exeter 2000, pp.341–43.
7. Seeing that the National Socialist racial categorizations, such as Jew and Aryan, were not at all transparant and self-evident categories, we enclose those terms in quotation marks. On the construction of these categories see C. Esser, *Die 'Nürmberger Gesetze' oder die Verwaltung des Rassenwahns 1933–1945*, Paderborn 2002; D. Fraser, 'Aryan and Jew in the Nazi Rechtsstaat', in *Thinking Through the Body of the Law*, ed. P. Cheah, D. Fraser and J. Grbich, Sydney and New York 1996, pp.63–79. On race-defilement investigations and trials see A. Przyrembel, *«Rassenschande». Reinheitsmythos und Vernichtungslegitimation im Nationalsozialismus*, Göttingen 2003; P. Szobar, 'Telling Sexual Stories in the Nazi Courts of Law: Race Defilement in

8. Germany, 1933 to 1945', *Journal of the History of Sexuality*, 11, 2002, pp.131–63.
8. H. Berschel, *Bürokratie und Terror. Das Judenreferat der Gestapo Düsseldorf, 1935–1945*, Essen 2001, pp.275–77; Tutas, *National-Sozialismus und Exil*, pp.105–16; J. Wacker, *Humaner als in Bern! Schweizer und Basler Asylpraxis gegenüber den jüdischen Flüchtlingen von 1933 bis 1943 im Vergleich*, Basel 1992, p.68; B. Eckert, *Die jüdische Emigration aus Deutschland 1933–1941. Die Geschichte einer Austreibung*, Frankfurt 1985, p.211; E. Johnson, *Nazi Terror. The Gestapo, Jews and Ordinary Germans*, New York 2000, p.114f.; G. Herz, *The Women's Camp in Moringer: A Memoir of Imprisonment in Germany 1936–1937*, New York 2006.
9. Dean, 'Nazi Denaturalization and Confiscation Policy', p.221; G. Maierhof, 'Selbsthilfe nach dem Novemberpogrom. Die Jüdische Gemeinde in Frankfurt an Main 1938 bis 1942' in *'Nach der Kirstallnacht'. Jüdisches Leben und antijüdische Politik in Frankfurt am Main 1938–1945*, ed. Monica Kingreen, Frankfurt 1999, pp.127–86.
10. Reports to and from the Sicherheitshauptamt Berlin, 1936, BBR 58, 994; Note German Ministry of Foreign Affairs to embassies in Berlin, 23.11.1938, BBR 58, 236; Report German Embassy in Paris, 21.5.1938, AA R 48907; H. Berschel, *Bürokratie und Terror*, pp.260–61.
11. W. Röder, 'The Political Exiles: Their Policies and Their Contribution to Post-War Reconstruction', in *International Biographical Dictionary of Central European Emigrés 1933–1945*, vol. II, ed. H. Strauss and W. Röder, Munich 1983, p.XXIX.
12. HSTAD RW 58, 9432.
13. In 1937, as many as 1,028 Germans were denaturalised: Dean, 'Nazi Denaturalization and Confiscation Policy', p.221ff.; Hepp, *Die Ausbürgerung*; see for example HSTAD RW 58, 44060 and 26250. Revoking of German citizenship of all Jewish emigrants was only decided in 1941, before such a bold decision was feared to endanger emigration opportunities: Berschel, *Bürokratie und Terror*, pp.262–74.
14. Reichsvereinigung der Juden in Deutschland, *Organisation und Auswanderung der Juden aus dem Altreich, 1933 bis 1941*, p.231 and 233, BBR 8150 (microfilm 31). See Aviva Halamish and Patrick von zur Mühlen in this volume.
15. B. Moore, *Refugees from Nazi Germany in the Netherlands, 1933–1940*, Dordrecht 1986, p.66f.; UEK, p.139; U. Gast, *Von der Kontrolle zur Abwehr. Die eidgenössische Fremdenpolizei im Spannungsfeld von Politik und Wirtschaft 1915–1933*, Zürich 1997, p.337.
16. L. London, 'British Immigration Control Procedures and Jewish Refugees, 1933–1939', in *Second Change: Two Centuries of German-Speaking Jew in the United Kingdom*, ed. W. Mosse, Tübingen 1991, p.490 and 500; L. London, *Whitehall and the Jews, 1933–1948: British Immigration Policy and the Holocaust*, Cambridge 2000, p.27ff.; B. Wasserstein, 'The British Government and the German Immigration 1933–1945', in *Exile in Great Britain: Refugees from Hitler's Germany*, ed. G. Hirschfeld, Leamington Spa 1984, p.67.
17. L. London, 'Jewish Refugees, Anglo-Jewry and British Government Policy, 1930–1940', *The Making of Anglo-Jewry*, ed. D. Cesarani, Oxford 1990, p.170. In line with contemporary political developments the concept 'temporary protection' is used if immigrants are considered refugees but are not entitled to this status and thus not granted (the prospect of) a permanent residence status. These refugees are however explicitly tolerated by giving them some temporary entitlement to stay. Temporary protection as a form of

explicit toleration is a concept which underlines the commitment to refugee protection in immigration policy, while implicit toleration (and other forms of explicit toleration) can be due to passively enduring immigration. While temporary protection is a positive choice, toleration is rather a negative choice due to indifference or impotence. The latter refers to the incapacity to enforce immigration rules which causes that the authorities halfheartedly give in and put up with immigrants who have not been authorised to enter and stay in the country.

18. Report of censors to Sicherheitshauptamt Berlin, 18.6.1936, Bundesarchiv Berlin-Lichterfelde (BABL) R 58/994.
19. Anne Grynberg, *Les camps de la honte: les internés juifs des camps français (1939–1944)*, Paris 1992, p.26ff.; B. Vormeier and H. Schramm, *Vivre à Gurs. Un Camp de Concentration français 1940–1941*, Paris 1977, p.201.
20. AAD 340.
21. J.C. Bonnet, *Les Pouvoirs publics français et l'immigration dans l'entre-deux-guerres*, Lyon 1976, p.235; V. Caron, *Uneasy Asylum: France and the Jewish Refugee Crisis, 1933–1942*, Stanford 1999, p.17ff.
22. V. Caron, 'Loyalties in Conflict: French Jewry and the Refugee Crisis, 1933–1935', *Leo Baeck Institute Yearbook*, 36, 1991, p.307f.
23. R. Thalmann, *L'immigration allemande et l'opinion publique en France de 1933 à 1936, La France et l'Allemagne 1932–1936. Actes du colloque franco-allemand tenu à Paris 10–12.3.1977*, Paris 1977, p.164f.; Caron, 'Loyalties in Conflict', p.307; J. Simpson, *The Refugee Problem, Report of a Survey*, London, New York and Toronto 1939, p.148f.
24. F. Caestecker, *Ongewenste gasten, joodse vluchtelingen en migranten in de dertiger jaren*, Brussel 1993, pp.38, 48–50; J. Deschodt and F. Huguenin, *La république xénophobe, 1917–1939*, Paris 2001, p.340.
25. Caestecker, *Ongewenste gasten*, p.43.
26. S. Mächler, *Hilfe und Ohnmacht. Der Schweizerische Israelitische Gemeindebund und die nationalsozialistische Verfolgung, 1933–1945*, Zürich 2005, p.35f. For more details see Regula Ludi, this volume.
27. Moore, *Refugees*, p.29; L. Rünitz, *Danmark og de jodiske flygtninge 1933–1940*, Copenhagen 2000, pp.178–79.
28. Thus for example, in Switzerland in 1936, only 6 Jewish refugees had a *Niederlassungsbewilligung* (settlement permit) and only 118 had a residence permit valid for more than one year: Mächler, *Hilfe und Ohnmacht*, p.17.
29. The Polish consular authorities in Paris knew of about a thousand Polish refugees from Nazi Germany who faced expulsion orders in the summer of 1933: Polish Embassy in Paris to Polish Ministry of Foreign Affairs, 1933 and 1934, Archivum Akt Nowych, Warsaw (AAN), Ambassada RP W Paryzu, 304; Caron, 'Loyalties in Conflict', pp.318ff.; Caron, *Uneasy Asylum*, p.35.
30. Vormeier and Schramm, *Vivre à Gurs*, p.201; Thalmann, *L'immigration allemande*, p.163.
31. Comité directeur de l'Union des Maires et Maire-adjoints de Paris to the préfet de police, 10.3.1934, quoted in C. Zalc, 'Des réfugiés aux indésirables: les pouvoirs publics français face aux émigrés du IIIe Reich entre 1933 et 1939', in *Construction des nationalités et immigration dans la France contemporaine*, ed. E. Guichard and G. Noiriel, Paris 1997, p.264.
32. For the French refugee policy see Vicki Caron, this volume.
33. For the Swiss refugee policy see Regula Ludi, this volume.

34. C. Ludwig, *Die Flüchtlingspolitik der Schweiz in den Jahre 1933 bis 1952. Bericht des Bundesrates an die Bundesversammlung*, Bern 1957, pp.331–49; Gast, *Von der Kontrolle zur Abwehr*, p.348f.
35. Rünitz, *Danmark*, p.175ff.
36. Y. Kapp and M. Mynatt, *British Policy and the Refugees 1933–1941*, London 1997, p.28; Caestecker, *Ongewenste gasten*, p.26.
37. In the Netherlands, the Jewish, Catholic and Matteotti committees rejected on principle any Germans convicted of (non-political) crimes and communists: Simpson, *The Refugee Problem*, p.350.
38. C. Van Eijl, *Al te goed is buurmans gek. Het Nederlandse vreemdelingenbeleid 1840-1940*, Amsterdam 2005, pp.183–84; Caron, 'Loyalties in Conflict', p.318.
39. Strauss, 'Jewish Emigration', p.329; Polish Embassy in Paris to Polish Ministry of Foreign Affairs, 1933 and 1934, AAN, Ambassada RP W Paryzu, 304; Moore, *Refugees*, pp.72–73; Van Eijl, *Al te goed*, pp.185–87; in the United Kingdom in 1933 a Pole and a Hungarian Jew fleeing Nazi Germany who had entered the country unlawfully were deported: London, 'British Immigration', p.500.
40. HSTAD RW 58, 4503; Rünitz, *Af hensyn*, p.413.
41. The yearly figure for 1933 for Belgium is calculated on the basis of the monthly intake of refugees. For Antwerp we only have figures for the period March–June, thus for July–December the figure of 1,000 is an estimate, a lower number than the 1,500 which Brussels registered in those months: Caestecker, *Ongewenste gasten*, pp.31–33; for the other countries: Moore, *Refugees*, p.83; Caron, *Uneasy Asylum*, p.389; Rünitz, *Danmark*, p. 178; Mächler, unpublished appendix in the original ms of *Hilfe und Ohnmacht*.
42. For Antwerp (Belgium) see the local journal, *Afweer*, 19.5.1933/3; Caron, *Uneasy Asylum*, p.40.
43. Van Eijl, *Al te goed*, pp.184–85.
44. Moore, *Refugees*, p.35; London, *Whitehall*, p.126f.
45. Caron, *Uneasy Asylum*, p.107; Moore, *Refugees*, p.28.
46. Mächler, *Hilfe und Ohnmacht*, p.66; Caron, *Uneasy Asylum*, p.40.
47. BBR 3426B; U. Langkau-Alex, *Deutsche Volksfront, 1932–1939. Zwischen Berlin, Paris, Prag und Moskau. Vorgeschichte und Gründung der Ausschusses zur Vorbereitung einer deutscher Volksfront*, Berlin 2004, pp.51–52; F. Caestecker, 'Het reëel bestaande socialisme in West-Europa en de vlucht uit Nazi-Duitsland, 1933–1934; een oefening in private internationale solidariteit', *Bijdragen tot de eigentijdse geschiedenis*, 15, 2005, pp.114–22.
48. Report of the meeting of the International Matteotti Committee, 6–7.1.1934, p.8, BBR 3426B; Langkau-Alex, *Deutsche Volksfront*, p.127; J.Omnès, 'L'accueil des émigrés politiques 1933–1938', in *Les Bannis de Hitler*, ed. Badia Gilbert et al., Paris 1984, pp.70–72.
49. Moore, *Refugees*, p.118; Caestecker, *Ongewenste gasten*, pp.93–94; Omnès, 'L'accueil des émigrés'; H. Wichers, *Im Kampf gegen Hitler. Deutsche Sozialisten im Schweizer Exil 1933–1940*, Zürich 1994, p.306. For a similar evolution of the British International Solidarity Fund see T. Kushner, 'Their Brothers' and Sisters' Keepers? The Nazi Persecution of the Jews and the Labour Movement', in *The Holocaust and the Liberal Imagination: A Social and Cultural History*, Oxford 1994, pp.70f.
50. Simpson, *The Refugee Problem*, p.189.
51. Moore, *Refugees*, p.123ff.; Brigitte Studer, *Un parti sous influence. Le parti communiste suisse, une section du Komintern, 1931 à 1939*, Lausanne 1994,

p.446; Caestecker, *Ongewenste gasten*, p.28, 99; R. Weijdeveld, *Rode Hulp. Opvang van Duitse vluchtelingen in Groningerland, 1933–1940*, Groningen 1986; B. Herlemann, *Die Anleitung des Widerstands der KPD durch die Exilierte Parteiführung in Frankreich, den Niederlanden und Belgien*, Taunus 1982.

52. B. De Cort, *Solidariteit in anonimiteit. De geschiedenis van de leden van de Onafhankelijke Socialistische Partij*, Breda 2004, pp.120–33; F. Battel, '*Wo es hell ist, dort is die Schweiz' Flüchtlinge und Fluchthilfe an der Schaffhauser Grenze zur Zeit des Nationalsozialismus*, Zürich 2000, pp.76–77; A. Hazekamp, 'Op de vlucht. Duitse anarchisten in Nederland 1933–1940', *De As*, 151, 2005, pp.3–13.

53. Decree of 30 October 1935, cited in Vormeier and Schramm, *Vivre à Gurs*, p.221; M. Livian, *Le parti socialiste et l'immigration*, Paris 1982, p.207.

54. S. Hoffmann, 'Les problèmes de l'immigration et la montée de la xénophobie et du racisme au Grand-Duché à la veille de la 2e Guerre Monidale', *Galerie* 4, no. 4, 1986, pp.521–36.

55. Kushner, 'Brothers'; in Luxemburg a new work permit was required with each change of job: S. Hoffmann, 'Les problèmes'.

56. Harouni Rahma, 'Le Débat autour du statut des étrangers dans les années 1930', *Le mouvement social*, 188, 1999, p.61ff.

57. V. Caron, 'The Politics of Frustration: French Jewry and the Refugee Crisis in the 1930s', *Journal of Modern History*, 65, 1993, p.338; Bonnet, 'Les Pouvoirs publics français', p.241; G. Cross, *Immigrant Workers in Industrial France: The Making of a New Laboring Class*, Philadelphia 1983, pp.207–10.

58. Moore, *Refugees*, p.74f.; Van Eijl, *Al te goed*, pp.153–55.

59. *Vrij Nederland*, 50, 6 May 1989, p.13. For psychiatrists' attempts to protect their profession from refugee colleagues, see *NRC Handelsblad*, 19 May 1984.

60. Internal note AJDC, 3.1937, JDC 658.

61. G. Noiriel, *Le Creuset Français. histoire de l'immigration XIX–XXe siècles*, Paris 1988, p.113; Caron, *Loyalties in Conflict*, p.329; R. Schor, *L'opinion française et les étrangers en France, 1919–1939*, Paris 1985, pp.156–61; Simpson, *The Refugee Problem*, p.276f.; C. Zalc, 'L'analyse d'une institution. Le registre de commerce et les étrangers dans l'entre-deux-guerres', *Genèses*, 31, 1998, p.99; C. Zalc, 'Contrôler et surveiller le commerce migrant. Nomades, forains et ambulants à Paris (1912–1940)', in *La police et les migrants*, Rennes 2001, pp.382–84 ; Caestecker, *Ongewenste gasten*, p.131ff. and 160ff.; Caestecker, *Alien Policy in Belgium*, p.248ff.; N. Manitakis, 'Etudiants étrangers, universités françaises et marché du travail intellectuel (fin du XIXe–années 1930)', in *Construction des nationalités et immigration dans la France contemporaine*, ed. E. Guichard and G. Noiriel, Paris 1997, p.151; Moore, *Refugees*, p.55 ; van Eijl, *Al te goed*, pp.157, 166–69; Deschodt and Huguenin, *La république xénophobe*, p.100.

62. Caestecker, *Alien Policy*, p.203.

63. Caron, 'Loyalties in Conflict', p.318; Grynberg, *Les camps de la honte*.

64. Bonnet, *Les Pouvoirs publics français*, p.290.

65. Gloden, 'Die Asylpolitik Luxemburgs', p.81.

66. Correspondence between Robert de Foy and Standaert,11.1934, AAD 226.

67. It is unclear if the 'so-called' is a qualification given by the refugee committee or that these Jews were expelled notwithstanding protection of the refugee committee. The latter is rather unlikely as the Jewish refugee committee boasted in September 1937 still of its perfect working relationship with the Amsterdam police. B. Moore, *Refugees from Nazi Germany in the Netherlands*,

1933–1940: The Political Problem and Government Response, PhD Thesis, University of Manchester, 1983, p.459; Gemeentearchief (GA) Amsterdam, Gemeentepolitie, arch.5225/5. The Dutch–German treaty of 1906 had established a formal procedure for removing German nationals from the Netherlands. Five Dutch agencies located at different border points were in charge of formally handing over the expellees to the German authorities at agreed times and places. Achim Korres underlines that in the archives of two such agencies, at Venlo and Heerlen in the south east of the Netherlands, there is no trace of extraditing refugees during the 1930s: A. Korres, 'Paspoortregime en migratie in het Duits-Nederlandse grensgebeid in de negentiende en twintigste eeuw tot ca.1940', *Jaarboek van het Sociaal Historisch Centrum voor Limburg*, 50, 2006, p.131.

68. The Danish authorities always asked the German authorities for the agreement on their return, prior to the expulsion: Rünitz, *Af hensyn*.
69. Wichers, *Im Kampf gegen Hitler*, p.59. It is unclear if the préfets of the French frontier départements only ordered undesirable aliens to leave the country, or forced them to do so, using the police as escorts.
70. M. Imboden and B. Lustenberger, 'Die Flüchtlingspolitik der Schweiz in den Jahren 1933 bis 1945', in *Zuflucht Schweiz. Der Umgang mit Asylproblemen im 19. und 20. Jahrhundert*, ed. C. Goehrke and W. Zimmermann, Zürich 1994, see also Regula Ludi, this volume.
71. Gloden, 'Die Asylpolitik Luxemburgs', pp.46, 79; Caestecker, *Ongewenste gasten*, p.38; Rünitz, *Af hensyn*.
72. Caron, *Uneasy Asylum*, p.61.
73. Also communist refugees in Luxemburg were habitually expelled, and they also were given a choice over which border they were sent: M. Gloden, *Die Asylpolitik Luxemburgs von 1933 bis 1940. Der Anspruch auf Kontrolle*, Wissenschaftliche Arbeit zur Erlangung des akademischen Titels eines Magister, Universität Trier, 2001, p.46
74. Moore, *Refugees*, p.143ff.
75. Moore, *Refugees*, p.453; Weijdeveld, *Rode Hulp*, pp.144–68; H. Weber and A. Herbst, *Deutsche Kommunisten. Biographisches Handbuch, 1918 bis 1945*, Berlin 2004, p.681. The same practice of open-ended detainment was applied to communist refugees in Sweden and Norway: Simpson, *The Refugee Problem*, p.257.
76. Caestecker, *Ongewenste gasten*, pp.48–49.
77. Caron, *Uneasy Asylum*, p.61.
78. Ibid., p.52.
79. Rünitz, *Af hensyn*, p.408, 76–88.
80. Wichers, *Im Kampf gegen Hitler*, pp.58–59; UEK, p.98; Studer, *Un parti sous influence*, p.439.
81. Rünitz, *Af hensyn*, pp.76–88, also the Netherlands sent unwanted communist refugees off to the USSR: Meershoek, *Dienaren*, p.95. For the refugee policy in the Soviet Union see C. Tischler, *Flucht in die Verfolgung. Deutsche Emigranten in sowjetischen Exil 1933 bis 1945*, Münster 1996.
82. This table is based on the biography of 1,400 persons who during the period 1918–1945 mostly had been officials of the German communist party, KPD, and were listed in Weber and Herbst, *Deutsche Kommunisten*.
83. M. Dewhurst Lewis, *The Boundaries of the Republic. Migrant Rights and the Limits of Universalism in France, 1818–1940*, Stanford 2007, pp.177–78.
84. Caestecker, *Ongewenste gasten*, p.38; Rünitz, *Af hensyn*.

85. 'Seront assimilés aux réfugiés politiques les étrangers qui, pour des raisons confessionneles ou raciales, seraient exposés à des persécutions ou soumis à un régime de discrimination', quoted in Omnès, 'L'accueil', p.98.
86. J. Rubinstein, 'Le Statut des réfugiés politiques', *Cahiers des Droits de l'homme*, 15.4.1937, pp.229–34.
87. See, for example, B. Wasserstein, 'Intellectual Émigrés in Britain, 1933–1939', in *The Muses Flee Hitler: Cultural Transfer and Adaptation, 1930–1945*, ed. J. Jackman and C. Borden, Washington 1983, pp.249–56; G. Hirschfeld, '"A High Tradition of Eagerness…" British Non-Jewish Organisations in Support of Refugees', in *Second Chance: Two Centuries of German-speaking Jews in the United Kingdom*, ed. W. Mosse, Tübingen 1991, pp.599–610.
88. H. Loebl, 'Refugees from the Third Reich and Industry in the Depressed Areas of Britain', in *Second Chance: Two Centuries of German-speaking Jews in the United Kingdom*, ed.W. Mosse, Tübingen 1991, pp.379–404.
89. D. Niederland, 'German Jews – Emigrants or Refugees?', in *Second Chance: Two Centuries of German-Speaking Jews in the United Kingdom*, ed. W. Mosse, Tübingen 1991, pp.61–63; B. Moore, 'Jewish Refugees in the Netherlands 1933–1940: The Structure and Pattern of Immigration from Nazi Germany', *LBIYB*, 39, 1984, pp.87–89; F. Caestecker, 'A Quantitative and Qualitative Analysis of the Volume and Direction of Migration Flows', in *Refugees from Nazi-Germany in West-European Border states, 1933–1939/1940*, Brussels 2004, p.131.
90. This graph is based on Appendix to Gottschalk to de Foy, 1936, AAD 783; YIVO, HICEM (Paris) – Emigration record group 245.5, Serie France I, Microfilms reel 16.11, folder 155 and microfilms reel 16.1. These figures refer to persons including minor-aged children. Also from the United Kingdom resettlement overseas was being organised, but we had no figures at our disposal: London, 'British immigration', p.501.
91. See Aviva Halamish, and Patrick von zur Muhlen, this volume.
92. According to the refugee committees they only organised repatriation at the refugees' request. On the policy of refugee committees forcing Germans to return to Germany see Caron, *Uneasy Asylum*, pp.108 and 144; Caestecker, *Ongewenste Gasten*, p.58; Mächler, *Hilfe und Ohnmacht*, pp.137–39; Moore, *Refugees*, p.96, 100; Simpson, *The Refugee Problem*, p.323; AAN, Ambassada RP in Paris, 304. According to German sources their numbers amounted to 10,000 by 1935: D. Niederland, 'German Jews – Emigrants or Refugees?', in *Second Chance: Two Centuries of German-Speaking Jews in the United Kingdom*, ed. W. Mosse, Tübingen 1991, p.67; Deschodt and Huguenin, *La république xénophobe*, p.104 .
93. O. Kulka and E. Jäckel, *Die Juden in den geheimen NS-Stimmungsberichten 1933–1945*, Dusseldorf 2004, pp.85, 88, 96; Y. Bauer, *My Brother's Keeper: A History of the American Jewish Joint Distribution Committee, 1929–1939*, Philadelphia 1974, p.152 mentions the return of 11,000 Jewish refugees to Germany, among them up to 1,500 Jewish refugees from the Netherlands and up to 3,000 from France.
94. Rünitz, *Af hensyn*, pp.76–88; H. Petersen, 'The Historical Perspective in Denmark: The Treatment of Refugees in the 1930s', in *Rescue-43: Xenophobia and Exile*, ed. John Strange, Ole Farver and Ove Nathan, Copenhagen 1993, pp.14–32; Caestecker, *Ongewenste Gasten*, p.67–74 ; Omnes, *'L'accueil'*, p.93ff.
95. For the international refugee regime see Susanne Heim, this volume.

96. Of the favourable recommendations the committee has already made, only about 5 per cent have been rejected by the Ministry. H.W.H. Sams, Report on Russian, Armenian, Spanish, Italian, Saar and German refugees in France (10–12.1937), p.116, Archives Royal Institute of International Affairs (Chatham House); F. Caestecker, 'Onverbiddelijk, maar ook clement. Het Belgische immigratiebeleid en de joodse vlucht uit nazi-Duitsland, maart 1938–augustus 1939', *Bijdragen tot de eigentijdse geschiedenis*, 13/14, 2004, pp.102ff.
97. Caestecker, *Ongewenste Gasten*, pp.65–66.
98. Noiriel, *La Tyrannie du National*, p.199; Caestecker, *Ongewenste gasten*, p.73.
99. B. Vormeier, 'Frankreich', in *Handbuch der deutschsprachigen Emigration 1933–1945*, ed. C. Krohn, P. von zur Mühlen, G. Paul and K. Winckler, Darmstadt 1998, p.221 quotes Grzesinski Albert, *Memorandum über die deutsche Emigration*, which documents that not one East European was eligible for refugee status although the commission had initially advocated for including those East Europeans whose only relation to their country of citizenship was their passport. Only very few applications of East European nationals were considered admissible by the prefects who administered the process all over France. Dewhurst Lewis, *The Boundaries of the Republic*, pp.180–82. For Belgium, from 1936 onwards, a refugee with a criminal record could be temporarily protected at most: Caestecker, *Ongewenste gasten*, p.38. For the latter issue we have no information on French eligibility policy.
100. The vicissitudes of the Communist MP from the city-state of Hamburg, Walter Hochmuth, provide ample illustration of the lack of criteria by which a country became responsible for asylum seekers. Hochmuth had fled from Germany to Denmark (1934–1935), then passed through Belgium on his way to the Netherlands where he stayed for three years (1935–1938), but he was finally expelled to Belgium, the country the Dutch considered his first country of asylum. The Belgians tried to pass him on, either to the Netherlands or to Denmark but both countries denied they were his 'first country of asylum': AAD, individual files, A 186757; UDL 47620.
101. Caestecker, *Ongewenste gasten*, pp.100f. German communist refugees were also not eager to divulge details on their political work, when the Danish authorities asked them to do so from 1936 onwards as part of the development of an autonomous, but still informal, eligibility procedure. In the Danish case, notwithstanding official policy, this information found its way to the German authorities as they had an informer within the Danish police until 1939: Rünitz, *Af hensyn*, pp.78–81
102. Only 3 per cent referred to racial persecution, while 6 per cent referred to religious persecution. Eighty per cent of the asylum seekers called themselves Jews and there were only slightly more male than female applicants (60 per cent): Rapport sur l'activité du comité consultative, 6.1938, AN F7 16073
103. R. Fabian Ruth and C. Coulmas, *Die deutsche Emigration in Frankreich nach 1933*, New York 1978, pp.38–45; Zalc, 'Des réfugiés aux indésirables', p.265, Omnes, 'Accueil',p.99.
104. F. Caestecker and D. Fraser, 'The Extraterritorial Application of the Nuremberg Laws. Rassenschande and "Mixed" Marriages in European Liberal Democracies', *Journal of The History of International Law*, 10, no. 1, 2008, pp.35–81; Caestecker, 'Onverbiddelijk', p.103ff.
105. See Lone Rünitz in this volume and Rünitz, *Af hensyn*, p.187.

106. Caestecker, *Ongewenste gasten*, p.84; Herlemann, *Die Anleitung des Widerstands des KPDs*, p.152; G. Seppen and W. Walraven, *Vreemdelingen en grensbewaking. Handleiding tot de kennis van het vreemdelingenvraagstuk en de grensbewakingsvoorschriften*, Alphen aan den Rijn 1950, p.513.
107. In 1937 the Swiss and Danish authorities respectively granted 20,000 SF and 25,000 kronen for all committees, except the communists: Mächler, *Hilfe und Ohnmacht*, p.146; Wichers, *Im Kampf gegen Hitler*, p.117; Battel, *'Wo es hell ist, dort is die Schweiz' Flüchtlinge und Fluchthilfe an der Schaffhauser Grenze zur Zeit des Nationalsozialismus*, Zürich 2000, p.164 mentions also cantonal subsidies for the co-financing of emigration and medical treatment; H. Petersen and L. Einhart, 'Fremdenpolitik und Asylpraxis der skandinavischen Staaten', in *'Ein sehr trübes Kapital'? Hitlerflüchtlinge im nordeuropäischen Exil 1933–1950*, ed. L. Einhart, K. Misgeld, H. Müssener and H. Petersen, Hamburg 1998, p.36 and 206; Rünitz, *Af hensyn*, pp.180–82; H. Petersen, 'Die Dänische Flüchtlingspolitik 1933–1941', in *Deutschsprachiges Exil in Dänemarken nach 1933. Zu methoden und Einzelergebenissen*, ed. R. Dinesen, B. Nielsen, H. Petersen, F. Schmoë, Copenhagen 1986, p.86.
108. Petersen, *Historical Perspective*, p.34.
109. Bonnet, *Les Pouvoirs publics*, p.299; Caron, *Uneasy Asylum*, pp.129ff.; Simpson, *The Refugee Problem*, p.324; Caestecker, *Ongewenste gasten*, pp.88–92; Moore, *Refugees*, p.75 and 117. Most refugees in the Netherlands were able to support themselves as the government adopted a liberal policy towards those refugees who had been in the Netherlands for a few years. Almost 70 per cent of the requests for work permits were granted to the protégées of the Amsterdam Jewish committee, while about half of the applicants supported by the Matteotti fund obtained a permission to work: Simpson, *The Refugee Problem*, p.349.
110. London, *British Immigration*, p.503.
111. A German 'Jew' who had to leave the Netherlands brought a legal case against the Dutch state in court. The court in Den Hague declared itself incompetent as this decision was part of the sovereign powers of the state. The plaintiff was repatriated on 18.5.1938: HSTAD RW 58, 45044; Dutch National Archive, Ministry of Foreign Affairs, A-dossiers 1815–1940, 20337.
112. London, *Jewish Refugees and British Government Policy*, p.174; C. Kotzin, *Christian Responses in Britain to Jewish Refugees from Europe: 1933–1939*, PhD Thesis, University of Southampton, 2000, p.52.
113. Of the 6,280 asylum applications only 19 declared they had arrived in France in 1937 of which 13 had left Germany in that year: *Rapport sur l'activité du comité consultatif*, 6.1938, AN F7, 16073.
114. Caron, *Uneasy asylum*, p.126 ; Livian, *Le parti socialiste*, pp.92–108.
115. Dormoy, circular no. 338 (confidential), July 9, 1937, quoted in Caron, *Uneasy Asylum*, p.163.
116. Caron, in a nuanced evaluation of the Popular Front policy in this volume and in *Uneasy Asylum* and based on a very broad research in private (Jewish) and public archives, is rather critical of Livian's claim that the Popular Front distinguished within immigration policy between economic and political immigration and still provided protection to the latter. She refutes, on the basis of the available evidence, Livian's assertion that the refugee commission had the right to review the applications of refugees arriving after 5 August 5 1936. Although the commission from a legal point of view had not the

competence exceptional cases were still put before it, but most importantly it seems to us that Caron does not take into account the centralised eligibility policy of the Ministry of Interior. Her research deals with 'Jewish' refugees and indeed she documents clearly that those fleeing racial persecution were no longer granted asylum, but it seems that she ignores, to a large extent, the distinct policy towards political refugees. Only a detailed analysis such as Rünitz' can give a clear answer.

117. Livian, *Le parti socialiste*, pp.104–8; D. Afoumado, 'Le Consistoire et les juifs immigrés en France pendant les années trente', *Revue d'histoire de la Shoah*, 172, 2001, p.276 quotes Philippe Serre, undersecretary of state for immigration in a meeting with representatives with the Jewish religious community in February 1938.
118. Noiriel, *Le Creuset*, p.116.
119. The Belgian asylum institution handled 53 cases of *Rassenschande* positively between July 1936 and July 1939. Mostly, but not exclusively, couples had arrived in 1936 (few in 1937 and 1938). It is also possible that victims of *Rassenschande* were autonomously considered refugees by the alien police. We found no decisions on cases of victims of *Rassenschande* in which the relationship started after 1935: Caestecker, *Onverbiddelijk*, p.106; Caestecker and Fraser, Extraterritorial application, p.77.
120. Internal service note, 23.5.1938, AAD 289.
121. Rünitz, *Af hensyn*, pp.187ff., see also Lone Rünitz, this volume.

Chapter II.3

The Deepening Crisis: March 1938–October 1938

Frank Caestecker and Bob Moore

The year 1938 is always seen as a watershed in the persecution of the 'Jews'[1] as it was the year when geopolitical changes brought more 'Jews' under German rule and when antisemitic policies were substantially radicalised. Yet even before the *Anschluss*, the Nazis were becoming increasingly worried about the slow pace of Jewish emigration. Their own policies, combined with immigration restrictions elsewhere, had served to limit the numbers able to leave. At the same time, Nazi strategy itself was contradictory, with 'Jews' being pressed to leave while simultaneously being stripped of the assets that would have made them acceptable immigrants in other countries. Nevertheless, individual emigration remained the Nazi strategy for making Germany *judenfrei* and in general, everything possible was done to hasten the emigration of the – albeit increasingly impoverished – 'Jews'. A number of official instructions were issued to facilitate this. For example, the police record of Jewish emigrants could be 'cleansed' to make them more acceptable to countries of immigration. Professional qualifications that were in demand were also included on passports, and the *Handwerkskammern* (Trade Associations) were authorised to issue papers certifying the professional knowledge of Jewish emigrants.[2]

A partial solution to the fundamental contradictions in Nazi policy was found in more overt state violence and schemes for collective forced emigration that removed individual initiative or choice in destination. The latter element was tried at the beginning of 1938. Five hundred 'Jews' with Soviet passports were ordered to leave the country. As the Soviet Union would not permit their repatriation, and since Germany had no common frontier with the Soviet Union, transit visas were required from third countries, but these were all refused. As a result, the experiment failed and in May 1938, all Soviet 'Jews' still residing in Germany were arrested and held in concentration camps until they could organise their emigration.

Their possessions were seized until the moment they left the country and they were given *Fremden* or Nansen Passports to facilitate their departure.³

In the meantime, the first expansion of Hitler's Germany had taken place with the *Anschluss* of Austria and its incorporation into the Reich. This had provoked a flight of political activists, albeit on much smaller scale than from Germany in 1933. The Austrian corporate state had already persecuted the parties of the left and their political activists had been emigrating since the coup of 12 February 1934. In 1938, former German émigrés who had found refuge in Austria after 1933, Austrian socialist and communist activists, and even a small group of Austrian conservative opponents of National-Socialism chose the path into exile.⁴ However, the vast majority of refugees from Austria were 'Jews'. The *Anschluss* prompted an almost immediate and unprecedented wave of violence against the 'Jews' in Vienna. Administratively, all the antisemitic legislation enacted in Germany over the previous five years was imposed overnight. In contrast to the *Altreich*, the SS took a much more prominent role in the organisation of antisemitic actions in Austria. Within a very short time, Adolf Eichmann had established the *Zentralstelle für jüdische Auswanderung* (Central Office for Jewish Emigration), an organisation that systematically deprived the 'Jews' of their assets, made sure they complied with all the antisemitic legislation, and provided them with the barest minimum of resources to expedite their emigration from the Reich.⁵ This radical dynamism was in direct response to the perception that the piecemeal persecution of the 'Jews' carried out in the *Altreich* had failed in removing them from Germany as expeditiously as possible.

The 'success' of the *Zentralstelle*, albeit in combination with a high level of terror, was spectacular when compared with the limited numbers of emigrants then leaving Germany. Nearly 50,000 'Jews' left Austria in the first six months after the *Anschluss*.⁶ Even given this level of terror and the fact that Eichmann benefited from an initial emigration of people with limited attachment to Austria, the idea that coercive pressure might be combined with a greater degree of administrative collusion was novel, but one that clearly got results. 'Jews' would now receive the necessary travel documents and police certificates required by countries of emigration, rather than being left to the whim of individual bureaucrats. However, even this success was not considered sufficient and, as pressures to make Austria *judenrein* mounted but opportunities for legal emigration became ever more severely restricted, the German police and border authorities increasingly flouted international law and local conventions by dumping 'Jews' across the frontiers of neighbouring countries.⁷

In the aftermath of the *Anschluss*, Hermann Goering took steps to regulate what had become a scramble for Jewish assets. The widespread profiteering that had taken place in Austria could not be allowed to continue, or be spread to Germany. The state had good financial reasons for wanting its share of every available asset in the country. In April 1938 all Jewish Property had to be registered and it could henceforward only be sold or leased with permission from the authorities. In this way, the state could keep track of assets that might otherwise have fallen into private hands undetected. During 1938 the 'Jews' were increasingly excluded from the German economy and the impoverishment of the 'Jews' threatened to add to the state's welfare burden. In the meantime, the Evian Refugee Conference had come and gone without result. There was to be no international solution to the question and the pressures on the 'Jews' continued to escalate. There was widespread antisemitic violence in the cities and June 1938 saw a wave of 10,000 arrests of asocials, including so-called 'Jewish criminals', encompassing anyone who had been convicted by the courts, even for minor offences, at some time in the past. Some 1,500 Jewish men were taken to Buchenwald concentration camp and told that they would not be released until they were able to emigrate.[8]

The practical outcome of Munich Settlement of 29 September 1938 was also a major watershed. German annexation of the Sudetenland caused a considerable flow of political activists to the unoccupied part of Czechoslovakia, including at least 5,000 anti-Nazi Germans. The 30,000 'Jews' resident in the Sudeten areas transferred to German control were forcibly arrested and expelled to Czechoslovakia. The Czechs refused to accept them and sent them on to Hungary, who in turn returned them to German soil. This continued until some ended up on a riverboat in the Danube and others in no-man's-land at Mischdorf, between Czechoslovakia and Hungary.[9] In the meantime, the newly autonomous Slovak state decreed that all non-Slovak Jews would have to leave the Slovak territory by 31 January 1939, while the Czech government decided that all German 'Jews' had to leave by 15 January 1939.[10]

The expansion of the German Reich and the radicalisation of antisemitic policy served to increase the steady flow of refugees from Nazi-controlled areas into a flood. Most countries surrounding Germany were subject to a form of human 'dumping'. In addition in Italy and in Eastern Europe, Jews were threatened and under pressure to emigrate. Until March 1938 the Fascist government in Italy had not limited the entry of Jewish refugees. On the contrary, Mussolini had granted asylum to German 'Jews' for diplomatic reasons, seeing Italy as the balance between Germany and the Western Powers. Italy also had no legislation to prevent foreigners from working and earning a living in the country.[11] From 1935 onwards this began to change as Italy and Nazi Germany became closer. In September 1938, Italy enacted anti-Jewish laws. Foreign Jews who had settled in Italy after 1 January 1919 had to leave the country within six months, that is, by the 12 March 1939.[12]

Slightly in advance of Italy, the Polish government embarked on a similar path. After the death of Marshal Josef Pilsudski in 1935, policies to tackle the country's 'Jewish problem' was extensively discussed among the Polish governing elite headed by Marshal Edouard Rydz-Smigly. The 3.5 million Jews in Poland in 1935 – 10 per cent of the population – were mostly urban and concentrated in the commercial sector and the liberal professions, both of which had been badly hit by the Depression. The

Polish regime embarked on a nationalist program in which the emigration of the Jewish minority figured prominently. The first coercive measure came in 1938 with a law that provided for the possibility that Poles who had lived outside Poland for more than five years and had shown no signs of attachment to their country of origin could be denationalised. Although the law did not specifically mention the Jews, they were undoubtedly the intended targets since the Polish government was determined to prevent the return of the 50,000 Polish 'Jews' still in Greater Germany who were threatened with expulsion. The Hungarian government followed suit and voted legislation by which Hungarian Jews living abroad could be stripped of their citizenship. All liberal states in Europe, fearing much greater refugee effluxes from Eastern Europe, adopted a firm stand against any attempts by these states with much larger Jewish populations to begin a policy of eviction. However diplomatic considerations – making these countries into allies and preventing them from slipping into the Nazi camp – meant that the message about Western objections to policies against the Jews was not always clearly received.[13]

In October 1938, Warsaw decided that all Polish citizens living abroad had to renew their papers, and if they did not do so their citizenship could be revoked. The first to react were the German authorities as they were aware that they were the chief targets of the Polish legislation. To pre-empt the creation of many thousands of stateless 'Jews', Himmler ordered the rounding up of all male Polish 'Jews' and their deportation to Poland by 29 October. Wives and children would have to follow. The Polish authorities reacted swiftly by closing their border. As a result about 16,000 'Jews' succeeded in entering Polish territory, while 6,500 Polish 'Jews' were stuck in no-man's-land at Zbaszyn. Although some were later allowed to return, some 20,000 'Jews' were removed from German territory.[14] The chaotic outcome of this experiment nevertheless taught the German authorities that any future mass deportations would have to be better prepared.

The Confidence of the European Liberal States in 'Remote Control'

The Anschluss on 11 March 1938 and fears of a new wave of refugees meant that several Western European states adjusted their policies almost immediately by introducing visa requirements that served to strengthen their remote controls and ensured that only a selected number of refugees could enter their territory legally. It had proven to be very difficult to make refugees leave once they were inside the country, so preventing them from arriving there in the first place was considered the most effective strategy.

By the end of March 1938, a few hundred Austrians were already being assisted by the Jewish refugee organisation in Switzerland. As those who were capable of supporting themselves did not need the help of refugee organisations, the numbers in the country must have been somewhat larger. From 1 April 1938 onwards, former Austrian citizens were required to apply for visas. As there was no longer an Austrian state, the Swiss were able to act unilaterally and promptly without any fear of international retribution. The British authorities were pushed into action by similar concerns. On the day of the *Anschluss*, the Jewish Refugees' Committee in London announced that it was unable to accept financial responsibility for any future entrants. The blank cheque that its predecessor had freely issued in 1933 – a time when they had not foreseen the possible explosion in refugee numbers – was withdrawn. The Jewish refugee relief organisation now insisted on a right to choose those it would support and thus ended its unlimited guarantee. This served to strengthen the British government's determination to control immigration from Germany. By 2 May 1938, the Home Office had imposed immediate visa requirements for all Austrian nationals, but properly notified its intention to do the same for German passport holders as the German government was entitled to reasonable notice of termination of the existing agreement. The Germans went to great lengths to accommodate British interests during negotiations with the Foreign Office in London. They proposed that an aspiring emigrant would only get a passport valid for the U.K. if (s)he could show written evidence that the British government had authorised admission. This did not meet the demands of the British authorities, as only those Germans who intended to leave directly from Germany for Britain would be pre-selected. All other Germans who succeeded in leaving Germany would be free to enter Britain. Beside this more pragmatic consideration, the British authorities also considered this proposal unacceptable in principle. The British did not want to outsource their immigration control to the Germans, as this would imply collusion with Berlin 'to detain people in the Reich'.[15] Visas for Germans coming to Britain became mandatory from 21 May 1938 onwards.

News of these decisions, coupled with Sweden and Norway also imposing a visa obligation for Austrian passport holders, caused the Danish Chief of Police, Eigil Thune Jacobsen, to insist on taking similar measures.[16] Since the *Anschluss* he had monitored the arrival of Austrians very closely. There had, in fact, been few arrivals and thus no immediate cause for alarm, but he feared that as Great Britain, Switzerland and the two neighbouring Scandinavian countries introduced visa requirements; Denmark would be a more likely destination for those fleeing Austria. He argued that Denmark, as the gate to Scandinavia, shouldered a heavy responsibility, but the Danish Foreign Office was reticent about imposing a visa requirement as this might adversely affect relations with Germany. When the Germans informed the Danish authorities that Austrian passports were being replaced by German documents from 15 August 1938 onwards and the former would be deemed invalid by the German authorities from 1 January 1939 onwards, a visa obligation for holders of Austrian passports was introduced in July 1938 as the Danish Foreign Office withdrew its opposition.[17] The Dutch were less charitable to former

Austrians citizens than their Danish counterparts. The Dutch Foreign Ministry was convinced that Austrian citizens would soon be issued with German papers and should be treated accordingly. Thus as early as 22 March 1938, the Dutch decided that Austrian passports were no longer valid travel documents.[18] The imposition of visa requirements during the spring and summer of 1938 meant that many more people from Austria and Germany had to obtain visas before entering France, Belgium, Denmark, Sweden, Norway and the United Kingdom. Confidence in this system for controlling immigration was again evident when, from September 1938 onwards, Italy and Czechoslovakia became sources of refugees. The authorities in several countries made access for Italians, Czechs and Slovaks to their territory more difficult by imposing a visa requirement.[19]

A new mechanism of remote control was introduced in early autumn 1938 when the Danish authorities, determined to stop the 'abuse' of temporary residence authorisations by German 'Jews', decreed that Germans admitted as temporary visitors would no longer be able to apply to settle in Denmark, even if they had enough means at their disposal, but would be obliged to leave the country in order to obtain a settlement visa from a Danish consulate abroad. The Netherlands had already introduced a similar scheme in March 1938. Germans who had entered the Netherlands as temporary visitors could only settle in the country if they had applied abroad for an authorisation to do so.[20] In this way, the Dutch and Danish authorities preserved unrestricted travel between their country and Germany, but at the same time prevented refugees from staying put. This new arrangement precluded jeopardising relations with Germany and it became popular as a policy all over Europe. The Belgian authorities, albeit already having the means to control all immigration from their consulates in Germany, saw the advantages of a second barrier in order to discourage anyone overstaying their visa. Thus from the autumn of 1938 onwards, the Belgian authorities prohibited the use of tourist visas for settlement purposes; foreigners wanting to settle in Belgium also had to leave the country first and apply abroad for a settlement visa.[21]

The visa requirements imposed across Western Europe, whether for entry or for settlement, were designed to stem the influx of uninvited aliens. Visa applications from German or Austrian 'Jews', even those with transferable assets, were looked on unfavourably and the vast majority were refused. Analysis of administrative practice clearly shows that the Jewish applicants were singled out for special scrutiny, based not so much on antisemitic or xenophobic feelings, but rather on a 'rational' bureaucratic reasoning that applicants had to be treated on their merits and on the likelihood that they would actually return to their country of origin. In this respect, such an assessment was compatible with the liberalism of these regimes bordering Germany. All West European countries refused visitors' visa to Germans and Austrians whom they suspected of wanting to remain in the country. Only a small minority of wealthy refugees whose immigration was considered in the interest of the country concerned were granted the necessary permits.[22] In addition, applications for (temporary) residence were sometimes approved when the individuals concerned could show they were able to leave for a destination overseas almost immediately.[23] A final category looked on more sympathetically were those with very close links to the country concerned.[24]

With the phasing out of Austrian passports, emigration from Austria to Switzerland and Scandinavia was no longer subject to visa control. Only by imposing a visa obligation on the holders of Germans passports could external control on immigration from Austria be retained. Switzerland (and Sweden) thus informed the German authorities that they wanted to impose a visa obligation on all German nationals. For their part, the German authorities made persistent efforts to avoid any travel restrictions for its 'Aryan' citizens, let alone the imposition of visas. Although the negotiations were separate, the Swiss and Swedish objectives were similar, namely to have a technical means to identify (and exclude) those – overwhelmingly 'Jews' – seeking entry into their countries with the intention of staying. At first, the Nazis opposed the idea, as it would make getting rid of the 'Jews' more difficult. However when it became clear that this was the only way 'Aryan' Germans would remain free from the requirement to obtain a visa, they conceded. This led to a new passport for German 'Jews' that included a three centimetres high red letter 'J', on the left-hand side of the first page, indicating their 'non-Aryan' status.[25] All German 'Jews' had to exchange their old passport for a new passport by 22 December 1938 and by 7 October 1938 all Austrian passports held by 'Jews' had also to be marked with a 'J'. In the meantime, the Swiss introduced a new visa requirement for the holders of the new Jewish passports, effective from the 6 October onwards.[26] This 'J' stamp was thus introduced by the Germans at the behest of the Swiss authorities to distinguish between Germans who did not have to carry a visa and those who did. Although the Swiss authorities introduced a clear-cut racial bias in their system, the authorities in the other liberal states were also not entirely free of antisemitism and even racism in their daily management of immigration. The denial of visa applications from Jews became routine in most consulates. Moreover, this attitude went beyond the German refugee crisis. Although the Polish authorities had given assurances that Polish Jews in Western Europe were not the intended targets of the Polish decree of 31 March 1938 designed to deprive Poles abroad of their citizenship, the immediate result was that Polish Jews were very rarely granted visas by any country.[27]

The category of 'Jew' also filtered through into the policy discussions of the authorities of the countries neighbouring Germany. For example, German 'Jews' were listed separately in the Dutch and Luxemburg immigration statistics for internal use.[28] The adoption of Nazi racial categorisation and Nazi terminology also penetrated the top level of decision making in Western European regimes. The guidelines for granting of visa are a clear case in point. These instructions served to make it far more difficult for 'Jews' than 'Aryans' to obtain visas. Mostly they were couched in moderate language and refrained from open use of antisemitic or racist language. Consulates were told to refuse visas to those applicants who wanted to settle in the country without having enough means to do so using ethnically and racially neutral terms, but in more detailed instructions one can see the use of coded language and even the term 'non-Aryan'.[29]

This overview of how external controls were imposed shows that all countries wanted to exercise a much tighter grip on immigration through their consular services. Remote control had the great advantage that the pressure of decision making was shifted away from the borders and now took place outside the country. Remote control was not necessarily meant to exclude refugees altogether, but to keep the flow at manageable levels. Consular instructions were sometimes explicit in saying that visa applications from political refugees were to be handled in a liberal manner.[30] Several thousand British visas were granted to German and Austrian subjects during the spring and summer of 1938,[31] including renewable permits for Jewish women to be employed as domestic servants in British households, and male Jewish entrepreneurs investing in Great Britain.[32] Most Austrians and Germans entering Great Britain were refugees who had private sponsors and intended to re-emigrate. The Jewish refugee organisations ceased to underwrite admissions generally, but created guarantee funds supported by people in Britain. Once an arrangement had been agreed, the sponsor had to deposit actual sums of money and to sign guarantees to defray costs of maintenance and re-emigration before the authorities granted a visa. Nevertheless, huge bottlenecks rapidly grew in the system for handling visa applications, and this served to delay the admission of many refugees to Great Britain.

Continental countries were seemingly less generous, as visas for these countries were granted only sparingly. However the porous nature of their borders made them much less capable of controlling the refugees entering their territory.[33] Thus, an important aspect of their migration control scheme was a stricter border and internal control policy, including the use of expulsion, as would be-immigrants would only respect the regulations if there was a high risk of being caught as an illegal resident. In addition to their remote control policies, the liberal states neighbouring Nazi Germany wanted to retain the right to repatriate unwanted immigrants, including those whose visas had expired. Thus, for example, a basic requirement for obtaining a Belgian visa from May 1938 onwards was that the holder's German passport was still valid for five years. In this way Germans who had resided lawfully in Belgium for several years could be deported as soon as they no longer satisfied the conditions by which they had entered.[34] The countries of continental Europe were therefore less confident in remote control as a means of stemming the refugee flow than Great Britain and insisted on additional safeguards.

The Desire to Exclude Jewish Refugees at the Border

In most countries, tighter frontier controls had been discussed during the course of 1937 but it was not until after the *Anschluss* that they were implemented. Officials had already been under strict instructions to turn away all foreigners without papers, but their competences were increased considerably after March 1938. Given its geographical position and linguistic affinity to Austria, Switzerland was the first state to experience the arrival of refugees, and also the first to strengthen its border controls. By the late spring, the authorities in other continental countries also noticed an increasing pressure at their borders. More and more people arrived from Austria without visas. A swift response followed. In May 1938, Luxemburg strengthened its frontier policing and mobilised the army to offset a shortage of suitable personnel. By July 1938, Belgium had supplemented its border police with 160 policemen stationed on the eastern frontier and mobile units on bicycles, popularly known in the border region as the 'Jew hunters'. The Netherlands deployed an extra 300 additional border guards and in France, police reinforcements were send to the border early in June, followed in July 1938 by the *Brigades de Gendarmerie Frontière* with 1,500 men who were assigned to securing the borders. In September 1938, Danish border control was also strengthened.[35]

Facilities for asylum seekers remained in place in all Continental European countries. In Switzerland, Austrians who had arrived after 28 March 1938 without the necessary visa (or prior to this without a passport), but who could make a plausible case that they were in mortal danger were treated as applicants for refugee status.[36] Numerous Jewish refugees who arrived at the Swiss border during the spring and early summer of 1938 were neither sent back by the Swiss central authorities nor considered eligible for refugee status. If they could prove they had been threatened with incarceration in a concentration camp, they were given 'temporary' permission to stay.[37] Sometimes these 'Jewish' refugees were pushed on into France. The Swiss Jewish refugee organisations could even pass on refugees to France legally by an arrangement with some French departmental authorities.[38] Initially, all countries kept to a generous admission policy in line with pre-1938 policy, distinguishing between permanent protection for 'refugees' and temporary protection for 'Jews'. Very soon this would all change.

In the Netherlands there was still no question of any formal asylum for refugees, but even providing temporary protection was brought into question shortly after the *Anschluss*. From March 1938 onwards, holders of Austrian passports arriving at the Dutch border were all refused access to Dutch territory. German passport holders could only be admitted if they had an official declaration that they could return at any time to Germany. The repatriation of such immigrants had to remain possible. The value of the assets they had to dispose of before being allowed to enter the Netherlands had also been considerably increased. This measure by the Dutch government was aimed specifically at German 'Jews', but as the issue was considered a particularly sensitive one, all Germans were subjected to the new rule. An exception was made for refugees. Even people without papers arriving at the Dutch border were to be admitted if they could prove that they were in mortal danger. Additional instructions were issued in May 1938 that talked not of mortal danger but 'imminent mortal danger' as being the only criterion for admission of people without papers. Restrictionism nevertheless went beyond this semantic change. The May 1938 circular letter abandoned all euphemistic language: there was no longer any question of scrutinising all Germans' travel plans, but it was stated explicitly that refugees, foreigners who had to leave their country 'under the pressure of circumstance', were to be considered as unwanted guests. Administrative practice was changed accordingly. While 'ordinary' German travellers were less severely scrutinised at the frontier, refugees were blatantly refused admission and even the possession of sufficient means of support was no longer accepted as a justification for admission. Only in few cases, where the Nazis had physically chased individuals across the border – thus substantiating the criteria of imminent mortal danger – could entry be granted.[39]

In all other liberal states of Western Europe, arriving Jewish refugees were still temporarily protected. The German dumping policy nonetheless placed great strains on this humanitarian policy. The high pressure on Jews to leave Austria meant that any rumour of an opportunity to emigrate was seized upon. According to interviews with Jewish refugees conducted by the French police, some Aachen residents had promised, out of greed, to assist Austrian 'Jews' in their flight abroad and the word had spread in Vienna. Other sources mention a rumour that the AJDC had set up an aid committee in Brussels for Austrian Jews. As a result, a large number of Austrian 'Jews' flocked to Aachen and some tried to cross into Belgium where they were apprehended by the Belgian border guards. The German authorities decided to incarcerate the Austrian 'Jews' and while in the local prison they were issued with short-term German passports and made to sign a declaration that they would never return to Germany. On the night of 22 May 1938, the German police sent fifty 'Jews' to Luxemburg. The following nights other batches of Jewish refugees were sent to Belgium and France, and possibly also to the Netherlands.[40]

While the Belgian authorities offered to protect those refugees who had circumvented its border guards and whom the Jewish refugee committees agreed to support, the Luxemburg authorities wanted to show the German authorities that dumping these people into Luxemburg was unacceptable. The Luxemburg authorities thus rounded up the fifty 'Jews', although the Jewish refugee committee had taken care of them. They were assembled at the military barracks in Luxemburg city, and then during the day brought under military escort to the Remich Bridge and handed over to German border guards. During this whole operation the soldiers were confronted with the despair of these refugees who tried to demonstrate that they could not return to Germany: one jumped into the Moselle and another tried to commit suicide with a razor.[41]

This example of gesture politics backfired as the Luxemburg government was castigated by the press and was strongly criticised for its inhuman treatment of these particular refugees. Even the American Joint Distribution Committee (JDC) intervened with the Luxemburg government – as Yehuda Bauer makes clear, a very rare thing for the JDC to have done – to stop further expulsions.[42] The fact that the expulsions had been ordered by the Minister in charge, the Socialist René Blum, meant that liberal elements in the Luxemburg political elite made no public protests. However, the experiment was not considered a success and alternatives to deportation such as internment were immediately discussed in government circles. The JDC provided undertakings to enable the local Jewish community to support refugees and assist them in finding countries of immigration overseas. The traditional policy of temporarily protecting refugees was thereby restored in the Grand Duchy and 'Jews' whom the local Jewish refugee committee were ready to support were admitted until they could organise their final emigration.

French border authorities were nevertheless inspired by the actions of their Luxembourgeois counterparts. When the fifty Austrian refugees who had been returned to Germany on 23 May by the Luxemburg authorities were dumped in small groups in France the following night they were arrested by the French border authorities. The next day they were returned in an official convoy along the main road to the German border so as to impress the German authorities. The official in charge executed these orders without any remorse and he pointed out that these 'Jews' protested dramatically, but he qualified them as 'ruined traders, Jews wanting to leave for abroad and victims of vengeance by their neighbours'. They were definitely not political refugees and could thus be returned.[43] As this French repatriation operation took place in the border region, it received no media attention and there were no civic protests.

A month later, in June 1938, the Danish Chief of Police, Eigil Thune Jacobsen, instructed the border police to hold Germans for questioning at the Danish border. They had to be interviewed about their destination, their family background and their economic means. Even travellers with Eastern European and Austrian passports containing the necessary visa were to be subjected to this control. With this information, the local police chiefs could then decide, usually after consultation with Copenhagen, whether these travellers really wanted to settle in Denmark and whether they possessed sufficient means to finance a permanent stay. As was the case in the Netherlands, the measure was implicitly directed against the 'Jewish' refugees from Nazi Germany. Suspicion of wanting to settle in Denmark was based on factors such as having so-called 'Semitic' facial expressions or travelling with family members and/or with a lot of baggage. The border control was so strict that the German ambassador in Copenhagen was moved to lodge a formal complaint against the long interrogations and resulting delays that all German travellers, in contrast to other foreigners, had to endure at the Danish border.[44]

On 12 September 1938, the Swedish authorities decided to impose stricter controls on the influx of 'Jewish' refugees: although Germans did not need a visa to enter Sweden those whom the border guards suspected of wanting to settle in Sweden were to be refused access unless they had a so-called 'border recommendation' from a Swedish consulate, a quasi-visa for German 'Jews', introduced to weed out refugees.[45] The Swedish example, together with the knowledge that the financial reserves of the Jewish aid committee were dwindling, and that existing Jewish refugees in the country would eventually become a public charge, moved the issue to the fore. Thus on 29 September 1938, the Danish council of ministers confirmed Jacobson's administrative directive of June 1938. Instructions were sent to the border guards and to consuls abroad to refuse entry to foreigners 'who, having left their country of origin with the intention of emigrating due to the difficulty of their situation, could not or did not wish to return to their country of origin'. Only if they had an entry permit authorised by the Ministry of Justice or a visa allowing them entry into a third country were they to be admitted. The radical strengthening of the border controls with regard to German 'Jews' thus became official policy.[46] Only 'persons who, due to political activities or political convictions, were liable to severe punishment should they remain in their country of origin' had to be protected. The official support for the strengthening of these border policies set the tone for the future. In a few cases the border guards even refused German 'Jews' who had a valid entry visa admission into Denmark. Likewise, Germans who had permission from the Danish consulate in Berlin to work in Denmark were refused entrance at the border when it became clear that these workers were regarded as 'Jews' in Germany and that they therefore came under the stricter regulations applied to German 'Jews'.[47] This 'mistake' by the Danish consulate in Berlin illustrates perfectly the difficult assignment given to both Danish and Dutch frontier guards: to allow 'bona fide' travellers in while excluding Jewish immigrants.

By the middle of August, the Swiss and Luxemburg authorities had rescinded the temporary protection for 'Jewish' refugees and orders were given to close the borders, except for political refugees. The Swiss border police was instructed to hand back to the German authorities those Austrians who attempted to cross into Switzerland without the necessary visa. The official excuse for this change of policy was that the German authorities would otherwise punish these refugees, as their involuntary return could not be documented. In fact, the real reason for this change was to improve efficiency rather than for any humanitarian concern. From 7 September 1938 onwards, the number of forced returnees increased as Swiss border officials were instructed to refuse entry to German 'Jews'. Even those with valid passports were kept out, although the rules in force indicated that they were, in fact, qualified to enter Switzerland.[48]

Although we have no conclusive evidence, it seems that France closed its borders on 18 August 1938 for 'Jewish' refugees, this did not imply that that these refugees were deported indiscriminately to Greater Germany: France had a preference for sending them on to neighbouring countries.[49] Switzerland strongly opposed this policy and reinforced its border controls at the Swiss–French border. The Belgian authorities were similarly indignant that their ally in devising an international refugee regime was now flouting its provisions. Thus from May 1938 onwards, refugees caught at the French–Belgian border attempting to enter illegally were returned to France and protests were made to the French authorities for not respecting the international refugee laws to which France had adhered. This attempt to take the moral high ground cut little ice with the French, who recalled the Belgian policy in 1933 of pushing their refugees into France.[50] However, this episode did serve to highlight the weakness of the French strategy of denying protection to refugees, but refusing to repatriate them back to Germany.

During the summer of 1938, the border authorities in those countries which had no visa requirement as a remote control mechanism had to investigate whether the would-be immigrants from Greater Germany were considered Jewish by the Nazis. The well-researched Danish and Swiss cases show that putting this policy into practice proved extremely difficult: it remained difficult to tell 'Jews' from other immigrants at the border, as passports bore no indication as to the bearer's religious denomination, let alone his or her racial categorisation. Travellers from Germany faced close interrogations at the borders to find out if they were Jewish and, if so, whether they qualified for entrance. Admission at these borders was discretionary and not set out clearly in published regulations. This meant that many refugees arrived at these frontiers not knowing if they would be admitted. Not only did the Dutch, Danish, Swiss and Luxemburg authorities have to deploy increasing resources to guard their frontiers, but they also placed great strain on their border and customs officials in having to carry out this exclusionary policy. Harrowing scenes at the border posts became daily occurrences. Threats of suicide that could easily become a reality only added to the border guards becoming desensitised. Confronted with the stubbornness of desperate refugees many lost any sympathy they might have had with the refugees and increasingly employed brutal methods to implement their instructions.[51] Central governments realised that their border guards had a difficult assignment and thus tried to give them some further assistance. For example, from September 1938 onwards, the Swiss border guards had to stamp, as having been 'turned back', the passports of Germans whom they considered as 'Jews' and had refused entry to Switzerland. In this way their colleagues at other border crossing points no longer had to decide themselves that these Germans were unwanted immigrants.[52]

While France, Belgium and to a lesser extent Great Britain, due to its geographical position, had to increase the policing of their frontiers, they did have the advantage of a clearly delineated set of regulations for entry.

Border guards did not have to conduct investigations to find out whether a would-be visitor from Greater Germany was a bona fide tourist or an immigrant. The burden of initial face-to-face contact with applicants had been shifted abroad to the consular officials who handled visa applications. For the border guards a visa requirement could make control of border crossings a bureaucratic routine. Yet even in countries where remote control was well developed and an effective administrative barrier to entrance, border authorities were still charged with exempting 'refugees' from the regulations.[53] In France, a decree law of 2 May 1938 stipulated that illegal aliens who petitioned for asylum upon their arrival in France had to receive an administrative hearing. No legislation was introduced to provide eligibility criteria for refugee status, but internal instructions for police use stipulated some principles of French asylum policy. France had to be the first country of asylum, so admission had to be refused to foreigners coming from a third country where they could have requested asylum, and those previously expelled were also excluded. Central to the definition of a refugee was evidence of forced departure because of a danger to life and the complete loss of possessions. The border guards had to grant access to those foreigners who could provide outline proof that made their status as a refugee plausible. These admissible asylum seekers were then sent to a municipality were they were granted (renewable) residence permits valid for a month. In the meantime the Minister of Interior investigated, on the basis of additional information, whether the applicant was eligible for refugee status.[54]

Notwithstanding the guarantees afforded to 'refugees' it seems that only a few people actually declared themselves as refugees to the border authorities. Germans and Austrians, and later also Italian and Czech nationals, were reluctant to do so if they saw a chance to gain admission by other means. They had little faith in the authorities of the countries to which they fled and were too afraid of being sent back to Germany if their petition for refugee status ultimately failed. Political as well as 'Jewish' refugees only declared themselves voluntarily to the authorities of the country of refuge after contacting 'their' refugee committees within the country of asylum. Armed with some local, albeit private, protection and already inside the country, they hoped to have a greater chance of being protected.

Although more systematic research needs to be done on the practical applications of policy at the border to compare and contrast with the well-documented Danish and Swiss cases, the findings suggest that border officials of all Continental European countries were directly involved in denying access to ('Jewish') immigrants. Judgements on both 'Jews' and 'Aryans' arriving from Germany and Austria, with or without the right papers, became a routine task for border guards from the summer of 1938 onwards. 'Jewish' refugees were turned away at the western borders of Germany in droves, albeit that border officials still had considerable discretion in these decisions.[55] In the countries that refused to impose a visa requirement on the Germans for economic and political reasons, the discretion given to border guards was much wider. These countries had to persist with an ad hoc and unsatisfactory compromise that nominally kept the border open, but effectively excluded a large number of people who wished to cross it but whom the border guards treated as unwanted 'Jewish' refugees. In countries with decentralised border controls such as Denmark and the Netherlands, border control was much less homogeneous and it was local authorities who decided on who was an unwanted immigrant and also who could eventually qualify for refugee status.[56]

No matter how stringent the security measures at the border were, they were incapable of securing the frontiers altogether. For all kind of motives, border guards sometimes turned a blind eye when refugees sought to cross the border, or in some cases even provided assistance.[57] Other refugees were able to circumvent border control altogether, and still others entered with a tourist visa or met other criteria of entrance and then stayed on, legally, quasi-legally, or illegally. The statistics of the Jewish refugee aid committees and the authorities (Figures 4 and 5, p.326)[58] clearly illustrate that there was an increasing number of mainly Austrian 'Jews' arriving in the spring and summer of 1938 who had been able either to circumvent frontier controls altogether or who had convinced the border guards that they met the criteria for entrance. For whatever reasons, efforts by the Western liberal states to stave off further influxes of uninvited foreigners were by no means totally successfully. Illegal immigration had not been uncommon before 1938, with both 'Jewish' and political activists contriving to avoid border controls, either because they did not have valid documents or the necessary means, but during and after 1938, the scale of this immigration increased enormously, as did the types of people involved. Now it was not just young and single males who were involved, but respectable bourgeois 'Jewish' families from Germany desperate to do anything to escape from the Nazis. Increasingly, there was a trade in people across the 'green frontiers' from Germany where smugglers were paid huge sums to conduct would-be refugees to safety.

Internal Control

Immediately after the *Anschluss*, once refugees had arrived in one of the liberal states of Europe, the old policy of providing some form of protection remained, although controls became stricter. From 1938 onwards, refugees were admitted to Great Britain with (renewable) three-month permits and in France permits valid for one month. In the Netherlands after March 1938, German travellers with papers and means obtained permits for no more than fourteen days that were non-renewable.[59] All foreigners living legally (and illegally) in the Western liberal states were subject to greater administrative control and refugees became a particular focus. This is most conspicuously illustrated by the Dutch case. Earlier in the twentieth century, the Netherlands had been a country of emigration rather than immigration, and this caused it to be relatively lax in updating its controls on aliens. Thus it was the refugee crisis of the 1930s that became the catalyst for the first fully fledged Dutch immigration control. Work permits had been introduced by the mid 1930s. By October 1938 internal controls had been considerably strengthened with all citizens obliged to inform the police authorities within 24 hours of the presence of foreigners in their homes. Before then, this obligation had existed only for hotels and guesthouses.[60] On 19 December 1938, the administrative web began closing around transit-refugees. 'Jews' and other 'non-Aryan' refugees who had arrived in the Netherlands after 1 March 1938 could no longer be registered in the aliens' register. They had to be registered in a newly created central refugee register that allowed the authorities to monitor them even more closely.[61]

The Protection of Political Refugees: A Sacrosanct Principle of Liberal States

In the aftermath of the *Anschluss*, the French authorities allowed all resident and newly arrived Austrians to express their dissatisfaction with the German annexation of their country by signing a declaration that they refused to be covered by German diplomatic protection. In this way, the French authorities effectively reinforced the idea that these immigrants still claimed their (temporarily suspended) Austrian citizenship. On their French identity papers they were listed as *Ex-Autrichien*. This administrative categorisation, an expression of the political stand taken by the second Blum government against the expansionist ambitions of Nazi Germany, became the basis for a refugee policy similar to the hospitality afforded to Germans who fled to France after the Nazi takeover in 1933. Also those who claimed that they were Austrians and opposed the Nazi regime were protected by a set of bureaucratic rules which were less restrictive than those applied to other foreigners. They were all granted a temporary residence permit. The Blum government did not last long and the more conservative Daladier government attacked the strategy outlined by its predecessor. In the autumn of 1938, Austrians who had arrived illegally but who did not want to avail themselves of German protection were still tolerated, but controls became more severe. They now had to provide documentary proof of them being refugees, and former Austrians arriving in France were no longer collectively a privileged category within alien policy. Even under the Blum regime, refugees from Nazi Germany with German passports had been excluded from this benevolence, but with the phasing out of the Austrian passports, more and more Austrian refugees were treated as Germans and handed an expulsion order. The final blow to the refugee policy created by the Blum government came in October 1938 when the Daladier cabinet decided that uninvited immigrants, even if they were Austrian refugees, had to be stopped, and only a very selective immigration was acceptable, controlled by consulates abroad. The immigrants who arrived in the country uninvited had to be returned. Only those travelling with German passports but claiming to be ex-Austrians *and* who could give firm proof that they were genuine refugees were to be tolerated. Only very few among those fleeing Greater Germany were granted an informal refugee status, exclusively political activists, and the same applied to later arrivals from the Sudetenland and Czechoslovakia.[62]

This humanitarian exception to a stricter immigration policy was only conceded half-heartedly, as can be seen by the attitude towards communist refugees, the political activists on the run least wanted by all the liberal states of Western Europe. The new political leaders in France, having ousted the French communists from the government, nonetheless still tolerated communist refugees. Those who had left France to join the International Brigades in Spain in 1936 and 1937 and who had returned in small batches by the end of 1938 were granted temporary residence permits, but at the same time they were banned from Paris and confined to small provincial towns cut off from their comrades.[63] This dispersal of political refugees was meant to limit their political activism so as not to endanger the potential for French–German reconciliation while appeasement still held sway within the Daladier regime.[64]

The privileged position afforded to political refugees remained a characteristic of the liberal states in Western Europe, and even the virulently anti-communist Netherlands officially became a sanctuary for 'subversive' refugees. This Dutch protection for these previously undeserving political refugees was a complete reversal of previous policy and prompted not by a spirit of greater tolerance, but by changes in the communist movement itself and the domestic and international pressure on the Netherlands. Since 1933, exiled German communists in Western Europe had been mobilised by the KPD for full-time political work to support the communist resistance in Germany, a prerequisite to qualify for help from the Red Help. By 1938 the political leadership of these refugees was in jeopardy. The Comintern had strongly criticised the inability of the KPD to maintain any meaningful resistance to the Nazis inside Germany itself, and also castigated its failure to implement a Popular Front strategy after 1935. The Stalinist purges and defeat in the Spanish Civil War added to a climate of demoralisation among German communists. Internal divisions and disorganisation of the KPD caused it to lose its hold over its members in exile. German communist refugees became dependent on the strategies of communist parties of the countries of asylum.

At the same time the communist Popular Front strategy had changed the priorities of the national sections of the Red Help. International solidarity had been directed away from supporting exiles and towards supporting the Spanish Republic. Likewise there were attempts to find political allies within the country in line with the Popular Front strategy. These new obligations for the Red Help were detrimental to the German communist refugees, who thus received a diminishing share of the organisation's scarce resources. The international communist movement decided to sacrifice the political activism of German communists in exile, so that its resources could be allocated for other (national) goals.

The refugees were forced to legalise their residence in host societies in order to enable them to provide for their own livelihood. Providing for their own income forced the refugees to limit their political activity.[65] When a refugee applied for legalisation of their stay, usually via the Red Help as intermediary, cessation of all political activity was mostly invariably imposed as a condition. However in the case of the Netherlands, the authorities refused to negotiate with the Dutch Red Help about the legalisation of communist refugees. Only when a 'neutral' refugee organisation was set up by mid 1938 – in the wake of the Popular Front strategy and in order to attract non-communist militants and to underline national solidarity – were the Dutch authorities ready to legalise the residence of most communist refugees in the Netherlands. Nevertheless, they continued to suppress any political activity by these 'subversive' refugees and in mid 1939 there were about fifty communist refugees in custody, and the few KPD refugees still in contact with the resistance in Germany itself had to remain underground.[66]

The Dutch change of policy cannot be entirely attributed to changes in the communist movement. They were also under strong international pressures to liberalise refugee policy. The bilateral treaty enacted with Belgium in April 1937 bound the Dutch to accept political refugees for whom the Netherlands was the first country of asylum. Unwanted political refugees could no longer be moved on to Belgium, and as repatriation to Germany was considered unacceptable, the Dutch authorities had to come to terms with these refugees. Nevertheless, the Belgian communists strongly criticised the 'extradition' of their comrades for whom the Netherlands was the first country of asylum. The Belgian authorities demanded guarantees that those returned would receive fair treatment from the Dutch authorities. From April 1938 onwards, the Dutch authorities agreed to inform the Belgians as to how the German political refugees were to be treated on their return: remaining at large in the Netherlands, interned or even repatriated to Germany. The Belgian decision was then made depending on what awaited the refugee in the Netherlands. As the Belgian authorities did not use force to make these political refugees leave the country, this information was also used to convince them to return to the Netherlands. The Dutch authorities were bound by this agreement for a year and were required to inform the Belgians of any alterations brought about by changing circumstances.[67] These concessions to the Belgian authorities increased the transparency and accountability of Dutch refugee policy at local, provincial and federal levels. A third factor explaining the Dutch change of course was the increasing use in public discussion of the notion of 'protecting political refugees' as a basic principle of the liberal state. Throughout 1938 it was repeated time and again that the Netherlands protected the 'real' refugees, those fleeing because of their political activities. This statement meant that the Dutch authorities had to live up to their promises and it became increasingly difficult to exclude communists from the group who were entitled to some privileges.

Jewish Refugees and the Loss of (Temporary) Protection

For domestic consumption, decision makers all over Western Europe claimed that they had strengthened immigration control, but at the same time they commonly expressed the mantra that this was done in a humanitarian way as the real, political refugees continued to be protected. The strengthening of immigration control had however a pernicious influence on the protection of Jewish refugees. The inflow of Jews was the subject of increasing opposition and repressive means to handle this uninvited immigration, be it forced deportation or imprisonment, gained increasing acceptance among policy makers and the public at large. Irrespective of the size of the local Jewish community and the number of the refugees already in the country, the arguments legitimising restrictive measures were very similar in all the countries considered. The dangers of economic competition and the need to curtail unemployment, which had been central in bolstering a protectionist alien policy in the first half of the 1930s, remained part of this restrictionist discourse. There was also the oft-expressed fear that the inflow of Jewish refugees would create a 'Jewish problem' as these new arrivals aroused antisemitic feeling among the population.[68] The notion of *Überfremdung* had been restricted to Swiss political discourse until the mid 1930s, but by the end of the decade it had found adherents among top-level bureaucrats and policy makers in all the liberal state of Europe. This xenophobic and even antisemitic discourse protected itself against accusations of illiberalism or a-humanitarianism by always underlining its commitment to national traditions of asylum. It was repeated time and again that political refugees were still granted asylum. The protection of 'refugees' thus remained assured. On the other hand it was argued that Jewish refugees were subject to less danger than political refugees and thus less in need of protection.[69]

The Netherlands was the first to abandon the policy for 'Jewish' refugees formulated in 1933, but here decision making was more complex and included local as well as national authorities. As mentioned before, by May 1938 the Dutch had changed their border policy by refusing admission to ('Jewish') refugees; at the same time the policy of temporary protection for these refugees was exchanged for a more coercive policy towards those refugees 'who had left their country under pressure of circumstances ... without being really in mortal danger'.[70] The Procurator-General in Amsterdam decided that imprisonment in a concentration camp was not sufficient reason for receiving refugee status and he even couched his decision in anti-Nazi terms by stating that 'the Netherlands will not submit to these questionable German practices'.[71] This tougher policy did not go unchallenged, even within the Dutch government. The Dutch Foreign Ministry was content to see a more robust policy at the border but was unwilling to countenance deporting Jewish refugees already in the country. These deportations tarnished the Dutch image as a country of asylum – just at a time when the Ministry was eager to polish up the country's image at the League of Nations.[72]

The harsh judgement on 'Jewish' refugees provoked a public reaction and when some Jewish refugees committed suicide during their repatriation, the protests became louder.[73] The path from legislation to implementation is often indistinct and we do not have conclusive data as to how many undocumented Jewish refugees were indeed deported as this was habitually carried out in secret, but tracking down refugees, detaining them and then deporting them was also extremely resource-intensive. The harsh language in the circular letters from government ministries tended to be moderated by the oral communication to local authorities given by the responsible civil servants. There was a certain reluctance to deny 'Jews' from Greater Germany protection completely. Thus for example, 'after fierce protest against expulsion' the asylum requests of alleged victims of persecution for *Rassenschande* or currency smuggling were to be submitted to the Minister of Justice. According to the civil servant in charge, granting this request would pose problems, because these persons 'had placed themselves in a position in which they knew to expect difficulties', but local authorities could in the meantime postpone the forced repatriation of alleged victims of persecution.[74] The autonomy afforded to local authorities added to this inconclusive picture. There are, however, indications of a radicalisation in Dutch deportation policy. Up to that point, repatriations had been mostly conducted on an individual basis, but some local authorities then began experimenting with collective deportations. In September 1938, forty-four 'Jews' from Vienna, including seven minors, embarked on a ship in Cologne, in collusion with the German police. The ship sailed to Rotterdam and crossed the frontier undetected by Dutch officials. Upon arrival in the port of Rotterdam the passengers were immediately arrested by the police, who decided to repatriate them in two buses. The police chief in Rotterdam considered that the advantage of a collective repatriation would be that suicide attempts would not occur so easily when the refugees were '*en famille*'.[75]

The Dutch authorities were not the only ones to take energetic action against the mass migration from Greater Germany. As Vicki Caron shows in her chapter in this volume, from May 1938 onwards, the French authorities used prison terms as a mean to convince 'Jewish' refugees to leave France. The French executive prevented any flexibility being exercised by the judiciary, as the courts were not permitted any discretion in taking account of specific individual circumstances. An internal crackdown of unprecedented severity followed and thousands of refugees landed in jail.[76]

As mentioned above, shortly after the Dutch decision to abort the protection for 'Jewish' refugees and the French decision to convict these refugees for illegal immigration, the Luxemburg authorities implemented a high profile show of strength policy towards 'Jewish' refugees dumped by the Germans on their territory. Dutch policy had also been induced by the dumping practices of the German authorities, but in Luxemburg the authorities responded to the German policy in an even more spectacular way. However, public criticism and the readiness of Jewish charities to guarantee the upkeep and re-emigration of the refugees caused the Luxembourg authorities to return to the old policy of temporarily protecting 'Jewish' refugees after this one incident, and there was a very quick increase in the number of 'Jewish' refugees in Luxemburg. By the middle of August, the Socialist Minister of Justice, René Blum, decided to close the border and also to repatriate 'Jewish' refugees. The local Jewish refugee committee, which did not have the means to meet the needs of this massive influx, agreed with the government that immigration had to be restricted. That same day, Blum gave instructions to his civil servants not to inform the press in any way about deportations. Blum had learned from the experience of May 1938 that expulsions were a sensitive issue and ones that should be kept as far as possible from the public.[77] As Regula Ludi shows in her chapter, the Swiss authorities decided to resort to the deportation of most 'Jewish' refugees at that time too. All those who had arrived illegally and had been found in the country after 19 August were to be returned to Greater Germany.

At the end of September 1938, Belgium joined Switzerland, the Netherlands and Luxemburg by deciding to abolish the temporary protection for 'Jewish' refugees and by enforcing their return to Greater Germany. On 30 September 1938, Joseph Pholien, the Catholic Minister of Justice, launched a secret operation. He gave instructions to the municipal police in Brussels to arrest any Austrian 'Jews' living illegally in the country. Roundups took place in hotels and refugees were arrested in police stations when they came to report their arrival to the authorities, after being told to do so by the Jewish refugee committee. This netted at least 250 Austrian 'Jews' in a fortnight and about 150 of them were rapidly repatriated to Germany. One of the repatriates managed to poison himself on the journey and had to be treated in a Belgian hospital close to the border.[78]

There was generally little public opposition to these increasingly restrictive practices and there was a consensus across Western Europe that a strict policy was necessary. Nevertheless, governments increasingly chose to alter policies through secret instructions and directives to the police forces and the local authorities, rather than to tinker with the legal framework, which would have involved a public debate. Yet this could not be avoided entirely as ministers had to defend their country's record on the admission of refugees in parliament. There was hardly any discussion on the general nature of border controls, but the arrest and expulsion of Jewish refugees already in the country became *causes célébres* and were sometimes hotly debated in both press and parliament.

Only in Belgium can parliamentary debate, buttressed by a wider public discussion, be seen to have changed the course of state policy. Treating

Jewish refugees like any other illegal immigrants and sending them back to their country of origin was a decision taken by the Catholic Minister of Justice, Joseph Pholien, in the Catholic-Socialist-Liberal government led by Paul-Henri Spaak. This decision also has to be situated within a political struggle among the conservatives. Since 1936, the conservative wing of the Catholic party had been in a severe crisis due to scandals and the desertion of conservative Catholic voters to the extremist Rex party. In 1936 the Brussels lawyer and newcomer Joseph Pholien was launched in national politics as the new face of the discredited conservative wing of the Catholic party. Pholien was a very individualistic politician with hardly any support within the party apparatus, but at that time the party machine became increasingly important as the locus of power where political strategies were designed and party members were disciplined. Pholien hoped that by bringing the antisemitic or xenophobic card into play, just as the rival Rex had seemingly successfully done, his party would be able to regain ground among traditionally conservative electors. Repressive measures pandering to the populist groundswell against immigration were therefore considered as an electoral advantage.

The expulsion of German 'Jews' immediately became known to Emile Vandervelde, the president of the Socialist Party, through an informer in the prison where the 'Jews' were being held prior to repatriation. Although Vandervelde led the Belgian Socialists, he was unaware of political deals struck by the independently minded socialist Prime Minister Spaak, who took a far more pragmatic line in trying to maintain his political coalition. These differences caused severe frictions between the two men. Vandervelde chose to champion the cause of the 'Jewish' refugees and lobbied within his party to preserve an (informal) asylum for all 'Jewish' refugees in Belgium. The Jewish refugee aid committee in Brussels also wanted to restore the temporary protection of their clientele, but a mere return to the old policy seemed unrealistic and they tried to kill two birds with one stone by proposing the creation of a refugee camp as a solution. Such a camp, they argued, would act as deterrent to immigration for all but the most desperate (and most deserving) of cases. Some months earlier the Jewish refugee committee had already proposed setting up a refugee camp, similar to Swiss experiments, largely as a means of reducing the costs for the upkeep of refugees and providing professional training to make them more attractive for countries overseas. Greater control was also sought in order to reduce the incidence of prostitution and swindling among refugees. In October the motivation for setting up a camp shifted to making the Jewish refugees much less visible and thus minimising the increasing antisemitic agitation in the country. The camp thus became a means of reducing the public perception of immigration rather than a means of deterring future arrivals. The Socialist leadership went along with this proposal and under pressure from his party colleagues, Prime Minister Spaak agreed to stop the expulsions and set up refugee camps.

Pholien was strongly opposed to this change of policy and highlighted the dangers of tolerating further illegal immigration of 'Jews' from Nazi

Germany. As neighbouring France and the Netherlands were toughening their policy, Belgium ran the risk of becoming the weak link in the chain and of being overwhelmed with refugees. He thus predicted, due to the increasing arrival of refugees and the slowing down of their departure to countries overseas, a rising antisemitism and the bankruptcy of the Jewish aid committee. A refugee camp would only attract would-be immigrants. In spite of his protests, Pholien had to back down completely: a refugee camp was set up in Merksplas and, on 15 October 1938, Pholien ordered a halt to the expulsions, although this latter decision was not made public. The next day, Emile Vandervelde, still unaware of the decision taken at top level, published a fierce protest against the expulsion of Jewish refugees in the Socialist daily *Le Peuple*. Vandervelde, having seen no result from his lobbying the previous week, took his demand for a humanitarian immigration policy to the street in order to bring his prime minister back to the ranks.

This public protest in Belgium caused immigration policy – which until then had been an uncontested prerogative of the executive power – to become a matter of public debate. Well-known members of the Jewish community and liberal politicians came out as advocates of the 'Jewish' refugees and criticised Joseph Pholien's expulsion policy. In the face of this, the hard-headed Pholien continued to defend the expulsion of 'Jewish' refugee albeit in an unsubtle manner, effectively portraying himself as a callous hard-liner with no empathy at all with the refugees' plight. He devalued their asylum claims by calling them economic immigrants and made a mockery of their suicide attempts. On 24 October, Vandervelde, obtained the backing of the council of the socialist party and ordered 'his' Prime Minister Paul-Henry Spaak to stop the (already abandoned) expulsions immediately.[79]

Enlisting German Cooperation in Immigration Control

The *Anschluss* of Austria brought individual protests from many Western European states against the German policy of dumping people across frontiers, albeit with no immediate results.[80] Consequently, the countries concerned developed preventive measures to arm themselves against future unwanted immigration. As the Nazi use of denaturalisation as a form of persecution became more widespread, Belgium and the Netherlands began to insist that German citizens applying for a visa or arriving at the border possessed an official German declaration that they could return at any time to Germany. The German authorities refused to issue such documents; affirming time and again that all Germans, including 'Jews', could always return to Germany.[81] This measure made travel for all Germans much more cumbersome and did lead to some German concessions to neighbouring states. A Belgian–German bilateral agreement concluded on 22 October 1938 stated explicitly that all German immigrants could return to Germany. In exchange for this guarantee the

Belgian authorities agreed to the normalisation of border controls for regular travellers from Germany.[82] Clarifying that it was possible for all Germans to return to Germany placed the onus firmly on the 'Jews' for not *wanting* to return.

The protests against the flight of Jews caused not only the German authorities to promise to allow their citizens to return, and as a result of negotiations with the Swiss and Swedish authorities, to mark their passports, but they made also promises that went beyond that. German–Swiss negotiations in September 1938 led to a German promise not only to mark the passports of the German 'Jews', but also to instruct the German border guards to prevent the holders of German 'J' passports from entering Switzerland if they did not have a Swiss visa.[83] Similarly, the German–Belgian agreement of 22 October 1938 stipulated that the German authorities would help to combat illegal immigration into Belgium. To honour these promises, the German authorities issued orders in early November 1938 to arrest all 'Jews' found near the border who did not have the documents necessary to enter Belgium, Switzerland or France. Male would-be emigrants were to be locked up in police prisons before transfer to a concentration camp, while women and children were merely removed from the border area. This German willingness to assist neighbouring countries was not entirely 'philanthropic' as it also served to prevent political activists from leaving the country and acted as a control to make sure that 'Jews' were stripped of all their assets prior to their departure.[84]

Numerous 'Jews' still tried to flee Nazi Germany by crossing the German border illegally and administrative capacities in the border areas were insufficient to enforce the orders properly. For example in November 1938 the Staatspolizei office in Aachen could not handle the large number of mostly Austrian 'Jews' who had tried to emigrate without permission and had been caught. As the local police prison was full to overflowing and as the transfer of these Jewish prisoners to a concentration camp could not be executed swiftly, the local authorities were obliged to set free a number of the Jewish would-be emigrants they had arrested. These 'Jews' were thus reprieved from a term in a concentration camp and were only removed from the border region.[85]

This cooperation in halting illegal immigration into neighbouring countries represented a change of course in the manner in which the Nazis attempted the ethnic cleansing of the German Reich.[86] While at the Eastern border the German authorities tried by every possible means to expedite emigration, on the western side they actively tried to prevent people from leaving.[87] Thus from November 1938 onwards, refugees trying to leave German soil for Belgium, France or Switzerland had to outwit the German as well as the Belgian, Swiss or French border guards and thus increasingly relied on the ever more expensive *'passeurs'*, who for substantial rewards would smuggle people across the frontier.

Notes

1. Seeing that the National Socialist racial categorisations, such as Jew and Aryan, were not at all transparant and self-evident categories, we enclose those terms in quotation marks.
2. Circular letter from the German Home Office, 24.8.1938: 'to hasten the exodus of German and stateless Jews, convictions are not to be mentioned automatically in the excerpt of the criminal record which is transmitted to the authorities of the immigration countries', AMIA, individual files, A 316.576. The politically motivated convictions because of communist activities were still to be mentioned: G. Anderl and D. Rupnow, *Die Zentralstelle für jüdische Auswanderung als Beraubungsinstitution*, Wien 2006, p.97; Krause to Home Offices of the German states beyond Prussia (ausserpreusssche Landesregierungen), 21.1.1939, BBR 276.
3. W. Gruner, 'Von der Kollektivausweisung zur Deportation der Juden aus Deutschland (1938–1945). Neue perspektiven und Dokumente', in *Die Deportation der Juden aus Deutschland*, ed. B. Kundrus and B. Meyer, Göttingen 2004, pp.23–24; BBR 276.
4. W. Röder, 'The Political Exiles: Their Policies and their Contribution to Post-War Reconstruction', in *International Biographical Dictionary of Central European Emigrés 1933–1945*, vol. II, part 1, ed. H. Strauss and W. Röder, Munich 1983, p.XXX.
5. Anderl and Rupnow, *Die Zentralstelle*.
6. J. Moser, 'Osterreich', in *Dimension des Völkermords: Die zahl der Jüdischen Opfer des Nationalsozialismus*, ed. W. Benz, Munich 1991, p.68. See also Zentralstelle für jüdische Auswanderung to SD-Hauptamt, 21.10.1938, BBR 486.
7. B. Moore, *Refugees from Nazi Germany in the Netherlands, 1933–1940*, Dordrecht 1986, pp.82, 96; J.Toury, '"Ein Auftakt zur Endlösung": Judenaustreibungen über nichtslawische Reichsgrenzen 1933–1939', in *Das Unrechts-Regime. Festschfit für Werner Jochmann zum 65. Geburtstag*, ed. U. Büttner, Hamburg 1986, vol. 2, pp.164–96.
8. S. Friedländer, *Nazi Germany and the Jews. I: The Years of Persecution, 1933–1939*, London 1998, pp.260ff.
9. J. Osterloh, *Nationalsozialistische Judenverfolgung im Reichsgau Sudetenland 1938–1945*, Munich 2006, pp.198ff.; Friedländer, *Nazi Germany and the Jews*, vol.1, pp.265f.
10. E. Mendelsohn, *The Jews of East Central Europe Between the World Wars*, Bloomington 1983, pp.164–67; P. Heumos, *Die Emigration aus der Tschechoslowakei nach Westeuropa und dem Nahen Osten 1938–1945*, Munich 1989, p.52.
11. K. Voigt, *Zuflucht auf Widerruf. Exil in Italien 1933–1945*, Stuttgart 1989; C. Villanci, *Zwischen Rassengesetzen und Deportation. Juden in Südtirol, im Trentino und in der Provinz Belluno, 1933–1945*, Innsbrück 2003.
12. Moreover, all foreign Jews who had been granted Italian citizenship after 1 January 1919 were stripped of it, a decree that affected approximately 9,000 Jews, for the most part formerly German and Polish citizens: M. Sarfatti, *Gli ebrei nell' Italia fascista. Vicende, identita, persucione*, Torino 2000; Klaus Voigt, *Zuflucht auf Widerruf*.
13. V. Caron,*Uneasy Asylum: France and the Jewish Refugee Crisis, 1933–1942*, Stanford 1999, pp.146ff.; Mendelsohn, *The Jews of East Central Europe*, pp.68–

83 and 112–28; Ben Eliahu Elissar, *Le facteur juif dans la politique étrangère du IIIe Reich (1933–1939)*, Paris 1969, pp.301–21.
14. The Polish authorities retaliated by expelling Germans, and those Poles stuck at the border could return to Germany. Later a Polish–German compromise was reached that those who had been able to enter Poland could stay and be joined by their family members still in Germany: S. Milton, 'The Expulsion of Polish Jews from Germany, October 1938 to July 1939', in *LBIYB*, 29, 1984, pp.169–74; Friedländer, *Nazi Germany and the Jews*, vol. 1, pp.266–68.
15. L. London, *Whitehall and the Jews, 1933–1948: British Immigration Policy and the Holocaust*, Cambridge 2000, p.63.
16. The Norwegian and Swedish authorities had imposed a visa requirement on Austrian travellers shortly after the Anschluss (April 1938): H. Müssener, *Das Exil in Schweden. Politische und kulturelle Emigration nach 1933*, Munich 1974, p.123; E. Lorenz, *Exil in Norwegen. Lebensbedingungen und Arbeit deutschsprachiger Flüchtlinge 1933–1943*, Baden-Baden 1992, p.51.
17. L. Rünitz, *Af hensyn til konsekvenserne, Danmark og flygtningesporgsmalet 1933–1939*, Odense 2005, pp.246ff.; Petersen, 'Viel Papier und wenig Erfolg. Dänemark und die internationale staatliche Hilfsarbeit für Flüchtlinge vor dem deutschen Fascismus 1933–1939', in *Exil, Forschung, Erkenntnisse, Ergebnisse*, 2, 1985, pp.60–84.
18. Report Belgian border police, 24.3.1938, AAD 37C9.
19. La Revue Communale de Belgique, *Journal de droit administratif et d'administration*, 68, 1939, pp.172–73; A. Sherman, *Island Refuge: Britain and Refugees from the Third Reich, 1933–1939*, London, 1973, p.190; Lorenz, *Exil in Norwegen*, p.51; Czecho-Slovakian nationals could travel throughout 1939 without visa to Denmark: Rünitz, *Af hensyn*, p.430.
20. C. Van Eijl, *Al te goed is buurmans gek. Het Nederlandse vreemdelingenbeleid 1840-1940*, Amsterdam 2005, p.188; Rünitz, *Af hensyn*.
21. Pholien to Spaak, 14.10.1938, but already since March 1938 this new procedure was being discussed (and possibly implemented), AAD 785; F. Caestecker, *Ongewenste gasten, joodse vluchtelingen en migranten in de dertiger jaren*, Brussels 1993, p.229.
22. F. Caestecker, 'Onverbiddelijk, maar ook clement. Het Belgische immigratiebeleid en de joodse vlucht uit nazi-Duitsland, maart 1938–augustus 1939', *Bijdragen tot de eigentijdse geschiedenis*, 13/14, 2004, pp.109–12; LSA J73/48. As Vicki Caron mentions in her chapter in this volume, a fully restrictive French visa policy was only introduced from April 1938 onwards. Immediately after the *Anschluss* the government of Léon Blum, briefly back in power, granted Austrian Jews entry visas. Once Daladier took power on 10 April, fear of an impending invasion of Austrian refugees took over and immediately instructions were given not to issue visa to Austrian refugees. For the Swiss administrative practice see Regula Ludi, this volume.
23. 358 Jews obtained a temporary residence permit in Denmark on their way overseas between July 1938 and September 1939, while in Luxemburg between November 1938 and September 1939, 793 such residence permits were granted: Rünitz, *Af hensyn*, pp.376–90; LSA J(ustice)73/53 and J 74/11.
24. Between July 1938 and September 1939, 266 Jews obtained an authorisation to settle permanently in Denmark because they had close relatives in Denmark. Danish restrictions were very harsh: follow-on migration was mostly limited to the single and very old family members, provided, however,

that the relatives were able to put up substantial guarantees that the person in question would not become a burden on public funds. The fact that one's parents, children or siblings lived in Denmark or even one's wife, gave an applicant no favorable treatment for a visa. These 'insignificant ties' could earn one at most a visa for a short visit, insofar as one was able to promptly return to Germany afterwards: Rünitz, *Af hensyn*, pp.273 and 376–90. In the Netherlands, Dutch-born women who had married a German and thus had lost their citizenship, and parents of residents of the Netherlands, if the latter could assure their upkeep, were mostly granted residence permits. In all categories combined, 800 persons were authorised to settle, mostly temporarily, in the Netherlands between May and October 1938: Van Eijl, *Al te goed*, pp.188–90; Moore, *Refugees*, p.84.

25. *Reichsgesetzblatt*, I, 7 October 1938, p.1342.
26. Anderl and Rupnow, *Die Zentralstelle*, p.156. Sweden and Switzerland became also knowledgeable of each other's negotiations and their common goal, but there was no coordination between the two countries. Sweden did refrain from using the word Jews in the Swedish–German agreement of 15 October 1938: C. Ludwig, *Die Flüchtlingspolitik der Schweiz in den Jahre 1933 bis 1952. Bericht des Bundesrates an die Bundesversammlung*, Bern 1957, p.124 ff.; UEK, pp.102–10. For the role of Switzerland in the introduction of the 'J'-stamp see Regula Ludi, this volume.
27. Caron, *Uneasy Asylum*, p.182. Rünitz, *Af hensyn*, pp.215–22.
28. From respectively 1933 and 1936 onwards: Van Eijl, *Al te goed*, p.174; LSA, Ministère de la Justice, J73/53, p.16.
29. Danish instruction to consular services of 6.10.1938 referred explicitly to non-Aryans from Central and Eastern Europe as a category to whom visas were to be granted only in exceptional circumstances and with explicit agreement of the Ministry of Justice: Runitz, *Af hensyn*, pp.273f. In Luxemburg, the office granting work permits made a distinction between non-Aryan German musicians and Aryan German musicians; for the former, their work permits were more limited in time: M. Gloden,*Die Asylpolitik Luxemburgs von 1933 bis 1940. Der Anspruch auf Kontrolle*, Wissenschaftliche Arbeit zur Erlangung des akademischen Titels eines Magister, Universität Trier, 2001, p.80. Applicants for British (tourist) visas who, according to the instructions of April 27 1938, 'appear to be of Jewish or partly Jewish origin or have non-Aryan affiliations' were ineligible as they were suspected of wanting to remain in Britain: London, *Whitehall*, p.56. In Norway, the authorities stated explicitly that Jews, defined as those of Mosaic faith, were to be refused visas: Einhart, *Exil in Norwegen*, p.51. In France, from May 1938 onwards, undocumented aliens had to fill in an identification card in which the French authorities asked for citizenship, religion and affiliation: J. Deschodt and F. Huguenin, *La république xénophobe, 1917–1939*, Paris 2001, p.271.
30. Caron, *Uneasy Asylum*, p.191; London, *Whitehall*, p.65; Rünitz, *Af hensyn*, p.274; Sherman, *Island Refuge*, pp.90ff.
31. By the end of June 1938 Great Britain had granted 2,740 visas to Austrian subjects: London, *Whitehall*, p.70.
32. T. Kushner, 'An Alien Occupation: Domestic Service and the Jewish Crisis, 1933 to 1939', in *The Holocaust and the Liberal Imagination: A Social and Cultural History*, ed. T. Kushner, Oxford 1994, pp.91–104; H. Loebl, 'Refugees from the Third Reich and Industry in the Depressed Areas of Britain', in *Second Chance: Two Centuries of German-Speaking Jew in the United Kingdom*, ed. W.

Mosse, Tübingen 1991, pp.379–403. See also Frank Caestecker and Bob Moore, 'Female Domestic Servants as Desirable Refugees: Gender Labour Needs and Immigration Policy in Belgium, the Netherlands and Great Britain' *European History Quarterly* (forthcoming)
33. Van Eijl, *Al te goed*, pp.188–90.
34. Caestecker, 'Onverbiddelijk', p.118.
35. Rünitz, *Af hensyn*, pp.271–76; Caron, *Uneasy Asylum*, pp.52 and 181; Noiriel, *La Tyrannie du National*, p.221; LSA, Ministère de la Justice, J73/45; G. Meershoek, *Dienaren van het gezag. De Amsterdamse politie tijdens de bezetting*, Amsterdam 1999, quotes Van den Hoek, *De geschiedenis van het Wapen der Koninklijke Marechaussee*, 1963, pp.340–41; Note Gestapo, 2.9.1938, BBR 800; H. Arntz, *Judenverfolgung und Fluchthilfe in deutsch-belgischen Grenzgebiet*, Euskirchen 1990, p.510; for Switzerland see Regula Ludi, this volume.
36. D. Bourgeois, 'La porte se ferme: la Suisse et le problème de l'immigration juive en 1938', *Relations Internationales*, 54, 1988, pp.188 ff.
37. Jews were mostly excluded from Swiss formal refugee status. The Swiss instructions of March 1938 to the border authorities considered those who had left Greater Germany via a regular German frontier post (Ausreisekontrolle) as not eligible for refugee status. Jews had no difficulty in passing through German border posts. The border guards had to send a copy of the written record of the arrest of a foreigner to the Federal Prosecutor's Office (Bundesanwaltschaft) who had to decide if the applicant was a genuine refugee and thus their competence. Jews were as a rule not considered refugees. S. Keller, *Grüningers Fall. Geschichte von Flucht und Hilfe*, Zurich 1993, pp.14f.; G. Koller, 'Entscheidungen über Leben und Tod. Die behördliche Praxis in der schweizerischen Flüchtlingspolitik während des Zweiten Weltkrieges', *Studien und Quellen. Zeitschrft des Schweizerischen Bundesarchivs*, 22, 1996, p.27.
38. J. Wacker, *Humaner als in Bern! Schweizer und Basler Asylpraxis gegenüber den jüdischen Flüchtlingen von 1933 bis 1943 im Vergleich*, Basel 1992, pp.96, 113 and 123; F. Battel, *'Wo es hell ist, dort is die Schweiz' Flüchtlinge und Fluchthilfe an der Schaffhauser Grenze zur Zeit des Nationalsozialismus*, Zürich 2000, p.151.
39. Moore, *Refugees in the Netherlands*, pp.77ff.; Van Eijl, *Al te goed*, p.188f.
40. Caestecker, *Ongewenste gasten*, p.182f.; Report prefect of Moselle, 27.5.1938, and report of the local police Thionville, 30.5.1938, AN F7/16072.
41. Belgian ambassador in Luxemburg to the Belgian Minister of Foreign Affairs, 26.5.1938, AAD 289; LSA, Ministère de la Justice, J73/47; Report prefect of Moselle, 27.5.1938 and report of the local police Thionville, 30.5.1938, AN F7/16072.
42. Y. Bauer, *My Brother's Keeper: A History of the American Jewish Joint Distribution Committee, 1929–1939*, Philadelphia 1974, p.242.
43. Report prefect of Moselle, 27.5.1938, AN F7/16072.
44. According to police records, of the 527 'Jewish' refugees who arrived at the Danish border in the period between 1 July and 1 October 1938, 291 of them were refused admission: Rünitz, *Af hensyn*, pp.271–76, 287, 428ff.
45. H. Müssener, *Das Exil in Schweden. Politische und kulturelle Emigration nach 1933*, Munich 1974, pp.124f.; P. Levine, *From Indifference to Activism: Swedish Diplomacy and the Holocaust (1938–1944)*, Uppsala 1996, p.105.
46. Rünitz, *Af hensyn*, pp.246–74, 415 and 410, 426; H. Petersen, 'Die Dänische Flüchtlingspoliitk 1933–1941', in *Deutschsprachiges Exil in Dänemaken nach*

1933. Zu methoden und Einzelergebenissen, ed. R. Dinesen, B.S. Nielsen, H. Petersen, F. Schmoë, Copenhagen 1986, p.80.
47. Rünitz, *Af hensyn*, p.429.
48. Not all Jews were deported to Germany, a few were pushed on the other neighbouring countries such as Belgium and France: LSA, Ministère de la Justice, J73/47 and 48. LSA, Ministère des Affaires Etrangères, 3309 (P.1–172). The Luxemburg border policy has hardly been investigated: Ludwig, *Die Flüchtlingspolitik der Schweiz*, pp.86f., 125, 90f., 156; Bourgeois, 'La porte se ferme', p.204, see also Regula Ludi, this volume.
49. Wacker, *Humaner als Bern*, p.113ff.; «Une seule solution s'impose, le "refiler" subrepticement à la Belgique»; G. Noiriel, *La Tyrannie du national. Le droit d'asile en Europe 1793–1993*, Paris 1991, p.116.
50. H. Bekaert, 'Note pour la 2e direction', 29.4.1938, AAD 1234; Note sur le libéralisme comparé des différents Etats. See also Lambert to Bérenger, 13.7.1938, AN F7 16072.
51. At least one report of the Dutch Marechaussee mentioned using rubber truncheons against would-be refugees: Moore, *Refugees*, p.83. See also LSA, Ministère de la Justice, J73/47.
52. See Regula Ludi, this volume.
53. London, *Whitehall*, p.66; Belgian border policy has hardly been investigated: border guards had less autonomy than in other countries as all decisions were to be taken by the alien police in Brussels. For the difficulties for such research see S. Kirschgens, *Wege durch das Niemandsland. Dokumentation und Analyse der Hilfe für Flüchtlinge im deutsch-belgisch-niederländisch Grenzland in den Jahre 1933 bis 1945*, Cologne 1998. Also British policy at the ports has hardly been investigated.
54. The authorities enumerated the possible forms of proof: 'Press clippings which deal with the evoked events which made the person leave the country, ... documents, letters which prove that the person was present at that place and at that time when the events happened ... documents which prove that the foreigner was opposed to the regime of his country and that this hostility exposed the person to the cruelty against his person or his belongings', Minister of Interior to the préfets, 1938, quoted in C. Zalc, 'Des réfugiés aux indésirables: les pouvoirs publics français face aux émigrés du IIIe Reich entre 1933 et 1939', in *Construction des nationalités et immigration dans la France contemporaine*, ed. E. Guichard and G. Noiriel, Paris 1997, p.265; Direction de la Police du Territoire et des Étrangers, 'Note sur l'applications de l'article 2, alinéa 2 du Décret du 3 Mai 1938', AN F7 16072; Caron, *Uneasy Asylum*, p.181; Noiriel, *La Tyrannie*, p.199.
55. H. Rozenkrans, 'Entrechtung, Verfolgung und Selbsthilfe der Juden in Oesterreich März bis Oktober 1938', in *Oesterreich, Deutschland und die Mächte. Internationale und Oesterreichische Aspekte des 'Anschlusses' vom März 1938*, ed. G. Stourzh and B. Zaar, Vienna 1990, p.402.
56. The Danish Red Help demanded, after the *refoulement* of communist refugees, a centralised decision making in this field, but to no avail: Rünitz, *Af hensyn*, pp.246–79, 408f. In Switzerland, border control became increasing centralised during this period.
57. For a personal testimony on how Belgian border guards brought Jewish refugees to the German border, but gave them indications on how to return safely to Belgium, see Walter Gersten, LBI-NY ME 185.

58. For Figure 4: the figures for France are based on the number of new arrivals (persons) from Germany (from March 1938 including Austria and from November 1938 including Czechoslovakia) in the monthly reports of the *Comité d'Assistance aux Réfugiés* (CAR) for Paris (AIU France X D 56); the figures for France, Luxemburg and Switzerland in 1939 are listed in a report of the AJDC (UCL, Van Zeeland, 906); for Belgium the figures are passed on a weekly basis by the Jewish refugee aid committees to the authorities (ADA 37C6) ; for Luxemburg in 1938 we used the figures in 'Note sur l'état actuel de l'émigration d'Allemagne et d'Autrich', 9.1938, YIVO HICEM (Paris) – Emigration record.group 245.5, Serie France I, Microfilms reel 16.11 ; the Dutch figures for the arrivals in 1939 refer to those who are registered by the Jewish committee in Amsterdam, but not all of them received aid from the Committee. Excluded are the so-called 2,551 transit refugees who mostly left the Netherlands shortly after arrival (only 2 per cent failed to leave as plans collided, those few were added to the other arrivals): Nederlands Instituut voor Oorlogsdocumentatie, 181 k, Comité voor Joodse Belangen Map 1a, annual report for 1938. In order to have the total number of refugees registered by the refugee committees, we should add up also the figures of the Jewish committees in other places and those registered by the Catholic, Protestant or non-religious refugee aid committees. Figure 5 refers, for Denmark, to all immigrants, thus not only 'Jews', who were registered in Denmark and who evoked that they had left Germany and other European countries because of persecution. The figures for Luxemburg are based on the official number of Jewish refugees from (Greater) Germany admitted. From November 1938 onwards these refugees were admitted on the basis of a temporary residence permit valid from between 2 days to 2 years. These figures are slightly higher than the figures we have for 1939 of the Jewish refugee committee in the AJDC report mentioned above, as not all Jewish refugees admitted passed through this committee: LSA, Justice Department J73/53, J74/11 and Foreign Affairs 3309 (P.1–172).
59. London, *Whitehall*, p.61; Noiriel, *La tyrannie*, p.183; Van Eijl, *Al te goed*, pp.189–90.
60. A violation of this rule could lead to a prison sentence of up to one month or a fine: R. Weijdeveld, *Rode Hulp. Opvang van Duitse vluchtelingen in Groningerland, 1933–1940*, Groningen 1986, p.111.
61. Kirschgens, *Wege durch das Niemandsland*, p.189. For a similar evolution in France, see Noiriel, *La Tyrannie*, p.194; M. Lewis, 'The Strangeness of Foreigners', *French Politics, Culture and Society*, 20, no. 3, 2002, p.10.
62. Deschodt and Huguenin, *La république xénophobe*, p.187 ; AN F7 16072; B. Vormeier and H. Schramm, *Vivre à Gurs. Un Camp de Concentration français 1940–1941*, Paris 1977, p.236; U. Weinzierl, *Oesterreicher im Exil. Frankreich 1938–1945. Eine Dokumentation*, Vienna 1984, p.44f.; U. Langkau-Alex, *Deutsche Volksfront, 1932–1939. Zwischen Berlin, Paris, Prag und Moskau. Vorgeschichte und Gründung der Ausschusses zur Vorbereitung einer deutscher Volksfront*, vol.2, Berlin 2004, p.447.
63. H. Walter, *Deutsche Exilliteratur 1933–1950 (Band 2), Europäisches Appeasement und uberseeische Asylpraxis*, Stuttgart 1984, p.105ff.
64. René Girault, 'La politique extérieure française de l'après-Munich (septembre 1938–avril 1939)', in *Deutschland und Frankreich 1936–1939*, ed. H. Klaus, K. Werner and K. Manfrass, Munich 1981, 507ff.

65. B. Herlemann, *Die Anleitung des Widerstands des KPD durch die Exilierte Parteiführung in Frankreich, die Niederlanden und Belgien*, Königstein im Taunus 1982, p.151ff.; Caestecker, *Ongewenste gasten*, p.98ff. and 230; Moore, *Refugees*, p.127.
66. A. Gerrits, '"Solidariteit zonder eenheidsfront". De Internationale Rode Hulp in Nederland, 1925–1938', *Cahiers over de geschiedenis van de CPN*, 10, 1985, pp.55–80; Weijdeveld, *Rode Hulp*, p.179; Moore, *Refugees*, p.128; Herlemann, *Widerstands des KPD*, p.151ff.
67. Circular letter Dutch Ministry of Justice (2e section/1135), 26.4.1938, Amsterdam archive, city police, 5225. Only in June 1939 did the Belgian authorities decide to deport to the Netherlands any refugee for whom the Netherlands was the first country of asylum: Caestecker, *Ongewenste gasten*, p.241.
68. London, *Whitehall*, p.61; Caestecker, 'Onverbiddelijk', pp.109ff.; Moore, *Refugees*, pp.107–8; Van Eijl, *Al te goed*, p.188. Even the Danish authorities evoked this argument in September 1938, notwithstanding the small Jewish community of 6,000 persons and the small number of refugees: Rünitz, *Af hensyn*, pp.272–74; H. Petersen and E. Lorenz, 'Fremdenpolitik und Asylpraxis der skandinavischen Staaten', in *'Ein sehr trübes Kapital'? Hitlerflüchtlinge im nordeuropäischen Exil 1933–1950*), ed. E. Lorenz, K. Misgeld, H. Müssener and H. Petersen, Hamburg 1998, p.28. For France and Switzerland see Vicki Caron, and Regula Ludi, this volume.
69. Rünitz, *Af hensyn*, p. 410; Petersen and Lorenz, 'Fremdenpolitik und Asylpraxis', p.28.
70. Strangely enough the Dutch authorities did not deny that these foreigners were refugees and stated explicitly that refugees had become undesirable elements: C. Berghuis, *Joodse vluchtelingen in Nederland 1938–1940*, Kampen 1990, pp.223–24.
71. Procurator-General Amsterdam to Jewish refugee committee, 6.1938, City archives Amsterdam, city police, arch. 5225, volume 16.
72. Van Eijl, *Al te goed*, p.191.
73. Van Eijl, *Al te goed*, p.189f.
74. Conference with Pannenborg of Ministry of Justice in relation to the instructions of May 1938, City archive of Amsterdam, archive of the police, arch. 5225/ 4 and 5.
75. All forty-four 'Jews' were extradited to the German border police on 17 September 1938. On 2 November 1938 the German border guards informed their superiors that the Dutch authorities had had no more recourse to similar operations: HSTAD 21.133; Van Eijl, *Al te goed*, p.194; K. Grossmann, *Emigration.Geschichte der Hitler-Flüchtlinge 1933–1945*, Frankfurt 1969, p.20.
76. See also M. Dewhurst Lewis, *The Boundaries of the Republic: Migrant Rights and the Limits of Universalism in France, 1818–1940*, Stanford 2007, pp.220–28.
77. LSA, Ministère de la Justice, J73/47 and 48; *Le Peuple*, 14 and 19 January 1939; Bauer, *My Brother's Keeper*, p.243.
78. Caestecker, 'Onverbiddelijk', p.113.
79. Caestecker, 'Onverbiddelijk', p.108ff.; Caestecker, *Ongewenste gasten*, p.188ff.
80. Caron, *Uneasy Asylum*, p.181; Regina M. Delacor, 'Die Reaktionen Frankreichs auf den Novemberpogrom 1938', in *Zeitschrift für Geschichtswissenschaft*, XLVI, 11, 1998, pp.998–1006; Rozenkrans, 'Entrechtung', p.402; Minister of

Foreign Affairs, P.H.Spaak to Belgian embassy in Berlin, 12.5.1938, AAD 785; Gloden, 'Die Asylpolitik Luxemburgs', p.100.
81. The Luxemburg authorities felt that they disposed of an assurance that they could always repatriated (ex-)German nationals. The Gotha Treaty of 1851 to which Luxemburg was a party entitled the Luxemburg authorities to return all German and ex-German nationals who had become stateless. The Luxemburg authorities considered this treaty the solution to eventual problems those leaving Germany would pose and repeated time and again the obligation of Germany to respect the terms of the treaty: LSA, Ministère de la Justice, J73/47 and 48. For the Gotha treaty see Andreas K. Fahrmeier, *Citizens and Aliens: Foreigners and the Law in Britain and the German States, 1789–1870*, New York 2000, pp.37–39.
82. Caestecker, *Ongewenstegasten*, p.208. The repatriation of (even undocumented) German Jews could proceed with few administrative difficulties as the German authorities could easily grant a laissez-passer for these German citizens. For the stateless, including the denaturalised German citizens and the holders of a *Fremdenpas*, the repatriation was more difficult to organise, as German consuls could only grant a laissez-passer when Berlin had agreed: Rünitz, *Af hensyn*, pp.414f.
83. Bourgeois, 'La porte se ferme', p.201.
84. Instructions Best and Lischka, Geheime Staatspolizei Berlin to Grensinspection West in Koblenz, 3.11.1938, BBR 276; see also Arntz, *Judenverfolgung*, p.533 and 'Note über die Einwanderung deutscher Staatsangehörige nach Belgien', Archive German Ministry of Foreign Affairs Bonn, R 48907; H. Berschel, *Bürokratie und Terror. Das Judenreferat der Gestapo Düsseldorf, 1935–1945*, Essen 2001, pp.280–85; Keller, *Grüningers Fall*, p.104ff.; Wacher, *Humaner als in Bern*, p.107.
85. Staatspolizeistelle Aachen, 23.11.1938, and information sheet, Ministry of Foreign Affairs, 10.12.1938, Archive Ministry of Foreign Affairs, Bonn, R 48907; Kirschgens, *Wege durch das Niemandsland*, pp.99ff.
86. Toury, 'Ein Auftakt zur Endlösung'.
87. Gruner, 'Von der Kollektivausweisung'.

Chapter II.4

From *Kristallnacht* to War, November 1938–August 1939

Frank Caestecker and Bob Moore

While the economic and administrative pressure on 'Jews' in Germany was already intense by the autumn of 1938, it was about to be made indescribably worse by the events of the *Kristallnacht*. An orgy of violence and destruction swept over Germany. Officially, 91 people were killed on the night of broken glass, but many hundreds more died of their wounds or in concentration camps in the following days and weeks. Approximately 30,000 male 'Jews' were arrested and taken to concentration camps.[1] Whatever funds or assets most 'Jews' had still possessed in November 1938 had been looted or destroyed in the pogrom, and the one billion mark fine levied on the community to pay for the damage, and various other impositions, effectively bankrupted most of its collective activities. All 'Jewish' business activity was to cease by 1 January 1939 and all remaining 'Jewish' assets and works of art were to be sold for the benefit of the Reich.[2]

Emigration from the Reich from 1933 had tended to claim the best candidates, and the 'Jews' who remained after November 1938 were less attractive for potential countries of refuge, but they were still placed under enormous pressure to leave. At the same time the German authorities sought to segregate them from all aspects of German life. Restrictions of all kinds rained down on the 'Jews', their pauperisation proceeded apace and 'apartheid' became a fact of daily life. They also became subject to segregated labour deployment as the Nazis chose to exploit those whose unemployment made them dependent on state welfare.[3] In March 1939, the German state annexed Bohemia-Moravia, a further 118,000 'Jews' came under Nazi control and it was not long before Adolf Eichmann established a branch of the *Zentralstelle* in Prague. Similarly in Germany, a *Reichszentrale für jüdische Auswanderung* was established in Berlin to centralise 'all work for 'Jewish' emigration'.

In this context, it should be remembered that the flow of people escaping from Greater Germany were by no means the only refugees in Europe at the end of the 1930s. There were well-founded fears in Western Europe that much larger numbers of Jewish refugees might be created by the states of Eastern Europe. Any generosity to refugees from Germany might well stimulate the impatience and rapacity of the Polish and Hungarian government to solve 'their' Jewish question in the same way as Nazi Germany had attempted to do. In January the Romanian government followed the Polish and Hungarian example and enacted legislation that stripped Jews naturalised after 1918 of their citizenship (and barred Jews from a broad range of professions). As the Romanian judiciary declared these laws unconstitutional they were never implemented, but the intent was clear and this potential efflux from Eastern Europe was a constant threat.[4] At the same time, there was also the reality of up to 400,000 Republican refugees from Spain as the civil war came to an end.

Forced emigration remained the goal of the Nazi leadership and it continued to use all the means at its disposal to remove impoverished 'Jews' from Reich territory, both legal and illegal.[5] 'Jewish' concentration camps inmates were only to be released if, and only if, they emigrated.[6] Emigration overseas was one option, but it remained costly. International Jewish charities provided some of the finance through Jewish organisations inside Germany. The Nazis also forced wealthy 'Jews' in Germany wanting to leave to co-finance the emigration of their less affluent co-religionists.[7] Emigration overseas nonetheless remained difficult. Immigration into Latin America became increasingly restricted as the authorities gave in to local protectionist and antisemitic forces.[8] There were only a few exceptions to the worldwide restrictive immigration policies. After *Kristallnacht*, Great Britain was the first state to introduce a more generous policy of temporary protection and even the United States opened its doors slightly to the victims of Nazi policy. As Bat-Ami Zucker explains in her chapter, President Roosevelt felt he had a moral obligation to aid the refugees, but for electoral reasons and the public mood of restrictionism he was unwilling to tamper with the fundamental principles of his country's immigration laws.

For those with nowhere else to go, the International Settlements at Shanghai provided a possible destination simply because it was a territory outside the international system of nation-states which, although under Japanese control, was self-governing and did not demand visas for entry. In spite of the lack of any real settlement opportunities there and the potential for abject poverty, many refugees chose, or were forced to take this as their only option. Some 1,500 had arrived by the end of 1938 and by September 1939, their numbers had grown to around 8,000.[9]

The pace of emigration was much too slow for the Nazis. The German authorities were fully aware that the J-stamp on the German passports had served to hinder their emigration programme. Hermann Göring's famous speech of 6 December 1938 to the Gauleiter, in which he outlined the anti-Jewish policy following the *Kristallnacht*, indicated how this difficulty might be overcome. 'Jews' who were able to finance their emigration, but whose J-stamped documents prevented them being considered as acceptable immigrants, could exceptionally be issued with regular German passports.[10]

The Nazis were also aware of how few places in the world would accept penniless 'Jews' as immigrants. Palestine was the favourite place to dump 'Jews' and the SS collaborated with revisionist Zionists from June 1938 and with the Jewish Agency from January 1939 onwards to organise illegal immigration into the mandate, largely by sea. When the Royal Navy began intercepting these ships in early 1939 and preventing the immigrants from landing, the refugees were dropped off in small boats just outside territorial waters and rowed the last few miles to the Palestinian coast.[11] Latin American ports also became targets for Nazi agencies anxious to export as many Jews as possible using schemes that involved transporting refugees en masse.[12] In January 1939 they allowed the steamship *Königstein* to leave for Barbados although fully aware that the passengers did not possess enough landing money.[13] The ship was not permitted to land and wandered the Caribbean for several days, while the AJDC looked for a destination. Finally the passengers were allowed to land in Venezuela. During 1939, the Gestapo organised numerous other steamship voyages containing Jews with dubious or non-existent travel documents to land refugees wherever the authorities might permit.[14] The *St Louis* was the most famous of these voyages, but it was by no means the only example.[15]

German Jewish organisations consistently warned the Nazi regime that this dumping strategy could be counterproductive, and from the beginning of January 1939, several outside organisations attempted to curb this brutal policy.[16] The main British and American aid organisations – the Council for German Jewry and the AJDC – threatened to remove their subsidies from all 'Jewish' emigration from Greater Germany if such damaging experiments continued.[17] Dumping refugees also created substantial risks for the steamship companies. If on arrival the refugees' travel documents were deemed insufficient or invalid and they were refused permission to land, the shipping companies were obliged to return them to their point of departure. As a result, many reputable Western European carriers became reluctant to transport Jewish refugees overseas and most of the journeys were made in chartered Italian or Greek ships.[18] The charter companies insured their risk by demanding that the refugees buy return tickets and also that they paid part of the fare in (hard) foreign currency.[19] The British government became determined to halt uncontrolled illegal immigration to Palestine and applied diplomatic pressure on the European states from which illegal vessels had departed. The states under whose flags of convenience the illegal ships operated also found themselves targeted by the British and by May 1939 British surveillance and diplomatic intervention had made it impossible to use Mediterranean ports as a means of reaching Palestine illegally.[20] The German authorities quickly took the necessary steps to assure that emigration overseas could continue, primarily by employing German shipping companies to carry out the task.[21] To expedite further illegal journeys to Palestine, the German authorities supported Zionist organised voyages that began in Vienna or Bratislava and used the Danube as a route to the Black Sea.[22]

According to the Jewish organisations, about 50,000 people left Greater Germany between 1 January 1939 and the outbreak of the Second World War in September. Palestine and Asia (overwhelmingly Shanghai) each took at least 10 per cent of these emigrants, but most who left for an overseas destination – nearly a third of the total – headed for the Americas. For the first time since 1933, the United States took nearly as many as the South American states. However for the first time since 1933, the majority of refugees from Greater Germany in 1939 remained in Europe. By 1939 legal emigration and resettlement overseas had been closed to the vast majority of 'Jews' still in the Greater German Reich.

For many, the countries bordering Germany represented the only possibility of escape.[23] While the German authorities turned a blind eye to illegal crossings into Eastern Europe, they carefully policed the frontiers with Western Europe after November 1938. Thus Jewish refugees wanting to flee to most countries of Western Europe had not only to outwit the border police of the country they were trying to enter, but also those of Germany. From early November 1938, the German authorities had issued orders to arrest all Jews found near the border without the necessary passport and a visa to enter Belgium, France or Switzerland and transfer the adult male Jews among them to concentration camps. By January 1939 this highly repressive policy was widened to include the whole Western border of Germany. The German border police stations at the German–Dutch border (*Grenzpolizeikommissariate*) were instructed to stop all German (and Austrian) Jews from entering Dutch territory. The slow communication of these instructions from Berlin indicates that the Dutch insistence upon cooperation to control the border had not been considered a priority. However, no such policy was even attempted at the Danish frontier, presumably because the Danish authorities saw no great problems at their frontier and had not pressed the German authorities to take any action.[24]

Although the pressures on 'Jews' to leave the Reich remained extremely brutal, it is clear that in general the German authorities no longer wanted to force 'Jews' into neighbouring Western countries. However, local examples of 'dumping' continued to take place. Thus for example, the Gestapo sent a group of 'Jewish' children on a train across the Dutch border to Nijmegen and then just abandoned them, thus more or less daring the Dutch authorities to send them back. A SOPADE[25] report noted in January 1939 that the 'Jews' of a town near the French frontier were herded into the square and then forced across the nearby border, only to return when the French authorities refused to admit them.[26]

Dumping of 'Jews' was, however, largely shifted away from the countries west of Germany and there was a good deal of cross-border co-operation. This cooperation was largely the result of continuing diplomatic pressure on the German authorities and the wish to maintain normal travel arrangements between states. The instructions to the German border police were easier to implement at the Belgian, Swiss and French border as the authorities only had to arrest and transfer all male 'Jews' without the necessary passport and visa to a concentration camp. However, throughout 1939, German policies at the Dutch frontier remained more lenient. This was primarily because entry to the Netherlands did not formally depend on having a visa – and therefore only 'Jews' whose entry to the Netherlands could *only* be made illegally were to be incarcerated.[27] The local German border police was hesitant about sending 'Jews' with valid passports to a concentration camp, and in March 1939 the Gestapostelle Düsseldorf decided that 'Jews' caught near the Dutch border who had a valid passport were not to be imprisoned, as there was no evidence that they intended to cross the border illegally. They were merely to be sent back to their place of origin, usually Vienna, and the authorities there were instructed only to (re-) issue passports if the individual had been given permission to enter another country.[28]

Changes in Western European Refugee Aid

The violence of *Kristallnacht* sent shock waves across Europe and provoked a sense of outrage in both the press and in public opinion. The urgency of providing aid became clear to many and the recognition that the pogrom had created new categories of victims meant that it became a matter that attracted interest beyond the left-wing organisations and the Jewish community. This broadening of interest can be seen in the creation of refugee aid committees for Jewish converts to Christianity, and in the non-sectarian appeals for refugee aid that followed the events of November 1938.

A number of new refugee committees were established across Europe to help the converts. There had been refugee aid groups that had given assistance to the small number of politically active Christian refugees since 1935, but it was only after *Kristallnacht* that the major Christian churches began to realise that they had converts among those persecuted as Jews in Germany. Christian aid organisations started to cater for these 'non-Aryan' Christians, as pressure on Jewish relief organisations increased. Until 1938, Jewish refugee organisations had helped all those categorised as Jews by the Nazis, without regard for their religion. Thus professing and non-professing 'Jews' were supported, as well as Christian converts. This inclusivity came to an end in 1939, when Jewish charitable resources were stretched beyond all limits and the organisations became increasingly selective. 'Jews' who could be helped by either Christian or left-wing organisations were directed elsewhere.[29] Nevertheless, the plight of these 'non-Aryan' Christians undoubtedly broadened the general public support for the refugees from Nazi Germany.

This wider support was particularly evident in Britain and the Netherlands. In Britain, Stanley Baldwin, the former Conservative Prime Minister, launched a national appeal. He called upon the British as Christians to support the non-Aryan refugees, be they Christians or Jews. His broadcast appeal was extremely successful and raised over £250,000 by the end of December. There was also a national appeal in the Netherlands, launched by a broadcast by Prime Minister Hendricus Colijn, and supported by many mayors that raised 473,000 guilders.[30] In other countries the general public was much less supportive and leading personalities were much less inclined to put their weight behind such a campaign. For example in Belgium, the Prime Minister Paul-Henri Spaak and the Belgian Red Cross refused to lead the campaign. In the same vein, the Belgian Roman Catholic church refused to canvass support from their parishioners for financial support for refugees, even if they were Christians.[31] Any widening social support for the refugees did not imply that the authorities were prepared to help finance refugee aid. Refugee aid remained a private, not a public affair. Only the Swiss and Danish authorities had given some token support to refugee aid and their subsidies were divided equally among the existing respectable refugee committees, but when the expenditure of the Jewish refugee aid committees increased, the public subsidy was even more of a drop in the ocean.[32]

Refugee and Immigration Policy in Continental Europe

Initial reactions to *Kristallnacht* in most liberal states were in tune with public opinion as restrictive policies were attenuated or promises were made that this would happen. In practice, however, governments remained cautious, realising that the apparently random fatalities gave any 'Jew' coming from Germany a prima facie claim to refugee status as being in mortal danger. Acknowledgement of this new facet of the persecution in Germany undermined the legitimacy of existing restrictive policies. However an open border policy could cause a mass immigration of destitute refugees: thus a selective immigration policy had to be pursued which safeguarded the possibility of expelling unwanted or uninvited 'Jews' from Germany.

Subcontracting and Strengthening External Control

All state authorities continued to believe that the flight of refugees from Nazi Germany had to be contained. The easiest way to do this was at the border and in their consulates abroad, without any public accountability for the decisions taken. Given the increased sympathy for those fleeing Nazi Germany from some sections of the public, the external controls became ever more important. The 'J'-stamp on German passports became the pivot of the external control of the liberal states of Continental Europe as it provided an instant distinction between 'genuine' visitors from Germany and those whose true purpose was to stay.

In order to ensure that refugees did not reach their territory, Western European states relied on several new forms of remote control beyond just a visa requirement. As mentioned before, states carrying out persecution were given inducements to stop unauthorised emigration, and this became a key part of the remote control policy as immigration control became largely dependent on German cooperation.[33] Other countries were also called upon to combat uninvited immigration from Nazi Germany. Every country considered itself a victim of 'lax' neighbours whose borders were too porous. In spite of ever more restrictive immigration policies, large numbers of refugees were still arriving and some states were castigated because they let refugees enter who just passed through their territory en route elsewhere.[34] The liberal European states thus continued to pressure each other to impose ever-tighter immigration restrictions; a trend that built up a momentum of it own that went beyond domestic considerations. Non-governmental agencies were also enlisted to stop the inflow of refugees. In some countries, transport companies were forced by the threat of sanctions to scrutinise their passengers' passports and visas for their validity, and refugee aid committees were pressured into advising would-be refugees not to leave Germany independently.[35]

Visa-issuing policies became increasingly restrictive. Consulates were in the front line and had to sift the wanted from the unwanted. Consular personnel were instructed to be particularly vigilant when dealing with both German and Eastern European Jewish applicants. Such people found it increasingly difficult to obtain a visa for a Western European country, even for a short stay, let alone for permanent settlement.[36] The fact that Luxemburg, the Netherlands and Denmark did not require visas for Germans had no meaning for German 'Jews' as, from 1938 onwards, while 'Aryan' Germans could still travel to these countries without a visa, they had to meet a semi-official obligation to have such a document in their passports.

Immediately after the Munich crisis in September 1938, although there were no official policy changes, a number of states became proactive in selecting 'deserving' refugees from those who had to leave the Sudetenland and promising visas. France initially undertook to provide 310, then 700, but in the end only about 100 visas were actually issued. Belgium granted 253 visas and Denmark 163.[37] The selection criteria used in these cases made the states' primary definition of who was a refugee deserving protection transparent.[38] In line with the hierarchy of persecution prevalent at that time, only political activists were granted visas. Being persecuted as 'Jew' did not, in itself, qualify anybody for protection within this scheme. Communist refugees were also excluded from the Belgian and Danish gestures towards the victims of Munich. However Belgium did agree to allow known German communists who had resided legally in Belgium before their departure to enlist in the International Brigades in Spain to return. Likewise Great Britain granted visas to communist political refugees, including former combatants of the International Brigades, but Denmark and Switzerland refused to do this.[39] Although there was little discussion, this positive discrimination towards political refugees was not perceived as unjust by the authorities. The fact that there were ostensibly so many organisations dedicated to the 'Jewish' refugees gave credence to the non-Jewish refugee organisations' claims that 'it was time to do something for the non-Jewish refugee'.[40]

The victims of racial persecution were not entirely neglected and some were actively afforded protection, but it was always kept in mind that they should not pose any problems for the receiving country, either qualitatively or quantitatively. As mentioned before, refugees with close personal ties to a country or those with economic assets were still eligible for a visa. Refugees who had definite emigration plans and all the necessary papers were sometimes given temporary residence. Such people had to guarantee that they would emigrate overseas within a few days or at most a few months.[41] Immediately after *Kristallnacht* only Swiss policy remained strictly on the course set before November 1938, other countries showed greater generosity and in particular more transit-refugees were allowed to wait in safety for the final issue of an immigration visa and the departure of their ship or flight. The Dutch even put forward a plan whereby Western Europe would act as a holding point for 'Jews' re-emigrating overseas, with all the costs borne by Jewish charities. The Dutch government was prepared to allow the legal admission of up to 2,000 'Jewish' refugees, a figure increased to 7,000 by public pressure. Selection remained in government hands with the Jewish refugee aid committee being allowed to recommend only 1,800 permits.[42] When the other European countries appeared lukewarm to the Dutch proposal it was quickly dropped.[43] This greater generosity towards transit-refugees soon disappeared when it became apparent that it was extremely difficult to get watertight guarantees that such refugees would receive all the necessary papers and be prepared to move on. In Switzerland the entry of transit refugees was soon further restricted. In December 1938 all three Scandinavian states curtailed their facilities for transit refugees and the Netherlands followed suit at the turn of the year.[44] These changes were sometimes justified on the spurious grounds that the treatment of Jews had improved and that immigration controls could now be 'normalised'.[45]

In total contradiction to this claim that the Jews were exposed to fewer dangers inside Germany, several countries decided during November 1938 to make unaccompanied Jewish children eligible for admission. The schemes to bring children to Western Europe epitomised the hopeless situation for 'Jews' in Greater Germany. Terrorised parents realised that their children's only hope of survival was in the hands of strangers. Jewish refugee organisations convinced various Western European governments to give their agreement to this rescue operation by referring to the precedent of the protection afforded to children during the Spanish Civil War. Ultimately, Switzerland and France took in a few hundred children each and Belgium and Denmark provided asylum to a thousand apiece while the Dutch record was more generous as the Netherlands accepted two thousand children.[46] The very limited initiatives by Continental European states for actively rescuing Jews from Greater Germany – initiatives which in any case did not last very long – are partly reflected in the figures indicating the Jewish refugees' official destination when they applied for a passports in Vienna and Prague.

Table II.3.1: Official Destination of 'Jewish' Refugees when Applying for Passports in Vienna and Prague 1938–1939

n=102.897 (with Bohemia and Moravia included n=111.666)[47]

	Austria 2 May 1938– 31 July 1939	Incl. Bohemia and Moravia 15 Mar–27 July 1939	Percentage of total applications granted
Great Britain	22,680	28,449	25
France	3,041	3,382	3
Switzerland*	3,021		3
Belgium*	1,680		1.6
Netherlands*	1,502		1.5
Denmark*	464		0.5
Luxemburg*	96		0.1

* Figures from Vienna only

Border controls that had already been strengthened during the course of 1938 became even more stringent. In November 1938 detention stations were set up on the French frontier to deal with illegal immigrants. At the French border, among the uninvited immigrants, only 'refugees' were to be admitted. An alternative for male refugees denied protection at the border was to volunteer for the French Foreign Legion, but due the high physical standards required to qualify as volunteer only a few hundred ('Jewish') refugees who put themselves forward were allowed entry into France.[48] In April 1939, controls were strengthened at the Italian-French border. Twelve *pelotons* of the Garde Mobile were deployed along the coastline. They were even active on the Mediterranean Sea and used fast boats, equipped with heavy lights to intercept vessels at night.[49] In the Netherlands, 1,000 border guards were made available to defend the 888 km frontier. Those in charge claimed that it would actually need 18–20,000 men to patrol it properly, but the civil servants, ever anxious to try and restrict expenditure, leapt at the idea of a more flexible employment of border personnel. From January 1939, men could be removed from areas where illegal entry was uncommon and redeployed as 'flying detachments' that could be moved to more critical areas.[50]

Inevitably, large numbers of refugees were turned away at the borders.[51] In countries with a visa requirement, whether for all Germans or only for German Jews, policy dictated that all those without the proper documentation should be refused entry. In Luxemburg, the Netherlands and Denmark, where there was no formal visa requirement, the 'J'-stamped passport served as a filter. This became the main criteria by which would-be immigrants were screened. However, even people carrying regular German passports were not always granted admission. Dutch instructions to the border guards on 17 October 1938 stipulated that German Jews without a 'J'-stamp on their passport had to be refused admission, as their documents were not valid. In February 1939, high-ranking officers expressed regret that it was difficult to stop Catholic spouses of 'Jewish' refugees at the border, as they legitimately had no red 'J' in their passports. As border guards could still not always distinguish easily between potential refugees and others, they had to stop or delay many other travellers.[52] In Denmark it appears that the border guards continued to identify unwanted entrants in an impressionistic way and questioned those whose presumed semitic facial features or strange travel patterns made them suspect as people wanting to settle in Denmark.[53]

In 1939, border controls in Western Europe were intensified to keep out unwanted refugees. In December 1938, French border guards had been specifically instructed to refuse entry to German Jewish children and in January 1939 the Belgian authorities followed suit. The Dutch, Danish and Swiss authorities were ready to do the same, but there were no formal instructions.[54] Transit refugees who had a steamship ticket and an entrance visa for a country overseas were usually allowed to enter the countries bordering Germany to embark at a Dutch, Belgian or French port, but supporting their ports and shipping lines did not imply that the authorities acknowledged the refugees' plight. From April 1939 onwards, France insisted that transit refugees were transported from the border to the ports under police surveillance.[55]

Attitudes at the border oscillated between outright refusal of entry for all Germans with a 'J'-passport and a more differentiated policy that examined the merits of individual cases. Luxembourg and Switzerland were the first countries to institute a blanket policy. From the middle of August 1938 onwards, the Swiss and Luxemburg authorities had adopted restrictive measures at the border and these were extended in Switzerland on 7 September and in Luxemburg shortly after *Kristallnacht*, on 25 November 1938, so that both borders was closed altogether for 'Jewish' refugees.[56] Denmark took a very similar position, but the Netherlands initially retained a case-by-case approach that did not automatically exclude 'Jews'. Until *Kristallnacht*, the Netherlands had admitted German refugees with papers and means to assure their upkeep, and even those without papers had been admitted if they could prove they were in imminent mortal danger. In the aftermath of *Kristallnacht*, even this criterion was amended. A circular from the Ministry of Justice made it clear that only those German refugees (with or without papers) who lived close to the Dutch border and could prove imminent mortal danger were henceforward to be admitted. Moreover, as with previous instructions, the terms of the directive were not to be made public lest they provoked a wave of new immigration from 'qualified' people. The only others with some chance of admission were those with family already in the Netherlands, people recommended by one of the relief agencies, and children. A month later, the Dutch government radically altered its border policy and decided that the sheer numbers being admitted could no longer be sustained. On 17 December 1938 the Minister of Justice gave orders for the border to be closed except for those Jews whom the Dutch authorities had already given permission to enter.[57] This implied that henceforward only those with existing permits would be admitted and that all others would be refused at the border. This regulation effectively introduced a visa-like system for Jewish refugees from Germany and to some extent informally duplicated Swiss practice. Now even Jewish refugees with sufficient means of support were no longer admitted. Only those who could demonstrate mortal danger (and until March 1939, unaccompanied women and children) were to be exempted. In fact this meant that only political refugees were to be admitted. Soon thereafter the Dutch authorities re-examined the effectiveness of their expulsion policy in the border region. By January 1939 the Minister of Justice Goseling decided that the practice of merely returning the refugees arrested in the border region was to no avail. These expellees just came back and thus an formal extradition mechanism along the lines of the Dutch–German agreement of 1906 would be more efficient.[58]

The tightening of remote and border control had the effect of increasing the number of refugees using smugglers.[59] The huge profits to be made in the clandestine transport of people as well as goods across frontiers meant that by 1939 smuggling had become increasingly modernised and almost professionalised. For example, bigger and faster motorboats replaced the traditional fishing boats of Ventimiglia and San Remo that had been used for smuggling 'Jews' from Italy into France in 1938. Action was taken against these human smugglers. Known smugglers were often prohibited from entering border regions and their travel documents were confiscated. Even repressive means were used: helping illegal aliens was criminalised in several countries and the judiciary used newly acquired powers to imprison smugglers or to confiscate their boats or cars.[60] The Belgian authorities relied mainly on the cooperation of the German authorities to stop the traffic. Known Belgian smugglers were, at the request of the Belgian authorities, refused entry to Germany, but more cooperation was sought. Drawing on the German–Belgian agreement of 22 October 1938, the Belgian authorities insisted that German authorities take steps to punish human smugglers.[61] The Germans complied and from March 1939 onwards, those caught with 'Jewish' would-be emigrants in the border regions of Western Germany were sent to concentration camps.[62] These higher risks for smugglers drove prices up even more and thus made this criminal trade even more lucrative for those prepared to take the risks.

Whatever state responses were to the threat of illegal immigration, borders remained permeable and many people were still able to slip through. The refugees from Nazi Germany were highly motivated and ready to make almost any sacrifice in order to cross frontiers. Human traffickers, in their turn motivated by the high profits involved, often anticipated changes made by the authorities. For example in the spring of 1939, with heightened control of the sea route across the Italian–French border, illegal immigration from Italy shifted to the mountain passes that were more difficult to monitor.[63] Each month several thousand refugees still succeeded in crossing the German borders illegally to look for asylum in the liberal countries bordering Nazi Germany (see Figures 4 and 5 p.326).

Internal Control

During the course of 1938, the combination of remote and border controls had been supplemented with an increased level of internal control on refugees who had arrived in West Europe. The very restrictive immigration policies across Europe inadvertently brought about a shift in the nature of immigration. Refugees continued to arrive as the pressures on 'Jews' in Germany to leave remained unabated, but the immigration of refugees became framed in terms of illegality and criminality. Smugglers were the conduits for refugees to cross frontiers, but once in a country of refuge, other supports were available to help people hide from the authorities. In effect, the inflow of refugees had been partly driven underground and states now assumed that there were large numbers of refugees living illegally in the country and escaping any control. The authorities' imperfect knowledge of their alien population meant that they were unable to assess the dangers to which society was exposed. These unknown aliens and the supposed abuse of the hospitality given to the legalised refugees became another obsession. Internal controls were intensified in order to control all immigrants and in particular to track down all undocumented refugees.[64] It became even more difficult for refugees to enter the territory of West European countries uninvited, although the exception was the continued granting of asylum to political refugees, including communists. France remained the country of asylum par excellence for these political refugees. This is illustrated by the dispersal of a sample of communist refugees within Europe as shown by Table II.3.2.

The predominance of France as country of asylum for German communists was mainly due to their flight from Spain after the civil war. The remnants of the International Brigades, some of whom had previously been refugees in other countries neighbouring Germany, found their only escape route across the Pyrenees with the hundreds of thousands of Spaniards fleeing in the same direction. Most were interned in camps but a few communist activists were allowed to leave the French camps and settle elsewhere, for example in Belgium and Great Britain where they had been offered hospitality. At the same time, the USSR became less important as a country of asylum, mainly due to its isolated political position and the murder of German communists during the Stalinist purges.[66]

Table II.3.2: Country of Asylum of a Sample of 333 German Communists, 1938–1939.[65]

	1938	1939		1938	1939
France	95	107	Denmark	18	19
Great Britain	14	28	Switzerland	13	12
USSR	39	31	Netherlands	11	17
Spain	47	20	Belgium	7	7

'Jewish' refugees who had succeeded in entering the territory of the liberal states, either legally or illegally, remained the main targets of restrictive measures. In Belgium, the publicity given to the deportation of illegal entrants in early October 1938 had led to widespread public discussion but the debate was radically altered by the wave of solidarity shown to the victims of the *Kristallnacht*. Reluctantly, but provoked by the hard-line attitudes of Minister of Justice Pholien, more and more politicians publicly advocated a more humanitarian immigration policy. On 22 November 1938, under enormous parliamentary pressure, Pholien finally made public the fact that the forced repatriation of Jewish refugees had been suspended. German Jews were again given temporary protection in order to prepare their re-emigration, but as they were prohibited from any economic activity, they usually had to be supported by Jewish refugee welfare organisations.[67]

Dutch policy changed as radically. From May 1938 onwards, those who entered the country illegally were supposed to be deported, but this stopped on 19 November.[68] During November and December 1938, 1,500 illegal entrants were granted temporary protection. Initially they had to report daily to the police, but were subsequently placed under close administrative supervision in camps at Veenhuizen and Hoek van Holland. Transfer to the camps was often delayed, as there were insufficient places for the numbers involved.[69] At the same time, prospects for re-emigration were shrinking as refugees found it increasingly difficult to gain admission overseas and on 17 December 1938 the Dutch Minister of Justice closed the border, which implied that refugees who had entered the country illegally would be escorted back to Germany. Indeed, Dutch practice and the terms of the Dutch–German agreement of 1906 dictated that illegal aliens were subject not just to expulsion, but also to repatriation. This began immediately after Christmas when 70 refugees were sent back in a bus from Amsterdam to Germany. This repatriation policy for ('Jewish') refugees meant that in Dutch eyes, charges of smuggling, tax evasion or *Rassenschande* (race defilement), threatened sterilisation or even internment in a concentration camp might not be considered prima facie grounds for protection.[70]

By the end of 1938, every Continental European country had its own pool of 'undesirable' refugees. There was no question of their being collectively dumped across another frontier for fear of creating diplomatic difficulties or tit-for-tat retaliation. Dumping refugees into neighbouring countries became increasingly difficult. Legal re-migration was possible, but proceeded at a slow pace. Figures for HICEM-sponsored travel from Western Europe gives a good indication of the nature of re-emigration (Figures 2 and 3). In the first seven months of 1939, 4,000 refugees re-emigrated under the auspices of HICEM, mainly to the U.S., but others left independently or used private agencies. Another possible avenue was to make use of the various Zionist organisations that were involved in schemes for illegal emigration to Palestine. Much to the disgust of the British, these were often tolerated by Western European states anxious to encourage refugees to leave. London even accused its continental neighbours of conniving with the Zionists in order to get rid of as many refugees as possible.[71] In practice, there seems to have been no active cooperation, but turning a blind eye to Zionist smuggling activities seems to have been common.

Three types of solution can be identified as having been tried by the states of Western Europe in 1939. Belgium was unique in continuing to provide temporary protection to all refugees entering its territory. The Danish, Luxemburg and Swiss responses were the exact opposite. 'Jewish' refugees were considered as illegal aliens and forced repatriation was used as a remedy. In between these two extremes, the Dutch and French response to refugees was more ambivalent, with some afforded temporary protection, either freely or interned in prisons and camps, while others were deported.

Belgian Retention of a Humanitarian Immigration Policy

After Minister of Justice Joseph Pholien had announced in Parliament that deportation of Jewish refugees had been suspended, about two thousand 'Jewish' refugees arrived illegally in Belgium every month (Figure 4, p.326). Upon registration they were granted a temporary residence permit as refugees in transit. No German 'Jews' were recorded as being repatriated between November 1938 and August 1939. The scope of persecution qualifying for protection was also extended: denationalised Polish Jews were also considered refugees worthy of temporary protection.[72] The head of the Belgian Sûreté, Robert de Foy, insisted that the Ministers in charge of immigration policy stop the flood and expel all the illegal entrants but regular cabinet reshuffles and the fear that intervening in this delicate and polarised matter would make one a second Pholien, provided a recipe for inertia. The expulsion of 'Jewish' refugees became a taboo for a long time to come and three successive Catholic Ministers of Justice between

November 1938 and March 1939 refused to take any initiatives on the matter.

The eligibility procedure used by the advisory refugee commission continued to distinguish between the 'voluntary' flight of the Jews from the 'forced' flight of political opponents. Although by 1938 both groups were subject to the same kind of brutal treatment that endangered their freedom and their lives, the criteria remained unaltered. In view of this unjustified discrimination it was suggested in early 1939 that Belgium should withdraw from the international refugee regime, but as the convention of 1938 left substantial discretion to the national authorities it was considered unnecessary to do so.[73] The artificial distinction between the 'Jewish' and political refugees could be justified by the authorities' claim that 'Jewish' refugees had no need for protection as they had no intention of settling in Belgium. Moreover, the refugee commission, a state institution that had the task of guaranteeing that Belgian alien policy met minimum humanitarian standards, did not oppose the political decision to exclude 'Jewish' refugees from the eligibility procedure and thus undermined its own prerogatives. The possibility for immigrants to apply for asylum, even if they had arrived illegally, was a principle fully entrenched in Belgian legislation since 1936, but 'Jewish' refugees were collectively excluded from the privileged category of immigrants whom the Belgian authorities could not, on principle, expel. In this way, the Belgian state retained the right to expel 'Jews' fleeing Nazi Germany. This 'statutory inferiority' conferred on the 'Jewish' refugees, an expression of the power of definition this independent asylum agency held, also served to undermine the validity of their reasons for leaving Nazi Germany. By denying 'Jews' refugee status, the Belgian authorities had a big stick at their disposal to coerce German Jewish transit refugees into organising their re-emigration, although no 'Jewish' refugees were actually expelled from Belgian territory. The fact that the refugee commission did not adjust its criteria to reflect the changing circumstances in Nazi Germany meant that couples in 'racially-mixed' marriages remained the only victims of Nazi racial policy eligible for protection. These *Rassenschande* applicants were the only 'Jewish' refugees whose asylum applications were still processed.

As more and more countries overseas closed their borders, 'transit' became largely a fiction. Belgian refugee aid committees made a great show of those 'Jews' who did depart overseas as it proved to public opinion that their refugees had not come to stay indefinitely. In the spring of 1939, when re-emigration had all but come to a halt, the main Jewish refugee organisation was so desperate to prove that 'Jewish' refugees who were temporarily protected in Belgium were still leaving that it tried to set up a cosmetic operation with Great Britain by pretending that German 'Jews' who had been selected in Germany for protection in Britain had actually been transit refugees in Belgium. Even the issue of camps for refugees made no headway. A refugee camp had been erected in Merksplas accommodating around 500 refugees. This first camp had been created to enable the refugee committees to save money and to enhance the chances of refugees finding a country of final settlement through the provision of occupational training. Segregating refugees in camps gave the refugees the clear message that they had not come to stay and most importantly it diminished their visibility. After October 1938 there were no further initiatives as the authorities considered that financing the restructuring of government property to create refugee camps went beyond the limits of a 'reasonable' refugee policy. The welfare of refugees had to remain the task of private charities.

The contradictions in these various policy strands meant that refugee policy became deadlocked. The Jewish relief committees had given the government assurances that no refugees would become public charges but the influx had continued unabated and the sheer weight of numbers had overwhelmed their financial resources. In April 1939, a new cabinet agreed to share the costs for the upkeep of Jewish refugees. In spite of intensifying xenophobia, there was a consensus among all the traditional political parties that repatriating Jewish refugees was impossible, even if this meant that their upkeep had to be partly subsidised by the Belgian treasury. The authorities were thus 'forced' into co-financing refugee relief and as this was more efficiently done in camps, the authorities quickly opened a second camp with 500 places and the Merksplas camp was enlarged to accommodate 700 people.[74]

Deporting Refugees: Jews Perceived as Illegal Immigrants

In Denmark and Switzerland the deportation of Jewish refugees continued unabated throughout 1939.[75] Between 1 March and 1 September 1939, 26 of the 70 Jewish refugees who had arrived illegally and 30 of around 700 who had entered Denmark legally were repatriated to Germany. These repatriations, which were sometimes contested by the refugee committees, were mostly due to misdemeanours committed by the individual or their failure to find a country willing to offer them permanent asylum. There was no attempt to disguise the nature of these expulsions, and by 1939 Minister of Justice Karl Steincke was justifying them by denying that those involved were refugees and by condemning the offences they had committed. The Danish-Jewish relief committee took a very pragmatic attitude to this restrictive policy. Henceforward the committee only protected those 'Jewish' refugees who could soon emigrate overseas and therefore only needed short-term support. As a rule, this protection usually exempted the individual from deportation, but this was not always the case. Some people were being repatriated before they could contact the Jewish relief committee and sometimes even the committee's support could not prevent the Danish authorities from deporting refugees.[76]

In Switzerland, 'Jews' continued to enter the country illegally although the border had been closed for 'Jewish' refugees from 9 September 1938.

As Regula Ludi writes, local officials could sometimes circumvent the intentions of federal policy. The case of the police chief of St Gallen, Paul Grüninger, is the most well-known example. He took a number of steps to prevent people being sent back, including antedating documents, thereby allowing, according to Stefan Keller, 3,601 'Jews' to enter Switzerland. The cantons Basel-Stadt and Schaffhausen, where social democrats had a substantial influence on policy, are other cases in point. Much to the annoyance of federal officials, these cantonal authorities largely stuck to the principle that once a 'Jewish' refugee had outwitted the federal and cantonal border guards and succeeded in entering the city of Basel or Schaffhausen they could be permitted to remain temporarily.[77] Nonetheless, the stringent Swiss border controls (assisted by the Germans) kept most 'Jewish' refugees away from Switzerland. By 1939 the few who did succeed in entering Swiss territory illegally were nearly all deported. The few cantonal authorities that advocated a more humane treatment of these refugees were placed under enormous pressure to toe the line by the federal authorities, but this was ultimately achieved by an increased centralisation of more and more issues related to asylum policy.[78]

Deportation also remained an instrument of migration control in France and the Netherlands. In the latter country, the only information on how this was administered comes from the police in Amsterdam, who seem to have taken a strict line. Many 'Jewish' refugees were forcibly repatriated and from 27 March 1939 even single women and children were no longer exempted from this process.[79] The Amsterdam figures indicate that although unauthorised immigration did not stop altogether, the number of recorded arrivals was drastically reduced.[80] The Dutch-Jewish welfare organisations' statistics on new arrivals in 1939 demonstrate that not all of them were forcibly removed from the Netherlands, although in contrast to Belgium, the authorities did not explicitly tolerate them. The basic criterion for being tolerated was that the refugee had to be in (imminent) mortal danger. Extreme left-wing political refugees who had entered illegally were exempted from deportation but those persecuted in Germany for crimes such as currency smuggling and *Rassenschande* were not granted asylum, as the Dutch did not interpret confinement in a concentration camp as constituting mortal danger. Dutch local authorities nevertheless continued to have considerable discretion in their actions. They were the ones to investigate the danger to which a deportee would be exposed. Only in cases of refugees fleeing charges of currency smuggling did deportation have to be the rule. The dangers to an illegal immigrant as a result of charges of *Rassenschande* and the dangers of a stay in a concentration camp were thus often investigated on a case-by-case basis.[81]

It seems that in line with tradition, the French authorities seldom resorted to deportation but policy did become far more heterogeneous.[82] The decree of May 1938 had given the prefects power to expel aliens who had entered illegally or overstayed the validity of their visas whereas previously this had required ministerial approval. According to a British

Passport control officer in Paris, the treatment of refugees in France lacked uniformity as there seemed to be little or no co-ordination among the provincial prefects who were entrusted with this work and who seemed to put all sorts of different interpretations on the regulations, resulting sometimes in unwarranted severity and at other times in the granting of unintentionally generous facilities.[83]

Deterring Refugees: French Prisons and Dutch Camps

The French authorities largely refrained from deporting refugees, but Vicki Caron points out that the French authorities believed that prison would deter illegal immigration and even the *Kristallnacht* did not alter this policy. Refugees arriving illegally were still treated on a par with criminals. According to estimates from the Jewish refugee committee, about 9,000 refugees had been sentenced to terms of imprisonment between May 1938 and July 1939, including about 3,000 Germans.[84] However, the implementation of this policy was not without its problems. Equating illegal immigrants with criminals had considerable disadvantages. Holding them in a high security facility was expensive and applying criminal procedures to refugees was ineffective. As Vicki Caron illustrates, invoking the law could be an impediment to a repressive policy as the courts showed considerable leniency in applying such laws.

Prisons remained the 'French home' for refugees, but elsewhere in continental Europe, refugee camps were increasingly created to house new arrivals. Jewish refugee committees in Switzerland and Belgium, in close cooperation with the authorities, had, during the moments of intense crisis in migration management, established a few camps to accommodate refugees in a more cost-effective way. In general authorities were reluctant to follow this example as the refugee camps were presumed to send a message that refugees were welcome to stay. However when the xenophobic mood among the French political elite waned, several refugee camps were set up in the course of 1939 where vocational training was provided, financed by the Jewish refugee committees.[85]

However, another kind of refugee camp was piloted in France and pursued with more vigour in the Netherlands. A French decree in May 1938 had deemed that prison was inappropriate for aliens who could not be deported, and such people had instead to be given an assigned residence under police supervision. As the ruling elite of that time had embarked on a conservative backlash against the Popular Front, the containment of subversive aliens was given a high priority. Also appeasement was still considered the best defence of French interests and the mere presence of the refugees, let alone their political activities, were considered an annoying impediment to French–German reconciliation.[86] The extensive use of close supervision of refugees rapidly got out of control as the Minister of Justice had to reprimand the prefects in November 1938 for their excessive zeal in using this means to supervise all kinds of refugees.

As too many refugees were put under police supervision, local gendarmes were overwhelmed by increase in work.[87] An emergency decree of 12 November 1938 enabled the executive to arbitrarily detain foreigners who constituted a 'security risk' in camps. As the executive received full power to deal with foreigners as it saw fit, it allowed the rule of law to be bypassed.[88]

When, in January 1939, 400,000 Republican refugees fled into France, the French authorities had to improvise emergency aid. All Spanish refugees were interned in makeshift camps and pressured to return to Spain. These camps were a solution to a very exceptional situation, but the experiment seems to have been considered successful.[89] In February 1939 a much more calculated decision was taken to erect a camp in Rieucros (Lozère) for undesirable refugees who could not be deported, with a capacity for 500 inmates. Forty foreigners were immediately interned there for an indeterminate period. German and Austrian refugees together with some Spaniards, Italians and Russians, most of whom had long criminal records, were thus rendered totally subject to the power of the administration. Although this camp remained an exception at that time, it would become *the* French tool for migration management from September 1939 onwards.[90]

In the Netherlands, the internment of refugees was already in full swing by 1939. The practice of interning so-called dangerous foreigners had been initiated in 1935 using powers obtained by the Dutch authorities in 1918. It was continued in the following years and refugees were invariably interned if it was felt that they were a danger to public order. At the end of 1938, the scale of internment grew dramatically (see Table II.3.3). From December onwards, all male refugees arriving in the Netherlands illegally or legally, were accommodated in camps scattered across the Dutch countryside. When they arrived, legal immigrants had to agree to be housed in camps financed by the Jewish refugee aid committee. Special camps for illegally immigrated refugees were established under the aegis of the Ministry of Justice with a far stricter regime. Only men were interned, so families were separated. Inmates of these camps were not allowed to go out, or to receive visits.[91]

These penal colonies attracted criticism even within government circles as it was argued that the 1918 law provided for full powers to confine dangerous aliens, but these refugees were harmless and were only distinguishable from refugees who had entered legally by their means of entry into the country. Their internment was considered an excessive interpretation of the powers given to the executive, but the Minister of Justice insisted that because there could be undesirable elements among the refugees that internment was necessary.[93] The existing small camps were difficult to supervise and expensive, and it was decided, mainly on economic grounds, that a central camp – Westerbork – was a better option. Also the costs of the camps for illegal refugees were borne by the guarantee fund established by the refugee committees, in spite of the fact that the committees had no control over the arrival of inmates.[94]

Table II.3.3: Number of Refugees Interned in Dutch Camps for Legal and Illegal Entrants, December 1938 – August 1939.[92]

	Inmates in camps for illegal (Jewish) refugees	Inmates in camps for legal refugees
Up to 31 December 1938	717	348
January 1939	(571)	
February	651 (638)	807
March	675 (658)	898
April	686 (665)	754
May	666 (640)	743
June	665 (645)	886
July	(672)	790
August 1939	(547)	731

Great Britain, a Proactive Refugee Policy

After the Munich agreements, the British authorities gradually developed a more proactive refugee policy. As Arich Sherman wrote, 'the moral ambiguities of the British position at Munich made the pressures on the Government to intervene more actively on behalf of these refugees well-nigh irresistible'.[95] At first, Britain had considered protective measures within the borders of the truncated Czechoslovak state but the negative attitude of the Czech authorities towards ethnic minorities pushed emigration to the fore as an alternative solution. In November 1938, the British government decided to grant asylum to 350 refugees and their families who were in imminent danger in Czechoslovakia. This number increased rapidly and by April 1939 between 2,000 and 3,000 persons benefited from this proactive refugee policy. This British readiness to accept refugees from Czechoslovakia did not deviate much from the minor humanitarian concessions made to the British immigration policy in the past. They received only a three-month temporary residence permit in expectation that they would re-emigrate elsewhere and all the costs involved were met by private relief organisations.

The first British quota of 350 was apportioned with two-thirds going to refugees who had just fled from the Sudetenland and one-third to refugees who had arrived in Czechoslovakia from Germany and Austria at an earlier date. The British refugee organisations in Czechoslovakia were asked to draw up a priority list of the most threatened individuals. Thus far, the British authorities had seen to it that asylum was not granted to communists, and although they wished to maintain this policy of exclusion, the refugee organisations had considerable left-wing representation and insisted that their rankings were respected. As a result, London finally accepted that communists were also to be included in those granted protection and to veil this far-reaching concession it was decided that only (communist) 'extremists' would be excluded. This excluded category seems not to have been used later on. Since 1917, Britain had been anything but welcoming to communist refugees, even temporarily, but their admission on condition that they would not engage in political activity was now accepted as the logical consequence of a more proactive refugee policy.[96] Thus, Great Britain became a more important place of asylum for communist refugees than in the preceding years (see Table II.3.2, p.288). In the course of 1939, the British authorities were 'forced' to make their proactive refugee policy even more generous. As it turned out to be difficult to find a country willing to receive the temporarily protected refugees, the average residence permits for transit refugees from Czechoslovakia were 'perforce' extended from 3 to 6 months in March 1939. From January 1939 onwards, the British subsidised refugee re-emigration. The money was taken from the £4 million which London had promised as financial support to Czechoslovakia. From this refugee fund, money could be taken only to arrange a permanent settlement elsewhere. The costs of temporary relief inside the United Kingdom continued to be met by charitable organisations.

Besides the above-mentioned organised immigration, there was also a spontaneous movement of Czech refugees posing as tourists. Possessing only a passport and some financial means, they could gain access to Great Britain. Yet, soon after September 1938, fears that refugees masquerading as tourists might try to settle meant that all Czechs were subjected to close scrutiny and interrogation at the ports of entry.[97] Immediately after the occupation of Bohemia-Moravia on 15 March 1939, the regulations were relaxed and refugees from Czechoslovakia who had fled immediately after the invasion of Prague and had succeeded in reaching British ports were usually granted admission if they possessed a valid passport. Thus, between September 1938 and April 1939, some 1,500 Czechs were given asylum in Great Britain of whom about a thousand were Jews, but others were turned away. The heavily publicised case of a group of 'Jewish' refugees from the protectorate who flew into Croydon airport from Warsaw on 31 March 1939 on a chartered plane and were immediately returned to Warsaw sent a clear message. This forcible return of Czech Jews had immediate repercussions on the continent. The Dutch authorities refused further passage to Czech 'Jews' travelling on trains from the protectorate to Dutch ports. These 'Jews' were ostensibly on their way to England, but in spite of direct intervention of the British Committee for Refugees from Czechoslovakia (BCRC) with the Dutch border officials, only a small number were allowed to cross into the Netherlands at Oldenzaal and most were left stranded in Bentheim on the German side of the border.[98]

After the introduction of a visa requirement for people from the protectorate in April 1939, the process of pre-selection could be applied as an administrative routine to Czech refugees. When such refugees presented themselves at British ports of entry they could be refused admission if they did not have the necessary documents – just like their German or Austrian counterparts. The British authorities wanted to preselect the refugees they admitted. From April 1939 onwards, British refugee policy explicitly extended its target group to ethnic Czechs and Czech 'Jews'.[99] The BCRC set up reception and clearing stations in Poland to select refugees who had fled the protectorate. Warsaw had agreed to admit illegally immigrating refugees provided that they departed quickly. Once arrived in Great Britain, the BCRC – for the first time in the history of British refugee policy – could apply for public funds to finance the (temporary) relief of these refugees. British groups supporting non-Jewish refugees argued that it was only their work that was truly resistance to Nazi Germany's policies. Help for Czech Jews to emigrate obviously played into the hands of the Nazis who wanted to purge the (Czech) protectorate of all its Jews. Berlin even proposed cooperation with the British authorities in this matter. The British rescue operation for those in danger in Czechoslovakia became exclusively focused on helping political refugees. The British acknowledgement of responsibility for the victims of the Munich agreement seemed to have had no advantages for Czech Jews, as they continued to be treated on a par with the Jews still residing in Germany or Austria and this in contrast to their politically active countrymen.

After *Kristallnacht*, 'Jewish' refugees in Germany and Austria also benefited from a more generous immigration policy. This liberalisation of entry for 'Jewish' refugees from Greater Germany remained almost exclusively dependent on private Jewish finances. By this stage, Neville Chamberlain, the British Prime Minister, had effectively given up all hope of moderating this aspect of Nazi policy and had assumed that the continuing pauperisation and expulsion of the Jews was irreversible. There was no doubt in his mind that the solution to the refugee question could only be found in the United States. He took the view that Great Britain could not cope with the massive inflow of refugees, and any increase in the quotas for Palestine was politically unacceptable. He was also convinced that the United States could only be persuaded to open its doors if it realised that there was no European solution to the problem. These political and humanitarian considerations explain Chamberlain's decision to grant temporary protection to considerably more refugees from Nazi Germany in Great Britain. Concessions were made to children and (female) workers prepared to become domestic servants.[100] In this manner about 10,000 children and 13,000, almost exclusively female, refugees had been admitted by September 1939. Both schemes officially offered only temporary protection, but these refugees were admitted for longer periods and the authorities were prepared to consider applications for permanent residence.

Chamberlain's decision meant that Britain was prepared to be far more generous in granting *temporary* asylum for 'Jewish' refugees, but the principles established in 1933 remained intact: relief measures for transit refugees and the costs of their journey to a final country of asylum were not to be at the expense of the public purse, but met either by the refugees themselves, or by private charities. This somewhat undermined any flood of refugees to the United Kingdom. From the *Anschluss* onwards, Anglo-Jewish relief organisations had limited their role to that of mediator between individual sponsors and candidate-refugees in Germany and Austria. This process of selective immigration was speeded up from November 1938 onwards as more civil servants were deployed to handle visa applications. At the same time, the criteria for being granted temporary asylum were drastically reduced. Thus, it was no longer necessary to provide evidence of imminent re-emigration and sometimes the mere fact that the applicant was deemed physically and socially suitable for re-emigration was considered sufficient. Recommendations from a refugee aid organisation became accepted as a substitute for official individual inquiries. Thus receiving a British visa became largely a decision taken by the relief organisations and the individual sponsors, who, after all, took on the financial responsibility for the persons they selected.[101]

The Jewish relief organisations concentrated their efforts almost exclusively on German (and Austrian) Jews while Czech Jews could not count on their support. The latter were not considered the responsibility of the British Jews, but of the British government, because the British authorities had accepted responsibility for victims of the Munich agreement by providing the resources for their re-emigration, and from April 1939 onwards, also for their temporary relief in the United Kingdom. These refugees were referred to the BCRC. This organisation, officially non-sectarian, was mainly a creation of the Left and its primary concern was with political activists. In agreement with the authorities, the BCRC thus privileged the political refugees, whereas Jews from Czechoslovakia were left out in the cold. Nevertheless, the possibility of reaching Great Britain via Poland continued to act as a magnet for Jews in Czechoslovakia. British refugee aid committees were told to pass on the message that it was useless for 'Jews' from Czechoslovakia to escape to Poland, because they stood no chance of obtaining a visa for the United Kingdom. This selective solidarity with the victims of Munich was also conditioned by British loyalty to her Polish ally who had little enthusiasm for this inflow of 'Jews'.[102] The British authorities claimed it was imperative to relieve the pressure on the Polish borders because the continuing 'Jewish' emigration from Czechoslovakia might even pose a threat to the Polish-Jewish population. As a result of the selective British refugee policy, the Polish authorities decided to give a clear signal to the 'Jews' in Czechoslovakia by starting to turn 'Jewish' refugees away at the frontier and even to expel them.[103]

By mid May 1939, the BCRC had already brought 5,000 refugees to Great Britain, but there were very few Jews among them.[104] In the battle for visas for Czechs, those representing the interests of Jewish refugees pointed out that there were many political activists among the 'Jewish' refugees in Poland and that they were in as much danger as activists of other ethnic groups from Czechoslovakia. The defence of the 'Jewish' refugees resulted in a serious crisis within the British refugee network. It was not until Czech Jews were represented in the selection committee that 'Jewish' Czechs were rescued through this operation.[105] In line with the British refugee policy the selection of Czech Jews was mainly based on their prospects of permanent overseas residence. An additional criterion, introduced by the BCRC and which concurred with its conception of a refugee, was the social engagement of Jews. Only those Jews who had taken part in public life, be it through membership of a professional, women's or youth organisation, could be selected for immigration.[106]

According to Louise London and Arieh Sherman, refugees caught trying to evade British immigration control were severely dealt with. They base their judgment mainly on a few cases which had been heavily publicised, possibly as part of a deliberate public relations campaign. Indeed illegal refugees were prosecuted in the United Kingdom, but the judges usually imposed mild sentences, albeit with a recommendation that the accused should be deported after the sentences had been served.[107] However, this was invariably back to their country of first asylum or to their point of departure, primarily the Netherlands, France or Belgium, and not to Nazi Germany. In most cases, such people had crossed the Channel illegally, as stowaways on ships from European continental ports. Some even made the journey in their own boats, as was the case of two refugees who, in the summer of 1939, left Belgium for England in a ten-foot dinghy.[108] Although, as mentioned before, the first country of asylum was not necessarily a safe haven, deportation from Britain directly to Germany seems to have been out of the question. As far as we know there were no cases of refugees deported directly to Germany, a point reinforced by the contemporary assessment by S. Adler-Rudel of the Council for German Jewry:

> The judges usually criticised the immigrant for entering the country illegally and imposed mild sentences. In all cases, including those in which the Law forced the judge to recommend deportation, he pleaded for clemency and hoped the Home Office would not deport these persons, as no one can assume the responsibility of sending a person to Germany.[109]

The St Louis: An Exceptional Case?

This overview of European refugee policy seems to contradict the most well-known episode in the rescue of German Jews from Nazi Germany in 1939: the saga of the *St Louis*. This story has been told many times in literature, in the press and in feature films, and underlines the myth of a generous European refugee policy. This 'trip of shame' is usually presented as a tribute to European solidarity with the refugees as opposed to American indifference.[110] On 13 May 1939, the *St Louis* sailed out of the port of Hamburg with 931 passengers on board, nearly all of whom were 'Jews'. They had purchased visas for Cuba, and hoped to find refuge in Havana. An economic crisis together with a corruption scandal in the immigration department caused a change in Cuban immigration policy on 5 May, but although the ship's owners, HAPAG, had been informed of the changes, they did not stop the *St Louis* from leaving Hamburg. In the event, only a very few of the refugees were allowed to disembark in Havana and the remaining 907 passengers were refused entry as the Cuban authorities refused to honour the visas issued by their consuls in Germany. In spite of intensive negotiations by the major Jewish charities, no other American state was prepared to accept any of these refugees and the *St Louis* was ultimately forced to set sail back to Europe and was destined to return to Hamburg. In an attempt to prevent this, the AJDC guaranteed to meet the costs of maintaining these people in any country ready to accept them, an undertaking discretely supported by the U.S. State Department. Initially the British and French authorities, worried about setting a precedent, refused to cooperate, as they considered calls to admit the *St Louis* passengers as giving in to German blackmail and a breach of the principle of pre-selecting refugees abroad.[111] It was probably also in British and French minds to send yet another message to would-be refugees that there was no sense in arriving at the French or British border uninvited.

In desperation, albeit with little hope, the AJDC contacted Max Gottschalk, the president of the Jewish refugee committee in Brussels, to see if Belgium would be ready to accept some passengers. On 10 June, Gottschalk obtained an agreement to take in 250 refugees still on board of the *St Louis* from the Belgian authorities.[112] This decision remained confidential and the AJDC then used it to lobby Belgium's neighbours. Two days later, on 12 June, the Dutch and French government also agreed to take in 194 and 250 Jews respectively. Britain was the last to follow and agreed to admit the remainder. Certainly the British and French, and even the Dutch, had been dragged somewhat unwillingly into this rescue operation, their hand forced by Belgian generosity. The British belated acceptance was also motivated by the desire to save the U.S. government any further embarrassment and in the hope that this would be rewarded by the Americans accepting more of the ever-increasing numbers of transit refugees waiting in the United Kingdom.

The actual selection of passengers destined for each of the four receiving countries took place on board ship in Antwerp harbour. The discussions between the governments over which refugees they should take resulted in some acrimony. The instructions for each official delegation were very similar. The Dutch were to take only people with a real chance of emigration, the stateless had to be refused categorically, and the quota should contain as few Poles as possible. Getting away with less than 194 refugees would be appreciated too. The French wanted the majority of 'their' refugees to have U.S. visas already in hand, while they refused to accept any Poles at all. By the same token, no country wanted to be saddled with an undue proportion of those who would be difficult to get rid of. The most desirable were those whose departure overseas was imminent. Different proposals on how to make the allocations were in circulation. One proposal was an arbitrary method of numerical selection. Another was to select on the basis of having friends or relatives in any of the four countries. This proposal emanated from the refugee aid organisations that wanted to minimise their expenses and was accepted. The British immediately produced a list of sponsors in Britain for 180 refugees, who turned out to be the ones with the best prospects and best credentials. This skimming off the cream of the list produced protests from the other three countries. As a compromise, Belgium and the Netherlands did not take their full quota and Britain had to accept the final residue of 'undesirables' and thus a larger number of people than originally intended. Thus Britain ended up with 287 refugees and France 224, of whom 162 already possessed U.S. visas. The Belgian group totalled 215 people and the Dutch took 181. When this last group arrived in Rotterdam, they were all placed in a temporary camp surrounded by guard dogs and barbed wire. The other groups fared somewhat better: In Belgium only those with no family in the country were housed in camps managed by the refugee committees. In France they were directed to an assigned residence in provincial refugee centres and in Britain they were housed privately.[113]

The rescue of the *St Louis* refugees remained an exceptional operation. Immediately afterwards, the JDC issued a statement of policy declaring that it would not be in a position to offer similar guarantees again. The liberal European states also all made it clear that this was not to constitute a precedent for the future and no similar actions would be taken in any subsequent cases.[114] And indeed, several other ships that had sailed in the expectation of dumping their 'Jewish' human cargoes were forced to return to Germany, thereby consigning their passengers to concentration camps. For these would-be refugees there was to be no international relief effort.[115]

Liberal Europe and the Impossibility of an Open-ended Humanitarian Commitment

In the summer of 1939 the pattern of immigration and asylum policies that had been established after *Kristallnacht* changed. Belgium decided to follow Switzerland, Luxemburg and Denmark and to deport all ('Jewish') refugees entering the country illegally. The local refugee committees were convinced that the hardliners now had the upper hand in Belgium and there would be no duplication of Dutch and French ambivalence.[116] At the same time, France and the Netherlands had pursued their own tortuous routes and both looked to soften their immigration policy. By the summer the French government was convinced that refugees could have some economic and military value, just like Frenchmen. The French authorities were more disposed to give a legal definition to the right of asylum and a decree dated 22 July 1939 to hold a census of all male refugees between

20 and 48 years of age was a clear step in this direction. This census had to list all foreigners protected in France and those refugees were to be summoned to perform some kind of French military service. The French authorities had not only to list those who had been qualified as 'refugees' and had received as such the right to stay in France, but also all those who because of the opinions they had expressed or the circumstances by which they had entered the country could be considered refugees. The stay of immigrants who were residing undocumented in France, but were categorised for this census as refugees, would be legalised.[117]

Likewise in the Netherlands, the hard line policy was brought into question. Although camps were still considered essential for immigration management and even greater powers of surveillance and control were given to the local authorities, changes in the other direction were also occurring. The Ministry of Justice was discussing the possibility of taking over the financing of the refugee camps with the Jewish refugee aid committee.[118] More importantly, the Amsterdam police reached an agreement with the refugee committees that encouraged illegal refugees to register with the police in exchange for an undertaking that they would not be pursued and become liable for deportation. This, it was thought, would give the police more information and a better insight into the refugee population.[119] It seems that even at cabinet level, the effectiveness of the hard-line policy was being questioned. In a confidential memorandum in July 1939, the Minister of Justice Goseling acknowledged that 'in the present circumstances repatriations to Germany were inconvenient' and secret instructions were issued which made it possible to systematically renew the residence permits of refugees on a monthly basis.[120]

Changes in refugee policy during the summer of 1939 also occurred in the United Kingdom where, although refugees remained a privileged category, generosity was increasingly limited. Not only did the channels of sponsorship dry up for Jewish refugees from Germany, but the authorities also sought to slow down the flow of new arrivals. The relief organisations had to cope with an increasing number of people who arrived in Britain and did not move on. In November 1938, the British government had estimated the number of refugees in the country at around eleven thousand. By July 1939, this number had multiplied fourfold, and some estimates suggest sixfold.[121] By that time, admissions to Palestine had been suspended as a punishment for Zionist-organised illegal immigration. This also had repercussions on refugees given temporary protection in the United Kingdom.[122] As a result, the authorities exercised greater scrutiny over the emigration prospects of those applying for admission.[123] The increasing financial burden on the Jewish refugee organisations in Great Britain as the result of the increasing inflow all but exhausted their resources. In August 1939 the Jewish refugee aid organisations realised that they could not take responsibility for more refugees and communicated this decision to the British authorities.[124] At the same time the BCRC, which had been conducting relief operations for refugees from Czechoslovakia in Poland also fell into financial problems.

The British refusal to co-finance the upkeep of refugees had been slowly eroded during 1939. The authorities had long been aware of the time bomb under its liberal admissions policy and in July 1939, seven months after they had decided to finance the re-emigration of Czech refugees, the British authorities agreed to do the same for Jewish refugees from Germany and Austria.[125] This decision went some way to alleviating the responsibility of private organisations for the temporary relief and re-emigration of refugees. The British authorities tried to muster international, and most importantly, American support for a private–public mix of refugee relief. In proposing this at the Intergovernmental Committee, the British representative, Earl Winterton, referred to the British public support for refugees from Czechoslovakia, the maintenance of 3,000 refugees by the Belgian government and the Dutch undertaking to build the camp at Westerbork and suggested a departure 'from the principle agreed unanimously at Evian, that no participating Government would give direct financial assistance to refugees'. He proposed that private subscription to an international fund to assist in defraying the expenses of overseas emigration of refugees might be encouraged by government participation, possibly on a basis proportionate to the amount of private subscription.[126] In spite of this, the British authorities refused to act unilaterally. When the news came that the BCRC was out of funds, the relief operations for refugees from Czechoslovakia in Poland had to cease immediately.[127]

When the war broke out in September 1939, a totally new political equilibrium was created in which liberal influences lost much of their clout and all the developments chronicled above were suspended. It also meant that the resolve of the Belgian authorities to carry out a blind deportation policy was never really put to the test and the Anglo-Jewish community never discovered if their financial difficulties would have led to a halt to Jewish refugee immigration. Even the very cautious Dutch reforms and the more resolute French steps towards a more liberal refugee policy could be pursued no further.

Notes

1. Seeing that the National Socialist racial categorisations, such as Jew and Aryan, were not at all transparent and self-evident categories we enclose those terms in quotation marks.
2. S. Friedländer, *Nazi Germany and the Jews. I: The Years of Persecution, 1933–1939*, London 1998, pp.272ff.
3. W. Gruner, *Jewish Forced Labor Under the Nazis: Economic Needs and Racial Aims, 1938–1944*, Cambridge 2006, pp.5–6.
4. V. Caron, *Uneasy Asylum: France and the Jewish Refugee Crisis, 1933–1942*, Stanford 1999, p.173; E. Mendelsohn, *The Jews of East Central Europe Between the World Wars*, Bloomington 1983, pp.202–11.
5. S. Heim, '"Deutschland muss ihnen ein Land ohne Zukunft sein". Die Zwangsmigration der Juden 1933–1938', in *Beiträge zur Nationalsozialistischen*

Gesundheits- und Sozialpolitik, II, 1993, pp.48–81; W. Gruner, 'Von der Kollektivausweisung zur Deportation der Juden aus Deutschland (1938–1945). Neue perspektiven und Dokumente', in *Die Deportation der Juden aus Deutschland*, ed. B. Kundrus and B. Meyer, Göttingen 2004, pp.21–62.

6. Only 'Jewish' communists and leading intellectuals were exempted from this policy: Krause to Interior Affairs, 21.1.1939, BBR 276; Report II 112.4, 16.2.1939, BBR 486.
7. While until 1938 only about 20 per cent of the 'Jews' who left Germany were financially assisted by Jewish organisations in Germany, this increased to 33 per cent for the first 8 months of 1939: 'Reichsvereinigung der Juden in Deutschland, Organisation und Auswanderung der Juden aus dem Altreich, 1933 bis 1941', pp.231–33, BBR 8150 (microfilm 31).
8. See Patrick von zur Muhlen, this volume.
9. See Steve Hochstadt, this volume.
10. S. Heim and A. Götz, 'Staatliche Ordnung und "Organische Lösung". Die Rede Hermann Görings "über die Judenfrage" vom 6. Dezember 1938', *Jahrbuch für Antisemitismusforschung*, 2, 1993, p.384.
11. J. Rohwer, 'Jüdische Flüchtlingsschiffe im Schwarzen Meer – 1934 bis 1944', in *Das Unrechtsregime: Internationale Forschung über den Nationalsozialismus*, ed. U. Büttner, W. Johe and A. Voss, Hamburg 1986, pp.197–214. See Aviva Halamish, this volume.
12. B. Mc Donald Stewart, *United States Government Policy and Refugees from Nazism, 1933–1940*, New York 1982, p.447.
13. Bericht der Israel, Kultusgemeinde Wien über ihre Tätigkeit in den ersten drei Monaten des Jahres 1939, p.2, Central Archives for the History of the Jewish People, Jerusalem (CAHJP), A/W 165,3.
14. L. Senkman, 'Argentina's Immigration Policy during the Holocaust (1938–1945)', *Yad Vashem Studies*, 21, 1991, p.165; JDC 666; AN F7 16080; D. Salzmann, *Mexico Frente a la inmigracion de refugiados judios 1934–1940*, Cordoba 2000, p.123f.; see also Patrik von zur Mühlen, this volume.
15. D. Afoumado, *L'exil impossible. L'errance des Juifs du paquebot St Louis*, Paris 2005 ; L. Senkman, 'Argentinien under der Holocaust. Die Einwanderungspolitik und die Frage der Flüchtlinge 1933–1945', in *Europäische Juden in Lateinamerika*, ed. A. Schrader and K.H. Rengstorf, St Ingbert 1989, p.65.
16. A. Margaliot, 'Emigration-Planung und Wirklichkeit', in *Der Juden in Nationalsozialistischen Deutschland*, ed. A. Paucker, Tübingen 1986, p.313.
17. Note of the HIAS-ICA Emigration Association (HICEM) on SS.Koenigstein and Caribia's transports: JDC 666; Bericht der Israel, Kultusgemeinde Wien über ihre Tätigkeit in den ersten drei Monaten des Jahres 1939, p.2f, CAHJP, A/W 165,3.
18. L. Rünitz, *Af hensyn til konsekvenserne, Danmark og flygtningesporgsmalet 1933–1939*, Odense 2005, p.429.
19. O. Kulka and E. Jäckel, *Die Juden in den geheimen NS-Stimmungsberichten 1933–1945*, Dusseldorf 2004, p.397; Afoumado, *L'exil impossible*, pp. 28f. See Steve Hochstadt, this volume.
20. Y. Bauer, *Jews for Sale? Nazi–Jewish Negotiations, 1933–1945*, New Haven 1995, pp.44ff.; A. Sherman, *Island Refuge: Britain and Refugees from the Third Reich, 1933–1939*, Berkeley 1973, p.239; K. Voigt, *Zuflucht auf Widerruf. Exil in Italien 1933–1945*, Stuttgart 1989, p.293ff. See Aviva Halamish, this volume.
21. As from 31 May 1939 onwards the German authorities cut shipping companies off from foreign currency for cruises, these companies became

much more willing to transport Jews: Report II 112, 16.5.1939, BBR 486; 'Reichsvereinigung der Juden in Deutschland, Organisation und Auswanderung 1933 bis 1941', p.212, BBR 8150.
22. Seeing this as a lucrative business, private entrepreneurs also provided these services: D. Ofer, *Escaping the Holocaust: Illegal Immigration to the Land of Israel 1939–1944*, Oxford 1990; Rohwer, 'Jüdische Flüchtlingsschiffe', pp.203ff.
23. Report II 112.4, 16.2.1939, BBR 486.
24. Rünitz, *Af hensyn*, pp.285f. We do not have any information on the German policy at the Luxemburg border.
25. SOPADE was the abbreviation used to denote the Sozialdemokratische Partei Deutschlands (SPD) in exile – in Prague from 1933.
26. Friedländer, *Nazi Germany and the Jews*, vol. 1, p.302; Moore, *Refugees*, p.96.
27. '"Für die nach Lage der Dinge nur eine illegale Auswandering in Frage käme" Erlass des Gestapa an die der Westgrenze des Reiches gelegenen Staatspolizeistellen', 23.12.1938, quoted in H. Berschel, *Bürokratie und Terror. Das Judenreferat der Gestapo Düsseldorf, 1935–1945*, Essen 2001, p.283.
28. Berschel, *Bürokratie und Terror*, pp.283–84.
29. F. Caestecker, *Ongewenste gasten, joodse vluchtelingen en migranten in de dertiger jaren*, Brussels 1993, p.205f., 231f.; H. Kocher, 'Rationierte Menschlichkeit'. *Schweizerischer Protestantismus im Spannungsfeld von Flüchtlingsnot und öffentlicher Flüchtlingspolitik der Schweiz 1933–1948*, Zürich 1996; C. Kotzin, *Christian Responses in Britain to Jewish Refugees from Europe: 1933–1939*, Southampton 2000 (unpublished manuscript), pp.192ff. In the Netherlands the Jewish committee had already passed its welfare clients to the newly founded Christian organisations in 1935–1936: D. Michman, 'The Committee for Jewish Refugees in Holland, 1933–1940', *Yad Vashem Studies*, 14, 1981, p.216.
30. In the Netherlands, the mayor was not an elected office, but a public servant: C. Berghuis, *Joodse vluchtelingen in Nederland, 1938–1940*, Kampen 1990, p.35f.; J. Michman Jozeph, B. Hartog and D. Michman, *Pinkas, geschiedenis van de joodse gemeenschap in Nederland*, Amsterdam 1999, pp.149f.
31. Caestecker, *Ongewenste gasten*, p.231, 234.
32. S. Mächler, *Hilfe und Ohnmacht. Der Schweizerische Israelitische Gemeindebund und die nationalsozialistische Verfolgung, 1933–1945*, Zürich 2005, p.168.
33. R. Thalmann, 'L'immigration allemande et l'opinion publique en France de 1936 à 1939', *Deutschland und Frankreich 1936–1939. Beihefte der Francia*, 10, 1981, p.64; R. Delacor, 'Die Reaktionen Frankreichs auf den Novemberpogrom 1938', *Zeitschrift für Geschichtswissenschaft*, 46, no. 11, 1998, p.1005. In August 1939, the French embassy in Rome protested about the illegal emigration of German Jews from Italy: P. Veziano, *Ombre di confine. L'emigrazione clandestina degli ebrei stranieri delle reviera dei Fiori verso la consta azzura (1938–1940)*, Pinerolo 2001, p.98.
34. Belgium, in the summer of 1938, and the Netherlands, in early 1939, asked Luxemburg to impose a visa obligation on Germans and Austrians and to stop the smuggling of refugees from Luxemburg: LSA, Ministère de la Justice, J 73/48.
35. For example in Belgium the authorities imposed sanctions on airline carriers which had enabled refugees to enter the country: Caestecker, *Ongewenste gasten*, p.182; Pholien to Spaak, 14.10.1938, AAD 785. See also Vicki Caron, this volume.

36. For France and Switzerland see Vicki Caron, and Regula Ludi, this volume; for France see also J. Deschodt and F. Huguenin, *La république xénophobe,1917–1939*, Paris 2001, pp.384–424.
37. W. Röder, 'The Political Exiles: Their Policies and their Contribution to Post-War Reconstruction', in *International Biographical Dictionary of Central European Emigrés 1933–1945*, vol. II, ed. H. Strauss and W. Röder, Munich 1983, pp.XXVII–XXXVI; P. Heumos, *Die Emigration aus der Tschechoslowakei nach Westeuropa und dem Nahen Osten 1938–1945*, Munich 1989, p.169ff.
38. Rünitz, *Af hensyn*, p.430; Heumos, *Die Emigration aus der Tschechoslowakei*, p.169; H. Petersen, 'Die Dänische Flüchtlingspolitik 1933–1941', in *Deutschsprachiges Exil in Dänemaken nach 1933. Zu methoden und Einzelergebenissen*, ed. R. Dinesen, B. Nielsen, H. Petersen, F. Schmoë, Copenhagen 1986, p.81; Conference on German Situation and Emigration, 14 and 15 December 1938, held at the offices of the JDC in Paris, 15.12.1938, p.9, JDC 363. See also Vicki Caron, this volume.
39. ABMFA 11.170; Rünitz, *Af hensyn*, p.88; H. Wichers, *Im kampf gegen Hitler. Deutsche Sozialisten im Schweizer Exil 1933–1940*, Zürich 1994, p.64.
40. Conference on German Situation and Emigration, 14 and 15 December 1938 held at the offices of the JDC in Paris, 15.12.1938, p.9, JDC 363; L. London, *Whitehall and the Jews, 1933–1948: British Immigration Policy and the Holocaust*, Cambridge 2000, p.61; F. Caestecker, 'Onverbiddelijk, maar ook clement. Het Belgische immigratiebeleid en de joodse vlucht uit nazi-Duitsland, maart 1938–augustus 1939', *Bijdragen tot de eigentijdse geschiedenis*, 13/14, 2004, p.110.
41. ESRA (Luxemburg Jewish Social Welfare Organisation), report on the situation in Luxemburg 22.8.1939, Université Catholique de Louvain (UCL) archives, Papers Van Zeeland 906; Rünitz, *Af hensyn*, pp.376–90.
42. Moore, *Refugees*, pp.87f.; Walter, *Deutsche Exilliteratur*, p.144; Michman 'The Committee', p.214.
43. R. Weingarten, *Die Hilfeleistung der westlichen Welt bei der Endlösung der deutchen Judenfrage. Das Intergouvernmental Committee on Political Refugees (ICG)*, Bern 1981, p.223; Berghuis, *Joodse* vluchtelingen, p.23ff.
44. 'Reichsvereinigung der Juden in Deutschland, Organisation und Auswanderung 1933 bis 1941', pp.147–49. BBR 8150.
45. Berghuis, *Joodse vluchtelingen*, p.45.
46. See Claudia Curio in this volume. The French record is unclear, through the regular Jewish channels only a few hundred were listed, but the French authorities promised more than a thousand visas. Sweden took in also a few hundred children: 'Reichsvereinigung der Juden in Deutschland, Organisation und Auswanderung 1933 bis 1941', BBR 8150; Bericht der Israel, Kultusgemeinde Wien, 1–25.3.1939, CAHJP, A/W 165,3. On the reception of Spanish children, a rescue operation from which the Netherlands remained aloof, see F. Caestecker and S. Eloy, 'Spaanse minderjarige oorlogsvluchtelingen in België' in *Los Niños, Tien vluchtelingenkinderen uit de Spaanse Burgeroorlog vertellen*, ed. H. Pauwels, Antwerpen 2007, pp.199–220; F. Caestecker, 'La acogida en Bélgica de niños refugiados de guerra españoles a partir de 1937', *Foro Hispanico* (in press). In Denmark, due to public pressure and as there was an unlimited demand for an inexpensive and highly motivated workforce in Danish agriculture, the Zionists succeeded in raising their quota of 200 Hechaluz to 600 youngsters in 1939 as well as an agreement to the temporary stay of a few hundred Aliyah children: J.

Haestrup, 'Auf den Weg von Deutschland nach Palästina. Jüdische Kinder und Jugendliche in Dänemark (1930–1945)', in *Deutschsprachiges Exil in Dänemarken nach 1933. Zu Methoden und Einzelergebnissen*, ed. R. Dinesen, H. Petersen, F. Schmoë and B. Nielsen, Copenhagen 1986, pp.57–66; Rünitz, *Af hensyn*, p.431.

47. The emigration data for Bohemia and Moravia for 1939 are listed in the attachment to the letter of the Police d'Israel to Zentralamt für die Regelung der Judenfrage in Böhmen und Mähren, 19.6.1944, Archives of the Centre de Documentation Juive Contemporaine (Paris), DXXI-1192 (with thanks to Diane Afoumado). The data for Austria for 2.5.1938 to 31.7.1939 are in Israel, Kultusgemeinde Wien, Emigration-Retraining-Social Care, UCL archives, Papers Van Zeeland, 906. Gertrude Stein, *Exile and Destruction*, Westport 1995, pp.153–56 mentions that, according to a document of the Vienna Jewish community of 10.11.1941, during 1938–1939, 4,270 Austrian Jews had left for Belgium, 1,650 for France and 1,151 for the Netherlands. The discrepancy with the figures in 'Reichsvereinigung der Juden in Deutschland, Organisation und Auswanderung der Juden aus dem Altreich, 1933 bis 1941', pp.231–33, BBR 8150 (microfilm 31) can probably be attributed to illegal immigration.

48. Due to the threat of war the French Legion started new recruitment: among the 3,645 recruited in 1938 there were 11 per cent Germans and 2 per cent Austrians. By September 1939, 500 Czechs and 2,500 Spaniards had been recruited and an unknown number of German and Austrians: E. Michels, *Deutsche in der Fremdenlegion, 1870–1965. Mythen und Realitäten*, Paderborn 2000, p.110; Note sur l'état de l'émigration d'Allemagne et d'Autriche, 8.1939, YIVO, HICEM (Paris), HIAS, Series II, France, I, 139; AN F7/16072; J. Simpson, *The Refugee Problem, Report of a Survey*, London, New York and Toronto 1939, p.377.

49. Veziano, *Ombre di confine*, pp.55ff.
50. Berghuis, *Joodse vluchtelingen*, pp.55f.
51. While in 1938, 7,797 foreigners had not been admitted at the Belgian border, in 1939 there were 5,842 aliens refused at the border. The refugee crisis was the most important cause of this rise: Caestecker, *Alien Policy*, p.231ff.
52. C. Van Eijl, *Al te goed is buurmans gek. Het Nederlandse vreemdelingenbeleid 1840-1940*, Amsterdam 2005, p.198f.
53. In the first nine months of 1939, border guards refused entry to Danish territory to 95 refugees, of whom 64 German citizens: Rünitz, *Af hensyn*, pp.428ff.
54. See Claudia Curio, and Vicki Caron, this volume.
55. AN F716080; Van Tijn in Conference on German Situation and Emigration, 14 and 15 December 1938, held at the offices of the AJDC in Paris, 15.12.1938, p.14, JDC 363; Caestecker, *Ongewenste gasten*, p.229; Delacor, 'Die Reaktionen Frankreichs', p.1001.
56. Mr Israel (Ezra Luxemburg), in Conference on German Situation and Emigration, 14 and 15 December 1938, held at the offices of the AJDC in Paris, 15.12.1938, JDC 363; Mc Donald Stewart, *United States Government Policy*, p.31.
57. Moore, *Refugees*, p.84ff.
58. Berghuis, *Joodse vluchtelingen*, p.58.
59. Rünitz, *Af hensyn*, p. 408.

60. Procureur Général d'État to Robert de Foy, 25.1.1939, AAD 293 ; H. Arntz, *Judenverfolgung und Fluchthilfe in deutsch-belgischen Grenzgebiet*, Euskirchen 1990, p.269ff., 542; Veziano, *Ombre di confine*, p.55ff. ; Berghuis, *Joodse vluchtelingen*, p.197. For France, see Vicki Caron, this volume.
61. Complaint Belgian embassy Berlin, 6.12.1938 and 1.1939. AA, R 48907.
62. Zimmermann, Geheime Staatspolizei Berlin to sections of the Staatspolizei in the west of Germany, 15.3.1939, BBR 2736; Arntz, *Judenverfolgung*, p.566; S. Kirschgens, *Wege durch das Niemandsland. Dokumentation und Analyse der Hilfe für Flüchtlinge im deutsch-belgisch-niederländisch Grenzland in den Jahre 1933 bis 1945*, Cologne 1998, pp.90f.; Berschel, *Bürokratie und Terror*, p.285.
63. Veziano, *Ombre di confine*, pp.55ff.
64. Berghuis, *Joodse vluchtelingen*, p.66ff.; B. Vormeier and H. Schramm, *Vivre à Gurs. Un Camp de Concentration français 1940–1941*, Paris 1977, p.241; Caestecker, *Alien Policy*, pp.231ff.
65. This table is based on the biographies of 333 persons, most of whom had been KPD functionaries and resident in one of our countries after 1933: H. Weber and A. Herbst, *Deutsche Kommunisten. Biographisches Handbuch, 1918 bis 1945*, Berlin 2004.
66. Austrian refugees had found asylum in the USSR from 1935 onwards. From 1938 onwards they were treated on a par with German communists, with concomitantly deadly results. Leading Czech communists also found asylum in the USSR in 1939: B. McLoughlin, H. Schafranek, W. Szevera, *Aufbruch-Hoffnung-Endstation. Oesterreicherinnen und Oesterreicher in der Sowjetunion 1925–1945*, Vienna 1997.
67. Caestecker, 'Onverbiddelijk', pp.116f.
68. Berghuis, *Joodse vluchtelingen*, p.24.
69. GA Amsterdam, Gemeentepolitie, arch. 5225, 30.
70. Also Rotterdam started then to deport refugees: Berghuis, *Joodse vluchtelingen*, pp.87, 160 and 113; Moore, *Refugees*, pp.87f.; Mrs Van Tijn in Minutes of Conference of Various Committees held on Thursday, 23 March 1939 in Paris, JDC 405; G. Meershoek, *Dienaren van het gezag. De Amsterdamse politie tijdens de bezetting*. Amsterdam 1999, pp.97–99; Alien office, report of meeting 4.5.1939, GA Amsterdam, Gemeentepolitie, arch.5225, 1938/2. See also the files of expelled refugees in HSTAD RW 58, 3960, 3210.
71. 'France, Italy and Switzerland and to a lesser degree Belgium actively connived at the illegal traffic by issuing sauf-conduits to groups of refugees whose stated destinations – China, Haiti, or other – were patently bogus', CID Jerusalem, a report on the organisation of illegal immigration to Palestine, 17.5.1939, quoted in London, *Whitehall*; Simpson, *The Refugee Problem*, p.236; G. Anderl, 'Emigration und Vertreibung', in *Vertreibung und Neubeginn. Israelische Bürger Oesterreichischer Herkunft*, ed. E. Weinzierl and O. Kulka, Vienna 1992, pp.256ff.
72. Illegally immigrated Jews who were still Polish citizens were repatriated: Antwerp Committee for Jewish Refugees, Report on the Belgian situation, UCL Archives, Papers van Zeeland, 906.
73. On the international refugee regime and the Convention of February 1938 see Susanne Heim, this volume.
74. Caestecker, *Ongewenste gasten*, pp.207ff.; Caestecker, 'Onverbiddelijk', pp.116ff.
75. With little hard evidence, the few indications we have indicate that Luxemburg deported Jewish refugees throughout 1939.

76. Runitz, *Af hensyn*, pp.390ff.
77. Basel did deport some refugees when the crisis was at its height from mid August to early December 1938: Ludwig, *Die Flüchtlingspolitik der Schweiz*, pp.151–56; J. Wacker, *Humaner als in Bern! Schweizer und Basler Asylpraxis gegenüber den jüdischen Flüchtlingen von 1933 bis 1943 im Vergleich*, Basel 1992, pp.100–41; S. Keller, *Grüningers Fall. Geschichte von Flucht und Hilfe*, Zürich 1993; F. Battel, *'Wo es hell ist, dort is die Schweiz' Flüchtlinge und Fluchthilfe an der Schaffhauser Grenze zur Zeit des Nationalsozialismus*, Zürich 2000, p.162.
78. The refugee policy in Liechtenstein was very similar to the Swiss one, also because the Swiss guarded the Liechtenstein–German border: U. Jud, *Liechtenstein und die Flüchtlinge zur Zeit des Nationalsozialismus*, Vaduz 2005.
79. Berghuis, *Joodse vluchtelingen*, pp.66ff.; Moore, *Refugees*, pp.87f.
80. Between 1 and 20 March 1939, the Jewish refugee aid committee registered 35 people who came to Amsterdam illegally and 112 who entered legally and 138 in transit: Mrs Van Tijn, in Minutes of Conference of Various Committees held on Thursday, 23 March 1939 in Paris, JDC 405.
81. Moore, *Refugees*, p.82; Berghuis, *Joodse vluchtelingen*, p.107, 113. On the, at times generous, attitude of local authorities, in contrast to central policy guidelines: M. Leenders, 'Joodse vluchtelingen aan de grens', in *Gelderland, 1900–2000*, ed. D.Verhoeven, Zwolle 2006, pp.41–45.
82. Minutes of Conference of Various Committees held on 23.3.1939 at the offices of the AJDC, Paris, JDC 405.
83. P. Heumos, *Die Emigration aus der Tschechoslowakei nach Westeuropa und dem Nahen Osten 1938–1945*, Munich 1989, p.166f.; see Vicki Caron, this volume.
84. Minutes of Conference of Various Committees held on 23.3.1939 at the offices of the AJDC, Paris, JDC 405. Migration Conference JDC/HICEM 22–23.8.1939, JDC 367; R. Pell, 'Letter to Pierrepont Moffat (US Foreign Affairs), 8.3.1939', in *Beiträge zur Nationalsozialistischen Gesundheids-und Sozialpolitik*, 15, 1999, p. 139.
85. Herbert Katzki to members of the Committee on Refugee Aid in Europe, 2.6.1939, JDC 111; Migration Conference JDC/HICEM 22–23.8.1939, JDC 367. See also Vicki Caron, this volume.
86. R. Girault, 'La politique extérieure française de l'après-Munich (septembre 1938–avril 1939)', in *Deutschland und Frankreich 1936–1939*, ed. H. Klaus, K. Werner and K. Manfrass, Munich 1981, pp.507ff.
87. Vormeier and Schramm, *Vivre à Gurs*, pp.235ff.; Noiriel, *La Tyrannie*, p.116; Deschodt and Huguenin, *La république xénophobe*, p.164.
88. N. Fischer, 'Les expulsés inexpulsables. Recomposition du contrôle des étrangers dans la France des années 1930', *Cultures et conflits*, 53, 2004.
89. L. Stein, *Beyond Death and Exil : the Spanish Republicans in France, 1939-1955*, Cambridge 1979.
90. R.Schor, *L'opinion française et les étrangers en France, 1919–1939*, Paris 1985, p.667 ; D. Peschanski, *La France des camps. L'internement, 1938–1946*, Paris 2002, p.21ff.; AN F7 14.711.
91. Mrs Van Tijn, in Minutes of Conference of Various Committees held on Thursday, 23 March 1939 in Paris, JDC 405; Berghuis, *Joodse vluchtelingen*, pp.45, 178, 195; H. Walter, *Deutsche Exilliteratur 1933–1950. Band 2: Europäisches Appeasement und uberseeische Asylpraxis*, Stuttgart 1984, pp.145ff.; A.L. Jonker, *Joodse vluchtelingen in Hellevoetsluis, 1938–1940*, Hellevoetsluis 1995; H. June, *Interneringskamp voor Duitse tegenstanders van Hitler, 1938–1940*,

Dortmund (n.d.); Pell, 'Letter to Pierrepont Moffat', p.141. As Claudia Curio mentions in her chapter, even unaccompanied children were confined in camps in the Netherlands.

92. Nederlands Instituut voor Oorlogsdocumentatie, 181 k, Comité voor Joodse Belangen Map 1a and 1b; D. Cohen, *Zwervend en Dolend*, Haarlem 1955.
93. Berghuis, *Joodse vluchtelingen*, pp.60f.
94. Berghuis, *Joodse vluchtelingen*, p.62. Attempts were made to reduce the numbers of people confined in camps by 'legalising' them after a period of six months – subject to their good behaviour: Moore, *Refugees*, p.97.
95. Sherman, *Island Refuge*, p.262.
96. Y. Kapp and Margaret Mynatt, *British Policy and the Refugees 1933–1941*, London 1997, p.61; Heumos, *Die Emigration aus der Tschechoslowakei*, pp.35f, 45; London, *Whitehall*, p.159
97. Heumos, *Die Emigration aus der Tschechoslowakei*, pp.53f.
98. The Croydon repatriation was probably based on the strict application of the principle of the first country of asylum. The flight came from Poland, thus from a country which could have offered asylum to 'Jews': Kapp and Mynatt, *British Policy*, p.20f.; H. Schmitt, *Quakers and Nazis. Inner Light in Outer Darkness*, Columbia and London 1997, p.141; London, *Whitehall*, p.160 and pp.65ff; Moore, *Refugees*, pp.104f.; Sherman, *Island Refuge*, p.75.
99. London, *Whitehall*, p.154.
100. See Claudia Curio, this volume; A. Stevens, *The Dispossessed: German Refugees in Britain*, London 1975, pp.149–50; Kushner, 'Alien Occupation'. Aviva Halamish in this volume also points out the British favouritism of German Jews in its Palestine immigration policy, but as the British took, for political reasons, an overall restrictive stand, this privilege brought little relief.
101. London, *Whitehall*, p.133; London, 'British Immigration Control', p.507.
102. London, *Whitehall*, p.158.
103. Heumos, *Die Emigration aus der Tschechoslowakei*, p.73.
104. London, *Whitehall*, p.161.
105. Heumos, *Die Emigration aus der Tschechoslowakei*, pp.79–85.
106. London, *Whitehall*, p.164.
107. The London Magistrate, Herbert Metcalfe, considered in August 1938 'that it was becoming an outrage the way in which stateless Jews were pouring in from every port of the country. As far as he was concerned, he intended to enforce the law to the fullest extent' and he sentenced three illegally immigrated 'Jewish' refugees to six months heavy labour and deportation. The British press strongly criticised the exceptional severity of his sentence: Walter, *Deutsche Exilliteratur*, p.123; Sherman, *Island Refuge*, p.125.
108. Antwerp Committee for Jewish refugees, Report on the Belgian Situation, 8.1939, UCL archives, Van Zeeland, 902bis; L. London, 'Jewish Refugees, Anglo-Jewry and British Government Policy, 1930–1940', in *The Making of Anglo-Jewry*, ed. D. Cesarani, Oxford 1990, p.177; London, 'British Immigration', p.511; London *Whitehall*, p.80; Sherman, *Island Refuge*, pp.125–27.
109. S. Adler-Rudel to Borchardt, 21.2.1939, JDC 658.
110. Afoumado, *L'exil impossible*; M. Bejarano,'La historia del buque St.Louis: la perspectiva cubana', in *Entre la aceptacion y el rechazo. America Latina y los refugiados judios del nazismo*, ed. A. Milgram, Jerusalem 2003, pp.212–47.
111. Home Office, 12.6.1939, AN AJ43, 36; Sherman, *Island Refuge*, p.252ff.

112. In the morning of 10 June the Belgian Minister of Justice, Paul-Emile Janson, and the Prime Minister, Hubert Pierlot, agreed to take 200 passengers, of which 150 had an affidavit for the U.S. and 50 had enough guarantees to leave within one year. In the afternoon the number of passengers was increased to 250, but all of them would have to have an affidavit for the U.S: AAD 37C6, JDC 386.
113. AN AJ43, 36; Caron, *Uneasy Asylum*; Caestecker, *Ongewenste gasten*, p.245ff.; Berghuis, *Joodse vluchtelingen*, p.120ff; Moore, *Refugees*, p.105; London, *Whitehall*, pp.137ff.
114. JCD 386 and 378. Emerson, Memorandum of conversation with Mr. Wohlthat, 20.7.1939, UCL archives, Van Zeeland, 899a.
115. Tagesmeldung II 112, 15.6.1939, BBR 992; JDC 666; L. Senkman, 'Argentinien under der Holocaust. Die Einwanderungspolitik und die Frage der Flüchtlinge 1933–1945', in *Europäische Juden in Lateinamerika*, ed. A. Schrader and K. Rengstorf, St Ingbert 1989, p.65.
116. Tolkovsky, representative of a Jewish committee in Belgium in Migration Conference JDC/HICEM in Paris, 22–23.8.1939, JDC 367; Caestecker, *Ongewenste gasten*, pp.180–255; Caestecker, *Alien Policy*, pp.232–35; Caestecker, 'Onverbiddelijk', p.134f.
117. Circular letter Ministry of Interiors, 5.8.1937; Journal officiel, 22.7.1939, AN F7, 14.711.
118. Moore, *Refugees*, p.97.
119. Meershoek, *Dienaren*, pp.98f; Alien office, report of meeting 4.5.1939, GA Amsterdam, Gemeentepolitie, arch.5225, 1938/2.
120. Minister of Justice to Procurator-Generals, 5.8.1939, archival document generously put at our disposal by Corrie Van Eijl.
121. Heumos, *Die Emigration aus der Tschechoslowakei*, p. 78; London, *Whitehall*, pp.103 and 132.
122. London, *Whitehall*, p.140; London, 'Jewish Refugees', p.183. See Aviva Halamish, this volume.
123. Pell, 'Letter to Pierrepont Moffat', p.142.
124. Sherman, *Island Refuge*, p.255; B. Wasserstein, *Britain and the Jews of Europe, 1939–1945*, Oxford 1979, pp.81f.; London, *Whitehall*, p.141; Heumos, *Die Emigration aus der Tschechoslowakei*, p.78; A. Gottlieb, *Men of Vision: Anglo-Jewry's Aid to Victims of the Nazi Regime, 1933–1945*, London 1998.
125. Sherman, *Island Refuge*, pp.156 and 242ff.; London, *Whitehall*, p.132.
126. Archives UCL, Van Zeeland, 902bis; Weingarten, *Die Hilfeleistung*, p.158f.
127. London, *Whitehall*, pp.159–68.

Conclusion

Frank Caestecker and Bob Moore

All the European countries surveyed here had alien policies based on slightly differing precepts that derived from their respective domestic social, economic, and political circumstances. The predominance of Liberalism in the nineteenth century and its strictures on the relationship between the individual and the state had an impact on alien legislation in all countries considered. Resident aliens were considered de facto members of the nation and therefore protected against abuses of state power. All other immigrants were granted some protection (equality before the law, basic rights), based on the provisions within each state's constitution, but this could go even further for those immigrants who were defined as refugees.

During and immediately after the First World War, these policies were adapted, initially to exclude unwanted political elements and to meet diplomatic imperatives. In particular, the fear of 'alien' ideologies such as Bolshevism being imported from abroad entailed a loss of the liberal protection based on the rights of man. Identifying these ideologies as alien reflected the strong push towards nation building in the early twentieth century as part of the integrative revolution in response to the democratisation of politics. Political elites wanted a state-community that shared a national identity. Policy towards aliens was also caught up in this integrative policy; imposing on immigrants the duty to assimilate in order to preserve a cultural status quo. However, the precise nature of this assimilation was subject of controversy, and attempts to homogenise the population or protect an established cultural order produced an exclusionary trend which perceived certain ethnic or religious groups as unassimilable.

Changes in alien policy during this period were nonetheless still predominantly determined by economic interests. Increasing democratisation gave a voice to the previously politically disenfranchised and enabled them to oppose state policies that were detrimental to what they perceived as their interests. A protectionist immigration policy was one of the innovations concomitant with the transformation of the liberal state into a nation-state. However, countervailing forces remained. There were the interests of tourism, international travel and trade that placed a premium on the free movement of peoples, but most importantly the interests of employers who wanted free access to the international labour market but at the same time wanted to recoup their investment in procuring manpower abroad. In practice, the turmoil in the years after 1918 was ultimately replaced with more relaxed policies before the economic recession of the early 1930s finally convinced each of the liberal Western European states to reappraise its immigration policies and led to restrictions on the admission of immigrants and especially foreign labour.

The transformation of alien policy that began at the end of the nineteenth century had thus two objectives: economic protection, a result of the increasing power of labour within the political system, and concerns about national identity that has been dubbed 'nativism'. In this process, the more ambitious use of alien policy by increasingly interventionist states meant that the liberal political culture that had traditionally acted to defend the individual against the state lost of its influence. Security measures taken as a result of the First World War dramatically changed the operation of prewar immigration and residence policies, and these were seldom completely restored after 1919. From a position of near equality, aliens were increasingly excluded from the rights afforded to citizens of these countries.

This demise of Liberalism can clearly be seen in changes to policies on refugees. Before 1914 there had been a general acceptance in liberal states that those who had to flee their country for political reasons had to be protected, but after 1918 the right to asylum had all but ceased to exist. Refugees arriving at the borders of the liberal states of Europe were now habitually dealt with under the terms of the newly erected protectionist immigration policies. Russian and Armenian refugees were the first victims of this change in attitude, but thanks to the political sympathy aroused by these anti-Bolshevist Russians their arrival was no lasting problem. Most importantly the need for additional labour in Western Europe at the moment of their arrival facilitated their reception.

Thus, it is important to realise that the arrival of refugees from Nazi Germany after January 1933 did not take place in a legislative vacuum, but against a background of existing structures, legal precedents and controls. Put another way, nearly all the factors that played some role in determining policy during and after 1933 were already in place long before the Nazis came to power. No national immigration policies were identical, but two basic models can be identified: the British model that emphasised external immigration control, comprising border controls and visa schemes, and the Continental model where control was much more a mixture of external and internal control. Within the Continental model we can distinguish two types: on the one hand the centralised one and on the other the decentralised type employed by countries such as Switzerland, Denmark and the Netherlands. In these latter countries, regional and local authorities had considerable influence on the practical application of aliens policy that created local variations within these countries. Another important difference within the Continental model was the manner in which undesirable immigrants from Central Europe were removed. For example, while France merely obliged such people to leave the country on their own initiative, the Belgian authorities physically took them to the border and the Dutch formally extradited them to the German authorities. These differences in national immigration policies would ultimately have important repercussions for the refugees from Nazi Germany.

On the eve of the refugee crisis of 1933 all countries had the legislative means to deal with people coming from Germany, but rapidly realised that practical solutions were difficult to enforce. The authorities baulked at expelling 'Jewish' and political refugees who had entered the countries illegally or whose visas or residence permits had expired. For humanitarian reasons deporting them to Germany was considered unacceptable, while passing them on to other states created diplomatic problems. National policies towards aliens continued to have many differences, but there was a general strengthening of internal controls in the countries of continental Europe that made it increasingly difficult for refugees to remain unnoticed or to stand in for their own upkeep. The arrival of 'Jewish' refugees played a crucial role in this process of restrictionism, but it has to be seen primarily as a continuation of the policies adopted to counter the effects of economic recession rather than directed specifically against those fleeing from Germany. Thus, while the numbers of people coming from Germany between 1933 and the summer of 1935 declined, the climate of increasing restrictionism nonetheless continued.

In effect, the main determinants of policy in this period remained the custom and practice of aliens policy combined with increasing economic nationalism, anti-Bolshevism, and (fears of) antisemitism. This development has to be seen more as an expression of the increasing power of representatives of labour and the middle classes in government, than as a reaction against the influx of refugees from Nazi Germany per se. The latter received a great deal of attention in the media, out of all proportion to their actual numbers. Their portrayal as a continuous and increasing flow of immigrants gave important ammunition to restrictionists who saw Jews (and communists) as 'alien' to the established cultural boundaries of the nation and undesirable as prospective citizens and even a danger to national unity. Although the measures enacted affected a much broader constituency, the arrival of the refugees from Germany was an important, albeit symbolic, catalyst in the final push for restrictive alien legislation in the later 1930s.

In those years there was also a convergence across Western Europe in both policy and treatment towards those regarded as refugees. A striking example is the way that Belgian and French refugee policies – which had operated on completely different lines in the summer of 1933 – had become so similar by the beginning of 1934. Although no Western European country had a legal provision for these fugitives, there was hardly any thought given to a blanket exclusion. Switzerland did have an administrative provision for refugees, and she was quickly followed by the other liberal states of Western Europe. Traditions of nineteenth-century liberalism were thus strong enough to force all liberal states to open their borders for refugees. The protection of refugees was a principle that liberal states upheld, it was an essential element of the national self-image and sections of public opinion could be mobilised for its defence. The creation of the 'refugee' as an administrative category within immigration policy was also the result of refugee resistance to being treated as normal immigrants. Refugees were increasingly dissociated from other forms of immigration and more benevolently treated. Only a geographically isolated Great Britain was to a large extent able to withstand this pressure for change. The British authorities accepted refugees, but they remained in a position to control who was admitted and under what circumstances. This was a luxury denied to their continental counterparts who, as frontline states, had to come to terms with large numbers of uninvited refugees.

Crucial in immigration policy was who the authorities defined as refugees. By 1935, political and 'Jewish' refugees were treated differently in most countries. Political refugees were given certain privileges such as longer-term residence status and even permission to work, whereas 'Jews' were given some form of temporary protection at most. This can be explained in part by the fact that political fugitives corresponded more closely to the traditional image of a refugee; of people who, because of their political ideas and deeds, had suddenly to flee their country to save their life or freedom. Such political refugees had not planned their flight and their departure was often in defiance of the authorities in their homeland. By force of circumstance they arrived suddenly and empty-handed in a neighbouring country. Such (political) refugees also benefited from support given to them inside countries of refuge by left-wing political parties. This led to a type of informal refugee status being afforded in most liberal states in Continental Europe and a more formal refugee status in Switzerland. Western European states continued to give asylum to political refugees even when they ignored restrictions placed on their working or engaging in political activities, but increasingly relied on prisons and internment camps as a deterrent. In comparative terms the Netherlands was definitely the least generous towards political refugees: its leniency towards them often only amounted to a choice of frontier over which to be expelled.

Conversely in both Belgium and France, the entry of socialists into government in the mid 1930s gave the impetus for some improved facilities for refugees. In France, concessions were limited to an amnesty for all refugees from Nazi Germany present in France in 1936, but the French Popular Front government refused to formalise refugee policy for new arrivals. Belgium on the other hand joined Switzerland by drawing a clear dividing line between refugees and immigrants in immigration policy. Refugees became legally entitled to claim asylum. Elsewhere there was an unwillingness to grant a specific legal status to those fleeing persecution and policy remained informal and discretionary.

Little changed before 1938 and only political activists whose lives or freedom were endangered were eligible for asylum. This was the case in Belgium and Switzerland, with a formal refugee policy, and in Denmark and France, which retained an informal refugee regime. These policies had few, if any, effects on those fleeing Germany's racial antisemitism. The 'Jewish' refugees' reasons for flight were not considered sufficient in themselves to accord them a privileged status as 'refugees'. Although 'Jews' fleeing Nazi Germany are nowadays often portrayed as refugees par excellence, before 1938 'Jews' were less visibly the victims of state persecution than political activists, and this helps to explain the less 'generous' response.

In 1933 it was possible for 'Jews' to arrive from Germany and be treated as regular immigrants, provided they could show sufficient means to establish themselves. However, increasing German restrictions on the export of goods and currency made this more difficult, and the increased imposition of work- and business-permit legislation meant that only very few 'Jewish' refugees were able to enter Western European states on this basis. For the vast majority, the only option was to arrive in a chosen country of refuge, and then look for support from the indigenous Jewish communities or their refugee committees. These committees effectively decided who were temporarily protected by granting financial aid. In this manner the authorities were able to fulfil their humanitarian 'obligations', without incurring any financial costs or adding any foreign workers to their labour market. The fact that the Jewish organisations provided a possible solution by arranging facilities for their re-emigration made further concessions unnecessary.

The political costs of a humanitarian policy towards ('Jewish') refugees should not be underestimated. Although the authorities made no binding commitments and left a great deal of discretion to its administrators, 'Jewish' immigration from Nazi Germany was largely uncontrolled. Aliens who had arrived illegally or overstayed their permits were not subject to expulsion if the Jewish refugee aid committees supported them. These committees therefore carried a heavy burden, as they were effectively sub-contracted by the state to make decisions and then supported those chosen on a temporary basis while at the same time expediting their re-emigration without incurring any costs for the host country. For potential refugees, the existence of even temporary protection could be a pull factor. Although the design of this informal refugee policy enabled the authorities to reaffirm immigration control at any time, it could also convey an impression of loss of control over the country's frontiers and this was often used against governments by political groups seeking to exploit anti-immigrant sentiment within the population.

The differential treatment of 'Jewish' and political refugees was undermined by the radicalisation of Nazi antisemitic policy in the aftermath of the Anschluss. At this point, all countries had to confront the reality of large numbers of 'Jews' arriving at the border or inside the country with genuine evidence that their lives might be in danger if they returned to Germany. Yet in spite of the overwhelming weight of evidence, refugee policy remained largely unaltered and by the summer of 1938, 'Jewish' refugees were even encountering outright hostility; from consular authorities, at the border and even inside the countries of refuge themselves. Most liberal states of Continental Europe started to deport refugees from within the country, which was the most conspicuous departure from previous policies. That refugees who had succeeded in entering the territory of a liberal state and were recommended by the local refugee committee for protection were removed by force amounted to a challenge to the moral codes of behaviour of these liberal states. France did not follow this trend, even though the French authorities only partly legalised the residence of refugees. France seldom physically deported people, but the reception was no more welcoming than elsewhere, as in France internment was used as a deterrent.

The reasons for this rupture in refugee policy were common to all countries. Most importantly 'Jewish' flight after the *Anschluss* (with the obvious connivance of German authorities) was raging out of control. The arrival of ever more refugees, stripped of their possessions, convinced the authorities that they should halt further 'Jewish' immigration, notwithstanding the guarantee of the Jewish committees. This restrictive attitude within Continental Europe has to be seen within its international context as it became increasingly difficult for those 'Jewish' refugees who had been granted provisional asylum in the liberal states in Continental Europe to find any country willing to take them as immigrants. While numerous states paid lip service to the idea of international negotiation to provide a solution to the problem of refugees from Germany and elsewhere, the lack of positive action from the Evian Conference in the summer of 1938 demonstrated a complete lack of collective political will. Thus the whole issue remained primarily a domestic one, tempered only by its effects on relations with Germany on the one hand, and relations with neighbouring states on the other. Each European government had to consider the other states' policy and each of them was afraid to become the magnet, implying that the policy of the most restrictive state set the tone. The fear of being out of step or too generous triggered pre-emptive actions and produced an upward spiral of restriction.

The illiberal policy of denying 'Jewish' refugees any protection was initially legitimised by the German policy of dumping. The liberal values which had guided refugee policy until then were exchanged for decisiveness in face of this violation of international law. However this resolve was only the trigger for a full-blown attack on the temporary protection of 'Jewish' refugees. The Dutch authorities even blatantly called (non-political) refugees 'unwanted', but it seems that the Netherlands was quickly surpassed by the other Continental European countries who eliminated most humanitarian considerations in daily migration management practice.

The increasing difficulty of denying that 'Jews' fleeing Germany were refugees meant that the authorities of the liberal countries bordering Nazi Germany preferred to stem the flow by border and remote controls: external controls that were largely invisible to the public and could be organised through administrative dictat and without scrutiny. Border control was strengthened, but it remained dependent on diplomatic considerations. Shortly after the *Anschluss*, several countries executed a straightforward bureaucratic border policy whereby insufficiently documented aliens, i.e., 'Jewish' refugees without visas, were collectively refused admission to the country. Other frontline states were not eager, for the sake of a more effective external control, to jeopardise their relations with Germany, and developed a more personalised system of border control to keep 'Jewish' refugees out. Both groups of countries had problems in making such a policy work and differentiating between the unwanted refugees and the mass of travellers. The introduction of the 'J'-stamp on German passports solved that problem and homogenised, to a large extent, the manner in which 'Jewish' refugees were routinely refused admission, not only at the borders of the liberal states of Western Europe, but also at the desks in their consulates.

Greater efficiency at the border was not the sole purpose of newly developed migration-control strategies in the course of 1938. Notwithstanding strengthened and more efficient control, the border remained permeable. To counter this defect, states increasingly focused on developing preventive measures outside their national frontiers. This strategy of remote control by liberal states aimed to control the movement of refugees before they arrived at their borders. The introduction of the 'J'-stamp is a striking example of how liberal countries – in this case Switzerland (and Sweden) – were manoeuvring to partly subcontract their selective immigration policy to Germany. In trying to reaffirm controls over immigration, liberal countries did not eschew even greater complicity with the Nazis. The most conspicuous example is that by insisting on German cooperation at the border, Swiss and Belgian authorities gave the impetus to the radical shift in German emigration policy in the autumn of 1938 that saw the complete cessation of their dumping policy on their Western borders.

This brutal immigration policy, including the deportation of refugees, was enacted through instructions issued to government agencies, local border officials and civil servants, rather than through new legislation that would have to be discussed, justified and formally promulgated. In this way, the executive authorities preserved their complete control of migration management; a control they did not want to relinquish as they strove to keep their actions away from any public scrutiny. However, when challenged, they were quite prepared to legitimise their stance by denying that the 'Jews' fleeing Germany were refugees. The seemingly persuasive argument was that these 'Jews' left Germany with the agreement of the German authorities, while (political) refugees had to flee surreptitiously. The liberal states of Western Europe, including the Netherlands, promoted the protection of the political adversaries of the Nazi regime, including the communists, to a fundamental principle in liberal migration management. This mantra gave persecuted political activists an entitlement to asylum and was the counterweight to the attack on temporary protection for Jewish refugees. By 1938 the rigid hierarchy of Nazi persecution employed by Western European refugee policy in 1933 was used to deny 'Jews' fleeing Germany any protection.

The violence of the *Reichskristallnacht* made it obvious that the Nazi state was at least complicit in the persecution of Jews. Switzerland, Luxemburg and Denmark, (although the latter was hardly exposed to migratory pressures) persisted in routine exclusionary practices at the border, but also in the countries themselves. Most people in need of protection remained excluded. In contrast, Belgium and the Netherlands softened the application of regulations which had dehumanised their immigration policies. In November 1938 the Netherlands reaffirmed its solidarity with the 'Jewish' victims of Nazi persecution, but only a month later the Dutch authorities considered that the sheer numbers admitted could no longer be sustained. Although the Dutch had followed the French example by confining refugees in camps, this was not considered a sufficient deterrent. Deportation of 'Jewish' refugees became again official Dutch policy, although this policy was full of ambiguity. During 1939 the Netherlands equivocated between a policy of forcible deportation and legalisation. Belgium, which in November 1938 resumed the policy of protecting 'Jewish' refugees by subcontracting large elements of internal immigration control to the aid committees, did not stop this until the outbreak of the Second World War. This consistency was the result of an assertive humanitarian lobby, expressing itself most virulently at the moment of the *Reichskristallnacht* and galvanised by a Minister in charge of immigration policy who had provocatively defended his inhumane 'realpolitik'. This coincidence of factors meant that internal migration control moved out of the closed forums of Belgian policy making and into the public arena. This outspoken politicisation of immigration policy meant that the influx of refugees could not be downgraded to a technical matter of migration control and the political elite had to take a watchful public into account.

Notwithstanding the existence of an institutionalised refugee policy, even in Belgium the relative merits of the politically and racially persecuted were still evaluated differently: while political refugees were granted a right of abode, 'Jewish' refugees were denied refugee status. 'Jews' from Germany remained 'only' temporarily protected as part of an informal refugee policy. Administrative discretion was preserved and the concessions to ('Jewish') refugees could be withdrawn. Concomitant with this dual refugee policy, the Belgian authorities also pressurised the German authorities to regulate cross-border traffic in line with existing agreements. These diplomatic initiatives underline the Janus-faced attitude of the Belgian authorities towards those fleeing Nazi Germany. Publicly all refugees were granted asylum, but 'Jewish' refugees received a lesser asylum and at the same time the Belgian authorities secretly tried to convince the Germans to keep their 'Jewish' persecutees 'at home'. The latter strategy of pressurising the German authorities to stop unauthorised immigration into their territory could also be seen in Switzerland, but was totally absent in Denmark and the Netherlands, countries which refrained from anything that could annoy their powerful neighbour.

The continental European liberal states had to deal with refugees who simply appeared inside their frontiers, but in contrast, Britain could develop a refugee policy without a similar pressing need to respond to the asylum claims of uninvited guests. After *Reichskristallnacht*, the British authorities made a conscious decision to offer asylum to people in danger in Germany and their intervention in offering a solution to a considerable number of victims was a clear departure from past policies. It remained an informal refugee policy financed by charitable sources, but private sponsors obtained considerably more leeway. Britain, as not being a country of first asylum and moreover protected by the North Sea, retained the ability to impose a pre-selection of the refugees she admitted. Still, it seems that those few who managed to arrive in the country illegally were treated in a humane manner, as there is no evidence of any direct repatriation to Nazi Germany. Outside Europe, no country developed a similar proactive refugee policy, on the contrary national protectionism held sway and refugees from Nazi Germany were usually the least welcome immigrants. Re-emigration from the first countries of asylum stalled, posing a problem for Britain and even more so for the frontline states which were left with an increasing number of uninvited and destitute refugees from Germany.

Explaining Different Refugee and Immigration Policies

In making direct comparisons between these Western European states, it is apparent that their national policies towards aliens in general and refugees in particular differed in 1933 and remained at variance throughout the 1930s. The evolution of policy in the liberal states of Western Europe was dependent on a myriad of factors. The historical legacy is clearly the most obvious element, involving as it does increasing state intervention in matters of immigration. The administrative structures of the state also had a direct influence on the development and execution of immigration policy and on the stances taken on the question of refugees in all countries. There were several other factors which had a direct, and perhaps a crucial, influence on the development and execution of immigration policy and on the stances taken on the question of refugees in all countries. The first was the role of the civil service in general and key individuals in particular. To some extent, the arrival of refugees from Germany after 1933 prompted fears in bureaucratic circles about the perceived lack of control over immigration. This can be seen against the background of growing concern during the interwar period about the general efficiency of government and its various agencies. All of this led to a continuing pressure for rules and regulations to be tightened in order to provide the civil servants with the necessary tools to carry out their tasks efficiently. Alongside this, it is essential to consider the role of key individuals in all countries whose specific position gave them a pivotal role in determining how individual states responded to the refugees and to immigration generally. It could be argued that men such as Robert de Foy, Heinrich Rothmund and Eigil Thune Jacobsen were all part of a new technocratic breed, basing their thinking on the precepts suggested above. However fears about the (Jewish and communist) refugees can clearly be seen in their writings of de Foy and Rothmund, suggesting that they also espoused deeply conservative opinions that were brought to bear on their work. Irrespective of this, their central role in the administration of border control, policing and the execution of admissions policy gave them enormous power in being able to instruct their subordinates on the one hand and to influence cabinet ministers through the provision of information and advice on the other. The role of key individuals and the administration thus has to be evaluated by positioning them within the power structures of both state and society. The Belgian case documents the importance of retaining a broad picture of decision making on this issue. Here, refugee policy became an issue of public importance in the autumn of 1938 and from then onwards, the responsible government Ministers were afraid of a negative political backlash if more selective refugee policies were introduced. Thus Robert de Foy in Belgium had to bow to political opposition, while his Swiss counterpart, Heinrich Rothmund, did not. Likewise in Luxemburg and Denmark, immigration policy remained largely isolated from public scrutiny and refugee policy largely evaporated in a process of tightened immigration policy.

It is important to underline the different ways in which policy was carried out. At one level, it is clear that legislation against aliens was not always fully implemented, or that there was a tacit understanding that some of its provisions would not be employed. Thus, there might be implicit toleration of people who, under a strict interpretation of the law, should have been expelled. At another level, it is also clear that the structures and systems in all countries provided a degree of autonomy, both for civil servants and the judiciary, and also for local officials. Centralisation appears to have been greatest in Belgium and Luxembourg. In Denmark and the Netherlands, policy implementation was far more decentralised and allowed greater scope for the autonomy of regional or local officials, while during the 1930s Switzerland shifted further towards the Belgian model, with questions of residence being added to border control and admissions policies that were already the responsibility of the federal government. These administrative structures undoubtedly served to influence policy making in a number of ways. For example, civil servants' autonomy to act independently of political influences or public opinion may have served either to strengthen the enforcement of regulations, or equally to have provided some amelioration of these same regulations. These freedoms, which undoubtedly varied from one country to another and also over time, may help to explain why it is so difficult to ascertain exactly how alien and immigration policies were implemented at the border or by the police and bureaucrats inside the country.

Last, but not least, we should also mention the refugees themselves. The refugees were not merely passive victims, but also agents of their own destiny, and their collective actions also influenced the aliens policy of the liberal states. The responses were highly interactive, as the closing of one border deflected refugees towards other borders. Empirical indications point that out. For example it is at the time when Switzerland closed its borders to Austrian Jews that emigration to the Benelux soared. This interactivity among asylum applicants of various countries is still a largely neglected subject. Further research needs to refine the correlation between the direction of flight, German emigration policy and West European immigration policies. To have a clear picture of this, it is essential to see how individual decisions coupled with the agency of the various indigenous and international refugee aid groups framed the ways in which Western European states tackled this most intractable of problem of the 1930s.

The open-ended situation at the outbreak of the Second World War is testimony of the quandary in which the policy makers in Western Europe found themselves. They were fully aware of Nazi persecution taking place within Germany and therefore carry some responsibility for the failures in maintaining their supposedly liberal values. However this responsibility is a shared one. When the situation in Germany became more and more acute, policy makers in countries outside Europe also tightened their immigration policy and refused to relieve the frontline states of their burden. Although increasing restrictions was always an attractive option, especially when the Nazis systematically stripped the refugees of all their possessions, the very different choices made in the various (frontline) states demonstrates that the outcome was by no means preordained. Respect for human rights remained a value that could be mobilised in political struggles, within the political elite and within society at large.

The sovereign right of the state to refuse an individual entry to its territory, even if he or she was identified as a refugee, was seldom ever contested. Once refugees crossed the frontier they were no longer merely emigrants, but became asylum applicants to whom national norms could be applied. This normative dimension in immigration policy was only partly the result of internationally agreed norms. The international refugee regime was accepted only by some of the liberal states, and in any case imposed few obligations on the immigration policies. Likewise national refugee regimes failed to enforce a humanitarian policy towards the mass of refugees. Even the agencies in Belgium and Switzerland in charge of immigration policy argued that the protection afforded to the (political) refugees was not applicable to the mass of 'Jewish' refugees. Yet even when Western European states resorted to the deportation of 'Jewish' refugees, they still had to legitimise this to liberal public opinion and the various aid and charitable organisations involved. Knowledge of such deportations often sparked off protests and their strength served to some extent to determine subsequent refugee policy. The liberal values, of which granting asylum to refugees was an intrinsic part, were only mobilised against a state when it used its coercive powers inside its own borders, but there was little or no protest against inhumane measures carried out in the form of external controls. The relevant authorities realised this all too well and therefore maintained their preference for external control exercised well away from domestic public scrutiny.

The liberal frontline states seem to have been successful in keeping out refugees only with the most draconian of policies against aliens. Thus only when forced repatriation was used to return those who had managed to enter illegally via the green frontiers was the migration pressure relieved. Even then, the real effectiveness of these policies remains open to question, but it did relieve the authorities of any responsibility for differentiating the refugees from the rest among these uninvited guests. By including refugees in the category of undocumented aliens who could be automatically deported, immigration procedures became more efficient, but this inevitably made it more difficult for the Western European states to keep up the appearance of being liberal regimes in every sense of the word.

Appendix

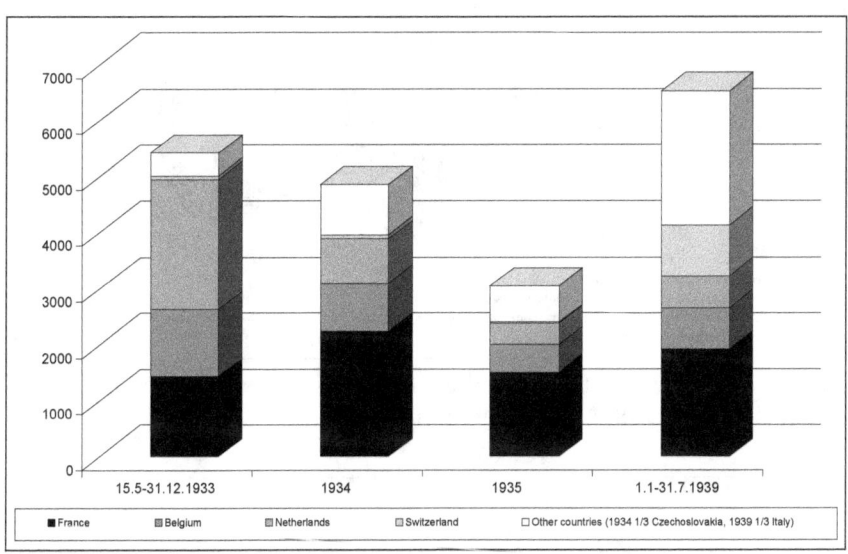

Figure 2. West European Countries from which HICEM Organized Emigration of German-Jewish Refugees, 1933–1935, 1939

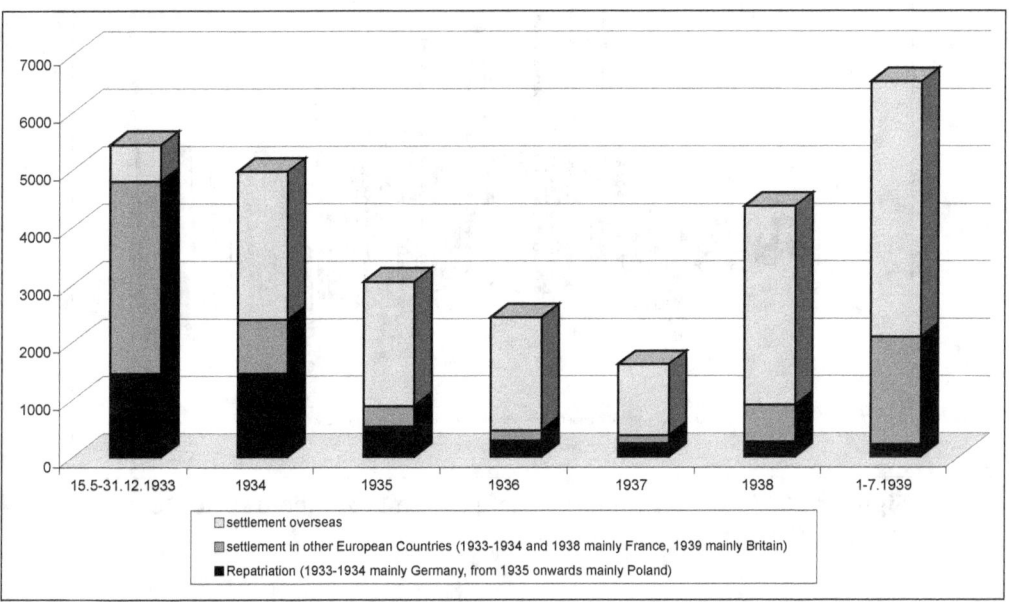

Figure 3. Destination of the HICEM-organized Emigration and Repatriation of German-Jewish Refugees from West European Countries, 1933–7.1939

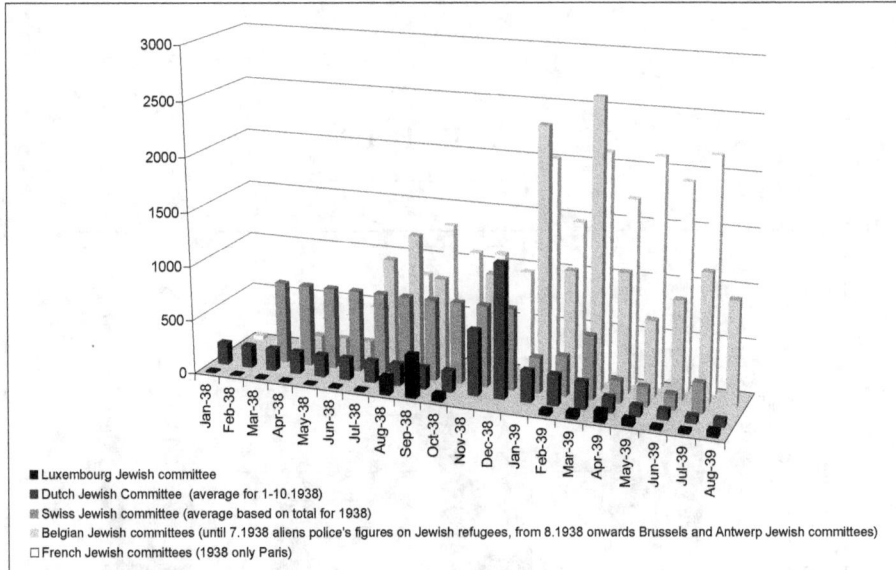

Figure 4. Newly registered (Jewish) Refugees by Jewish Refugee Organisations, 1938–8.1939 (by month)

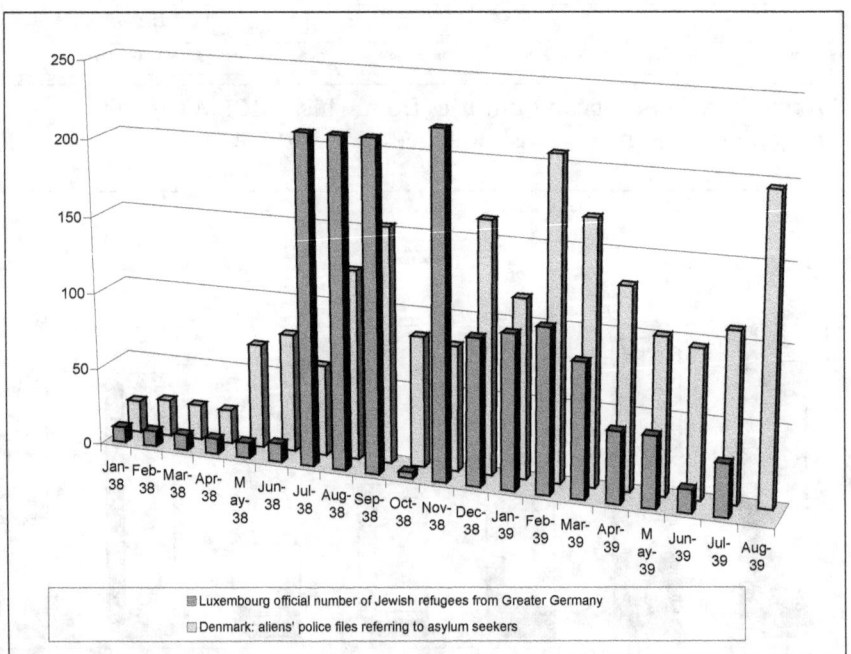

Figure 5. Official Registration of Refugees in Luxembourg and Denmark 1938–9.1939 (by month)

Notes on Contributors

Frank Caestecker, PhD (1994) European University Institute. Senior researcher at University of Ghent, Department of Modern and Contemporary History. Former eligibility officer UNHCR and asylum agency in Belgium. Main publications: *Vluchtelingenbeleid in de Naoorlogse periode (*Brussels: VUBPress, 1991); *Ongewenste Gasten. Joodse Vluchtelingen en Migranten in de Dertiger Jaren in België* (Brussels: VUBPress, 1993). *Alien Policy in Belgium, 1840–1940: The Creation of Guest Workers, Refugees and Illegal Aliens* (Oxford: Berghahn, 2000).

Vicki Caron, PhD (1983) Columbia University. Thomas and Diann Mann Professor of Modern Jewish Studies, History Department and Jewish Studies Program, Cornell University. Main publications: *Uneasy Asylum: France and the Jewish Refugee Crisis, 1933–1942* (Stanford: Stanford University Press, 1999, 2001); *Between France and Germany: The Jews of Alsace-Lorraine, 1871–1918* (Stanford: Stanford University Press, l988); *Jewish Emancipation Reconsidered: The French and German Models*, co-edited with Michael Brenner and Uri R. Kaufmann (Tübingen: Mohr Siebeck, 2003).

Claudia Curio, PhD (2005) Technical University Berlin. Research associate at the Zentrum für Antisemitismusforschung, Technische Universität Berlin. Main publications: *Verfolgung, Flucht, Rettung. Die Kindertransporte nach Großbritannien 1938/39* (Berlin: Metropol, 2006); *Die Kindertransporte 1938–1939 nach Großbritannien. Rettung und Integration* (co-edited with Wolfgang Benz and Andrea Hammel) (Frankfurt am Main: Fischer Taschenbuch, 2003).

Aviva Halamish, PhD (1996) Tel Aviv University. Professor of History at The Open University of Israel. Main publications: *The Exodus Affair: Holocaust Survivors and the Struggle for Palestine* (London: Syracuse University Press and Vallentine Mitchell, 1998); 'Refugees', entry to the *Holocaust Encyclopedia* (Walter Laqueur, General Editor), Yale University Press, 2000, pp. 519–24; *A Dual Race Against Time: Zionist Immigration Policy in the 1930s* (Jeruzalem: Yad Ben-Zvi Press, 2006) [Hebrew].

Susanne Heim, PhD Habilitation in political science (2002), Free University Berlin. Charles Revson Fellow at the United States Holocaust Memorial Museum in Washington (2003). Project coordinator at the editorial project: 'The Persecution and Extermination of the European Jews by Nazi Germany 1933–1945'. Main publications: *Kalorien, Kautschuk, Karrieren. Pflanzenzüchtung und landwirtschaftliche Forschung in Kaiser-Wilhelm-Instituten 1933–1945*, (Göttingen: Wallstein, 2003); with Götz Aly, *Architects of Annihilation. Auschwitz and the Logic of Destruction* (London: Weidenfeld and Nicolson, 2003 (German edition: Hamburg, 1991); with Ulrike Schaz, *Berechnung und Beschwörung. Überbevölkerung - Kritik einer Debatte* (Berlin/Göttingen: Schwarze Risse, 1996).

Steve Hochstadt, PhD (1983) Brown University, Dept. of History. Professor of History, Illinois College. Main publications: *Mobility and Modernity: Migration in Germany 1820–1989* (Ann Arbor: University of Michigan Press, 1999); *Sources of the Holocaust* (Houndmills, UK, and New York: Palgrave Macmillan, 2004); *Shanghai-Geschichten: Die juedische Flucht nach China* (Berlin: Hentrich und Hentrich, 2007).

Regula Ludi, PhD (1997) Karman Center for Advanced Studies in the Humanities, University of Bern. Researcher for the Independent Commission of Experts Switzerland – Second World War (1997–2000) and co-author of the reports on Swiss refugee policy (1999) and Swiss policy towards Roma and Sinti (2000). She held fellowships at Harvard University, UCLA and the Holocaust Memorial Museum, Washington DC. Her current project is on the history of reparations for Nazi victims in France, Germany and Switzerland (1945–1965). Main publications: *Die Fabrikation des Verbrechens. Zur Geschichte der modernen Kriminalpolitik 1750–1850* (Tübingen: Tübingen Academica, 1999); 'Post-War Reparations for Nazi Victims: Priorities, Omissions, and Memory Politics', *Journal of Contemporary History* 41, no. 3 (July 2006), pp.421–50.

Bob Moore, PhD (1983) University of Manchester. Professor of Twentieth Century European History at the University of Sheffield. He has published extensively on the history of the Netherlands and on the Second World War, including *Refugees from Nazi Germany in the Netherlands, 1933–40* (Dordrecht, Boston and Lancaster: Nijhoff, 1986) and *Victims and Survivors: the Nazi Persecution of the Jews in the Netherlands 1940–1945* (London: Arnold, 1997). More recently he co-wrote *The British Empire and its Italian Prisoners of War* with Kent Fedorowich (Basingstoke: Palgrave, 2003), and has edited *Resistance in Western Europe* (Oxford: Berg, 2000) and with Barbara Hately-Broad *Prisoners of War, Prisoners of Peace* (Oxford: Berg, 2005).

Lone Rünitz, MA (1995) University of Copenhagen. Researcher at the Danish Institute for International Studies, the Department for Holocaust and Genocide Studies, with a project on Danish refugee policy 1933–1945. Main publications: *Danmark og de jødiske flygtninge 1933–1940* [Denmark and the Jewish refugees 1933–1940] (Copenhagen: Museum

Tusculanum Press, 2000) and *Af hensyn til konsekvenserne – Danmark and flygtningespørgsmålet 1933–1940* [Considering the consequences – Denmark and the refugee question 1933–1940] (Odense: Syddansk Universitetsforlag, 2005).

Patrik von zur Mühlen, PhD (1971) studies of history, political science and philosophy University/Institute Berlin and Bonn. Member of the Historical Department of the Friedrich Ebert Stiftung, Bonn since 1975, editor-in-chief of Archiv für Sozialgeschichte, 2001–2003. Main publications: *Fluchtweg Spanien-Portugal. Die deutsche Emigration und der Exodus aus Europa 1933–1945* (Bonn: Dietz, 1992); *Fluchtziel Lateinamerika. Die deutsche Emigration 1933–1945: politische Aktivitäten und soziokulturelle Integration* (Bonn: Neue Gesellschaft, 1988); books and essays on German Emigration 1933–1945, Spanish Civil War, Baltic countries and East German history (DDR).

Bat-Ami Zucker, PhD (1981) University of Bar-Ilan. Professor emeritus of American History at the University of Bar-Ilan where she specialised in American legal history. Main publications: she has published on the history of the United States and in particular on immigration and refugee policy, including *In Search of Refuge: Jews and U.S. Consuls in Nazi Germany 1933–1941* (Portland: Vallentine Mitchell, 2001).

Select Bibliography

Afoumado, Diane. (2005). *L'exil impossible. L'errance des Juifs du paquebot St Louis.* Paris: L'Harmattan.
Arntz, H. Dieter. (1990). *Judenverfolgung und Fluchthilfe in deutsch-belgischen Grenzgebiet.* Euskirchen: Kümpel.
Badia, Gilbert et al. (ed.). (1984). *Les Bannis de Hitler.* Paris: Editions sociales.
Battel, Franco. (2000). *'Wo es hell ist, dort is die Schweiz' Flüchtlinge und Fluchthilfe an der Schaffhauser Grenze zur Zeit des Nationalsozialismus.* Zürich: Chronos.
Bauer, Yehuda. (1974). *My Brother's Keeper: A History of the American Jewish Joint Distribution Committee, 1929–1939.* Philadelphia: Jewish Publication Society.
———. (1995). *Jews for Sale? Nazi-Jewish Negotiations, 1933–1945.* New Haven: Yale University Press.
Ben Elissar, Eliahu. (1969). *Le facteur juif dans la politique étrangère du IIIe Reich (1933–1939).* Paris: Julliard.
Berghuis, Corrie K. (1990). *Joodse vluchtelingen in Nederland 1938–1940.* Kampen: Kok.
Berghahn, Marion. (2006). *Continental Britons: German-Jewish Refugees from Nazi Germany.* Oxford: Berghahn.
Berschel, Holger. (2001). *Bürokratie und Terror. Das Judenreferat der Gestapo Düsseldorf, 1935–1945.* Essen: Klartext.
Breitman, Richard and Alan Kraut. (1987). *American Refugee Policy and European Jewry, 1933–1945.* Bloomington: Indiana University Press.
Büttner, Ursula, Werner Johe, Angelika Voss (ed.). (1986). *Das Unrechtsregime: Internationale Forschung über den Nationalsozialismus.* Hamburg: Christians.
Caestecker, Frank. (1993). *Ongewenste gasten, joodse vluchtelingen en migranten in de dertiger jaren.* Brussels: VUBpress.
———. (2000). *Alien Policy in Belgium, 1840–1940. The Creation of Guest Workers, Refugees and Illegal Aliens.* Oxford: Berghahn.
———. (2004). 'Onverbiddelijk, maar ook clement. Het Belgische immigratiebeleid en de joodse vlucht uit nazi-Duitsland, maart 1938–augustus 1939', *Bijdragen tot de eigentijdse geschiedenis*, 13/14, pp.99–139.
Caron, Vicki. (1991). 'Loyalties in Conflict: French Jewry and the Refugee Crisis, 1933–1935', *Leo Baeck Institute Yearbook*, 36, pp.305–38.
———. (1993). 'The Politics of Frustration: French Jewry and the Refugee Crisis in the 1930s', *Journal of Modern History*, 65, pp.311–56.
———. (1999). *Uneasy Asylum: France and the Jewish Refugee Crisis, 1933–1942.* Stanford: Stanford University Press.

Curio, Claudia. (2006). *Verfolgung, Flucht, Rettung. Die Kindertransporte nach Großbritannien 1938–39.* Berlin: Metropol.
De Cort, Bart. (2004). *Solidariteit in anonimiteit. De geschiedenis van de leden van de Onafhankelijke Socialistische Partij.* Breda: Papieren Tijger.
Dean, Martin. (2002). 'The Development and Implementation of Nazi Denaturalization and Confiscation Policy up to the Eleventh Decree to the Reich Citizenship Law', *Holocaust and Genocide Studies*, 16, no. 2, pp.217–42.
Deschodt, Jean-Pierre and François Huguenin. (2001). *La république xénophobe, 1917–1939.* Paris: JC Lattès.
Dinesen, Ruth, Birgit S. Nielsen, Hans Uwe Petersen, Friederich Schmoë (ed.). (1986). *Deutschsprachiges Exil in Dänemaken nach 1933. Zu Methoden und Einzelergebenissen.* Copenhagen: Wilhelm Fink.
Lorenz, Einhart. (1992). *Exil in Norwegen. Lebensbedingungen und Arbeit deutschsprachiger Flüchtlinge 1933–1943.* Baden-Baden: Nomos.
Einhart, Lorenz, Klaus Misgeld, Helmut Müssener and Hans Uwe Petersen (ed.). (1989). *'Ein sehr trübes Kapital'? Hitlerflüchtlinge im nordeuropäischen Exil 1933–1950.* Hamburg: Ergebnisse.
Fabian, Ruth and Corinne Coulmas. (1978). *Die deutsche Emigration in Frankreich nach 1933.* New York: Saur K.G.
Feingold, Henry L. (1970). *The Politics of Rescue: The Roosevelt Administration and the Holocaust, 1938–1945.* New Brunswick: Rutgers University Press.
Fischer, Nicolas. (2004). 'Les expulsés inexpulsables. Recomposition du contrôle des étrangers dans la France des années 1930', *Cultures et conflits*, 53, no. 1, pp.25–41.
Franke, Julia. (2000). *Paris- eine neue Heimat. Jüdische Emigranten aus Deutschland, 1933–1939.* Berlin: Dunck and Humblot.
Friedländer, S. (1998). *Nazi Germany and the Jews. I: The years of persecution, 1933–1939.* London: Weidenfeld and Nicolson.
Gerhard, Paul. (1997). *'Flensburg meldet.' Flensburg und das deutsch-dänische Grenzgebiet im Dritten Reich im Spiegel der Berichterstattung der Gestapo und das Sicherheitsdienstes (SD) der SS.* Flensburg: Gesellschaft für Flensburger Stadtgeschichte.
Gerrits, André. (1985). '"Solidariteit zonder eenheidsfront". De Internationale Rode Hulp in Nederland, 1925–1938', *Cahiers over de geschiedenis van de CPN*, 10, pp.55–80.
Gordon, Daniel A. (2004). 'The Back Door of the Nation State: Expulsions of Foreigners and Continuity in Twentieth-Century France', *Past and Present*, 186, no. 1, pp.201–32.
Gottlieb, Amy Zahl. (1998). *Men of Vision: Anglo-Jewry's Aid to Victims of the Nazi Regime, 1933–1945.* London: Weidenfeld and Nicolson.
Grossmann, Kurt R. (1969). *Emigration. Geschichte der Hitler-Flüchtlinge 1933–1945.* Frankfurt: Europäische Verlagsanstalt.
Gousseff, C. (2008). *L'exil russe 1920–1939. La fabrique du réfugié apatride.* Paris: CNRS.
Gruner, Wolf. (1997). *Der Geschlossene Arbeidsinsatz deutscher Juden. Zur Zwangsarbeit als Element der Verfolgung 1938–1943.* Berlin: Metropol.
———. (2004). *Zwangsarbeit und Verfolgung. Osterreichische Juden im NS-Staat 1938–45.* Innsbruck: Studien.
Halamish, Aviva. (2006). *A Dual Race Against Time: Zionist Immigration Policy in the 1930s* (in Hebrew). Jeruzalem: Yad Ben-Zvi Press.

Heim, Susanne. (1999). 'Vertreibung, Raub und Umverteilung. Die jüdischen Flüchtline aus Deutschland und die Vermehrung des "Volksvermögens"', in *Flüchtlingspolitik und Fluchthilfe* (Beiträge zur Nationalsozialistischen Gesundheids und Sozialpolitik 15, pp.107–138). Berlin: Schwarze Risse.

Heim, Susanne and Götz Aly. (1993). 'Staatliche Ordnung und "Organische Lösung". Die Rede Hermann Görings "über die Judenfrage" vom 6. Dezember 1938', *Jahrbuch für Antisemitismusforschung*, 2, pp.378–404.

Hepp, Michael. (1985–88). *Die Ausbürgerung deutscher Staatsangehöriger 1933–45 nach den im Reichsanzeiger veröffentlichten Listen*. Munich: K.G.Saur.

Herlemann, Beatrix. (1982). *Die Anleitung des Widerstands des KPD durch die Exilierte Parteiführung in Frankreich, die Niederlanden und Belgien*. Königstein im Taunus: Hain.

Heumos, Peter. (1989). *Die Emigration aus der Tschechoslowakei nach Westeuropa und dem Nahen Osten 1938–1945*. Munich: R. Oldenbourg.

Hirschfeld, Gerhard (ed.). (1984). *Exile in Great Britain: Refugees from Hitler's Germany*. Leamington Spa: Berg.

Hochstadt, Steve. (2007). *Shanghai-Geschichten: Die jüdische Flucht nach China*. Berlin: Hentrich und Hentrich.

Jud, Ursina. (2005). *Liechtenstein und die Flüchtlinge zur Zeit des Nationalsozialismus*. Vaduz: Historischer Verein für das Fürstentum Liechtenstein.

Kapp, Yvonne and Margaret Mynatt. (1997). *British Policy and the Refugees 1933–1941*. London: Frank Cass.

Keller, Stefan. (1993). *Grüningers Fall. Geschichte von Flucht und Hilfe*. Zürich: Rotpunktverlag.

Kirschgens, Stefan. (1998). *Wege durch das Niemandsland. Dokumentation und Analyse der Hilfe für Flüchtlinge im deutsch-belgisch-niederländisch Grenzland in den Jahre 1933 bis 1945*. Cologne: Rheinland.

Krohn, Claus Dieter, Patrick von zur Mühlen, Gerhard Paul and Lutz Winckler (ed.). (1998). *Handbuch der deutschsprachigen Emigration 1933–1945*. Darmstadt: Primus.

Kulka, Otto D. and Jäckel Eberhard (ed.). (2004). *Die Juden in den geheimen NS-Stimmungsberichten 1933–1945*. Dusseldorf: Droste Verlag.

Kundrus, Brith and Meyer Beate (ed.). (2004). *Die Deportation der Juden aus Deutschland* (Beiträge zur Geschichte des nationalsozialismus, 20). Göttingen: Wallstein.

Kushner, Tony. (1994). *The Holocaust and the Liberal Imagination: A Social and Cultural History*. Oxford: Blackwell.

Langkau-Alex, Ursula. (2004). *Deutsche Volksfront, 1932–1939. Zwischen Berlin, Paris, Prag und Moskau. Vorgeschichte und Gründung der Ausschusses zur Vorbereitung einer deutscher Volksfront*. Berlin: Akademie.

Leenders, Marij. (1993). *Ongenode gasten. Het vluchtelingenbeleid in Nederland, 1815–1938*. Verloren: Rijksuniversiteit Utrecht.

Lesser, Jeffrey. (1995). *Welcoming the Undesirables: Brazil and the Jewish Question*. Berkeley: University of California Press.

Levine Paul, A. (1996). *From Indifference to Activism: Swedish Diplomacy and the Holocaust (1938–1944)*. Uppsala: Acta universitatis Upsaliensis.

Livian, Marcel. (1982). *Le parti socialiste et l'immigration*. Paris: Anthropos.

London, Louise. (1990). 'Jewish Refugees, Anglo-Jewry and British Government Policy, 1930-1940', in David Cesarani (ed.), *The Making of Anglo-Jewry* (pp.163–90). Oxford: Blackwell.

———. (2000). *Whitehall and the Jews, 1933–1948: British Immigration Policy and the Holocaust*. Cambridge: Cambridge University Press.

Ludwig, C. (1957). *Die Flüchtlingspolitik der Schweiz in den Jahre 1933 bis 1952. Bericht des Bundesrates an die Bundesversammlung*. Bern: n.p.

Michman, Dan. (1981). 'The Committee for Jewish Refugees in Holland 1933–1940', *Yad Vashem Studies*, 14, pp.205–32.

Mächler, Stefan. (2005). *Hilfe und Ohnmacht. Der Schweizerische Israelitische Gemeindebund und die nationalsozialistische Verfolgung, 1933–1945*. Zürich: Chronos.

Milgram, Avraham (ed.). (2003). *Entre la aceptacion y el rechazo. America Latina y los refugiados judios del nazismo*. Jerusalem: Yad Vashem

Moore, Bob. (1986). *Refugees from Nazi Germany in the Netherlands, 1933–1940*. Dordrecht, Boston and Lancaster: Nijhoff.

Mosse, Werner (ed.). (1991). *Second Chance: Two Centuries of German-Speaking Jews in the United Kingdom*. Tübingen: JCB Mohr.

Mühlen, Patrik von zur. (1992). *Fluchtweg Spanien-Portugal. Die deutsche Emigration und der Exodus aus Europa 1933–1945*. Bonn: Dietz.

Müssener, H. (1974). *Das Exil in Schweden. Politische und kulturelle Emigration nach 1933*. Munich: Hanser.

Niederland, Doron. (1988). 'Jewish Emigration form Germany in the First Years of Nazi Rule', *Leo Baeck Institute Yearbook*, pp.285–300.

Noiriel, Gérard. (1991). *La Tyrannie du national. Le droit d'asile en Europe 1793–1993*. Paris: Calmann-Lévy.

Petersen, Hans Uwe. (1991). *Hitlerflüchtlinge im Norden. Asyl und politischen Exil 1933–1945*. Kiel: Neuer Malik.

Rünitz, Lone. (2000). *Danmark og de jødiske flygtninge 1933–1940*. Copenhagen: Museum Tusculanum Press.

———. (2003). 'The Politics of Asylum in Denmark in the Wake of the *Kristallnacht* - A Case Study', in John Strange, Ole Farver and Ove Nathan (ed.), *Denmark and the Holocaust* (pp.14–32). Copenhagen: Institute for International Studies, Department for Holocaust and Genocide Studies.

———. (2005). *Af hensyn til konsekvenserne, Danmark og flygtningespørgsmålet 1933–1940*. Odense: Syddansk Universitetsforlag.

Senkman, Leonardo. (1989). 'Argentinien under der Holocaust. Die Einwanderungspolitik und die Frage der Flüchtlinge 1933–1945', in Achim Schrader and Karl Heinrich Rengstorf (ed.), *Europäische Juden in Lateinamerika* (pp.49–68). St Ingbert: Werner J. Röhrig.

Simpson, John. (1939). *The Refugee Problem, Report of a Survey*. London, New York and Toronto: Oxford Univeristy Press.

Sherman, A.J. (1973). *Island Refuge: Britain and Refugees from the Third Reich, 1933–1939*. Berkeley: University of California Press.

Stevens, A. (1975). *The Dispossessed: German Refugees in Britain*. London: Barrie and Jenkins.

Strauss, Herbert. (1980). 'Jewish Emigration from Germany. Nazi policies and Jewish responses', *Leo Baeck Institute Yearbook*, 25, pp.318–61 and 26, 343–409.

Strauss, Herbert and Werner Röder (ed.). (1983). *International Biographical Dictionary of Central European Emigrés 1933–1945*. Munich: KG Saur.

Studer, Brigitte. (1994). *Un parti sous influence. Le parti communiste suisse, une section du Komintern, 1931 à 1939*. Lausanne: l'Age d'Homme.

Index

administrative discretion in refugee policy, 203, 229 *see also* executive authorities, refugee definition
airline carriers, 305n35
aliens' registration, 196, 259
American Jewish Joint Distribution Committee, 22–23, 30, 64–65, 89, 106, 112, 218, 254, 278, 300
amnesty for illegal aliens, 30, 62–63, 65, 71–77, 92, 104, 228
Anschluss, 65, 106, 130
anti-Bolshevism, 9, 86, 313–14
antisemitism, 3–4, 27, 53, 55, 64–65, 88, 105, 107, 127, 173–176, 184, 315
appeasement, 18, 134, 172, 260, 293, 297
Argentina, 103, 105–106
Armenians, 20, 58, 202, 314
Aryan, 48–51, 91,947, 175, 209, 234n7, 250, 257, 259, 282
assigned residence, 66, 293–94, 301
asylum as right or favor, 39, 49, 203, 232
Australia, 43n55, 110, 169
Austria
 as a country of asylum, 23
 imposing German citizenship, 259
 Jewish persecution 90, 112, 171, 245
 seizure of Jewish property, 90
 see also Germany

Barbados, 278
Belgium
 agreement with the Netherlands on refugees, 224, 231, 229, 261, 274n67
border policy, 213, 223, 252, 307n51, 285
child refugees, 283
communist refugees, 224, 229, 282
definition of refugee, 282, 290
economic protectionism, 222
eligibility procedure, 290
expulsion of Jewish refugees, 264, 301–2
expulsion policy, 195, 223, 315
financial aspects of refugee reception, 242n107
German assistance in combating unwanted immigration, 267, 279–80
international refugee regime 22, 30–32, 36, 290
Jewish community 179, 214, 265
labour market protectionism, 200–1, 221
polity, 265–66
pressure on other asylum countries, 282, 305n34
proactive refugee policy, 282
public opinion, 180, 264–66
refugee policy, 196, 223, 229, 281, 288–91, 300–1, 316–17, 320
refugee policy and labour market protectionism, 214, 231
refugees pushed on by first countries of asylum, 256, 272n48
shoving of refugees on other countries of asylum, 213

temporary protection for Jewish refugees, 214, 233–34
travel agreement with Germany, 267, 286
visa policy, 179, 197, 212, 249
Ben-Gurion, David, 132–35
Bérenger, Henry, 22, 68
Berthoin, Jean, 67–68, 74
bilateral agreements in the field of refugee protection, 224, 229, 231, 261, 274n67
see also international agreements
Blum, Léon, 62, 65, 67, 71, 259
Blum, René, 254, 264
Bolsheviks, see communists
Bolivia, 104, 107
Bonnet, George, 65, 68, 72–74
border choice for expellees, 194, 203, 224–25, 240n73
border control, 252, 272n53, 285
   border guards, 61, 92, 256–58
   green border, 7, 258
   returning visa-holders, 61, 255
   see also recognizing 'Jews'
Brazil, 103–5, 107

Canada, 169–170
Catholic Church, 281, 296
centralized versus decentralized immigration policy, 194, 198, 272n56, 292, 314, 322,
Chamberlain, Neville, 174, 297
Chautemps, Camille, 57, 59, 64
Child refugees
   Jewish children, 69, 72, 134, 169–89, 279, 283–84, 306n46, 285, 292, 297
   Spanish Civil War refugees, 283, 30n46
Chili, 103, 105, 107
Christian refugees, 180, 285
Christians of Jewish origin, see non-aryan Christians
civil servants, 319, see also de Foy, Robert; Rothmund, Heinrich; Jacobsen, Eigil Thune; Berthoin, Jean
Comintern, 203, 260
communism and Jews, 128

communist refugees, 49, 203, 212, 219, 224–5, 229, 231, 237n37, 228–31, 260–1, 282–83, 287–88, 320
   in Soviet Union, 225, 240n81
   see also expulsion of communist refugees, KPD, individual countries
communist refugee aid committee, see Red Help
corruption, 71, 104–5, 107
Council of German Jewry, 130, 134, 174, 278, 299
criminalization of assisting undocumented immigrants, 66, 286
criminalization of illegal immigration, 34, 58, 66, 228
Croydon airport, 296, 310n98
Cuba, 300–1
currency smuggling, 24–25, 263, 288, 292
Czech Jews, 296–299
Czechia, 295
Czechoslovakia, 7, 22, 30, 246
   see also Munich agreement
competition between Jewish persecutees, 128–33, 142, 298
competition between political and racial persecutees, 52, 87, 298

Daladier, Edouard, 65, 67, 69, 73, 76, 259–60
decree laws, 58
definition of refugee, see refugee
de Foy, Robert, 181, 289, 322
democratisation 313, see also political power of labour and middle classes
Denmark
   border policy, 258–59, 271n44, 272n56, 285
   border policy and refugees, 307 n53
   child refugees, 306n46, 283
   communist refugees, 225, 241n101, 282–83
   definition of refugee, 231, 282, 291

expulsion policy, 223, 249, 291
expulsion of subversive refugees, 225
financial support for refugees' reception, 242n107
German assistance in combating unwanted immigration, 279
historiography, 4,5
immigration policy, 193, 248–250, 314
international refugee regime, 22, 30, 32
Jewish refugee aid committee, 50–51, 64, 291
labour market protectionism 23, 52–53, 199
labour market protectionism and refugees, 231
polity, 199
proactive refugee policy, 282
recognizing Jewish refugees, 254–58
refugee policy, 216, 223, 281, 317
relations with Germany, 248
repatriation of subversive refugees, 225, 291
temporary protection for Jewish refugees, 214, 234
visa policy, 197, 248–49
visa policy and refugees, 282
deportation, *see* expulsion
deserters, 198
diplomatic protest against German deportation policy, 70
diplomatic protest against shoving off refugees, 213, 224–25, 266
dispersal of refugees, 176, 260
Dominican Republic, 104, 107, 109
domino effect in refugee policy, 220, 305n35, 220
see also upward spiral of restriction
Dormoy, Marx, 64, 233
drielandenpunt, 224
due process, 232

East European immigrants/refugees, 59, 64–66, 211, 229, 241n99
see also repatriation
East European Jews residing in Germany, 211–12, 215–16
Ecuador, 104–5, 107
Eichmann, Adolf, 90, 141, 245, 276
Emerson, Sir Herbert, 47, 118
entrepreneurs *see* industrialists
Evian Conference, 19, 29, 34–39, 67–68, 90, 114, 131, 135, 173, 246, 318
executive authorities and immigration policy, 86, 197–99, 231–32, 319
expulsion and bilateral agreements, 195, 201, 221, 224
expulsion of aliens, 194
expulsion of children, 69, 180, 182
expulsion of communist refugees, 203, 223–24, 231, 240n73, 275n81
expulsion of Jewish refugees, 36, 215, 223, 242n111, 253, 256, 263–64, 296, 310–11, 318
expulsion of refugees 32
exile, 119n14
extermination of Jews, 6, 82
extradition, 5, 194, 261, 280
see also repatriation

fear of political subversion, 198
Federal Prosecutor's office, 97, 216
financing refugee aid
private fund raising, 92, 143, 219, 281, 298
public funding, 242n107
Finland, 7
first country of asylum, 32, 59, 195, 213, 229, 241n100, 257, 299, 310n98
Flandin, Pierre-Etienne 59–61, 220
foreign students, 221
fort Honswijk, 224
France
assigned residence, 293–94
asylum in prison, 58, 60, 263, 284, 293–94
attitude towards Anschluss, 259
border policy, 59, 63, 69, 92, 222, 252, 284–85
border policy and refugees, 58, 61, 257, 279, 284

child refugees, 69, 72, 232, 283, 306n46
communist refugees, 225, 229, 287–88, 293
conviction of illegal aliens, 220
definition of refugee, 233
economic protectionism, 58, 222
eligibility procedure for refugees, 58–59, 64–64, 67, 228–230, 233, 257, 259–260, 272n54, 302
expulsion of communist refugees, 224
expulsion of Jewish refugees, 60, 215, 256
expulsion policy, 292
expulsion policy of refugees, 195, 212, 215, 315
German assistance in combating illegal immigration, 279–80
historiography, 4, 242n116
illegal immigration to Palestine, 30n71
immigration policy, 196
immigration to Shanghai's international Settlement, 114, 117
international refugee regime, 22, 30, 36, 228
Jewish refugee aid committee, 64–65, 67
judiciary, 70–71, 74, 195, 263, 293
labour market protectionism, 200–1, 221
labour market protectionism and refugees, 231
political activists, 293
private interest groups, 59
proactive refugee policy, 282
pro-refugee lobby, 72–76
refugee policy, 106, 202–3, 228–232, 259, 293, 300–1, 316–17
refugees pushed out by first country of asylum, 58, 70, 92, 213, 252, 272n48
refugees shoved off to other countries of asylum, 256

resettlement of refugees, 64, 73
street level bureaucracies, 70–71
temporary protection of Jewish refugees, 215
transit refugees, 285
visa policy, 57, 59, 63, 65, 68, 197, 212
visa policy and refugees, 59, 61, 65
Fremdenpass, 210, 212, 245, 275n82
French Foreign Legion, 76, 307n48, 284
French Guiana, 73
frontline states, 316, 321–324
fund-raising *see* financing refugee aid

German Jews and Zionism, 128
German shipping lines, 115, 278, 300, 304n21
Germany
control of emigration, 267, 279–80, 282, 286, 321
definition of Jew, 35, 207, 209
deportation and violation of international law, 318
deporting of Jews, 6, 37, 91, 112, 115, 141, 182, 244, 247, 253, 267, 278
emigration dynamic, 169, 245, 258, 276, 279
foreign currency needs, 35
international refugee regime, 31
Jewish persecution, 24, 208, 244, 277
League of Nations, 21
migration agreement with the Netherlands, 195, 201, 221, 286, 288
minority protection, 17
persecution 17, 207–10, 276
policy towards returnees, 208, 266, 275nn81–82
revoking citizenship 85, 208, 236n13, 266
seizure of Jewish property, 22, 24, 26, 112–13, 245–46, 276
trade balance, 25, 137

travel agreement with Belgium, 266, 286
travel restrictions for Aryans, 248, 250, 255, 266
Gestapo, 19, 24
Great Britain
 antisemitism, 3, 173
 border policy, 203, 296
 border policy and refugees, 197–98, 212
 communist refugees, 212, 282–83, 295–96
 eligibility procedure, 197
 expulsion of Jewish refugees, 296
 expulsion policy, 238n39
 immigration policy, 193, 196, 314–15
 immigration to Palestine, 134, 138, 278
 immigration to Shanghai's international Settlement, 114
 international refugee regime, 22, 30, 32, 62
 Jewish community 4, 212, 248, 251
 judiciary, 196, 199, 299
 labour market protectionism, 176
 labour market protectionism and refugees, 212
 polity, 172, 176
 preselection, 232, 297–299
 proactive refugee policy, 227, 295–99
 pro-refugee lobby, 173
 refugee aid organisations, 295–299
 refugee policy, 173–176., 197, 290, 297, 300–301
 repatriation to first country of asylum, 299
 repatriation to Germany, 299
 visa policy, 172, 197, 211, 248, 297
 visa policy and refugees, 199, 270n29, 270n31
Goering, Hermann, 35, 37, 39, 245
Gotha Treaty, 275n81
Greek shipping lines, 278

Grüninger, Paul, 93, 96, 177, 292

Ha'avarah Agreement, 25–26, 35, 129
Hamburg, 241n100
Hapag, 300
Hebrew Intergovernmental Committee for European Migration (HICEM), 29, 106, 117, 227, 289, 325
Hechaluzn, 54, 306n46
High Commissioner of Refugees from Germany, 21–23, 29–33, 47–48, 118, 163
Hilfsverein der deutschen Juden, 28, 111, 218
human rights, 91, 232
Hungary, 55, 65, 246

identity certificate, *see* residence permit
illegal immigration, 141, 177, 180, 182, 212, 217, 251, 258, 281–283
illegal immigration to Palestine, 308n71
illegal work, 28
immigration control
 agencies, 282
 external versus internal control, 197, 199–200, 217, 222, 227, 251, 281, 287, 314, 319
 remote control, 319
 subcontracting to private
 upward spiral of restriction, 282, , 318
immigration crimes, 70–71, 85
immigration policy, *see* individual countries, centralized versus decentralized
industrialists, 227, 251, 232
integration of refugees, 232
Intergovernmental Committee on Refugees, 35, 39
international relations, 213, 248, 279, 321 *see also* individual countries, diplomatic protest
international refugee regime, 6, 18–23, 30, 32, 36, 62, 228–232

Austrian refugees, 33
expulsion of refugees, 30, 32
stabilising actual refugee situation, 30, 32, 63
Sudeten refugees, 33
see also first country of asylum, sovereign powers of the state, international relations
internment camps, 67, 92, 182, 294
internment of subversive refugees, 224
Italian shipping lines, 113, 115
Italy, 7, 22, 246, 286
International Brigade members, 260, 282–83, 287–88

Jacobsen, Eigil Thune, 248, 254, 322
Japan and antisemitism, 115
Japan and Germany, 115
Japan and immigration to Shanghai, 114
jail, see prison
'Jew', 209, 235n7, 250–51, *see also* non-Aryan
Jewish Agency for Palestine, 22, 129, 132, 146n9
Jewish Colonization Agency, 22, 227
Jewish community in countries of asylum, 89, 104–107, 183, 317
anti-refugee attitude, 23
assistance of refugees, 65, 218, 251
boycott of German goods, 25, 137–38
fear of growing antisemitism, 23
fund-raising, 89, 218
national interests, 28, 163
and Zionism, 27, 125–26
Jewish community in Germany
improving Jewish position, 27
its organisations, 27, 37
and professional retraining, 28–29
promoting/organizing emigration, 27, 29, 170
and Zionism, 128
Jewish refugees and choice of destination, 123, 151, 227
Jewish refugees and the need for protection, 226, 230–31, 233–34, 262
Jewish refugees and Zionism, 123, 128
'J'-stamp, see passport
judiciary, 70–71, 74, 193, 195–96, 199, 232, 242n111, 263, 293, 299, 322

Kindertransporte, 171–184, *see also* child refugees
KPD, 207, 225, 230, 241nn100–101, 260–61
political strategy for communist refugees, 219, 260–61
and the Soviet Union, 225, 230
see also communist refugees, Red Help
Kristallnacht, 65, 135, 141, 277–78, 280–81, 285, 320–21

labelling of refugees, 85–86, 119n14, 204n11
Latin America, 103–107, 228, 277
corruption 71, 104–5, 107
see also individual countries
labour market protection and refugees, 31–32, 89, 212, 231
Laval, Pierre, 59, 61, 67
legal profession and refugees, 221
liberal values, 7, 163, *see also* rule of law, human rights
liberalism, 193, 313–14
Luxembourg
border policy, 223, 252, 285
expulsion of Jewish refugees, 253, 264
expulsion of communist refugees, 240n73
immigration policy, 196
international refugee regime, 6
Jewish community, 254, 264
labour market protectionism, 200–1.
polity, 264
pressure of other asylum countries, 305n35
refugee policy, 223
repatriation of communist refugees, 275n81
temporary protection for Jewish refugees, 214

visa policy, 270n29, 282
League for the Rights of Man and Citizen, 60, 213
law enforcement officials and disobedience, 71, 91, 98
liberal professions *see* medical profession, legal profession
Long Breckinridge,165n17, 160
LPC (Likely to be a public charge), 153, 155, 159–60

Madagascar, 8, 73
manufacturers *see* industrialists
marriages of convenience, 49, 53, 69, 139
marriages, mixed by nationality, 53
Matteotti fund, 218–219
Mauritius, 141
McDonald, James, 21–28, 163
medical profession and aliens/refugees, 115, 201
Merksplas, 266, 291
Mexico, 104–5, 107
middle-class interests, 58–59, 88, 222
minority protection, 18
Mischlinge, 209
Munich agreement, 7, 246, 282, 295

Nansen international office 1, 20, 32, 62
Nansen refugees, 58–59, 75, 245
nation state, 88, 196, 313
National Socialist racial categorization, *see* 'Jew', Aryan, non-Aryan
nativism , 86, 88, 107, 152, 178, 198, 314
nationality legislation and marriage, 53–54
naturalisation, 63, 97
navigation companies, 69, 112, 197, 285
Netherlands
    agreement on refugees with Belgium, 224, 229, 231, 261, 274n67
    asylum in prison, 231, 261

border policy, 222–23, 249, 252–53, 279, 284–88, 292, 296
child refugees, 286, 292
definition of refugee, 288–89, 292
economic protectionism, 222
expulsion of Jewish refugees, 36, 223, 242n111, 263
expulsion policy, 32, 195, 239n67, 315
expulsion of subversive refugees, 203, 224, 231
German assistance in combating unwanted immigration, 279–80
historiography, 3,5
immigration policy, 196, 211, 249, 270n24
immigration to Shanghai's international Settlement, 118
international refugee regime, 30, 32, 36, 218
internment of refugees, 224, 294
Jewish refugee aid committee, 3, 292, 294
judiciary, 242n111
labour market protectionism, 23, 182, 200–202 , 221, 259
migration agreement with Germany, 195, 201, 221, 286, 288
political activities of refugees, 261
polity, 123, 262
pro-refugee lobby, 263
protection of communist refugees, 231, 261
refugee policy, 196, 203, 231, 259, 263, 281, 283, 288, 300–303, 316
refugees shoved of by first countries of asylum, 213
repatriation of refugees, 286
temporary protection of Jewish refugees, 214
transit refugees, 296
visa policy, 197, 211, 249, 270n24, 282–83
New Caledonia, 73

non-Aryan Christians, 20, 107, 217, 280–81
non-Aryans, 180, 207, 209, 251, 270n29
Norway, 6, 30, 32, 36, 46n109, 62, 248, 270
Nuremberg laws, 48, 53, 61, 63, 68, 104, 130, 158, 209

open-ended detention, 224, 240n75, 294

Palestine, 122–146, 172, 228, 278, 297
  labour market protectionism, 123
  refugee policy, 123, 125, 127–28, 169
Paraguay, 104–6.
passports, 208–210, 248
  Austrians, 248–49
  'J' marked on, 84, 94–95, 250, 277, 281–82, 285, 319
Peru, 103
Pholien, Joseph, 179, 181, 264–266
Poland
  immigration policy, 216–17, 298
  international refugee regime, 22
  refugee policy, 297
  revoking citizenship, 247, 250
Polish Jews, 215, 237n29, 247, 250, 289, 308n72 see also East European Jews
political power of labour and middle classes, 200, 314–15
political refugees, 36, 48–52, 86–87, 105–6, 162, 196, 202–203, 208, 230, 233, 260
Popular Front, 62–65, 228, 230, 233
Portugal, 7, 117
préfecture de police, 215
préfets in frontier départements, 194, 212, 214, 240n69, 233
pre-selection, 174–176, 232
prison as place of asylum, 58, 60,67, 70, 224, 231, 261, 263, 284, 293–94
private aid, 89, 173, 254, 291, 296–97, 302–3

proactive refugee policy, 282, 295–299
pro-refugee lobby, 104, 162–63, 173, 254, 263, 320
provisional agreement on refugees from Germany, 29
public opinion, 280–81, 320, 324
public scrutiny of immigration policy, 319

racism in immigration policy, 250, 270n29
Rassenschande, 48–52, 209, 263, 288, 290, 292
recognizing 'Jewish' refugees, 93–95, 254–257
Red Cross, 179–180, 281
Red Help, 219, 225, 228, 230–31, 260
  see also communist refugees, KPD, private aid, financing refugee aid
refoulement, 60, 196
refugee aid as a public matter 291, 296–97, 302–3
refugee aid committees and refugee policy, 216–17, 220, 228, 231, 260–61, 280, 290, 295–299, 317
  see also private aid, financing refugee aid
refugee, administrative definition, 49, 86, 196, 203, 212, 215, 214, 229, 231, 254, 257, 290, 316, 319–20
refugee camp, 265, 288, 290–91, 293
refugee, civil society definition, 226
refugee eligibility procedure 33, 58, 61–62, 175, 228–29, 290, 317
refugee, legal definition, 6, 29, 31, 63, 87, 202–3, 224
refugee protection encourages further immigration, 65, 317
refugee ships, 113, 139 see also shipping lines
refugee, sociological definition, 204n11
refugees as army recruits, 72

refugees and their assets, 208
refugees' choice of destination, 84–85, 105, 111, 209, 211
refugees and criminal record, 241n99
refugees and gender, 28, 175
refugees and political activities, 2–4, 87, 11n5, 208, 261
refugees as security risk, 58, 63–64, 69, 76, 87
refugees as transmigrants, 87, 174, 197, 283, 290
refugees as undesirable foreigners, 88–89, 94–96
refugees and their visibility, 173, 176, 265–66, 291
Reichskristallnacht, see Kristallnacht
remote migration control, 197, 249, 251, 319
repatriation to Germany, 61, 180, 203, 214, 225, 228, 231, 240nn92–93, 299, 324, *see also* return
repatriation to Poland, 216–17, 228
residence permit, 30, 60, 201, 206n30, *see also* unconditional leave to remain
return to Germany, 84, 209, 228
revoking citizenship, *see* Hungary, Poland, Germany, Romania
Rieucros, 294
Rollin, Louis 72, 74
Romania, 277
Roosevelt, Franklin Delano, 34, 164, 277
Rothmund, Heinrich, 2, 31, 36, 86, 92, 94–95, 178, 184, 322
Rothschild, de 26, 75
rule of law, 294
rupture de ban, 194–95
Russian Jews, 196
Russian refugees, 20, 29, 111, 202, 314

Saar refugees, 60–61, 106, 225
Scandinavia, 283
  coordination of refugee policy, 32, 36, 46n109, 248
Schacht, Hjalmar, 26, 35, 208
Schacht-Rublee Plan, 35–36, 39

Serre Philippe, 64–65, 243n117
Shanghai, 109–117, 277
Slovakia, 246
smuggling, 180, 258, 267, 286–87
Social Democratic refugee aid committees, *see* Matteotti fund
Social Democratic refugee policy, 51, 218
sovereign powers of the state, 33, 209, 232, 242n111,
Soviet Union
  refugee policy 225–26., 288, 308n66
  return policy, 244
  see also Russian refugees, communist refugees
Spaak, Paul-Henri, 265–66, 281
Spain, 7
  international refugee regime, 32
  civil war refugees, 30n46, 58, 283
  communist refugees, 225, 260
  see also International Brigade
SPD, 27
sponsorship *see* financing refugee aid
spouses of Jewish refugees, 285
St Louis, 45n105, 278, 299–301
statelessness, 85, 99n19, 210, 217, 229, 275nn81–82
Steinecke Karl, 49, 230, 291
Sterilisation, 49, 61, 231, 288
Sudenten refugees, 68
Sudeten refugees, 172, 246
Sudetenland, 246, 282
Suicides of refugees, 60, 70, 224, 254, 256, 263
Sweden, 7, 22, 51, 95, 250
  visa policy, 248, 250, 255
Switzerland
  antisemitism, 88
  border policy, 178, 285, 292
  border policy and refugees, 92, 94, 96
  cantons, 92–96, 177, 198, 203, 206n30, 292, 322
  eligibility procedure, 203–4, 215–16, 223, 252, 255, 271n37
  expulsion of refugees, 89
  expulsion of subversive refugees, 203, 223
  financial support for refugees'

reception, 242n107
German assistance in combating unwanted immigration, 267, 279–80.
historiography, 2,5, 83, 98n5, 99n6
illegal immigration to Palestine, 308n71
immigration policy, 88, 281, 314
international refugee regime, 22
Jewish community, 11, 46–47, 89, 92, 96
labour market protectionism, 88, 200–1
labour market protectionism and refugees, 89, 231
polity, 82, 86, 198
private interest groups, 59, 85, 88, 94
recognizing Jewish refugees, 256
refugee policy, 86, 283, 292
refugees, 214, 252
refugees shoved of by France, 256
shoving of refugees to France, 92, 252
street level bureaucracies, 91, 98
temporary protection for Jewish visa policy, 197, 211, 247, 250
visa policy for refugees, 90, 93–94, 96, 98, 177

tax evasion *see* currency smuggling
Taylor Myron, C., 29, 162
technocrats, 322
temporary protection, 71, 158, 214–15, 226, 233–34, 236n17, 252
toleration implicit, 224, 236n17, 322
  explicit *see* temporary protection
tourism, 94, 104, 198, 313 *see also* German, Italian, Greek shipping lines and navigation companies
transport companies, 282 *see also* shipping lines, airline carriers

Überfremdung see nativism

unconditional leave to remain, 206n30, 220, 222, *see also* residence permit
United States, 151–164, 289, 297
  immigration to Shanghai's international Settlement, 114
  international refugee regime, 21–22, 62
Uruguay, 103, 105–6

vagabondage, 60, 62, 199
Vargas Get'ulio, 104, 107
Vatican, 107
Venezuela, 103, 278
visas, 57, 59, 63, 65, 68, 155, 172, 179, 197–98, 211–12, 222, 248–251, 270n24, 282, 297
  abolition agreement, 248
  Austrians, 248–49
  for 'Jews' and non-Aryans, 91, 255, 270n29, 282
  for refugees, 30, 61, 65, 93–94, 96, 98, 177, 199, 251
visa overstayers, 39–40, 157–58, 213, 249
voluntary aid, see private aid

Warburg, Max, 25–26.
Weiss, Louise, 72–73
Weizmann, Chaim, 131, 133
Westerbork, 294, 303
Wohlthat, Helmut, 35, 39
women, *see* refugees and gender

Youth Aliya, 55, 131, 138–39, 185n2, 306n46

Zionists, 125, 128,
  and Evian, 131–32, 135, 162
  and Ha'avara Agreement, 25, 135–36.
  and illegal immigration to Palestine, 139–142, 278–79, 289
  and Palestine, 123

Thalmann, Rita. (1981). 'L'immigration allemande et l'opinion publique en France de 1936 à 1939', *Deutschland und Frankreich 1936–1939. Beihefte der Francia*, 10, pp.47–70.
Tutas, H.E. (1975). *National-Sozialismus und Exil. Die Politik gegenüber der deutschen politischen Emigration*. Vienna: C. Hauser.
Unabhängige Expertenkommission Schweiz-Zweiter Weltkrieg (UEK). (2001). *Die Schweiz und die Flüchtlinge zur Zeit des Nationalsozialismus*. Bern: Chronos.
Van Eijl, Corrie. (2005). *Al te goed is buurmans gek. Het Nederlandse vreemdelingenbeleid 1840-1940*. Amsterdam: Aksant.
Veziano, Paolo. (2001). *Ombre di confine. L'emigrazione clandestina degli ebrei stranieri della riviera dei Fiori verso la costa azzura (1938–1940)*. Pinerolo: Alzani.
Villanci, Cinzia. (2003). *Zwischen Rassengesetzen und Deportation. Juden in Südtirol, im Trentino und in der Provinz Belluno, 1933–1945*. Innsbrück: Wagner.
Voigt, Klaus. (1989). *Zuflucht auf Widerruf. Exil in Italien 1933–1945*. Stuttgart: Klett-Cotta.
von zur Mühlen Patrik *(1988)*. *Fluchtziel Lateinamerika. Die deutsche Emigration 1933-1945: politische Aktivitäten und soziokulturelle Integration*. Bonn: Neue Gesellschaft.
Vormeier, Barbara and Hanna Schramm. (1977). *Vivre à Gurs. Un Camp de Concentration français 1940–1941*. Paris: Maspero.
Wacker, Jean-Claude. (1992). *Humaner als in Bern! Schweizer und Basler Asylpraxis gegenüber den jüdischen Flüchtlingen von 1933 bis 1943 im Vergleich*. Basel: Reinhardt.
Walter, Hans-Albert. (1984). *Deutsche Exilliteratur 1933–1950. Band 2: Europäisches Appeasement und uberseeische Asylpraxis*. Stuttgart: J.B. Metzler.
Weber, Hermann and Andreas Herbst. (2004). *Deutsche Kommunisten. Biographisches Handbuch, 1918 bis 1945*. Berlin: Karl Dietz.
Weingarten, Ralph. (1981). *Die Hilfeleistung der westlichen Welt bei der Endlösung der deutschen Judenfrage. Das 'Intergovernmental Committee on Political Refugees (ICG)'*. Bern: Peter Lang.
Weinzierl, Ulrich (ed.). (1984). *Oesterreicher im Exil. Frankreich 1938–1945. Eine Dokumentation*. Vienna: Oesterreichischer Bundesverlag.
Wichers, Hermann. (1994). *Im kampf gegen Hitler. Deutsche Sozialisten im Schweizer Exil 1933–1940*. Zürich: Chronos.
Wyman, David S. (1968). *Paper Walls: America and the Refugee Crisis 1938–1941*. Amherst: University of Massachusetts Press.
Zalc, Claire. (1997). 'Des réfugiés aux indésirables: les pouvoirs publics français face aux émigrés du IIIe Reich entre 1933 et 1939', in Eric Guichard and Gérard Noiriel (ed.), *Construction des nationalités et immigration dans la France contemporaine* (pp.259–74). Paris: Presses de l'Ecole normale supérieure.
Zucker, Bat-Ami. (2001). *In Search of Refuge: Jews and U.S.Consuls in Nazi Germany 1933–1941*. Portland: Vallentine Mitchell.

www.ingramcontent.com/pod-product-compliance
Lightning Source LLC
Chambersburg PA
CBHW072143100526
44589CB00015B/2061